T0257039

Building Secure Cars

Building Secure Cars

Assuring the Automotive Software Development Lifecycle

Dennis Kengo Oka

This edition first published 2021
© 2021 John Wiley & Sons Ltd

All rights reserved. No part of this publication may be reproduced, stored in a retrieval system, or transmitted, in any form or by any means, electronic, mechanical, photocopying, recording or otherwise, except as permitted by law. Advice on how to obtain permission to reuse material from this title is available at http://www.wiley.com/go/permissions.

The right of Dennis Kengo Oka to be identified as the author of this work has been asserted in accordance with law.

Registered Offices
John Wiley & Sons, Inc., 111 River Street, Hoboken, NJ 07030, USA
John Wiley & Sons Ltd, The Atrium, Southern Gate, Chichester, West Sussex, PO19 8SQ, UK

Editorial Office
The Atrium, Southern Gate, Chichester, West Sussex, PO19 8SQ, UK

For details of our global editorial offices, customer services, and more information about Wiley products visit us at www.wiley.com.

Wiley also publishes its books in a variety of electronic formats and by print-on-demand. Some content that appears in standard print versions of this book may not be available in other formats.

Limit of Liability/Disclaimer of Warranty
In view of ongoing research, equipment modifications, changes in governmental regulations, and the constant flow of information relating to the use of experimental reagents, equipment, and devices, the reader is urged to review and evaluate the information provided in the package insert or instructions for each chemical, piece of equipment, reagent, or device for, among other things, any changes in the instructions or indication of usage and for added warnings and precautions. While the publisher and authors have used their best efforts in preparing this work, they make no representations or warranties with respect to the accuracy or completeness of the contents of this work and specifically disclaim all warranties, including without limitation any implied warranties of merchantability or fitness for a particular purpose. No warranty may be created or extended by sales representatives, written sales materials or promotional statements for this work. The fact that an organization, website, or product is referred to in this work as a citation and/or potential source of further information does not mean that the publisher and authors endorse the information or services the organization, website, or product may provide or recommendations it may make. This work is sold with the understanding that the publisher is not engaged in rendering professional services. The advice and strategies contained herein may not be suitable for your situation. You should consult with a specialist where appropriate. Further, readers should be aware that websites listed in this work may have changed or disappeared between when this work was written and when it is read. Neither the publisher nor authors shall be liable for any loss of profit or any other commercial damages, including but not limited to special, incidental, consequential, or other damages.

Library of Congress Cataloging-in-Publication Data
Name: Oka, Dennis Kengo, author.
Title: Building secure cars : assuring the automotive software development lifecycle / Dennis Kengo Oka.
Description: First edition. | Hoboken, NJ : John Wiley & Sons, Inc., 2021. | Includes bibliographical references and index.
Identifiers: LCCN 2020041114 (print) | LCCN 2020041115 (ebook) | ISBN 9781119710745 (cloth) | ISBN 9781119710769 (adobe pdf) | ISBN 9781119710776 (epub)
Subjects: LCSH: Automotive telematics–Security measures. | Automotive computers–Programming.
Classification: LCC TL272.53 .O42 2021 (print) | LCC TL272.53 (ebook) | DDC 629.2/72–dc23
LC record available at https://lccn.loc.gov/2020041114
LC ebook record available at https://lccn.loc.gov/2020041115
Cover Design: Wiley
Cover Image: nadla/iStock/Getty Images
Set in 9.5/12.5pt STIXTwoText by SPi Global, Chennai, India
C9781119710745_040321

Contents

organizations involved in building automotive systems to incorporate security into their software development lifecycle.

I would like to extend my gratitude to the staff members at Wiley who supported and guided me throughout the entire process of writing this book. I would also like to thank all my colleagues and research collaborators over the years. I am extremely grateful to have had the opportunity to work with so many bright and talented people who have inspired and supported me. On a personal note, I would like to thank my wonderful wife Mai for being extremely patient and providing me with her full support while I was writing this book, and my three beautiful daughters Mia, Elina, and Alyssa for making me smile every day :) I would also like to thank my parents Sven and Etsuko, and my brother Alex and sister Linda, for always keeping me motivated and focused on the important things in life.

About the Author

Dr. Dennis Kengo Oka is an automotive cybersecurity expert with more than 15 years of global experience in the automotive industry. He received his Ph.D. in Computer Science and Engineering, with a focus on automotive security, from Chalmers University of Technology in Sweden. In the past, Dennis has worked with Volvo Car Corporation in Sweden where he bootstrapped automotive security research for remote diagnostics and over-the-air updates on vehicles. He has also worked for the Bosch Group in Japan serving both Japanese and global customers. Specifically, Dennis co-launched the automotive security practice (ESCRYPT) in Japan and was the Head of Engineering and Consulting Asia-Pacific. Dennis has also been involved in several automotive standardization activities, including the development of fuzz testing guidelines and cybersecurity testing frameworks. He has over 60 publications consisting of conference papers, journal articles, and book chapters, and is a frequent public speaker at international automotive and cybersecurity conferences and events.

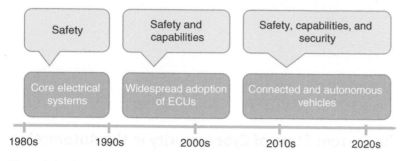

Figure 1.1 Overview of automotive technology trends.

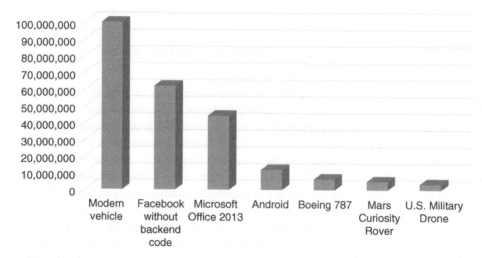

Figure 1.2 Comparison of software sizes of different systems in terms of lines of code. Source: Data from [1].

wireless connectivity and autonomous driving functionality need to be both designed and developed securely, as well as properly security tested.

A modern vehicle can contain up to 150 ECUs and more than 100 million lines of software code, which is projected to rise to 300 million lines of code by 2030. For reference, Figure 1.2 shows a comparison of software on vehicles with that of other systems in order to highlight the enormous volume of software the automotive industry is engaged in. As can be seen in the figure, a modern vehicle contains more software than Facebook without the backend code (62 million lines of code). A vehicle also has more than double the code of Microsoft Office 2013, more than six times the code of the Android OS, more than 15 times the code of a Boeing 787, and more than 20 times the code of the Mars Curiosity Rover and a US military drone [1]. As more software is included in vehicles, there is a risk of introducing software bugs and vulnerabilities that, if abused by malicious attackers, could potentially have disastrous consequences, including on safety, privacy, and operation of the vehicles.

For reference, the statistical average for software used in critical systems (e.g. flight control and air traffic control) indicates 10–12 errors for every 1000 lines of code. However, this level of error rate is unacceptable for NASA regarding software used on space shuttles. It was shown that software for the unfortunate Space Shuttle Challenger had a latent defect rate of just 0.11 errors per 1000 lines of code [2]. Considering even this minuscule error rate of 0.11 errors per 1000 lines of code, mathematically speaking, a modern vehicle would contain more than 11 000 defects!

As highlighted by the technology trends and the large volume of software, cybersecurity is an ever-increasing important topic that the automotive industry must seriously consider. To this end, the automotive industry has been working on and has produced several cybersecurity related standards, best practices, and guidelines. A few examples of these are presented in this chapter to provide some background on the current state of cybersecurity. Additionally, automotive organizations are going through process changes and organizational changes based on these standards, best practices, and guidelines, which are explored further in detail. Moreover, some results from a survey conducted on the current state of cybersecurity practices in the automotive industry are presented to provide some further insight. Finally, this chapter discusses a few examples of vulnerabilities identified in the automotive industry to better understand the consequences caused by the lack of adequate cybersecurity activities during the development lifecycle.

The main points of this chapter are:

- We present an overview of the current automotive cybersecurity landscape, including cybersecurity standards, guidelines, and activities.
- We discuss the necessary process changes, organizational changes, and new solutions that need to be adopted by automotive organizations based on the aforementioned cybersecurity standards and guidelines.
- We review results from a recent study on automotive cybersecurity practices and highlight existing challenges at automotive organizations.

1.1 Cybersecurity Standards, Guidelines, and Activities

The automotive industry is well-known for following a rigorous development process based on standards such as ISO 26262 for functional safety [3], ISO 21448 for safety of the intended functionality (SOTIF) [4] and ASPICE (Automotive Software Process Improvement and Capability dEtermination) [5], and for following coding guidelines provided by MISRA (Motor Industry Software Reliability Association) for development of safety-relevant software [6]. However, besides safety, cybersecurity has become a major concern and, consequently, there are several standards, best practices and guidelines regarding cybersecurity. For example, the SAE J3061 [7], released in January 2016, is the world's first cybersecurity standard for the automotive industry. The *SAE J3061: Cybersecurity Guidebook for Cyber-Physical Vehicle Systems* provides guidance and recommendations for designing cybersecurity into the system including product design, validation, deployment, and communication tasks. It also states that, for a system to be safe, it also needs to be secure. This concept is depicted in Figure 1.3, where all safety-critical systems also need to be cybersecurity-critical systems; highlighting the mantra that *there is no safety without security*.

The SAE J3061 has now been superseded by the ISO/SAE 21434 standard [8]. In previous years, there were several ongoing activities on automotive security in both ISO and

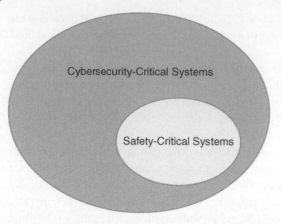

Figure 1.3 All safety-critical systems are cybersecurity-critical systems.

SAE, so, in November 2016, the Partnership Standards Development Organization (PSDO) was created as a cooperation agreement between ISO and SAE in two areas: Road Vehicles and Intelligent Transportation Systems. As a result, SAE and ISO agreed to work together to develop a cybersecurity standard, namely the ISO/SAE 21434, which is the first standard to be created under this new agreement. This standard will be jointly released by both SAE and ISO. The DIS (draft international standard) version of ISO/SAE 21434 was released in February 2020, and the final document for publication is expected to be published sometime in the first half of 2021. Proposed contents of the ISO/SAE 21434 divided into different clauses include Overall cybersecurity management, Continuous cybersecurity activities, Risk assessment methods, Concept phase, Product development, Production, Operations and Maintenance, among others [9]. An overview of how the relevant clauses in ISO/SAE 21434 are mapped onto the product lifecycle is illustrated in Figure 1.4. Please

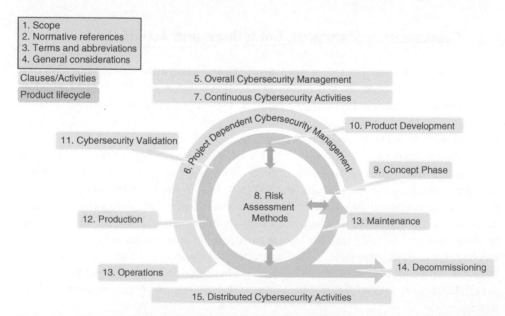

Figure 1.4 Clauses in ISO/SAE 21434 mapped onto the product lifecycle. Source: Based on [8].

Focusing on software development, besides standards, regulations and best practices, there exist several secure coding guidelines. For example, MISRA [6] was initially focused on providing coding rules to ensure safe development of safety-relevant systems, however the MISRA C:2012 Amendment 1 released in 2016 [18] included a number of security-relevant rules as well. The CERT (Computer Emergency Response Team) C/C++ coding standards [19, 20] are often used by developers to develop secure code in other industries and, lately, are becoming more adopted in the automotive industry. The AUTOSAR (AUTomotive Open System ARchitecture) C++ 14 guidelines [21] can be followed for developing safe and secure AUTOSAR software. Although technically not a coding guideline, the CWE (Common Weakness Enumeration) [22] contains a broad categorization of security flaws that can be used by developers to check whether their code contains certain weaknesses.

Furthermore, the automotive industry has a very complex supply chain, traditionally starting with an OEM (original equipment manufacturer) at the top and then branching out into several tiers of suppliers providing anything from entire systems, hardware devices, fully functional software, individual hardware components, standalone software stacks, components, libraries, specific firmware etc. To properly manage the risks in the supply chain, especially considering the fluid and fast development of software components, the National Telecommunications and Information Administration (NTIA) of the United States Department of Commerce has established a task force focusing on Software Component Transparency [23]. This task force focuses on promoting SBOM (software bill of materials) both as a concept and for practical deployment, building awareness and providing information on strategies, use cases, organizational roles etc. It also looks at universal approaches on how to identify and name components, how to share SBOMs, how to automate SBOM in production and use, including what tools and standards could be used for creating SBOMs in the specific formats identified.

1.2 Process Changes, Organizational Changes, and New Solutions

Based on the standards, regulations, best practices, and guidelines presented in the previous section, the automotive industry is going through a transformation. To follow and meet the standards and regulations requires several process and organizational changes. Moreover, for automotive organizations to realize these process changes requires implementation of several new technical solutions. This three-step activity is illustrated in Figure 1.5 and is described in more detail in the following.

Changes may need to be made to the software development lifecycle (SDLC). One example is is to be compliant with certain coding standards (e.g. MISRA or AUTOSAR). Another example is the addition of new security gates, e.g. adding a security gate requiring fuzz testing to be performed as part of the process before the next step in the product development phase is allowed. To realize coding standards compliance, solutions based on various automated static code analysis tools that perform scans of the source code and generate reports of the results could be used. These tools can be built into the development process to run as an automated step. To realize fuzz testing as part of the process, it is

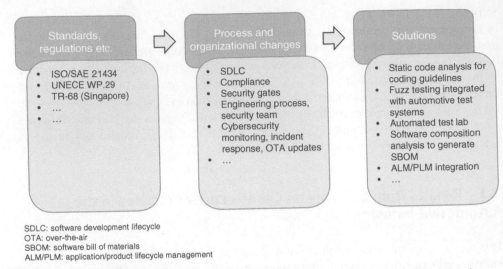

SDLC: software development lifecycle
OTA: over-the-air
SBOM: software bill of materials
ALM/PLM: application/product lifecycle management

Figure 1.5 Three-step activity from standards and regulations to process and organizational changes to solutions.

possible to employ a technical solution that consists of an automated fuzz testing tool that tests the target system and stores the results of the tests in a log file. The fuzz testing tool could be integrated with existing automotive test systems to enable automated fuzz testing as part of the test process.

Some other examples are changes to the engineering process by including testing in an automated manner and the establishment of dedicated security teams. The corresponding technical solution is to create a test lab which the dedicated security team is responsible for. The test lab should, using automation, be used to perform several different types of testing, e.g. security functional testing, source code/binary scans, vulnerability scanning, fuzz testing, and penetration testing. In addition, the test lab could be used to allow the target system to be tested in multiple different environments, such as standalone, in combination with other systems, in various states, on virtual platforms etc.

Furthermore, there may be new process requirements for cybersecurity monitoring, incident response, and over-the-air (OTA) updates. These process requirements require technical solutions based on, for example, software composition analysis tools to generate SBOM during the release management process and store the relevant data in some database. For instance, the SBOM generation can be integrated with ALM/PLM (application lifecycle management/product lifecycle management) systems so that it is clear exactly which component or vehicle contains what software and which versions of the software. Cybersecurity monitoring services or tools that give alerts on new vulnerabilities can be used to provide input to an automotive security operations center (SOC). Using the information stored in the ALM/PLM systems allows for organizations to identify the impact of a certain newly identified vulnerability. First, it is necessary to assess which software versions are affected by the identified vulnerability, as well as the exploitability and impact of said vulnerability. Second, it is possible to assess how many components/vehicles are affected by the specific vulnerability by using the information stored in the ALM/PLM systems to know exactly which components or vehicles contain the vulnera-

software. Third, based on the number of affected components or vehicles and the severity of the vulnerability, an appropriate response can be taken, e.g. urgently providing an updated software which includes a fix. To fulfill the OTA update process requirements, the organization requires a technical OTA solution or service to be employed. As a response to the identified vulnerability, the organization can then provide the patched software through the OTA solution to reach as many vehicles as fast as possible.

These are just a couple of examples of where standards, regulations, best practices, and guidelines lead to process and organizational changes that finally require new technical solutions to be deployed in automotive organizations.

1.3 Results from a Survey on Cybersecurity Practices in the Automotive Industry

This section presents some results from a survey on cybersecurity practices in the automotive industry to get a better understanding of the common challenges automotive organizations are facing. In February 2019, a report based on a survey of the automotive industry called "Securing the Modern Vehicle: A Study of Automotive Industry Cybersecurity Practices" [24] was released. Synopsys and SAE International collaborated to commission this independent survey. The objective was to understand the current automotive industry's cybersecurity posture and its capability to address software security risks inherent in connected, software-enabled vehicles based on data. Up to this point, there had been a gap that had existed far too long – the lack of data to understand the current state of cybersecurity in the automotive industry. The Ponemon Institute was selected to conduct the study and researchers surveyed 593 professionals at auto manufacturers and parts suppliers responsible for contributing to or assessing the security of automotive components.

1.3.1 Survey Methods

The target of this survey was IT security practitioners and engineers in the automotive industry. To ensure relevant responses, all the participants in the study are contributing to or assessing the security of automotive components. A total of 15 900 participants were selected to participate in a web-based survey. All survey responses were captured during a two-week period from July 19, 2019 through August 3, 2019. Initially, responses from a total of 677 surveys were received; however, screening and reliability checks led to the removal of 84 surveys. Thus, the final sample used for this report consisted of responses from 593 surveys, or a 3.7% response rate.

Some additional details about the participants of this survey are provided with the following percentage breakdowns as follows. Regarding the participants' current position within their organization, there is a good mix of different roles and positions, such as Senior Executive/VP (3%), Director (12%), Manager (19%), Supervisor (11%), Engineer (15%), and Technician (21%), among others. It is worth noting that more than half of the respondents hold engineer or higher-ranked positions. Exploring deeper into the organization and the primary person the survey participant reports to, shows, among others, Chief Information Officer (23%), Head, Product Engineering (21%), Head, DevOps

note that clauses 1 through 4 are general clauses covering the Scope, Normative references, Terms and abbreviations, and General considerations. Clauses 5 through 15 contain specific cybersecurity requirements for the respective activities that automotive organizations need to fulfill.

Moreover, there are currently ongoing activities for new UNECE (United Nations Economic Commission for Europe) regulations regarding cybersecurity and software updates. There are currently two groups in the World Forum for Harmonization of Vehicle Regulations Working Party (WP.29) working on these activities: *Proposal for a new UN Regulation on uniform provisions concerning the approval of vehicles with regards to cyber security and cyber security management system (CSMS)* and *Proposal for a new UN Regulation on uniform provisions concerning the approval of vehicles with regards to software update and software updates management system (SUMS)*.

These documents are still in draft form at the time of writing this book, however the currently proposed contents include: Risk assessment processes, Threats to vehicles, Mitigations, Measures to detect and prevent cyberattacks, CSMS required for type approval, SUMS required for secure delivery of software updates.

The UN regulations will apply to passenger cars, trucks, and buses and will enter into force in January 2021. These regulations will require:

- Vehicle manufacturer to obtain a certificate of compliance for their CSMS.
- Vehicle manufacturer to obtain a certificate of compliance for their SUMS.
- Vehicle type approval with regard to cybersecurity and software updates based on the CSMS and SUMS certificates and vehicle-specific material.

In the European Union, the regulation on cybersecurity will be mandatory for all new vehicle types from July 2022 and for all new vehicles produced from July 2024 [10].

There has also been regional work to promote cybersecurity. For instance, in Singapore a technical reference document called TR-68 [11] was released in January 2019 focusing on giving guidance on cybersecurity principles and assessment framework for autonomous vehicles.

Moreover, ENISA (European Union Agency for Cybersecurity) has published a couple of reports on the topics of cybersecurity and resilience of smart cars [12], and good practices for the security of smart cars [13]. These reports cover various topics including threats and attack scenarios, and security measures and good practices such as policies, organizational practices, and technical practices.

Furthermore, NHTSA (National Highway Traffic Safety Authority) released a document called *Cybersecurity Best Practices for Modern Vehicles* [14] in October 2016. This document provides best practices for developing a risk-based approach and processes to cover cybersecurity issues for organizations manufacturing and designing vehicle systems and software. Moreover, there have been several proposals for legislation, e.g. in 2015 the US Congress SPY CAR (Security and Privacy in Your Car) Act [15] was proposed. This act focuses on the need for auto manufacturers to handle cybersecurity and employ proper methods considering privacy of data collected in vehicles. This bill was reintroduced in 2017 [16] and 2019 [17], focusing on a *cyber dashboard* with easy to understand graphics to inform consumers about the vehicle's protection from cybersecurity threats and its ability to protect personal information.

(15%), Chief Information Security Officer (15%), and Chief Technology Officer (9%). Further, the organizations the participants belong to are headquartered in the following regions: Unites States (60%), Europe (12%), Canada (10%), Latin America including Mexico (9%), Asia-Pacific (8%), and Middle East and Africa (1%). As can be seen, a majority of the respondents are headquartered in the United States. The organization sizes based on the worldwide headcount for the participating organizations were captured as follows: fewer than 5000 (34%), 5000–10 000 (31%), 10 001–25 000 (16%), 25 001–75 000 (11%), and more than 75 000 (8%). Thus, 66% of the respondents belong to organizations with a worldwide headcount of more than 5000 employees. Finally, the total yearly investment on automotive component security for these organizations in terms of technologies, personnel, and managed and outsourced services ranges from $1–$100 000 (2%), $100 001–$250 000 (9%), $250 001–$500 000 (13%), $500 001–$1 000 000 (19%), $1 000 001–$2 500 000 (23%), $2 500 001–$5 000 000 (17%), $5 000 001–$10 000 000 (9%), $10 000 001–$25 000 000 (2%), $25 000 001–$50 000 000 (3%), $50 000 001–$100 000 000 (2%), and more than $100 000 000 (1%). It is noteworthy that more than half of the participating organizations spend more than $1 million per year on automotive security.

1.3.2 Report Results

The contents of the automotive industry cybersecurity practices report are divided into four sections, focusing on challenges in the respective areas of *organizational topics*, *technical areas*, *product development and security testing practices*, and finally *supply chain topics*. Examples from each of these areas are briefly presented as follows.

1.3.2.1 Organizational Challenges

Regarding organizational challenges, 52% of the respondents say that they are aware of potential harm to drivers that could be caused by insecure automotive technologies. Sixty-two percent say that a malicious or proof-of-concept attack against the automotive technologies or systems developed by their organizations is likely or very likely in the next 12 months. However, there is a critical disconnect in the organizations since even though the security experts within these organizations have concerns about security, only 31% of the respondents feel empowered to raise such concerns up their chain of command. This begs the question: Why do cybersecurity experts not feel empowered to raise their concerns? One reason could be that 30% of the organizations do not have any established cybersecurity program or team. So, this could mean that even if a cybersecurity expert wants to raise a certain concern, there is no structured approach on who to report this concern to and, even if it is reported, there is no defined process how to handle the concern. Breaking down the responses based on OEMs and suppliers shows that OEMs are generally better since only 18% of OEMs do not have any established cybersecurity program or team. In contrast, roughly two out of five suppliers (41%) do not have any established cybersecurity program or team. Moreover, one reason for organizations not having an established cybersecurity program or team could be due to the lack of necessary cybersecurity resources and skills. Fifty-one percent of respondents say that the organizations do not allocate enough budget and human resources to cybersecurity. On average, there are only nine FTE (full-time equivalent) per organization dedicated to product cybersecurity

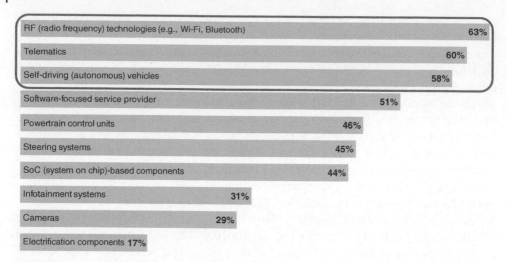

Figure 1.6 Technologies posing the greatest cybersecurity risks. Source: Data from [24].

management programs. Furthermore, 62% of the respondents believe they do not have the necessary cybersecurity skills in product development [24].

1.3.2.2 Technical Challenges

Regarding the technical challenges, 84% of the respondents state that they are concerned that cybersecurity practices are not keeping pace with changing technologies. In particular, the three main technologies that pose the greatest cybersecurity risk, as shown in Figure 1.6, are related to wireless and autonomous driving technologies, such as Wi-Fi, Bluetooth (63%), telematics (60%), and self-driving (autonomous) vehicles (58%) [24]. These technologies are also driving the trends in the automotive industry as explained in Chapter 2. Moreover, the famous Jeep hack presented at the Black Hat and Defcon conferences in 2015 [25] focused on exploiting vulnerabilities and security issues in these technologies, namely, connecting remotely to the vehicle over Wi-Fi and telematics (over a cellular network) and abusing assisted driving (partially self-driving) functionality, e.g. the park assist function.

As software complexity grows to support new technologies, and as with any software, it is evident that there will be software bugs in automotive software. However, a technical challenge that 61% of the organizations face is being able to address critical security vulnerabilities in a timely manner through a software update delivery model. For example, only 37% of the participants state that their organizations provide OTA capabilities to deliver security patches and updates. Last, since organizations apply security solutions to their automotive systems, and since these security solutions often rely on cryptographic algorithms, there is a strong need for management of cryptographic keys, including the generation, exchange, storage, use and replacement of keys. While 56% of the respondents answered that their organizations use central key management systems, a challenge is that 43% of the participants say that their organizations use a manual process, including spreadsheets and paper-based approaches, which limits the usefulness of cryptographic keys and hampers security [24].

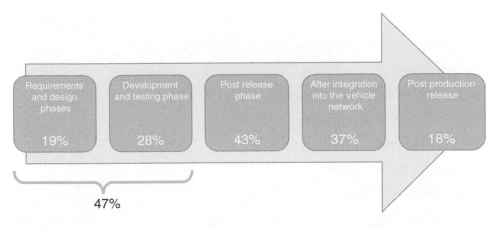

Figure 1.7 Overview of when security assessments occur in the development lifecycle. Source: Data from [24].

1.3.2.3 Product Development and Security Testing Challenges

In terms of the challenges regarding product development and security testing, only 47% of the organizations say that they perform security assessments of their products early in the product release process, namely in the "requirements and design," and "development and testing" phases. Thus, the results show that a majority of the organizations assess vulnerabilities too late in the process such as after release, after integration, or post production release. This fact is illustrated in Figure 1.7.

Testing for vulnerabilities late in the development lifecycle is often also very costly, as providing fixes to identified critical issues may require redesign or major changes to the target system. It is important to note that an established best practice is to use a risk-based, process-driven approach to cybersecurity throughout the entire product development lifecycle. The survey also shows that 63% of the organizations test less than half of their hardware, software, and other technologies for vulnerabilities. Even more surprising is that 25% of the organizations do not perform any cybersecurity testing at all of their automotive software and systems. One main reason for organizations not performing cybersecurity testing could be that a secure software development lifecycle (SSDLC) process, which defines the cybersecurity activities is not followed. As can be seen from the survey, 36% of the organizations do not follow an SSDLC process. Investigating further the main causes for vulnerabilities in automotive software and systems, the survey reveals that the primary factors that lead to vulnerabilities, shown in Figure 1.8, include the pressure to meet deadlines (71%), lack of secure practices for *coding* (60%) and accidental *coding* errors (55%), lack of procedures for *testing* (50%), and the use of insecure *open-source software* (40%). In addition, while 60% of the respondents say that a lack of understanding or training on secure coding practices is a primary factor that leads to vulnerabilities, only 33% of the organizations educate their developers on secure coding methods [24].

Thus, to summarize, the top three primary factors – besides the pressure to meet deadlines – are related to *coding*, *testing*, and *open-source software*.

1.3.2.4 Supply Chain and Third-Party Components Challenges

Regarding challenges for supply chain and third-party components, 73% of the respondents answered that they are very concerned about the cybersecurity posture of automotive

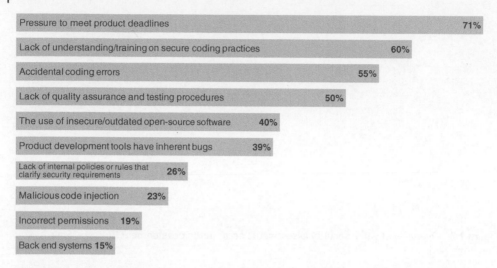

Figure 1.8 Primary factors that lead to vulnerabilities in automotive systems. Source: Data from [24].

technologies supplied by third parties. OEMs often integrate a number of different systems from multiple suppliers, who in turn integrate various third-party components, software, communication stacks, and applications, which may include vulnerabilities that the OEMs need to be aware of and be ready to handle. Thus, vulnerabilities in the complex automotive supply chain present a major risk. Moreover, 68% of the participants are very concerned about the cybersecurity posture of the industry as a whole. In addition, 56% of the organizations do not impose cybersecurity requirements on the products provided by their suppliers. Even for the organizations that do provide cybersecurity requirements to their suppliers, 40% of them have no defined formal process to verify that the suppliers actually adhere to the provided security requirements. Instead, 51% of the organizations rely on the suppliers to perform self-assessments and subsequently provide relevant artifacts for verification and validation that the suppliers have fulfilled the received requirements [24].

1.3.3 How to Address the Challenges

Based on the results from the survey on cybersecurity practices in the automotive industry presented in Section 1.3.2, this section highlights major takeaways for automotive organizations to address the identified challenges. Relevant takeaways for each of the four categories, namely organizational topics, technical areas, product development and security testing practices, and supply chain topics are presented.

1.3.3.1 Organizational Takeaways

The main takeaways from the organizational challenges are, first, for an automotive organization to ensure that cybersecurity is made a priority within the organization. It is a necessity that the organization has a formal leader who is driving the internal cybersecurity activities, e.g. a CISO (Chief Information Security Officer) or VP of Cybersecurity in a leadership role. This leader sends the message in the organization that cybersecurity priority is top-down and therefore empowers the security experts in the organization to speak up if they recognize any security concerns. Second, it is important that organizations establish a cybersecurity program or team that is responsible for establishing internal cybersecurity processes, creating guidelines, and ensuring and enforcing compliance within the organization. Third, it is imperative that the organizations have the necessary cybersecurity resources in place, which includes hiring more people with relevant cybersecurity skills, offering cybersecurity training to existing staff, including secure coding practices education for developers, and preparing more budget for cybersecurity activities to allow the organizations to acquire necessary cybersecurity resources, equipment, and tools.

1.3.3.2 Technical Takeaways

The main takeaways from the technical challenges are, first, for organizations to put increased security focus on, in particular, the high-risk technology areas, namely self-driving (autonomous and ADAS) technologies, and remote wireless communication interfaces including Wi-Fi, Bluetooth, and telematics. Second, organizations must have the understanding that software bugs and vulnerabilities will be detected in their automotive systems after vehicles have been released and that such vulnerabilities need to be addressed in a timely manner. Therefore, organizations must prepare technical solutions to allow OTA software updates and security patches in a secure manner. Third, as organizations are deploying more security solutions in automotive systems, and consequently more cryptographic keys are required to keep such systems secure, it is imperative that automotive organizations avoid manual processes for key management and instead employ best practices including the usage of secure key management systems.

1.3.3.3 Product Development and Security Testing Takeaways

The main takeaways from the challenges regarding product development and security testing are, first, for organizations to *shift left* and systematically assess risks and vulnerabilities in the early phases of development including the requirements, concept, design, and development phases. By conducting, for example, proper requirements reviews, design reviews, and threat analysis and risk assessments, an organization can build in security by incorporating the appropriate security controls early in the requirements and designs. Second, it is important that automotive organizations employ and follow a defined SSDLC process by applying appropriate security activities at each step in the development lifecycle. This includes, for example, defined procedures, security measures and activities to address *coding*, *testing*, and the use of *open-source software*, which are among the primary factors that lead to vulnerabilities. This could also include a security gate to ensure that the automotive software is tested before it is shipped. Third, to alleviate the pressure to meet deadlines, which is considered the top factor leading to vulnerabilities, it is imperative to improve efficiency and automation using automated tools. Thus, it is recommended that automotive organizations use automated tools as much as possible as part of the process. In particular, such tools can help organizations detect vulnerabilities in the software during coding, identify vulnerable open-source software, and detect vulnerabilities by performing automated security testing.

1.3.3.4 Supply Chain and Third-Party Components Takeaways

The main takeaways for the supply chain and third-party components challenges are, first, for automotive organizations to start providing downstream security requirements.

It is imperative that the OEMs, who are at the top of the supply chain, create and provide relevant security requirements to their suppliers. There should be both process-level requirements and product-level requirements. The process-level requirements should include requirements on the processes and product development, e.g. requiring suppliers to use certain type of approaches or tools to test for vulnerabilities. The product-level requirements would be product-specific requirements, e.g. a requirement for device authentication or storage of secret keys on the automotive system. These types of security requirements, if they are not applicable for the supplier in question, should then be passed on from the tier 1 supplier to the tier 2 supplier and so on. Second, once a supplier provides a product upstream, the receiving organization should have an established process for enforcing and verifying that the supplier has adhered to the provided security requirements. There are various approaches for conducting this type of assessment. For instance, the supplier can perform a self-assessment and provide the necessary artifacts, including documents, test results, log files, reports, etc., along with the deliverable to provide assurance that the requirements have been met. Alternatively, the receiving organization can perform the assessment by running various tests on the received automotive system or going onsite to the supplier to perform a supplier audit. Furthermore, the assessments could also be performed by an independent third party that tests the product or reviews the necessary processes, documents, and reports from the supplier. Regardless of the type of assessment, ultimately, the goal is to provide assurance that the deliverable fulfills the provided security requirements. Third, since the use of vulnerable open-source software components is one of the primary factors leading to vulnerabilities in automotive systems, it is imperative that automotive organizations have an established process for conducting open-source software management. Mainly, this means that organizations should know what open-source software components they are including in their automotive systems, which versions of the software are included and what the associated known vulnerabilities of those software versions are. Moreover, as a side-note as this is not directly related to cybersecurity, from a legal perspective considering open-source license compliance, it is important that organizations also know what the associated open-source software licenses are in order to be aware of potential legal risks [26].

1.3.3.5 Getting Started

Although the above-mentioned takeaways are general in nature to address the major concerns outlined in the automotive survey, it is imperative that an organization considers what approaches and solutions are appropriate for their organization. To this end, an organization may proceed with the following simple four steps illustrated by finding a treasure on a treasure map in Figure 1.9 to get started:

(1) Understand where you are;
(2) Identify where you want to go;
(3) Map out the way to go there;
(4) Start the journey and track the progress.

The first step is for the organization to understand where they are, i.e. the current state. This step includes organizing all internal relevant process documents, requirements documents, organizational charts, roles and responsibilities charts, security methodologies and

designed by 🌀 freepik.com

Figure 1.9 Four steps for automotive organizations to get started. Source: Freepik.com.

test approaches documents, lists of relevant test tools and test equipment, etc., to have a clear view of what the current cybersecurity posture looks like. The second step involves identifying what the goals for the organization are, i.e. the desired state. This step encompasses gathering and processing relevant material on standards, regulations, best practices, and guidelines to be able to define what the desired state should look like. Examples include new organizational charts with defined security roles and teams, process documents with new cybersecurity activities and cybersecurity gates, new test approaches requiring new test benches and test labs etc. Then, the third step consists of mapping out the activities and milestones to reach the desired state. This step includes creating a roadmap defining, for example, hiring of key security personnel over a certain time period, a timeline for updating the relevant internal process documents, and a plan for introducing new test tools within the organization and gradually deploying such tools further in the organization to expand its usage in a more automated fashion. Last, the fourth step comprises the organization starting the journey from the current state along the path indicated by the roadmap defined in the third step. During this journey, which involves a transformational change on an organizational level, it is important to track the progress of the activities to the milestones laid out in the roadmap, to finally reach the desired state.

1.3.3.6 Practical Examples of Organizations Who Have Started
This section highlights some practical examples of activities that some automotive organizations have already started in order to address the various challenges from the automotive survey. Considering the organizational challenges and takeaways, e.g. to help with empowerment and top-down priorities and strategies on cybersecurity, there are automotive organizations who have appointed cybersecurity leaders with titles such as cybersecurity chief and vice president, cybersecurity [27, 28]. Moreover, there are organizations with established security engineering processes [29], and in order to tackle the challenge with limited cybersecurity resources, there are several automotive organizations who acquire or establish joint ventures with automotive security companies [30–33].

Regarding the technical challenges and takeaways, organizations are putting more emphasis on security for the high-risk technology areas [34], and there are organizations working on secure OTA update solutions [35, 36].

In terms of the product development and security challenges and takeaways, there are organizations establishing cybersecurity lifecycle processes where risks and vulnerabilities are assessed early in the analysis and design phases to allow for appropriate security controls to be applied. Cybersecurity test labs are established in these organizations to improve efficiency and automation of security testing [37, 38].

Finally, regarding the supply chain and third party components challenges and takeaways, there are organizations who provide requirements and evaluate suppliers as part of the process [29].

As shown in this section, many organizations have already started the journey toward building secure cars by overcoming some of the highlighted challenges, and it is imperative that all relevant organizations in the automotive industry proceed in this direction by continuously tracking the progress and finally reaching the desired states.

1.3.3.7
This section is left intentionally blank.

1.4   Examples of Vulnerabilities in the Automotive Industry

While there have been numerous vulnerabilities and weaknesses identified in various automotive systems over the years, this section focuses on three examples. These examples highlight the top three factors, namely *coding*, *testing*, and *open-source software*, that lead to vulnerabilities, besides the high pressure to meet deadlines as indicated in the automotive survey [24].

The first example is regarding *coding* and highlights a buffer overflow vulnerability in an automotive system [39]. In this example, a certain modem software running on a telematics unit is used to create a link between the telematics unit and a remote telematics call center. This software explicitly supports receiving packet sizes up to 1024 bytes. Moreover, there is some custom code used to glue the modem software to a command program software which parses the packets from the modem software and passes them on to the command program. The command program then executes the commands included in the packets. Security researchers analyzed the software and identified that this custom code accepts packet sizes up to around only 100 bytes, which is assumed to be the maximum length of the commands. This difference in acceptable packet sizes between the modem software and the custom code leads to a buffer overflow vulnerability caused by a coding mistake. This buffer overflow vulnerability is remotely exploitable as illustrated in Figure 1.10. Please note that since this attack occurs on the lowest level of the protocol stack, it completely bypasses higher-level authentication checks implemented by the command program. An attacker is thus able to send a packet containing around 300 bytes exploit code, which is accepted by the modem software since it is less than 1024 bytes; however, it exploits the buffer overflow vulnerability in the custom code since the packet is larger than 100 bytes. This results in the attacker taking full control of the target system and consequently being able to send

Figure 1.10 Buffer overflow vulnerability caused by coding mistake.

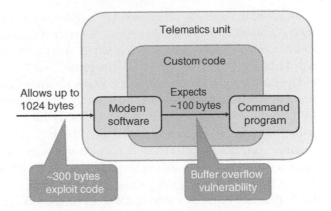

arbitrary CAN (controller area network) messages on the CAN bus, resulting in being able to control or disrupt vehicle functionality.

The second example is regarding *testing*. This example is based on an attack that involves exploiting several weaknesses and vulnerabilities in multiple steps [25]. For each step, it would be possible to apply appropriate test procedures or execute relevant test cases in order to identify the corresponding issues. Although the attack itself is sophisticated, the attack steps involved have been simplified for brevity as follows. First, the target vehicle is connected to a certain cellular network provider using a network address space of 21.0.0.0/8 or 25.0.0.0/8. This network provider did not block intra-device communication, meaning that an attacker device connected to the same network address space would be able to communicate with other devices, or vehicles in this case, connected to the same network address space. Security researchers scanned the cellular network with a network scanning tool called Nmap [40] and found 2695 vehicles connected to the network with a listening D-Bus service (port 6667), which is a software bus used for inter-process communication. In the second step, the security researchers remotely connected to the open D-Bus service on port 6667 on a target vehicle. This service was accessible remotely without any authentication. Next, in the third step, an "execute" method included in one of the services available through the D-Bus service was abused to execute arbitrary commands on the target system. As a result, the security researchers gained a remote root shell. Finally, in the fourth step, using access through the root shell, the security researchers updated the microcontroller responsible for CAN communication with an arbitrary firmware, which allows one to remotely inject arbitrary CAN messages. Thus, an attacker who is able to perform these steps would be able to take full control of the target system and consequently be able to send arbitrary CAN messages on the CAN bus.

For these four steps, the following test procedures or test cases could be used to identify the corresponding issues. For the first step, performing a test whether intra-device communication on the cellular network is possible. For the second step, conducting a test whether the open ports on the target system are remotely accessible without authentication. For the third step, perform testing to verify if any existing methods available through the D-Bus service allows executing arbitrary commands. For the fourth step, conduct testing of the firmware update process to verify whether digital signature verification is used and if the verification function has been implemented correctly.

Please note there may be many other weaknesses and vulnerabilities in automotive systems so, besides the specific test approaches related to these four steps, organizations should follow a secure development lifecycle where appropriate test cases and procedures are identified and applied in the process (cf. Chapters 2 and 7).

The third example is regarding *open-source software*, in particular focusing on known vulnerabilities in such software used in automotive systems that can be exploited by attackers [41]. In this example, a certain in-vehicle infotainment system is running a web browser using an old version (around 2.2.x.) of QtWebkit, which is an open-source web content rendering engine. Security researchers achieved code execution by exploiting two vulnerabilities in QtWebkit. The first vulnerability is a new vulnerability identified by the security researchers and exists in the function JSArray::sort(). It is a memory corruption vulnerability that can be used to alter contents of memory locations. The second vulnerability is a known vulnerability and has an assigned Common Vulnerabilities and Exposures (CVE) identifier CVE-2011-3928 [42]. It is a use-after-free vulnerability that can be used to leak memory. The security researchers developed exploit code that chains together these two vulnerabilities in the web browser. Consequently, this exploit code is used to gain a remote shell with web browser privileges on the target system. Since an attacker at this point would have restricted capabilities on the target system based on the web browser's process context, the natural next step for an attacker is to gain root privileges to be able to execute arbitrary commands. The target system is based on the Linux kernel, which is an open-source operating system kernel. Linux kernel version 2.6.36 is used, which is an old version containing nearly no exploit mitigations. Moreover, this Linux kernel version contains a known vulnerability, assigned CVE-2013-6282 [43], which allows an attacker to read or modify arbitrary kernel memory locations via a crafted application. In the next step, the security researchers crafted exploit code which exploits this known Linux kernel vulnerability to gain remote root privileges. An attacker would now have full control of this system achieved by only exploiting vulnerable open-source software. As a side-note, while the following step does not include open-source software, it is worth noting that an attacker can flash a modified firmware to the Gateway ECU, which allows one to send arbitrary CAN messages on the CAN bus. Thus, this attack is made possible initially through vulnerable open-source software, in particular by exploiting two known vulnerabilities.

1.5 Chapter Summary

This chapter provided an overview of the current state of cybersecurity in the automotive industry. First, an introduction to various relevant cybersecurity standards, guidelines and activities is given to provide some background on the current automotive cybersecurity landscape. Examples covered in this chapter include SAE J3061, the first cybersecurity standard for the automotive industry, the upcoming ISO/SAE 21434, which supersedes the SAE J3061, and the two UNECE WP.29 regulations on cybersecurity and software updates. Besides standards, there are specific coding guidelines often used in the automotive industry such as MISRA and AUTOSAR coding guidelines to help develop safe and secure code. Moreover, considering the complex supply chain in the automotive industry, there are ongoing activities to help manage the risks in the supply chain by the usage of SBOM. For example, NTIA of the United States Department of Commerce has established a task force focusing on software component transparency promoting SBOM for practical deployment. As a result of these cybersecurity related standards, regulations, guidelines, and activities, the automotive industry is going through a transformation driven by cybersecurity. To this end, automotive organizations need to update their internal processes and make changes to their organizational structures. Additionally, to effectively realize these process changes requires organizations to deploy new technical solutions. An example is the addition of a security gate to perform fuzz testing as part of the development process, and deployment of the corresponding technical solution to perform the testing required for the security gate. Furthermore, to get an insight into what the common challenges in the automotive industry are, an independent study on cybersecurity practices in the automotive industry was conducted by the Ponemon Institute and the corresponding results were released in 2019. Highlights from this study are presented in this chapter, and are organized into four categories: organizational challenges, technical challenges, product development and security testing practices, and supply chain and third-party component challenges. Based on these challenges, this chapter provided a number of takeaways to help organizations address the corresponding challenges for each of the four categories. Last, this chapter gave a few examples of how vulnerabilities in automotive systems can be exploited by attackers to get a better understanding of potential consequences caused by not adequately addressing cybersecurity during the development lifecycle.

References

1 Visualcapitalist (2017). How many millions of lines of code does it take? https://www .visualcapitalist.com/millions-lines-of-code (accessed 30 July 2020).

2 NASA (2001). Advanced vehicle automation and computers aboard the shuttle. https:// history.nasa.gov/sts1/pages/computer.html (accessed 30 July 2020).

3 International Organization for Standardization (ISO) (2018). *ISO 26262-1:2018 – road vehicles — functional safety*. Geneva, Switzerland: ISO.

4 International Organization for Standardization (ISO) (2019). *ISO/PAS 21448:2019 – road vehicles — safety of the intended functionality*. Geneva, Switzerland: ISO.

5 VDA QMC Working Group 13/Automotive SIG (2017). Automotive SPICE process reference model/process assessment model version 3.1. VDA QMC.

6 MISRA. MISRA publications. www.misra.org.uk/Publications/tabid/57/Default.aspx (accessed 30 July 2020).

7 Society of Automotive Engineers (SAE) International (2016). SAE J3061 – cybersecurity guidebook for cyber-physical vehicle systems. USA: SAE International.

8 International Organization for Standardization (ISO)/Society of Automotive Engineers (SAE) International (2020). *ISO/SAE DIS 21434 – road vehicles — cybersecurity engineering*. Geneva, Switzerland: ISO and USA: SAE International.

9 Lin, C. K. (2020). Implementing automotive cybersecurity based on ISO/SAE 21434 and WP 29. *Automotive Software Frontier*, Tokyo, Japan.

10 UNECE (2020). UN regulations on cybersecurity and software updates to pave the way for mass roll out of connected vehicles. https://unece.org/press/un-regulations-cybersecurity-and-software-updates-pave-way-mass-roll-out-connected-vehicles (accessed 30 July 2020).

11 Singapore Standards Council (2019). Technical reference for autonomous vehicles – part 3: cybersecurity principles and assessment. Singapore: Enterprise Singapore.

12 ENISA (2017). Cyber security and resilience of smart cars.

13 ENISA (2019). ENISA good practices for security of smart cars.

14 NHTSA (2016). Cybersecurity best practices for modern vehicles.

15 Congress (2015). S.1806 – SPY car act of 2015. https://www.congress.gov/bill/114th-congress/senate-bill/1806/text (accessed 30 July 2020).

16 Congress (2017). S.680 – SPY car act of 2017. https://www.congress.gov/bill/115th-congress/senate-bill/680/text (accessed 30 July 2020).

17 Congress (2019). S.2182 – SPY car act of 2019. https://www.congress.gov/bill/116th-congress/senate-bill/2182/text (accessed 30 July 2020).

18 MISRA (2016). MISRA C:2012 Amendment 1 – additional security guidelines for MISRA C:2012.

19 SEI (2016). CERT C coding standard – rules for developing safe, reliable, and secure systems.

20 SEI (2016). CERT C++ coding standard – rules for developing safe, reliable, and secure systems in C++.

21 AUTOSAR (2019). Guidelines for the use of the C++14 language in critical and safety-related systems.

22 MITRE (2020). CWE common weakness enumeration. https://cwe.mitre.org (accessed 30 July 2020).

23 NTIA (2020). NTIA software component transparency. https://www.ntia.doc.gov/SoftwareTransparency (accessed 30 July 2020).

24 Ponemon Institute - SAE International and Synopsys (2019). Securing the modern vehicle: a study of automotive industry cybersecurity practices. Synopsys, Inc. and SAE International.

25 Miller, C. and Valasek, C. Remote exploitation of an unaltered passenger vehicle. *Black Hat USA*, Las Vegas, NV, USA.

26 Synopsys (2019). Top open source licenses and legal risk for developers. https://www.synopsys.com/blogs/software-security/top-open-source-licenses (accessed 30 July 2020).

27 Reuters (2014). General motors appoints its first cybersecurity chief. https://www.reuters.com/article/us-gm-cybersecurity/general-motors-appoints-its-first-cybersecurity-chiefidUSKCN0HI2M020140923 (accessed 30 July 2020).

28 aftermarketNews (2016). Lear appoints industry expert to lead cyber security for E-systems https://www.aftermarketnews.com/lear-appoints-industry-expert-to-lead-cyber-security-for-e-systems (accessed 30 July 2020).

29 Bosch (2018). Product security at Bosch. https://www.boschsecurity.com/xe/en/support/product-security (accessed 30 July 2020).

30 ETAS (2012). ETAS acquires system house ESCRYPT. https://www.etas.com/en/company/news_archive_2012-etas_acquires_system_house_escrypt.php (accessed 30 July 2020).

31 Businesswire (2016). HARMAN completes acquisition of TowerSec automotive cyber security. https://www.businesswire.com/news/home/20160311005083/en/HARMAN-Completes-Acquisition-TowerSec-Automotive-Cyber-Security (accessed 30 July 2020).

32 Reuters (2017). Germany's continental buys Israeli auto cyber firm Argus. https://www.reuters.com/article/us-argus-m-a-continental/germanys-continental-buys-israeli-autocyber-firm-argus-idUSKBN1D31DR (accessed 30 July 2020).

33 Denso (2018). DENSO and NRI SecureTechnologies agree to establish a joint venture for the growing automotive cybersecurity market. https://www.denso.com/global/en/news/newsroom/2018/20180927-g01 (accessed 30 July 2020).

34 Aptiv (2020). Connectivity & security. https://www.aptiv.com/solutions/connectivity-and-security (accessed 30 July 2020).

35 Harman (2020). HARMAN OTA (over-the-air) solution. https://car.harman.com/solutions/ota/harman-ota-over-air-solution (accessed 30 July 2020).

36 Vector (2020). Automotive over-the-air. https://www.vector.com/int/en/know-how/technologies/automotive-connectivity/automotive-ota (accessed 30 July 2020).

37 Chen, B. (2019). Security development by China FAW Group. *escar Asia,* Tokyo, Japan.

38 Auto-ISAC (2019). Auto-ISAC fall summit 2019. https://www.automotiveisac.com/wp-content/uploads/2019/02/2019-11-14-Auto-ISAC-2019-Summit-Slides.pdf (accessed 30 July 2020).

39 Checkoway, S., McCoy, D., Kantor, B. et al. (2011). Comprehensive experimental analyses of automotive attack surfaces. *USENIX Security,* San Francisco, CA, USA.

40 Nmap (2020). Nmap free security scanner. https://nmap.org. (accessed 30 July 2020).

41 Nie, S., Liu, L., and Du, Y. (2017). Free-fall: hacking Tesla from wireless to CAN bus. *Black Hat USA,* Las Vegas, NV, USA.

42 NIST (2012). National vulnerability database – CVE-2011-3928. https://nvd.nist.gov/vuln/detail/CVE-2011-3928 (accessed 30 July 2020).

43 NIST (2013). National vulnerability database – CVE-2013-6282. https://nvd.nist.gov/vuln/detail/CVE-2013-6282 (accessed 30 July 2020).

2

Introduction to Security in the Automotive Software Development Lifecycle

Security is not a feature, it is a necessity

There are currently four major trends in the automotive industry. These trends are commonly known by the acronym CASE: *Connected, Autonomous, Shared and services,* and *Electric*. These four trends are the main drivers for the unprecedented increase of software in the automotive domain. *Connectivity* software allows for more use cases for the connected car scenario by adding support for more communication interfaces, such as Wi-Fi, Bluetooth, cellular, etc., and allowing control of various vehicle functions remotely, such as remote engine start and door lock/unlock features. *Autonomous* vehicles or various advanced driving assistance systems (ADAS) require more software for processing data from sensors and cameras, logic for decision making, safety and vehicle control, etc. Software solutions for *Shared and services* allow for a larger vehicle eco-system going beyond a specific vehicle to enable mobility services provided by backend systems and mobile apps, including ride-sharing, ride-hailing, car-sharing, and various location-based services. Finally, software required for *electrification* allows for the efficient use of electric vehicles (EVs), including battery management systems, charging functionality and motor control. As a result, vehicles today contain more than 100 million lines of code. Further, software in vehicles is growing at an incredible rate, and it is projected that semi-autonomous vehicles (SAE J3016 [1] level 3) will contain more than 300 million lines of code and a fully autonomous vehicle (level 5) more than 1 billion lines of code! [2]. It is forecast that there will be 80 million autonomous vehicles (level 4 or level 5) in 2030 [3]. It is also forecast that there will be 125 million connected vehicles in 2022 [4] and 470 million connected vehicles in 2025 [3]. To support the development of these connected and autonomous vehicles, the automotive industry is growing at a fast pace. Studies indicate that the ADAS global market will more than double from $27 billion in 2020 to $83 billion by 2030 with the main demands coming from semi-autonomous driving systems [5]. Moreover, the automotive software market is estimated to grow from $19 billion in 2018 to reach $60 billion by 2025, with the driving forces being communication systems and software for passenger vehicles, including more software to improve user experience [6]. As a result of more software with growing complexities and an increasing number of connected vehicles, cybersecurity threats targeting vehicles will also increase. Increased connectivity presents more attack surfaces,

Building Secure Cars: Assuring the Automotive Software Development Lifecycle, First Edition. Dennis Kengo Oka.
© 2021 John Wiley & Sons Ltd. Published 2021 by John Wiley & Sons Ltd.

and complex software increases the risk for critical software vulnerabilities. As a result, there is a need to consider security throughout the entire automotive development lifecycle to reduce the risk of vulnerabilities. This growing need for security is evident from forecasts showing that the automotive cybersecurity market is projected to grow from $1.34 billion in 2018 to $5.77 billion by 2025 with a focus on in-vehicle application security [7].

The main points of this chapter are:

- We analyze the current automotive development lifecycle and existing challenges.
- We give recommendations on how to address security at each step in the automotive software development lifecycle.
- We discuss new technical challenges and present suggestions for how to tackle such challenges.

More details about security in the automotive software development lifecycle can be found in [8].

2.1 V-Model Software Development Process

The traditional development process in the automotive industry follows the ASPICE (Automotive Software Process Improvement and Capability dEtermination) V-model [9]. This development process is illustrated in Figure 2.1, and shows the different activities and steps included in the automotive development lifecycle.

Previously, one focus area for development of automotive software was on functional safety according to standards such as ISO 26262 [10]. This standard offers guidance on approaches to reduce the risk of systematic failures and random hardware failures. Because of new developments, including increased connectivity and more complex software responsible for various vehicle controls such as steering and braking, the automotive industry needs to consider not only safety risks but emerging cybersecurity-related threats and risks. To counter such threats and risks, the response from the automotive industry has been to engage in various security initiatives. For example, there have been standardization activities to improve automotive cybersecurity in recent years, including SAE J3061

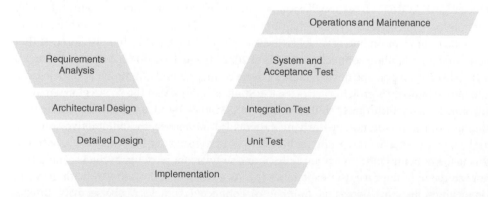

Figure 2.1 Traditional V-model development process used in the automotive industry.

"Cybersecurity Guidebook for Cyber-Physical Vehicle Systems" [11] and ISO/SAE 21434 "Road Vehicles – Cybersecurity Engineering" [12]. These standards provide a process framework, guidance to identify and assess cybersecurity threats, and guidance to design cybersecurity into cyber-physical vehicle systems through the entire development lifecycle. In addition, these documents highlight the fact that safety-critical systems are a subset of cybersecurity-critical systems, i.e. emphasizing the mantra *"there is no safety without security."* Consequently, it is imperative to consider how to incorporate security at each step in the automotive development lifecycle since software mistakes and vulnerabilities introduced during development could have serious safety-related consequences during operation. Moreover, it is also imperative to consider that, besides safety-related consequences, cybersecurity attacks can have impacts on finance, operations, and privacy.

2.2 Challenges in Automotive Software Development

It is well-known that, traditionally, development cycles in the automotive industry span several years, which means that the notion of security-by-design must happen years in advance of a vehicle being released. As a result, a huge challenge is that when a vehicle is released, the state-of-the-art security level, concept and software that is typically included in the vehicle may be outdated, as it is from years ago. Additionally, vehicles have long life spans, ranging from 10 to 15 years, which means that security needs to be designed such that vehicles can stay secure for their entire lifetimes. Yet another challenge is that many vehicles often have limited functionality to perform software updates remotely; thus, there are difficulties providing fixes to any identified vulnerabilities in a reasonable amount of time, as highlighted in Section 1.3.2.2. If vulnerabilities are found in software running on vehicles in the field and there is no possibility to perform over-the-air updates of the affected software, an auto manufacturer may be forced to recall the vulnerable vehicles, which is extremely costly. For example, in 2015, Chrysler recalled 1.4 million vehicles due to a software vulnerability in Chrysler's uConnect system [13].

Although the introduction of several wireless communication interfaces – such as Wi-Fi, Bluetooth, cellular, and V2X (vehicle-to-X) – allows for more advanced functionality and allows for providing better services to the users, it also increases the attack surface of the vehicle by introducing potential entry points to attackers. These wireless interfaces may also include newly developed communication stacks, such as for V2X, that perhaps have not had the benefit of enduring years of testing in other industries, such as common communication stacks for Wi-Fi and Bluetooth.

Further challenges include the large and growing volume of software used in automotive systems and the fact that software is developed and supplied to OEMs (original equipment manufacturers) in an often complex supply chain. There are several tiers of software suppliers providing various software components including drivers, libraries, OSs (operating systems), and applications. These software components may include a combination of proprietary own-developed software, third-party developed software, commercial software, as well as open-source software. Consequently, it may be difficult for OEMs to know exactly what software is included in the automotive systems that are delivered to them and what level of security a certain piece of software may have. For example, a vulnerability in a software component provided by a supplier may lead to a full compromise of a vehicle. Take the example of the Tesla hack presented at Black Hat [14], also described in more detail in Section 1.4, where the initial entry point was exploiting a vulnerability in a piece of open-source software related to the web browser in the infotainment system, followed by several steps that finally allowed an attacker to send arbitrary messages on the CAN (controller area network) bus to control vehicle functionality. This example shows the levels of complexity in software where one vulnerability in one system can lead to a compromise, and further lead to finding vulnerabilities in a different system that can be exploited, and so forth. Moreover, the development of new technologies such as ADAS and autonomous driving, and more advanced infotainment and telematics systems require larger software bases, which often means more complex software. Consequently, the development of large and complex software increases the risk for introduction of software vulnerabilities.

2.3 Security Solutions at each Step in the V-Model

For each step in the V-model there are security solutions that automotive organizations can employ. To reduce the risk of software vulnerabilities, the following recommendations on how to address security in each stage of the software development cycle are provided. The security recommendations are mapped onto each step, as illustrated in Figure 2.2. This figure is based on an overview of the product development phases from SAE J3061 and ISO/SAE 21434, containing the respective security steps. The recommended security activities presented can be conducted internally by various development teams and

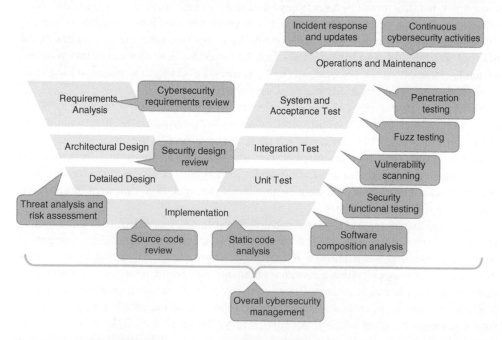

Figure 2.2 V-model development process used in the automotive industry with security activities mapped to each step.

security teams with the necessary expertise and experience or, in some cases, performed externally by third-party security vendors. Besides the security activities during the product development phases, this chapter also briefly mentions some considerations for the post-development phases as well as the overarching cybersecurity management that needs to be considered for the organization.

2.3.1 Cybersecurity Requirements Review

Product development at software level is initiated in the top-left corner of the V-model. Typically, as functional requirements are defined, it is necessary to also define the required software cybersecurity requirements. Here it is important to verify that the software cybersecurity requirements are appropriate for the target system. Therefore, at this step it is recommended that a *cybersecurity requirements review* is conducted. The purpose of the cybersecurity requirements review is to identify any missing cybersecurity requirements or detect any critical security flaws in the specified requirements at a very early stage in the development cycle. It also allows for a better understanding of the overall cybersecurity goals and cybersecurity concept. Moreover, the requirements are reviewed to ensure that the defined cybersecurity requirements are aligned with best practices. The review of the cybersecurity requirements should include, among others, analyzing requirements regarding authentication, authorization, usage of cryptographic algorithms and keys, input validation, mechanisms for monitoring and detecting attacks, countermeasures for detected attacks, and requirements for storage of sensitive data such as passwords or log files.

2.3.2 Security Design Review

In the next steps during the design activities it is recommended for automotive organizations to perform a *security design review*. By carefully examining the software architecture and application design it is possible to detect weaknesses in the design that attackers may be able to abuse. For example, by analyzing the design and how it fulfills the previously defined cybersecurity requirements to achieve the cybersecurity goals, it is possible to verify that there are no weaknesses in the design itself. While security design reviews can be performed during different stages of the development lifecycle, it is recommended to perform these reviews as early as possible to be able to rectify the design before coding has started. Any changes made to the design after software has been written may require rewriting large parts of the software. Security design reviews are useful to identify any issues regarding the design of security controls that should be implemented based on the requirements. For example, a security design review can detect that isolation between applications is insufficient or that storage of sensitive data is not protected adequately.

2.3.3 Threat Analysis and Risk Assessment

Threat analysis and risk assessment (TARA) is an activity that should occur several times during the product development, and initially during the concept phase when the initial goals and requirements are defined. Per the ISO/SAE DIS 21434 standard it is a requirement to perform TARA. This activity includes several steps such as identifying assets and threat scenarios, performing impact rating, analyzing the attack paths and conducting an attack feasibility rating, and finally determining risk values and making risk treatment decisions. This activity helps to refine the cybersecurity requirements and software design. The TARA is performed by using known attack patterns and system-specific attacks targeting the defined assets. The risks are assessed by combining the impact, e.g. based on safety, financial, operational and privacy, with the likelihood, e.g. derived from time, expertise, knowledge of target, window of opportunity and equipment. The result of the TARA is a prioritized list of risks and, for each identified risk, the organization must make a decision: to *accept* the risk as identified, to *transfer* the risk to another entity in the eco-system that is capable of taking the risk, to *take action* by implementing, for example, a security control to reduce the risk, or *avoid* the risk entirely by, for example, removing the specific feature or requirement that is associated with the risk.

2.3.4 Source Code Review

In the next step, during implementation the software development is started, and it is recommended that the organization performs *source code reviews*. Source code reviews can involve both automated code scanning using tools and risk-based manual code reviews. Automated code scanning tools can be run directly in the IDE (integrated development environment) and can automatically detect common vulnerabilities and offer practical remediation guidance directly while the developer is typing the code. This also has the added benefit that it assists in teaching secure coding practices and improves the security awareness of developers. In a manual code review, the source code is read line-by-line by an experienced code reviewer to identify any potential vulnerabilities. While this approach may allow better understanding of the intentions of the developer, it is time-consuming and costly, and requires human code reviewers with appropriate skills and experience. The main advantage is that source code reviews helps to identify potential security issues early and allows software coding mistakes to be fixed as they arise.

2.3.5 Static Code Analysis

Furthermore, while software is being developed, it is recommended to perform *static code analysis*. Static code analysis helps reduce risk and overall project costs by identifying critical quality defects and weaknesses in the code that can lead to security vulnerabilities, such as CWE (Common Weakness Enumeration) [15] by just scanning source code. The added benefits are that there is no need to write test cases or execute the code. Moreover, static code analysis tools can be integrated with the existing tools and systems used in the current development process in an organization, such as source code management systems, build and continuous integration tools, and bug tracking and application lifecycle management solutions. Static code analysis tools also provide developers with reliable, actionable information and remediation guidance so that the developers can address vulnerabilities quickly. Such tools typically include checkers to find, for example, buffer overflows, deadlocks, hard-coded credentials, integer overflows, memory corruptions, and illegal accesses. Furthermore, the ISO/SAE DIS 21434 standard requires software to follow coding guidelines where necessary, and since static code analysis tools scans the source code they are suitable to run checkers for such guidelines, like CERT (Computer Emergency Response Team) C coding standards [16]. Additionally, automotive software is often required to be MISRA compliant, traditionally from a safety point of view; however, in 2016, MISRA published an amendment to MISRA C:2012 to also include security guidelines [17]. Static code analysis tools can scan source code and perform MISRA coding guidelines checks to assist automotive organizations to develop MISRA-compliant code.

2.3.6 Software Composition Analysis

As part of implementation it is common to integrate various software components and it is therefore recommended that these various integrated software components are tested for vulnerabilities. There are two types of vulnerabilities to consider: known vulnerabilities and unknown vulnerabilities. Known vulnerabilities can be identified using, for example, *software composition analysis* tools. Software composition analysis can be performed on source code or binaries. For example, a supplier that is developing software can run software composition analysis on the accessible source code. Similarly, a supplier or an OEM that receives software as binaries can run software composition analysis on the received binaries. These types of software can contain open-source software components, such as various libraries. By running software composition analysis on the software, it is possible to identify third-party and open-source software components, known vulnerabilities, associated license types and other potential risks. Additional information from the National Institute of Standards and Technology (NIST) National Vulnerability Database (NVD) [18], including the Common Vulnerabilities and Exposures (CVE) [19] identifier and the associated severity level of the detected vulnerabilities, can typically be provided by the software composition analysis tools. This analysis allows an OEM or supplier to gain visibility into the composition of the developed or received software, to make better buying decisions or help make decisions on which open-source software to include, and to manage the ongoing risks of operating complex systems and software.

2.3.7 Security Functional Testing

Functional testing is typically performed in the next step to verify the functionality of the implementation. In this step, it is recommended to also perform *security functional testing*. The main focus is on testing the implementation of security-related functionality – e.g. authentication and encryption subsystems, and access control – to detect implementation errors, discrepancies to the specification, and unspecified functionality. Any issues detected at this point may have impacts on the security of the system as a whole. Therefore, it is imperative to test the implementation of security functionality in regard to correctness, performance, compliance, and robustness.

2.3.8 Vulnerability Scanning

During the next step, as the target implementation becomes more functional, it is recommended to perform *vulnerability scanning*. Typically, vulnerability scanning is conducted based on a dynamic application security testing approach which provides various inputs to the target software and observes the responses. These inputs are formatted by the vulnerability scanning tool to test the target implementation for known common security vulnerabilities and configurations with known weaknesses. Besides testing for known vulnerabilities, it is also possible to detect unknown vulnerabilities in the target software by performing vulnerability scanning using known attack patterns. For example, vulnerability scanning may detect that it is possible to bypass authentication and access critical functionality on the target system due to an implementation mistake or misconfiguration of the system.

2.3.9   Fuzz Testing

While software composition analysis is useful for identifying known vulnerabilities, and vulnerability scanning may be useful for detecting some types of unknown vulnerabilities, it is recommended in the next step to use fuzzing as a technique to test for and find unknown vulnerabilities. There are different automated *fuzz testing* tools that use various techniques of fuzzing. In general, the tools provide malformed inputs to the system under test and observe the behavior to uncover failure modes and unexpected behavior. The approaches to generate the malformed input may differ. For example, some simple fuzzers, often called dumb fuzzers, just provide random input and may in some cases not even be aware of the input structure. Some fuzzers are mutation-based, meaning that they generate fuzzed data based on some specific seed inputs, e.g. valid files or communication protocol logs. The mutation-based fuzzer then modifies certain bits of the seeds to generate semi-valid inputs. The third type of fuzzer is a generation-based fuzzer or model-based fuzzer. The strength of this fuzzer is that it is intelligent and typically understands the network protocols and file formats being used, for example, message sequences and specific fields, such as checksums. With such information, it intelligently generates fuzzed data from scratch to yield optimal results, where, for example, the necessary fuzzed data is in the data field and a correct checksum of this data is calculated and included in the message. In contrast, a random dumb fuzzer would be able to include fuzzed data but would be unaware of the checksum field and therefore not generate the correct checksum value. As a result, the target system would reject the data based on the incorrect checksum even before the application that is to be tested can process the fuzzed data. Consequently, serious consideration should be taken when choosing the type of fuzzer to use.

2.3.10   Penetration Testing

As a final step before release, the developed system is tested against the cybersecurity goals in a step typically knows as validation. In this step, it is recommended to perform *penetration testing* of the target system. There are different approaches for penetration testing depending on the purpose, including black-box, gray-box and white-box approaches [20]. Black-box testing has the advantage that the penetration tester simulates a real-world attacker who has access to only publicly available information, and this approach could be useful to an organization to get a realistic understanding of what a real-world attacker could potentially do. The disadvantage is that the pentester must spend significant time on reverse-engineering tasks to understand certain protocols or commands, or to bypass certain access controls, which may lead to missing deeper issues. In gray-box testing the pentester is provided with certain pieces of information regarding the target system, which allows the pentester to save time on reverse-engineering tasks and, as a result, can achieve better coverage. This approach can uncover deeper issues in the system and is often the preferred approach for penetration testing. In white-box testing, the pentester is provided with full documentation and necessary information about the target system, which can help uncover specific weaknesses in the system. The disadvantage is that such attack conditions are typically not realistic and may give the wrong estimate of attack difficulty and likelihood, which could lead to incorrect risk treatment decisions. There are generally two types of penetration testing: system testing and hardware testing. The system testing applies to the target system communications and target system software. Penetration testing activities include, among other things, reconnaissance, configuration analysis, network communication analysis, wireless communication analysis, and reverse-engineering of software. The hardware testing applies to the target system hardware and requires physical access. Reconnaissance, physical analysis, chip and bus analysis, system-specific attack analysis, and firmware extraction and analysis are examples of activities commonly included for this type of penetration testing. It is important that the penetration testers are aware of the cybersecurity goals for the target system, e.g. protection of secret keys, so that the focus of testing is targeting the validation of such goals. Consequently, penetration testing can assist in finding issues in configuration, implementation, and design of the system that may have been missed in earlier stages in the development lifecycle, and is thus an important step in creating a secure product.

2.3.11 Incident Response and Updates

After a product has gone through all the cybersecurity-related activities in the product development phases – including cybersecurity requirements review, security design review, TARA, source code review, static code analysis, software composition analysis, security functional testing, vulnerability scanning, fuzz testing, and penetration testing, as part of the entire product lifecycle – it is also necessary to consider cybersecurity-related activities in the operations and maintenance phases. These activities include *incident response and updates* of the target systems [12]. If there is an incident occurring in the field – for example, there is a report about a software vulnerability that has been exploited and that can cause serious impact to the driver of the vulnerable vehicle – the automotive organization has to be ready to provide a response to that particular incident. This includes establishing the necessary incident response teams and processes, including the internal reviewing steps to verify the vulnerability and the decision on how to fix it, and approval processes on how to deliver the fixed software through updates to the affected vehicles. There are technical solutions that need to deployed, such as systems to, for example, handle reporting of incidents, make decisions on how to address vulnerabilities, and allow for software updates on the affected vehicles. Additionally, there are organizational solutions that need to be established, such as defining new processes or modifying existing processes for handling incidents and updates, creating responsibility matrixes for handling incidents and approving fixes and updates, and defining communication matrixes between the incident response teams, development teams, verification teams, and delivery teams.

2.3.12 Continuous Cybersecurity Activities

Continuing on activities for the operations and maintenance phases, it is also necessary for automotive organizations to consider *continuous cybersecurity activities*, such as cybersecurity monitoring, cybersecurity event assessment, vulnerability analysis and vulnerability management [12]. Cybersecurity monitoring entails activities to collect cybersecurity relevant information regarding threats, vulnerabilities and mitigations, which is used as the input to vulnerability management and cybersecurity incident response activities. For example, the information collected is processed and used by concept and development teams to avoid known vulnerabilities and to consider new threats and possible countermeasures. Cybersecurity event assessment focuses on analyzing information regarding a specific cybersecurity event to determine the criticality and decide whether to proceed with a certain cybersecurity incident response. Vulnerability analysis is conducted to further analyze a specific vulnerability identified during the cybersecurity event assessment, to determine the potential attack paths and how feasible it is to exploit the vulnerability. As a result of this vulnerability analysis, vulnerability management involves determining the risk of attacks and the corresponding countermeasure to handle the risk.

2.3.13 Overall Cybersecurity Management

In addition to all the previously mentioned cybersecurity activities at each step of the product development phases, and operations and maintenance phases, automotive organizations also need to consider and implement an overarching security culture and governance as part of the *overall cybersecurity management*. This includes, for example, embracing a cybersecurity awareness program, competence management and continuous improvement [12]. The organization has to define cybersecurity policies and create cybersecurity process requirements documents to enable a cybersecurity engineering framework, where the above-mentioned activities in the product lifecycle development and the continuous cybersecurity activities can be fulfilled. These documents could also include specific templates and step-by-step guidelines used in various activities such as TARAs. In addition, these process requirements documents should be reviewed over time to ensure best practices are employed in the entire development lifecycle. Furthermore, the overall cybersecurity management should also encompass cybersecurity considerations for the automotive organization in terms of responsibilities and resources. This includes ensuring that the organization has enough resources dedicated to cybersecurity activities, that the resources have the necessary cybersecurity competences, including receiving cybersecurity training when deemed needed, and that the responsibilities are clearly defined for the resources; for example, it is clearly defined who is responsible for risk management and who is responsible for incident response, etc.

2.4 New Technical Challenges

The recommendations presented in this chapter will lead to improvements of cybersecurity in the automotive software development lifecycle; however, employing these recommendations may incur new technical challenges. For example, if static code analysis is performed on a target software with CERT C or MISRA C checkers enabled, and the software originally has not been developed according to these respective coding guidelines, the target software will generate a large number of violations that may be impractical to handle. Another example is if a software contains many third-party components that have not been developed according to these coding guidelines, and similarly static code analysis is conducted on the entire software with the coding guideline checkers enabled. This will also generate a great number of violations. Triaging this large number of findings is going to take an unnecessarily long time and, in some cases, would be infeasible due to time constraints. Moreover, many of the violations may not be fixable since they are included in third-party code and modifying that code may have unknown adverse effects. Therefore, it may not be as easy for an organization to just enable checkers in the static code analysis tool at this particular step in the development lifecycle and believe that security will automatically be improved. For example, further analysis is required to understand which parts of the software should adhere to the CERT C or MISRA C coding guidelines and how to, for example, segment the codebase so that the static code analysis tool only checks the relevant parts of the software, especially if the software includes third-party components. This approach allows for an efficient and effective use of static code analysis and reduces unnecessary time spent on triaging irrelevant findings.

Yet another example that may introduce new technical challenges is adopting the fuzz testing activity in the development lifecycle. When performing fuzz testing on a specific software component it is necessary to consider how much fuzz testing is needed for the relevant interfaces including network protocols and file formats. One suggested approach is to use results from the TARA activity conducted earlier in the development lifecycle for that specific component combined with some internal guidelines based on, for instance, a Fuzz Testing Maturity Model (FTMM) [21]. The FTMM provides a set of standard levels for fuzz testing. There are five different levels specified in the FTMM: (i) Initial, (ii) Defined, (iii) Managed, (iv) Integrated, and (v) Optimized. The different levels define, for example, the type of fuzzing (e.g. generation or template), how many test cases or how many hours are required at a minimum, and what is required to be documented in the fuzz testing report. The internal guidelines could be used to indicate that for high-risk interfaces identified in the TARA, such as Wi-Fi or Bluetooth, fuzz testing has to be performed to a level equal to 4 or 5 in the FTMM, and, conversely, for low-risk interfaces such OBD-2 (on-board diagnostics) or USB, an FTMM level of 1 or 2 should be achieved.

Additionally, included in the ISO/SAE DIS 21434 is an informative annex describing Cybersecurity Assurance Levels (CALs). Following an approach using CALs together with the FTMM, it would be possible to create a matrix defining how much fuzz testing is required for each level of the specified CALs. A simple example matrix is presented in Table 2.1.

Based on the results from the TARA, high-risk interfaces can then be assigned a certain CAL, which then indicates how much fuzz testing should be performed for that level. An example of this mapping is shown in a matrix in Table 2.2.

For example, the L2CAP (logical link control and adaptation protocol) layer in Bluetooth is remotely accessible before pairing is initiated and is thus more likely to be targeted in an attack based on results from an example TARA. Therefore, L2CAP is assigned CAL 4. Moreover, the TARA results indicate that the damage impact associated with a successful

Table 2.1 Test activities mapped to CALS.

Test activity	CAL 1	CAL 2	CAL 3	CAL 4
Fuzz testing	8 h	16 h	40 h	160 h
...	...	...	...	...

Table 2.2 Mapping of interfaces and protocols to CALS.

Interface	Sub-interface/Protocol layer	CAL	Rationale based on TARA
Bluetooth	L2CAP	4	Accessible before pairing
	HFP	3	...
	A2DP	3	...
Wi-Fi	802.11	3	...
	DHCP	2	Damage impact is low
	HTTP	3	...
	TLS	3	...
File parser	zip	3	Update file can change behavior of system
	jpg	2	...
	mp3	2	...

attack on DHCP (Dynamic Host Configuration Protocol) over Wi-Fi is low and therefore the assigned CAL value is 2. Finally, the TARA shows that an attacker can use malicious zip files to update the target system to change the system behavior, and therefore the zip file format is assigned CAL 3. An organization can use these results combined with the values in Table 2.1 to help determine the amount of fuzz testing for the various interfaces and protocols on the target system.

In addition, to be able to effectively and efficiently perform the necessary fuzz testing, a proper test environment needs to be prepared to allow for automation of test cases to be sent to the target system as well as detection of exceptions. Therefore, when introducing fuzz testing in the automotive development lifecycle, it may not be as easy for an organization to just have a requirements document stating that fuzz testing needs to be done. Automotive organizations need to carefully consider the level and depth of fuzz testing that is suitable for the target software and interfaces, e.g. based on the FTMM and CAL, as well as take into consideration the necessary test environment required to achieve a high level of automation.

2.5 Chapter Summary

Considering how to incorporate cybersecurity in the automotive development lifecycle is imperative. This chapter provided several examples of cybersecurity activities that can be performed at each step in the development lifecycle. Specifically, the following activities are recommended to be performed early in the development lifecycle: cybersecurity requirements review, security design review, and TARA. Moreover, during the product development phases, it is recommended to perform source code reviews and static code analysis to identify and fix potential vulnerabilities in the source code early during development. Additionally, as various software components, including open-source software, are integrated into the codebase, it is recommended to conduct software composition analysis to identify known vulnerabilities. Further, various approaches of dynamic security testing, including security functional testing, vulnerability scanning, and fuzz testing, should be performed to detect known and unknown vulnerabilities. Finally, as a last step in the product development, it is recommended to perform penetration testing to uncover any potential vulnerabilities that may have been missed earlier in the development lifecycle and to validate the cybersecurity goals. By addressing security at each step in the automotive development lifecycle, it is possible for an organization to find and reduce potential vulnerabilities throughout the development lifecycle. Besides the activities throughout the development lifecycle, it is equally imperative to consider solutions during the operations and maintenance phases, such as incident response, and solutions that allow for software updates to be provided to vulnerable vehicles. In addition, organizations need to be constantly aware of new threats and vulnerabilities by conducting ongoing cybersecurity monitoring. Finally, to enable organizations to fully incorporate cybersecurity, an overall cybersecurity management approach, including cybersecurity culture, policies, and processes is needed. As more complex software is developed to handle use cases such as autonomous driving capabilities, and as more connectivity interfaces are included on vehicles to support various connected car use cases, cybersecurity threats targeting vehicles will also increase. Thus, it is imperative that security is considered throughout the entire automotive development lifecycle.

References

1 Society of Automotive Engineers (SAE) International (2018). SAE J3016 - taxonomy and definitions for terms related to driving automation systems for on-road motor vehicles. USA: SAE International.

2 Talisman Executive (2017). What needs to happen to make autonomous vehicles a reality?. https://www.talismanexecutive.com/blog/needs-happen-make-autonomous-vehicles-reality (accessed 30 July 2020).

3 ITS Digest (2018). 470 million connected vehicles on the road by 2025. https://www.itsdigest.com/470-million-connected-vehicles-road-2025 (accessed 30 July 2020).

4 Internet of Business (2018). Connected cars report: 125 million vehicles by 2022, 5G coming. https://internetofbusiness.com/worldwide-connected-car-market-to-top-125-million-by-2022 (accessed 30 July 2020).

5 MarketsandMarkets (2020). ADAS market. https://www.marketsandmarkets.com/Market-Reports/driver-assistance-systems-market-1201.html (accessed 30 July 2020).

6 MarketsandMarkets (2020). Automotive software market. https://www .marketsandmarkets.com/Market-Reports/automotive-software-market-200707066.html (accessed 30 July 2020).

7 MarketsandMarkets (2019). Automotive cyber security market. https://www .marketsandmarkets.com/PressReleases/cyber-security-automotive-industry.asp (accessed 30 July 2020).

8 Oka, D. K. (2018). Security in the automotive software development lifecycle. *Symposium on Cryptography and Information Security (SCIS)*, Niigata, Japan.

9 VDA QMC Working Group 13/Automotive SIG (2017). Automotive SPICE process assessment/reference model version 3.1.

10 International Organization for Standardization (ISO) (2018). *ISO 26262-1:2018 – road vehicles — functional safety*. Geneva, Switzerland: ISO.

11 Society of Automotive Engineers (SAE) International (2016). SAE J3061 – cybersecurity guidebook for cyber-physical vehicle systems. USA: SAE International.

12 International Organization for Standardization (ISO)/Society of Automotive Engineers (SAE) International (2020). *ISO/SAE DIS 21434 – road vehicles — cybersecurity engineering*. Geneva, Switzerland: ISO and USA: SAE International.

13 Wired (2015). After jeep hack, Chrysler Recalls 1.4M vehicles for bug fix. https://www .wired.com/2015/07/jeep-hack-chrysler-recalls-1-4m-vehicles-bug-fix (accessed 30 July 2020).

14 Nie, S., Liu, L., and Du, Y. (2017). Free-fall: hacking tesla from wireless to CAN bus. *Black Hat USA*, Las Vegas, NV, USA.

15 MITRE (2020). CWE common weakness enumeration. https://cwe.mitre.org (accessed 30 July 2020).

16 SEI (2016). CERT C coding standard – rules for developing safe, reliable, and secure systems.

17 MISRA (2016). MISRA C:2012 Amendment 1 – additional security guidelines for MISRA C:2012.

18 NIST. (2020). National vulnerability database. https://nvd.nist.gov (accessed 30 July 2020).

19 MITRE (2020). CVE – common vulnerabilities and exposures. https://cve.mitre.org (accessed 30 July 2020).

20 Bayer, S., Enderle, T., Oka, D. K., and Wolf, M. (2015). Security crash test — practical security evaluations of automotive onboard IT components. *Automotive — Safety & Security 2015*, Stuttgart, Germany.

21 Synopsys (2017). Fuzz testing maturity model.

3

Automotive-Grade Secure Hardware

TRUST IS BUILT ON LAYERS STARTING WITH A FIRST LAYER

This chapter provides a brief introduction to automotive-grade secure hardware, specifically automotive hardware security modules (HSMs). Although the main focus of this book is on secure software development for the automotive industry, the overall security of a vehicle or automotive system relies not only on secure software but also on the security of the underlying hardware. Therefore, we will briefly discuss automotive HSMs and how it is possible to build secure software on top of secure hardware.

The automotive industry has experienced several cases of software-based attacks on vehicles, which highlights the need for automotive HSMs. A couple of examples are presented as follows to provide some insight into the challenges. The UDS (Unified Diagnostic Services) Security Access [1] function is typically used for providing authentication of a diagnostic tester against an ECU (electronic control unit) to enable certain diagnostics operations. A simple example of the authentication sequence is illustrated in Figure 3.1 to show the messages involved.

As shown in the figure, the diagnostic tester first sends a seed request message (0x27 0x01) to the target ECU. The target ECU generates a random seed value, e.g. a four-byte value, and replies with the seed value in the following message (0x67 0x01 0xXX 0xXX 0xXX 0xXX), where "X" represents a hexadecimal value. Both the diagnostic tester and the target ECU use the seed value as input to a known cryptographic or secret function, together with a secret key, and calculate the key value, respectively. The diagnostic tester then sends the calculated key value as a response in the next message to the target ECU (0x27 0x02 0xXX 0xXX 0xXX 0xXX). Finally, the target ECU compares the received key value with the calculated key value, and if it is a match, the diagnostic tester has been successfully authenticated to the ECU. Thus, the ECU can assume that the diagnostic tester knows the secret key and if used, the secret function.

One software-based attack is made possible due to secrets stored in software. Typically, due to limitations in computing power and memory, proprietary and often simple functions have been used to implement Security Access on some ECUs. These functions are implemented in software and thus are susceptible to reverse-engineering. Security researchers have shown that it is easy to extract ECU software and identify the secret

Building Secure Cars: Assuring the Automotive Software Development Lifecycle, First Edition. Dennis Kengo Oka.
© 2021 John Wiley & Sons Ltd. Published 2021 by John Wiley & Sons Ltd.

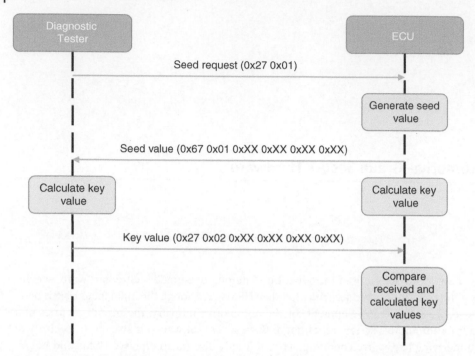

Figure 3.1 Example sequence of exchanged messages for UDS Security Access authentication. Source: Based on [1].

keys and reverse-engineer the secret functions used to calculate the key values [2, 3]. Another software-based attack is made possible due to the fact that the random seed used in the authentication protocol is often not randomly generated on the target ECU. In this particular example, the seed is hard-coded and always outputs the same seed. An attacker could sniff valid communication of a diagnostic tester performing Security Access authentication to the target ECU and then replay the captured key value. Alternatively, since the seed is always the same it is possible to brute-force the key value [2]. These examples show that software-based only security solutions are susceptible to attacks and that underlying hardware security to provide and protect these solutions is required.

In an effort to create more secure vehicles, automotive organizations have introduced more security solutions implemented on automotive systems. These security solutions are often based on cryptography; consequently, there is an increased need for secure key management and protecting the secret keys. For example, there are approaches for performing secure in-vehicle key management in order to securely establish session keys on different ECUs used for secure in-vehicle communication [4]. For some advanced use cases there may also be a need for a secure execution environment on the ECU, where operations are executed in a separate environment out of reach of potential software-based attacks.

More details on the need for automotive secure hardware solutions is explained in Section 3.1. Furthermore, automotive-grade secure hardware comes in various flavors. To provide additional insight, some background on the types of automotive HSMs that have emerged through the years is presented in Section 3.2. Finally, to show how automotive HSMs can be used as the root of trust to overcome the software-based only challenges, some practical example use cases for automotive systems using HSMs – including secure boot, secure in-vehicle communication, secure host flashing, secure debug, and secure logging – are discussed in Section 3.3.

The main points of this chapter are:

- We explain the need for secure hardware in the automotive industry.
- We provide an introduction to different types of automotive HSMs.
- We present example use cases of using automotive HSMs as the root of trust.

3.1   Need for Automotive Secure Hardware

First, to give a short background of the need for automotive hardware security, we first need to consider physical attacks on vehicles, including theft of vehicles. One of the early uses of hardware security solutions in the automotive industry was to counter theft of vehicles, namely by the use of the immobilizer. Although the concept of an immobilizer is not new – the first electric immobilizer was invented and patented in 1919! – it was not until much later that immobilizers started using hardware security solutions. A modern immobilizer typically consists of two parts as a keyless entry system: a transponder in the key fob and a receiver in the car. The purpose of the immobilizer is to prevent the engine from running unless the correct transponder is present. This prevents an attacker from being able to start the engine without having the right key; thus, an immobilizer works as a security solution against car theft. Immobilizers were made mandatory in EU countries in the late 1990s and gradually, as more vehicles with immobilizers were deployed in the field, the number of car thefts reduced drastically. For instance, the costs associated with car thefts in Germany steadily decreased from €800 million in 1993 to €176 million in 2008 as shown in Figure 3.2 [5]. The electronic immobilizer was introduced in the early 1990s and it is clear from Figure 3.2 that this had an impact on reducing the costs associated with car thefts.

However, these early electronic immobilizers were often based on proprietary cryptographic solutions, such as DST40, Hitag2, and Megamos Crypto. These solutions were analyzed by security researchers and found to be vulnerable to several types of attacks. Attacks include recovering the secret key by eavesdropping on wireless communication and cracking the key, and recovering the secret key by exploiting a weakness in the key update function. The recovered key allows an attacker to bypass the cryptographic authentication [6–8]. Another famous proprietary cryptographic solution for electronic immobilizers is KeeLoq. Details about the proprietary algorithm used in KeeLoq were leaked in 2006 and, using this information, security researchers in 2007 identified a practical attack which allows recovery of the secret key [9]. From Figure 3.2, it can be seen that after a steady decrease in previous years, costs associated with car thefts started to increase in 2009 to €219 million and continued to increase steadily until 2017, to €324 million. It is possible to consider that, as a result of the shortcomings in proprietary solutions being publicly released, real attackers are able to mount attacks to bypass the security solutions to steal vehicles, which correlates with the data that costs associated with car thefts slowly increased after 2008. These types of attacks have continued over the past few years with criminals using more sophisticated approaches to steal vehicles. In one case, thieves had stolen at least 34 vehicles, worth $1.6

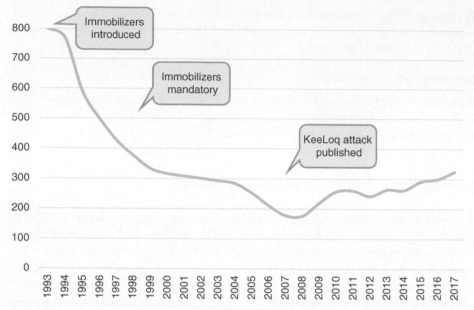

Figure 3.2 Costs in million euro associated with car thefts in Germany over the years. Source: Data from [5].

million, by seemingly cracking keyless entry systems [10]. To combat the increase of costs associated with car thefts, new automotive hardware security solutions for immobilizers and keyless entry systems are needed that address these shortcomings and that can perform proper authentication using standardized cryptography, can securely store cryptographic keys, and properly generate random numbers.

Another example of attacks on vehicles is the manipulation of the odometer value, i.e. the mileage value showing how far the vehicle has traveled, stored in the vehicle. According to a study by the European Parliamentary Research Service [11], estimated costs for EU member states of such odometer fraud attacks is between €5.6 billion and €9.6B billion yearly. Since the odometer value typically is stored in software on an ECU in the vehicle, attackers who are able to exploit software weaknesses can easily modify the value, e.g. rolling back the value by 30 000 km on a used car to increase the second-hand value by on average €3000. Therefore, to prevent unauthorized modification of this value and other important data stored in ECUs, there is a need to store such data in secure storage in automotive hardware.

Moreover, as more use cases and security approaches for software solutions based on cryptographic solutions arise, such as authentication, encryption, and verification and generation of digital signatures, there is a need to securely use standardized cryptographic algorithms, e.g. Advanced Encryption Standard (AES), with increasingly higher performance requirements, and to securely generate, store and use cryptographic keys. Consequently, there is a strong need for automotive-grade secure hardware.

To sum up, there are two main features for automotive HSMs:

- Security component separate from software (e.g. secure execution environment and secure storage).
- Hardware acceleration (e.g. AES crypto engine).

Additionally, since automotive systems are typically operating in environments with potentially harsh conditions compared with enterprise solutions, there are specific requirements on, for example, temperature ranges that the hardware needs to support. Thus, typical IT-based security IC (integrated circuit) solutions would not be applicable. There are also automotive-specific needs for secure debugging to allow for failure analysis, which is not possible on IT-based security IC solutions that are missing debug interfaces. Finally, costs for IT-based security IC are too high to be applicable for the automotive industry. Therefore, it is not possible to apply an IT-based security IC solution as is, for use in an ECU; instead, an automotive-grade secure hardware solution is needed.

The main goal of automotive HSMs is to protect software using hardware. Although there are many approaches to improve software security, such as following secure coding guidelines, using static code analysis, performing fuzz testing and penetration testing, it is most likely not possible to create 100% vulnerability-free software. However, by using security features provided by an HSM it is possible to mitigate and reduce the impact of potential software vulnerabilities.

3.2   Different Types of HSMs

This section provides some history on automotive hardware security to give insight into the development and progress in the industry over the years. Around 2005, HIS (Hersteller Initiative Software), a consortium consisting of German OEMs (original equipment manufacturers), suppliers and security companies, started work on what later become the first secure automotive hardware specification, called SHE (Secure Hardware Extension). The SHE specification was released in 2009 and, based on this specification, a number of semiconductor manufacturers started to develop SHE-enabled automotive microcontrollers. The SHE specification was republished by AUTOSAR (AUTomotive Open System ARchitecture) in 2019 in a technical report called "Specification of Secure Hardware Extensions" [12]. The SHE specification states that a hardware crypto accelerator (an AES engine), some secure storage for cryptographic keys, and a hash function built on the MP (Miyaguchi-Preneel) function are required. These features allow for the implementation of several security-related functions based on these primitives, such as encryption and decryption of data, and generation and verification of MACs (message authentication codes). Using these primitives would allow solutions for secure communication, authentication of messages, secure and authenticated boot, etc. However, since there is no dedicated secure core and there are restrictions on the size of the secure storage, use cases for SHE-enabled microcontrollers are also limited.

From mid-2008 to the end of 2011, as part of the European Framework Program 7, work was done on defining requirements for secure automotive hardware in a project called EVITA (E-safety Vehicle Intrusion proTected Applications) [13]. The EVITA project defined requirements for three levels of automotive HSMs, given the names *EVITA light, EVITA medium,* and *EVITA full.* The reason for defining three levels of hardware security was to allow for considering the appropriate level of security for different ECUs in the vehicle depending on the security features required, costs, and risks. Since there are a large number of ECUs in a vehicle, it would be impractical to only have one defined level of hardware security. For example, simple automotive components such as door ECUs or immobilizers

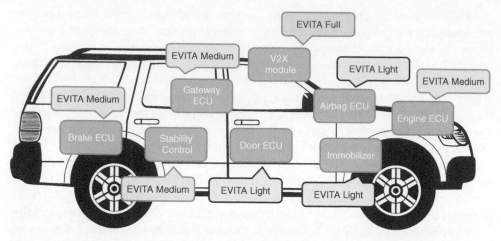

Figure 3.3 Different levels of hardware security are applicable to different ECUs in a vehicle.

may only require EVITA light, whereas a more sophisticated system, such as a Gateway ECU, may require an EVITA medium level, and for a high-performance communication device, such as a V2X module, EVITA full would be suitable. Figure 3.3 gives some examples of how the different levels of hardware security can be used by different ECUs in a vehicle.

Due to the limited use cases supported by the SHE specification, which is almost equivalent to the EVITA light level, Bosch created a Bosch HSM specification, which is seen as an equivalent to the EVITA medium level. The Bosch HSM specifies, for example, the requirement for a crypto accelerator (specifically an AES-128 engine), a separate secure core (different from the host core), and its own secure memory (both RAM (random-access memory) and ROM (read-only memory)). Because there is a separate secure core it requires a separate HSM firmware to perform secure execution on the secure core. Since the secure core can technically perform code execution securely, separate from the host core, it provides a Trusted Execution Environment (TEE). The TEE supports the implementation and processing of multiple security solutions, such as secure flashing, secure debug, secure runtime checks, and securely executing arbitrary code in a secure environment, e.g. executing code to allow for verifying digital signatures based on public key cryptography in a secure environment [14, 15].

While an EVITA medium equivalent automotive microcontroller is useful for numerous use cases, with the advent of new technologies, new use cases, and requirements for higher performance, it has become more common for recent automotive microcontrollers to provide security features to support EVITA full [16–18], including, for example, asymmetric cryptography accelerators and hash functions in hardware.

It is also worth mentioning that in 2015 the Trusted Computing Group (TCG) released a specification for a TPM (trusted platform module) for automotive use cases called TPM 2.0 Automotive Thin Profile [19]. While TPMs are widely used in the IT industry, such a solution is not suitable for the automotive industry due to different use cases and deployment scenarios. Therefore, the TCG created the automotive TPM specification intended for use on ECUs. A traditional TPM typically contains, for example, a secure cryptoprocessor, secure key storage, and a random number generator. The automotive TPM builds on the typical features that TPMs offer in terms of integrity reporting of software and cryptographic key management, including creation, storage, and use of cryptographic keys. For automotive use cases, the specification describes support for proving ECU identity, reporting of ECU software in use, and remote deployment of updates [20]. In 2018, the first microcontroller including a TPM specifically for automotive applications was released [21].

Because of different use cases, security risks, and specific hardware requirements, e.g. in performance, size, and power, it is important for automotive organizations to consider the SoC (system-on-chip) design for automotive HSMs. The previous sentence mentions just a few examples, but microcontroller manufacturers can further customize the design of SoCs to specific detailed requirements. When developing the SoC, similar to the software development lifecycle where various security activities take place, such as cybersecurity requirements review, security design review, threat analysis and risk assessment, secure development, and verification and validation, security activities for the hardware development should be performed. Since a vulnerability in the hardware, such as Meltdown and Spectre [22], could be very costly to fix, it is imperative to check security at every stage in the development process. Typically, it is recommended to take four main steps [23]. The first step is to specify the security threat model, e.g. accessing secure memory from malicious unprivileged programs in normal mode should not be possible. Based on this, there could be a security rule that says that data from a secure memory region should never flow to a normal memory region. The second step is to generate the security model for the design based on the design RTL (register-transfer level) and security rules, which are defined in the first step. In the third step, the security model is inserted into a functional verification environment. The security model is executed in parallel with the original RTL and the processor software using existing verification environments to detect security violations. The fourth step, which is the last step, is to perform an analysis of the results to identify security rule violations. For example, the analysis can detect that certain data from secure memory is leaking to normal memory due to configuration mistakes or other errors. To help hardware designers and developers there are various tools that can be used to maximize effectiveness and coverage of detecting different types of vulnerabilities. These tools can also automate complex analyses that when performed manually are often error-prone. Similar to how establishing a proper process for secure software development leads to reducing the number of software vulnerabilities introduced in the final product, establishing a proper process for secure hardware development reduces the likelihood of vulnerabilities in the final SoC.

3.3 Root of Trust: Security Features Provided by Automotive HSM

Since the automotive HSM acts as a root of trust for the automotive component, it can provide support for securing a number of different use cases [24]. Common use cases include:

- Secure boot
- Secure in-vehicle communication
- Secure host flashing

- Secure debug access
- Secure logging

A brief explanation of each use case is presented below. These explanations are based on an EVITA medium or higher automotive HSM, i.e. containing a separate secure core, crypto accelerator, etc. It is important to note that the root of trust provides the security foundation for these use cases and needs to be secure by design, as mentioned in the previous section regarding designing secure SoC.

3.3.1 Secure Boot

Secure boot is a feature to ensure that the microcontroller boots from a safe and trusted state. For example, it provides security protection even if an attacker is able to reprogram some memory related to the host core. Secure boot is performed when the microcontroller boots up to verify the integrity and authenticity of, for example, the bootloader and the application code. It is often performed by calculating a MAC of the sensitive memory areas that are to be checked. However, calculating a MAC of several MB (megabytes) of memory takes time and it is impractical and unacceptable to have the HSM check the entire memory before giving a decision whether the host core is allowed to boot or not. Instead, since the HSM serves as a root of trust, it begins by checking only a small part of the memory, called the *Host Boot Manager*, stored in the HSM. An example flow of this secure boot process is depicted in Figure 3.4. If the Host Boot Manager passes the integrity checks, the HSM instructs the host core to boot. The host core executes the Host Boot Manager, which then first checks the integrity of the *ECU bootloader*. The ECU bootloader in turn then checks the *ECU application(s)* and if the security checks pass, starts the application(s). Even though the

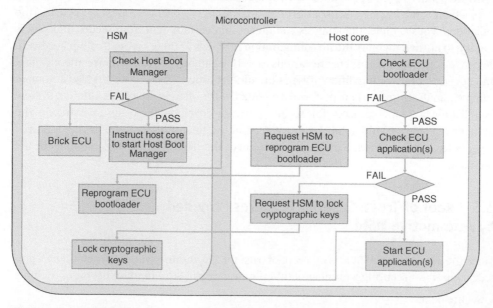

Figure 3.4 Example flow of a secure boot process using HSM.

host core is executing the instructions to perform these security checks, the HSM performs the cryptographic operations using its hardware acceleration engine and using the necessary cryptographic keys stored securely in the HSM. Thus, in this example, it is possible for the secure boot process to be defined by the host core, e.g. by using security checkers in the Host Boot Manager and ECU bootloader to check the next pieces of software before they are executed; however, the HSM acts as a root of trust to first verify that the initial software and security checkers used by the host core are correct and have not been tampered with. The HSM is also responsible for executing the necessary operations to support additional security checks performed by the host core and reporting the results of those operations to the host core. Moreover, it is required to define how the host core and the HSM should handle failed security checks. For instance, the HSM can prevent the host core from running any insecure code at all, which in some cases may lead to "bricking" the ECU. That is, if the security checks of the Host Boot Manager fail then the host core does not start and the ECU is effectively bricked, leaving it inoperable. If this approach is not acceptable, the HSM could, for example, lock access to the cryptographic keys that are securely stored in the HSM, and then allow the host core to run potentially insecure applications. In this example, if secure in-vehicle communication is used, a compromised host core may be able to receive messages but would not be able to send correct messages on the in-vehicle network and thus would have some restricted functionality. Since the cryptographic keys are locked, the HSM will not be able to calculate the MACs needed to create valid in-vehicle network messages. Consequently, an attacker who has compromised the host core is prevented from being able to send arbitrary messages on the in-vehicle network in this case.

3.3.2 Secure In-Vehicle Communication

Secure in-vehicle communication ensures integrity and authenticity of in-vehicle network messages. AUTOSAR provides a specification for secure onboard communication (SecOC) describing a practical approach of how secure in-vehicle communication can be achieved [25]. Although SecOC can be implemented in different ways, it is typically based on a MAC calculated over a concatenation of the message and a freshness value using a cryptographic algorithm and a shared secret key. A non-HSM implementation of SecOC would be susceptible to several types of software attacks targeting the freshness value stored on the ECU, the random number generator as well as the cryptographic keys and cryptographic algorithms used in the SecOC calculations. Some examples of these attacks on software implementations are explained in more detail as follows, and the corresponding HSM solutions to prevent such attacks are also briefly discussed.

An attacker who successfully modifies the freshness value stored in software on the ECU can break the replay protection. That is, the ECU can be tricked to accept old legitimate messages by setting the freshness value to a previously used value. To prevent such attacks, the HSM stores the freshness value securely inside the HSM where it is protected from any software vulnerabilities on the host core.

Additionally, an attacker may be able to tamper with a random number generator implemented in software on the ECU through software vulnerabilities. Random numbers are often used in key derivation and challenge–response authentication. This type of attack may allow the attacker to, for example, set the random number on the ECU to a certain value to be able to use a derived key of the attacker's choosing. Moreover, while not directly related to SecOC, this type of attack could also allow an attacker to bypass the Security Access authentication by setting the random seed value to a previously used value and replaying a previously captured valid key response. To prevent such attacks, the HSM internally generates random numbers based on a TRNG (true random number generator). Thus, an attacker exploiting software vulnerabilities on the host core is not able to tamper with the random number generation.

Furthermore, an attacker may be able to read out cryptographic keys stored in software that are accessible by the host core, or modify cryptographic algorithms implemented in software and used by the host core. An attacker can reuse the secret keys extracted from a target ECU to spoof valid messages to other ECUs that share the same secret keys. Furthermore, by modifying the cryptographic algorithms implemented in software on an ECU, the ECU can be tricked to accept specifically crafted messages that match the modified algorithm. To prevent such attacks, the HSM stores cryptographic keys securely in the HSM so that they are only accessible by the HSM itself. An attacker exploiting software vulnerabilities on the host core may only be able to request the HSM to use a certain key in an operation but will never be able to extract or read the key itself. Regarding the cryptographic algorithms, they are either implemented in hardware, e.g. an AES engine, or implemented and run in the protected execution environment on the HSM, i.e. the TEE, and therefore cannot be tampered with through any software vulnerabilities on the host core.

3.3.3 Secure Host Flashing

Secure host flashing refers to the HSM securely flashing the host core software. Given the complexity of automotive software and the risk for software bugs and vulnerabilities, it is imperative to ensure that ECUs can be securely updated. A common approach for securing software updates comprises generating a digital signature on a hash of the software data. In some cases, a digital certificate is also included in the update package. With no protection, an attacker is able to flash arbitrary software to the ECU. With a software-only protection mechanism, an attacker may be able to modify the cryptographic keys or algorithm stored in software and used for signature verification on the ECU, and thus successfully pass the verification using a specifically crafted digital signature. An attacker may also be able to find a vulnerability in the software update process implemented in software on the ECU and bypass the security checks and directly jump to the reflashing instructions. Even if the above-mentioned attacks are not possible, another attack is to downgrade the ECU with a valid, old, and vulnerable version of the software if no proper version control on the ECU is implemented. This will pass the security checks since the digital signature for the old legitimate vulnerable software package is valid; however, if there is a version check function on the ECU, an attacker may have to bypass it through modification of the version number stored in software on the ECU. It is possible to overcome the above-mentioned challenges by using an HSM, where the cryptographic keys and the software version numbers can be stored securely in the HSM. Moreover, the cryptographic algorithms and the verification process for the software updates can be executed securely by the HSM. Thus, before updating the host core, the HSM first checks the version, certificate, and digital signature of the update package. These instructions occur within the protected execution environment on the HSM. If the security checks pass, the HSM saves a hash of the data to be written, releases the flash controller, and instructs the host core to perform the update. Once the update is completed, the HSM calculates a hash of the updated memory areas and compares it to the previously saved hash. This final check allows the HSM to verify that the correct data have been written to the ECU memory. This solution prevents attacks where an attacker presents valid data during verification but then replaces it with attacker-controlled data during the flashing process by exploiting race conditions [26].

3.3.4 Secure Debug Access

In the automotive industry, it is necessary to be able to perform failure analysis on faulty automotive systems that are, for example, returned from the field. The failure analysis is typically conducted through a physical debug interface, e.g. a JTAG (Joint Test Action Group) interface on the PCB (printed circuit board). Since debug access often provides various features that allow direct reading or writing memory areas, it would allow an attacker who abuses the debug access to, for example, dump data from the flash memory to extract the firmware [27]. To make it more difficult for attackers to abuse the JTAG interface, some manufacturers apply some rudimentary countermeasures such as obfuscation by cutting tracks or removing resistors on the PCB, reconfiguration of the JTAG pins in software, or protecting the debug port with a simple password. Using an HSM, debug access can be controlled by logic in the HSM itself instead. For instance, a more sophisticated authentication protocol can be implemented and securely executed in the HSM. When an external debugger is connected to the JTAG interface, the external debugger first has to perform authentication to the HSM, using, for example, a challenge–response protocol. If the external debugger passes authentication, the HSM opens up debug features on the host core to allow debugging of the device.

3.3.5 Secure Logging

Similar to debug access, to be able to determine failure causes during failure analysis it is equally important to be able to access various logs on the ECU. These logs can contain valuable information about the ECU state, vehicle state, failure modes, and various activities leading up to the failure. If such log data are stored unsecured in flash memory, an attacker may be able to modify the contents of the data. Using an HSM there are typically two approaches that can be taken to ensure that log files are stored securely. First, log files can be stored in the HSM data section of the flash memory. The host core cannot access the HSM data section due to hardware restrictions and therefore any software vulnerabilities on the host core will not allow an attacker to read or modify the log data. However, since the HSM data section is often limited in size, for larger data logs that need to stored securely the second approach is for the HSM to encrypt the relevant log files and store the encrypted data in the shared flash section. The encrypted data acts as a secure storage. Although the host core has access to the encrypted data stored in the shared flash section, the host core does not have access to the cryptographic keys. Therefore, an attacker exploiting software vulnerabilities on the host core will not be able to decrypt the encrypted storage and access the contents, i.e. the log data. The corresponding cryptographic keys used to encrypt and decrypt the log file data are stored securely in the HSM. Any cryptographic operations on these data are performed by the HSM, which means that any unencrypted form of these data is only stored in HSM RAM and not accessible by the host core. Please note that secure logging could be considered a subset of a more general secure storage use case, since other types of data can be stored securely using the same approach.

3.4 Chapter Summary

This chapter provided a brief introduction to automotive-grade secure hardware, specifically automotive HSMs. It is important to understand how secure hardware plays a major role in providing comprehensive security for an entire vehicle. The overall security depends on a strong foundation based on secure hardware and building secure software on top of it. Only by using a combination of secure hardware and secure software approaches is it possible to build secure products and, in turn, secure vehicles. Some examples of common software-based attacks which justify the need for secure hardware in the automotive industry have been presented. Specifically, two main features for automotive HSMs have been highlighted, namely, a security component separate from software, e.g. a TEE which provides a secure execution environment and secure storage, and hardware acceleration, e.g. an AES crypto engine. A few different automotive HSM types were described, including EVITA, SHE, and Bosch HSM. In addition, some considerations for designing secure SoCs for automotive HSMs were briefly discussed. The highlights include the importance of specifying a security threat model, defining security rules, and testing the SoC design for vulnerabilities. There are various automated tools to help hardware designers and developers detect vulnerabilities before the SoC is finalized. Since fixing hardware vulnerabilities after development is very costly, it is crucial to establish a proper secure hardware development process. Finally, using an HSM as the root of trust allows automotive systems to support a number of security use cases including secure boot, secure in-vehicle communication, secure host flashing, secure debug access, and secure logging.

References

1 International Organization for Standardization (ISO) (2013). *ISO 14229-1:2013 – road vehicles — unified diagnostic services (UDS)*. Geneva, Switzerland: ISO.

2 Miller, C. and Valasek, C. (2013). Adventures in automotive networks and control units. *Defcon*, Las Vegas, NV, USA.

3 Milburn, A., Timmers, N., Wiersma, N., et al. (2018). There will be glitches: extracting and analyzing automotive firmware efficiently. *Black Hat USA*, Las Vegas, NV, USA.

4 Sugashima, T., Oka, D. K., and Vuillaume, C. (2016). Approaches for secure and efficient in-vehicle key management. *SAE 2016 World Congress and Exhibition*, Detroit, MI, USA.

5 Car Sales Statistics (2018). 2017 Germany: most-frequently stolen car brands and models. https://www.best-selling-cars.com/germany/2017-germany-most-frequently-stolen-car-brands-and-models (accessed 30 July 2020).

6 Bono, S. C., Green, M., Stubblefield, A., et al. (2005). Security analysis of a cryptographically-enabled RFID device. *USENIX Security Symposium*, Baltimore, MD, USA.

7 Verdult, R., Garcia, F. D., and Balasch, J. (2012). Gone in 360 seconds: hijacking with Hitag2. *USENIX Security Symposium*, Bellevue, WA, USA.

8 Verdult, R., Garcia, R., and Ege, B. (2015). Dismantling megamos crypto: wirelessly lockpicking a vehicle immobilizer. *USENIX Security Symposium*, Washington, D.C., USA.

9 Biham, E., Dunkelman, O., Indesteege, S., et al. (2007). A practical attack on KeeLoq. *CRYPTO International Cryptology Conference*, Santa Barbara, CA, USA.

10 Cyberscoop (2020). European police bust Polish gang suspected of hacking and stealing cars. https://www.cyberscoop.com/europol-poland-car-hacking-keyless-go (accessed 30 July 2020).

11 European Parliamentary Research Service (2018). Odometer manipulation in motor vehicles in the EU.

12 AUTOSAR (2019). Specification of secure hardware extensions.

13 EVITA (2011). E-safety vehicle intrusion proTected applications – EVITA. https://www.evita-project.org (accessed 30 July 2020).

14 Pohl, C. and Stumpf, F. (2014). An automotive-qualified hardware security module. *escar EU*, Hamburg, Germany.

15 Synopsys (2018). Safety and security from the inside — a SoC's perspective.

16 Renesas (2020). RH850/U2A16. https://www.renesas.com/us/en/products/microcontrollers-microprocessors/rh850/rh850u2x/rh850u2a16.html. (accessed 30 July 2020).

17 NXP (2020). S32S microcontrollers for safe vehicle dynamics. https://www.nxp.com/products/processors-and-microcontrollers/arm-processors/s32-automotive-platform/s32smicrocontrollers-for-safe-vehicle-dynamics:S32S24 (accessed 30 July 2020).

18 Infineon (2020). AURIX family – TC39xXX. https://www.infineon.com/cms/en/product/microcontroller/32-bit-tricore-microcontroller/32-bit-tricore-aurix-tc3xx/aurix-family-tc39xxx (accessed 30 July 2020).

19 Trusted Computing Group (TCG) (2015). TCG TPM 2.0 automotive thin profile, version 1.0. TCG.

20 Trusted Computing Group (TCG) (2018). TCG TPM 2.0 automotive thin profile, version 1.01 revision 15. TCG.

21 Infineon (2018). World's first TPM for cybersecurity in the connected car. https://www.infineon.com/cms/en/about-infineon/press/press-releases/2018/INFDSS201810-004.html (accessed 30 July 2020).

22 Graz University of Technology (2018). Meltdown and spectre. https://meltdownattack.com. (accessed 30 July 2020).

23 Synopsys (2019). Configure, confirm, ship: build secure processor-based systems with faster time-to-market.

24 Gay, C. and Oka, D. K. (2017). Software vulnerabilities mitigations using automotive HSMs. *Symposium on Cryptography and Information Security (SCIS)*, Naha, Japan.

25 AUTOSAR (2017). Specification of secure onboard communication.

26 MITRE (2020). CWE-367: time-of-check time-of-use (TOCTOU) race condition. https://cwe.mitre.org/data/definitions/367.html (accessed 30 July 2020).

27 embeddedbits (2020). Extracting firmware from devices using JTAG. https://embeddedbits.org/2020-02-20-extracting-firmware-from-devices-using-jtag (accessed 30 July 2020).

4

Need for Automated Security Solutions in the Automotive Software Development Lifecycle

SECURITY IS BUILT ON AUTOMATION

Recent results from a survey conducted on the cybersecurity posture in the automotive industry [1] provide valuable insight into the current challenges the automotive industry is facing. This chapter briefly reviews a couple of examples from the survey and highlights the main challenges regarding vulnerabilities in automotive systems. Based on these challenges, this chapter provides some ideas on effective and suitable solutions for automotive organizations to consider in the software development lifecycle. Please note that when discussing automated security solutions in the automotive software development lifecycle, the focus is on security solutions and tools that help organizations develop secure software. These tools are commonly known as *application security testing tools*, and cover various techniques and approaches for testing such as static code analysis, software composition analysis, dynamic application security testing, fuzz testing, and penetration testing.

As automotive software is growing in complexity and volume, it is useful for the automotive industry to investigate how other software-based industries are managing their software development lifecycle. A common theme for software-heavy industries is a culture shift toward *DevOps*, where an organization can rapidly build, operate, and continuously improve software applications. That is, DevOps aims at building an organizational culture to allow a deeper collaboration between software development (Dev) and IT operations (Ops) who traditionally operate in isolated separate departments or teams. This closer collaboration enables shortening the development lifecycle and provides continuous delivery with high software quality into operation. Moreover, there is a further shift toward *DevSecOps*, which expands DevOps by integrating security at every stage of the process. That is, DevSecOps is a *shift-left* culture shift that aims to integrate security practices within the DevOps process and bridge the gap that typically exist between development and security teams. This requires a closer collaboration between development (Dev), security (Sec) and operations (Ops), including establishing automated security processes often handled by the development team earlier in the development lifecycle. Thus, DevSecOps focuses on people, processes, and technologies to be able to develop and release more secure high-quality code faster [2]. Especially, in terms of technologies, there exists several different application security testing tools that can be integrated and automated into the build and release

Building Secure Cars: Assuring the Automotive Software Development Lifecycle, First Edition. Dennis Kengo Oka.
© 2021 John Wiley & Sons Ltd. Published 2021 by John Wiley & Sons Ltd.

pipeline. This continuous approach is often known as a CI/CD (continuous integration, continuous delivery) workflow.

A few results from a survey on DevSecOps [3] conducted in 2018 comprising 350 IT decision makers at large enterprises from various industry sectors including high-tech products, professional services, healthcare services, software-as-a-service (SaaS), and traditional retail among others are highlighted as follows. The survey shows that 36% of the organizations are focused on continuous integration, 35% on continuous delivery and 35% on DevOps. As seen from these results, there are already several organizations who have an increased focus on the of speed of development and releases. For example, 22% of the respondents state that code changes or releases are deployed in a matter of hours, 49% indicate code changes or releases occur in a matter of days, while 22% say the frequency of code changes or releases are measured in weeks. Moreover, the survey highlights the top industries where CI/CD workflow implementations already include application security testing elements. The leading industries are high-tech products (56%), SaaS (55%), and professional services (50%), followed by traditional retail (44%) and healthcare (40%). These industries are already moving toward a DevSecOps culture. While there is a small difference between the different industries, generally as can be seen from the results, there is significant room for improvement in all industries. To this end, to improve application security testing in the CI/CD workflows, the survey posed a question asking which elements of application security testing are most critical. The results emphasize the following application security testing elements to be added to the CI/CD workflows:

- software composition analysis (61%)
- dynamic application security testing (59%)
- penetration testing (57%)
- static code analysis (51%)
- fuzz testing (31%)

To successfully integrate relevant application security testing tools, it is important to understand at which steps in the CI/CD workflow which types of application security testing tools should be used to maximize the benefits and to allow automation of such tools [4]. An overview of the type of application security testing tools that can be integrated and automated into the CI/CD workflow to support DevSecOps is illustrated in Figure 4.1. Please note that some testing can occur after release as well; however, since the focus is on finding vulnerabilities as early as possible in the development lifecycle, the figure shows only application security testing tools before release.

There is also a notion of a security development lifecycle (SDL). For example, Microsoft SDL was first released in 2008 highlighting the security considerations organizations need to address in all phases of the development process to help build secure software and reduce development costs. Microsoft SDL contains guidance, best practices, tools, and processes to improve security in the software development lifecycle [5].

Although the automotive industry is often following a more traditional V-model development process and therefore approaches for DevSecOps, integrated security tools in CI/CD workflows, and SDLs established in other industries may not be fully compatible and applicable as is, there are useful ideas that can be considered and adopted from other software-heavy industries to enable the deployment of automated security solutions in the automotive software development lifecycle.

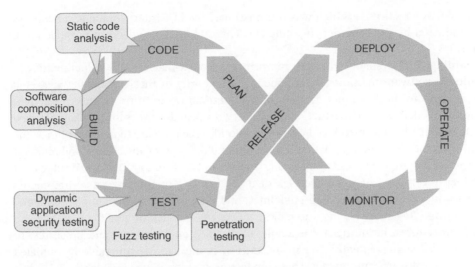

Figure 4.1 Application security testing tools mapped to stages in DevOps to shift toward DevSecOps.

In this chapter, the main challenges in the automotive industry leading to vulnerabilities in automotive systems, including challenges related to coding, testing and the use of open-source software, are first reviewed in Section 4.1. To overcome the challenges, automotive organizations can apply a number of automated security solutions in the product development phases as presented in Section 4.2. These solutions comprise static code analysis, software composition analysis, and security testing approaches including security functional testing, vulnerability scanning, and fuzz testing. Finally, some examples of security solutions that automotive organizations can apply during the operation and maintenance phases are discussed in Section 4.3. These solutions and activities encompass cybersecurity monitoring, vulnerability management, incident response, and over-the-air (OTA) updates.

The main points of this chapter are:

- We highlight the major challenges in the automotive industry leading to vulnerable automotive systems.
- We present automated security solutions that can be used during automotive software development to help reduce vulnerabilities in automotive systems before release.
- Besides solutions for the development phase, we provide input on security solutions for the operation and maintenance phases to address detecting and fixing vulnerabilities after vehicles have been released.

4.1 Main Challenges in the Automotive Industry

This section presents some of the main challenges in the automotive industry. We start the discussion based on some results from a recent survey on cybersecurity posture in the automotive industry – called "Securing the Modern Vehicle: A Study of Automotive Industry

Cybersecurity Practices" – which was commissioned by SAE International and Synopsys and conducted by the Ponemon Institute [1]. This survey is described in more detail in Section 1.3.

Regarding the question "what are the primary factors that lead to vulnerabilities in automotive software/technology/components," a majority of the respondents answered "the pressure to meet product deadlines." The automotive industry is known for tight development, delivery, and production schedules with clear deadlines for, for example, new vehicle models that are introduced every year. Besides the pressure to meet deadlines, the top three factors from the survey that lead to vulnerabilities being introduced and remnant in automotive systems are regarding *coding*, *testing*, and *open-source software*. With respect to *coding*, the main issues include lack of understanding or training on secure coding practices, including secure coding guidelines, and developers making simple accidental coding errors. Regarding *testing*, the main challenge is the lack of quality assurance and testing procedures, including, for example, proper test environments and processes. In terms of *open-source software*, the main concern is the use of vulnerable or outdated open-source software components. These top factors are highlighted in Figure 4.2.

Besides the product development challenges surrounding coding, testing and use of open-source software components described in more detail in Section 1.3.2.3, the automotive cybersecurity survey also mentions organizational challenges, which are described in more detail in Section 1.3.2.1. Specifically, the survey results show that organizations do not have enough cybersecurity resources, on average there are only nine full-time equivalent working on cybersecurity management programs, and the the majority of resources available do not have the necessary cybersecurity skills. Considering the technical challenges coupled with the limited resources available in organizations, tied with the high pressure to meet product deadlines, the automotive industry needs to deploy security solutions that are efficient and require little interaction or control by skilled cybersecurity resources. Consequently, automotive organizations should focus on deploying *automated* security solutions in the development, operations, and maintenance phases of the software development lifecycle.

Moreover, the survey mentions that 61% of the organizations are unable to address critical security vulnerabilities in their products in a timely manner through a software

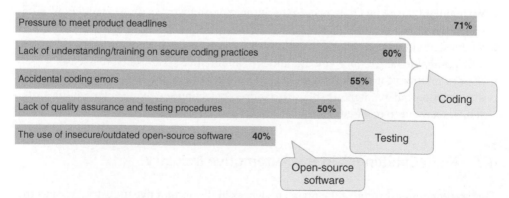

Figure 4.2 Top three factors, besides pressure to meet deadlines, are related to coding, testing, and open-source software. Source: Data from [1].

update delivery model. Only 30% of the organizations have a cybersecurity program or team that would be responsible to establish the proper processes and procedures to handle cybersecurity activities and solutions. Therefore, deploying automated security solutions in the product development phases to reduce the number of vulnerabilities before release is a great start but only a partial solution. Organizations must also establish the proper security solutions and activities during the operations and maintenance phases including cybersecurity monitoring, vulnerability management, incident response, and OTA updates.

4.2 Automated Security Solutions During the Product Development Phases

For the product development phases, the focus is on automated security solutions for the three main areas of concern, namely, coding, testing, and use of open-source software components, highlighted by the automotive cybersecurity survey. This section gives a brief introduction to various application security testing tools and approaches to address these concerns, including static code analysis, software composition analysis, and multiple security testing techniques. Lastly, a short introduction to automation and requirements traceability is provided.

4.2.1 Static Code Analysis

This section gives a brief introduction to static code analysis tools. Even though an organization is performing proper cybersecurity requirements reviews and security design reviews, coding mistakes during the software development phase may introduce vulnerabilities in the final product. To assist developers identify such vulnerabilities early in the code as it is being developed, automated tools such as static code analysis tools can be used to perform static application security testing (SAST). Static code analysis tools analyze the software source code or compiled code itself without running the code (hence, *static*) to identify vulnerabilities. Since there is no need to execute the software, there is also no need to write any test cases, thus the effort to run such tools is ordinarily very low. Some tools can scan only the source code as is; however, often tools require the proper build environment to be present to be able to compile the code. While compiling the code, the tool builds call graphs, which help identify the sources of data and data sink.

There are some static code analysis tools that can be integrated into the developer IDE (integrated development environment) and thus can run instantly as soon as the developer is writing the code into the IDE. These tools can be run at any point during the development phase. Other static code analysis tools target scanning the code during the build process and are thus more suitable to be run at a later stage in the development phase when the code available is in a more stable state and can be compiled properly.

To simplify, static code analysis tools typically work in two steps, as illustrated in Figure 4.3. In the first step, the tool builds a model based on the source code it takes as input. This model is a standardized model that the analysis engine can interpret. In the second step, the tool performs the analysis using the model as input. As an additional input at this step, the tool uses security knowledge such as various rules on what to assess within the source code. It is important to note that these rules can be controlled

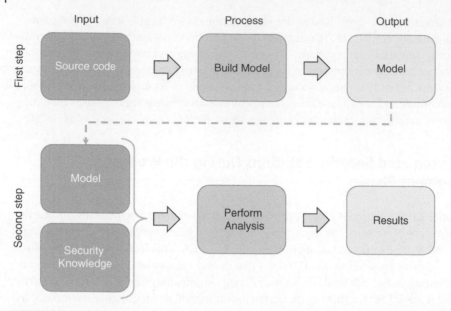

Figure 4.3 Steps involved for static code analysis tools to process source code and generate results.

by the user. Fine-tuning the rules to the target software allows achieving more accurate and high-quality findings. The results generated from the second step of performing the analysis are the specific findings the tool has identified during the scan.

The advantages of static code analysis tools include coverage and speed. Such tools have the ability to scan 100% of the codebase and are much faster than manual code reviews. For instance, these tools can scan millions of lines of code in just a few minutes. Additionally, these tools contain security knowledge to identify security issues developers may not be able to detect themselves while doing, for example, manual code reviews. Moreover, these tools can automatically provide information about identified vulnerabilities to developers, such as a description of the issue, the specific lines of code where the vulnerability exists, and CWE (Common Weakness Enumeration) [6] information. Equally important, these tools typically provide suggestions for remediation on any issues found, which helps developers to quickly fix the issues while also learning how to avoid making such mistakes in the future. Furthermore, static code analysis tools can also provide coverage of various coding guidelines such as CERT (Computer Emergency Response Team), MISRA (Motor Industry Software Reliability Association), and AUTOSAR (AUTomotive Open System ARchitecture). These guidelines help developers avoid coding and implementation errors in the software and are often used in the automotive industry. To assist in verifying whether a software codebase is conforming to the coding guidelines, it is possible to use static code analysis tools that can detect violations of coding rules in a practical and consistent manner [7]. More details about static code analysis tools can be found in [8].

Chapter 5 provides a deeper discussion on automotive industry challenges and solutions regarding using static code analysis on automotive software to verify that the code complies with coding guidelines such as MISRA and AUTOSAR coding guidelines.

4.2.2 Software Composition Analysis

This section gives a brief introduction to software composition analysis tools. The three main objectives with software composition analysis tools are to: *discover*, *protect*, and *manage*.

The first objective, to *discover*, includes identifying open-source software that exists in the source codebase, binaries, and containers. The tools should also be able to detect partial or modified open-source components. Often these tools require little effort and can run automated as part of the development toolchain, e.g. when software is added to the codebase or when the software is built.

The next objective is to *protect*, which involves mapping the identified open-source components to known vulnerabilities in a vulnerability database, e.g. the National Institute of Standards and Technology (NIST) National Vulnerability Database (NVD) [9]. Many tools also maintain their own vulnerability databases which contain additional entries that typically are not available in NVD. Moreover, although not directly security related, software composition analysis tools can also be used to identify license and component quality risks. For example, certain open-source software may have very restrictive licenses and if an organization does not comply with the license conditions the organization may be subject to a lawsuit and be forced to pay costly fines. Alternatively, an organization may be forced to, for example, release its own software as open source under the same license conditions, thus potentially having to publicly release proprietary IP (intellectual property) or secret data that may be stored in the software. Regarding quality risks, since vehicles have long lifespans of 10–15 years, automotive organizations are required to take careful consideration when deciding to include a certain open-source software component. It is important that organizations investigate how many active developers are contributing to the specific open-source software project, how long ago was the last commit to the specific project, and how often are new versions of the software released, etc. For example, consider a scenario where an organization is including an open-source cryptographic library in an automotive system, and imagine that several years in the future there is a critical vulnerability detected in this library that requires a fix, or that there is a need to support a new cryptographic algorithm in the future, can the automotive organization rely on the open-source software project team to address these needs in a timely manner? It is crucial for an organization to understand how many active developers are still working on this project, and what the expectation is on how fast an updated version can be developed and released. It is imperative that automotive organizations scrutinize the type of open-source software to be included for use in vehicles by performing this type of investigation.

Thus, using software composition analysis tools in the development phase is useful to understand, for example, what open-source software is used and to identify associated known vulnerabilities. As well as the usage of such tools in the development phase, software composition analysis tools also play an important role during the operations and maintenance phases as part of the continuous cybersecurity activities. That is, software composition analysis tools can provide alerts on newly identified vulnerabilities that exist in open-source software components included in the previously scanned software packages and therefore serve as valuable input to the cybersecurity monitoring activities.

The third objective is to *manage* open-source software, which means that automotive organizations can use software composition analysis tools to set and enforce policies for open-source software usage and security. To reduce manual effort, these policies can be automated using various integrations with other tools in the toolchain. For instance, there may be policies on which open-source software are allowed to be included in certain projects, e.g. using whitelists of open-source components detailing specific versions that are allowed. There may also be policies defining a maximum age of acceptable open-source software to be included in projects, e.g. open-source software components older than one year are not allowed to be used if there exist newer versions. Another example of a policy is defining how many of a certain type of vulnerability are allowed for a particular open-source software component to be included in an automotive system, e.g. zero critical vulnerabilities and fewer than 10 medium vulnerabilities are acceptable. Organizations can also use software composition analysis tools to manage how to handle the identified vulnerabilities. For example, an organization can prioritize and track remediation activities such as including a patched version in the software package or having the internal development team fix the vulnerability themselves.

Chapter 6 presents an example of software composition analysis applied to real-world software in the automotive industry.

4.2.3 Security Testing

This section gives a brief introduction to security testing in general in the automotive industry. There are various approaches ranging from *security functional testing*, to *vulnerability scanning*, to *fuzz testing* to *penetration testing*. Each approach has a different level of manual effort associated with it and, additionally, some of the approaches allow for more automated tools to be used.

Testing traditionally occurs on the right-hand side of the V-model during the development lifecycle. As automotive organizations finalize the development of security functionality, it is possible for these organizations to test the implementation by performing *security functional testing* to verify, for example, the correctness and robustness of the implementation. Once the developed software for the automotive system is more or less functional, organizations can perform *vulnerability scanning* using known attacks and attack patterns to identify vulnerabilities in the software. Moreover, *fuzz testing* can be performed by sending malformed input to the target software, including through application protocol interfaces (APIs), network protocol interfaces, and file parsers. Different tools are used to perform security functional testing, vulnerability scanning, and fuzz testing; however, these tools are often required to be configured to the specific target system and, in some instances, may require to be modified/enhanced to support the specific test cases. Once support is available, the tests can often run in an automated fashion. Thus, there are typically some security resources required during the initial configuration and setup phase of the test tools and test environment; however, once the preparations are done and the tools are performing security testing of the specific target system, the required manual effort is low. Finally, once the product is more or less complete, as a last step the automotive organization can perform *penetration testing*. Typically, security experts with penetration testing experience and expertise are required to perform this step. It is possible to reduce some of the manual effort by using various tools and customs scripts; however, there are several activities that require expertise, time, and manual effort including analyzing results, investigating new attack techniques, and developing exploits for detected vulnerabilities.

Chapter 7 provides more details about automotive security testing approaches. Specifically, regarding fuzz testing, Chapter 8 describes more details about automating fuzz testing of in-vehicle systems, Chapter 9 presents a solution for improving fuzz testing coverage by using agent instrumentation, and Chapter 10 gives an approach for automating file fuzzing over USB for automotive systems.

4.2.4 Automation and Traceability During Software Development

While automated security solutions discussed in previous section can be used during the software development process, it is equally important for an automotive organization to handle *requirements traceability* for software security requirements. In other words, an organization needs to keep up-to-date information on which software security requirements are verifiable using which tools and configurations, and additionally be able to trace the actual test results from such tools to serve as evidence that the requirements have been fulfilled. Examples of test cases that can be used for verifying software security requirements include the use of static code analysis tools with certain configurations, the use of software composition analysis tools with certain configured policies, and the use of vulnerability scanning tools and fuzz testing tools with specific configurations for the target systems and software. These type of software requirements and test cases can be defined in ALM (application lifecycle management) systems. By integrating application security testing tools with ALM systems, it is possible to automate the security testing and requirements traceability during the software development lifecycle. That is, it is possible to automatically launch the appropriate application security testing tools based on the requirements and test cases defined in the ALM system, to scan and test the target software and system, and finally upload the actual test results from the application security testing tools back into the ALM system. This approach allows an organization to trace the software security requirements to actual test results in the ALM system that are used as evidence to verify that the requirements have been fulfilled.

Chapter 11 provides more details about how automotive organizations can achieve automation and traceability by integrating application security testing tools into ALM systems in the automotive software development lifecycle.

4.3 Solutions During Operations and Maintenance Phases

After a product has been developed and released, it is imperative to consider ongoing cybersecurity activities during the operations and maintenance phases. These activities include cybersecurity monitoring, vulnerability management, incident response, and OTA updates.

4.3.1 Cybersecurity Monitoring, Vulnerability Management, Incident Response, and OTA Updates

This section gives a brief introduction to some of the cybersecurity activities that automotive organizations need consider besides the previously mentioned security solutions for the product development phases in Section 4.2. Specifically, organizations need to establish processes and teams in the post-development phases to enable *cybersecurity monitoring, vulnerability management, incident response,* and *OTA updates. Cybersecurity monitoring* involves, for example, being able to actively and passively monitor for cybersecurity-related activities and events to learn about new threats and vulnerabilities as well as possible mitigations. For example, security teams can actively search for newly identified vulnerabilities that are published online, and actively monitor and process information gathered from deployed vehicles to detect attack patterns. To this end, one technical solution that can be applied to vehicles is an automotive intrusion detection system (IDS). An automotive IDS is responsible for monitoring the in-vehicle network traffic to detect anomalies and attack patterns in the communication between electronic control units (ECUs). Information about any detected events can be gathered from a fleet of vehicles and processed in a backend analytics center where the data are actively monitored by security teams. Additionally, organizations can passively receive information from various sources, including certain tools, e.g. software composition analysis tools can provide alerts on newly identified open-source software vulnerabilities, or communities and organizations, e.g. Auto-ISAC (Automotive Information Sharing and Analysis Center) [10] provides information on emerging cybersecurity risks to vehicles and automotive systems. This type of information collected by the cybersecurity monitoring activities can then be used as input to the vulnerability management and incident response activities. *Vulnerability management* involves identifying how critical a certain threat or vulnerability is in regards to the specific products. For instance, if there is a newly found vulnerability in a certain function of a cryptographic library but that function is not used in the product then the risk for attackers exploiting that particular vulnerability may be very low. On the other hand, if the vulnerable function is commonly used in the product, the risk for attackers exploiting the vulnerability may be very high. Additionally, organizations should use ALM/PLM (product lifecycle management) systems to create an inventory of the included software and hardware in their products. It would then be possible for an organization to assess exactly which products contain this specific vulnerability by using the inventory in the ALM/PLM systems. Based on this type of analysis, the organization can then decide on the next steps in the incident response activity. During *incident response*, the organization needs to determine how it should handle a certain vulnerability or event. For example, if the risk is low, the software may be patched during a regular service update and no particular urgent activity is therefore required. On the contrary, if the risk is critical, the vulnerability may need to be patched immediately through an OTA update solution. As part of the *OTA updates*, the organization needs to establish a technical solution that allows vulnerable software to be updated timely, and in a safe and secure manner. For instance, the new software updates need to be stored in a secure manner in the backend as well as in the vehicle. Automotive organizations can use various cryptographic solutions and key management systems to provide confidentiality, integrity, and authenticity of the software updates. The OTA infrastructure could look as follows: a backend solution communicates securely with the vehicle's communication unit, e.g. a telematics unit. The new software update is securely transferred from the backend server to the vehicle through the telematics unit. On the vehicle side, the software may be managed by a Gateway ECU that is responsible for the in-vehicle ECU flashing. The Gateway ECU contains the security features to verify the downloaded software prior to flashing, commences the flashing of the target ECU and provides some controls to verify that the flashing of the target ECU was successful.

Chapter 12 provides some example solutions pertaining to cybersecurity monitoring, vulnerability management, incident response, and secure OTA updates.

4.4 Chapter Summary

This chapter discussed the need for automated security solutions in the automotive software development lifecycle. First, this chapter provided some background on the need for such solutions by highlighting the main challenges based on a recent survey on the cybersecurity posture in the automotive industry. Besides the pressure to meet deadlines, the top three factors that lead to vulnerabilities in automotive systems are related to coding, testing, and open-source software. More specifically, the top three technical factors include coding mistakes or insufficient training on coding guidelines, lack of testing procedures, and the use of vulnerable open-source software. Moreover, besides these product development challenges, organizations are also facing organizational challenges, namely personnel with limited cybersecurity skills, or even if an organization does have team members with the right cybersecurity skills they do not have enough of them. Therefore, organizations in the automotive industry battling with the product development challenges in conjunction with the organizational challenges, as well as considering the high pressure to meet product deadlines, have a strong need for automated security solutions in the software development lifecycle. To address the product development challenges, organizations can employ static code analysis tools to help reduce vulnerabilities in the code, software composition analysis tools to assist with management of open-source software vulnerabilities, and security testing tools and methods to improve test procedures. Considering the organizational challenges, the various tools used during the software development process should be automated to the greatest extent possible. Moreover, besides the above-mentioned security solutions applicable during the software development phase, automotive organizations also need to consider employing solutions during the operations and maintenance phases to be able to detect and fix vulnerabilities after vehicles have been released. A majority of organizations in the automotive industry are currently unable to address critical security vulnerabilities in automotive systems in a timely manner through a software update delivery model. Consequently, organizations need to establish appropriate processes and apply technical solutions to enable cybersecurity monitoring, vulnerability management, incident response, and OTA updates.

References

1 Ponemon Institute – SAE International and Synopsys (2019). Securing the modern vehicle: a study of automotive industry cybersecurity practices. Synopsys, Inc. and SAE International.

2 Synopsys (2020). DevSecOps - build secure software at the speed of DevOps. https://www.synopsys.com/software-integrity/solutions/by-security-need/devsecops.html (accessed 30 July 2020).

3 451 Research (2018). DevSecOps realities and opportunities.

4 Synopsys (2020). How to navigate the intersection of DevOps and security.

5 Microsoft (2020). Microsoft security development lifecycle (SDL). https://www.microsoft .com/en-us/securityengineering/sdl (accessed 30 July 2020).

6 MITRE (2020). CWE common weakness enumeration. https://cwe.mitre.org (accessed 30 July 2020).

7 SEI (2020). How to use static analysis to enforce SEI CERT coding standards for IoT applications. https://insights.sei.cmu.edu/sei_blog/2019/04/how-to-use-static-analysis-to-enforce-sei-cert-coding-standards-for-iot-applications.html (accessed 30 July 2020).

8 Synopsys (2020). Why static application security testing (SAST) tools aren't just glorified grep.

9 NIST (2020). National vulnerability database. https://nvd.nist.gov (accessed 30 July 2020).

10 Auto-ISAC (2020). Automotive information sharing and analysis center. https://www .automotiveisac.com (accessed 30 July 2020).

5

Static Code Analysis for Automotive Software

YOU MUST FIRST LOOK WITHIN BEFORE YOU LOOK WITHOUT

Static code analysis is typically used as part of improving software security during the development phase. Two main topics related to static code analysis are covered in this chapter. First, static code analysis can be used to detect weakness patterns and vulnerabilities in the software early during development. Second, static code analysis can be used to check the code for compliance to various coding guidelines such as CERT (Computer Emergency Response Team), MISRA (Motor Industry Software Reliability Association), and AUTOSAR (AUTomotive Open System ARchitecture) coding guidelines. These measures can help automotive organizations address security, safety, and quality concerns early in the software development lifecycle. Analyzing the software code can be performed at any stage of the software development once some code is available; however, the earlier this activity is performed, the lower the costs for an organization to detect and fix vulnerabilities and defects in the software. More details about where static code analysis fits into the software development lifecycle is explained in Chapter 2.

Regarding the first topic of using static code analysis to find weakness patterns and vulnerabilities in the software, the approaches and tools for the automotive industry and for automotive software are similar to other industries and other software, and are therefore discussed in general terms. The main goal of static code analysis is to identify as many common coding issues in the software early in the development. Static code analysis examines the software statically, i.e. without running the application, and instead is performed by only analyzing the source code or byte code.

While it is possible for organizations to perform manual source code reviews as a form of static code analysis, it is time-consuming and requires team members with specific skills who are able to review and understand the code, and know what type of errors they are trying to find to achieve the best results. Manual code reviews can typically be performed through the implementation of self-reviews or peer reviews. For self-reviews, the developer reviews his or her own written code, tries to identify any issues and subsequently fix the code. An organization may establish a process with guidance for self-reviews that all developers follow, e.g. not reviewing the code right after it has been written, use a checklist to detect common mistakes, and allocate enough time for reviews. For peer reviews, the code written by a developer is reviewed by another person, e.g. a colleague or an external third party. Similarly, an established process may be used, including definitions for review goals, participants, review steps, checklists, and format of the review report.

Since manual code reviews are time-consuming and may miss various defects and vulnerabilities, due to the fact that they rely on the experience and skills of the developers and reviewers involved, it is recommended to use automated static code analysis tools where applicable. The main advantages with static code analysis tools are speed and coverage. These tools are much faster than manual code reviews and are able to scan 100% of the codebase in a consistent manner. A static code analysis tool can scan millions of lines of code in just a few minutes – a task that is impossible for a human reviewer or would require an enormous amount of effort and time to conduct. While there are various static code analysis tools available, it is important for an organization to ensure that the specific static code analysis tool used provides strong support for the programming languages the developers are using. For example, in the automotive industry there is a heavy focus on the programming languages C and C++ for the development of automotive software.

In addition, static code analysis tools contain knowledge to perform the detection of defects and vulnerabilities, meaning that the tool operator is not required to have the equivalent level of experience and skills that is required by a human reviewer. That is, it is imperative that an organization uses a static code analysis tool that has a broad coverage of weaknesses that it can detect, e.g. CWE (Common Weakness Enumeration) [1] and SANS (SysAdmin, Audit, Network, and Security) Top 25 Most Dangerous Software Errors [2]. Moreover, static code analysis tools can generally provide additional information about identified vulnerabilities, such as descriptions of the identified defects, the specific lines of code where the defects are found, and any relevant CWE information to assist developers to further investigate the detected issues. In addition, these tools can help developers by providing suggestions for remediation of the defects identified, allowing for quicker fixes. This information also helps developers learn about the specific defects in order to avoid making the same coding mistakes in the future.

More specifically, static code analysis tools can reach deeper into the software code to track the flow of data to determine whether input is validated before use, using so called *data-flow analysis* [3]. This is based on the concept of identifying *taint*, or potentially harmful input. Applying an attacker model where input to the software is considered harmful, i.e. tainted, requires the target software to properly conduct *input validation* before the appropriate logic in the application processes the input. Static code analysis tools should be able to identify the data flow in the software, from the *sources* where external data are passed into the application to the *sinks*, where the input data are used. A simple overview of the data flow in an application is illustrated in Figure 5.1.

From an attacker point of view, the sources are where the attacker can influence the data by, for example, providing malicious or malformed data to the target software, and the sinks are where the malicious data are processed and, as a result, where an attack may be executed. Imagine an application receives some data over a network-connected socket using the `recv()` function, which represents the source. These data are then copied into a buffer using the `strcpy()` function, which represents the sink. An attacker may be able to provide malicious data or unexpected data to the `recv()` function, leading to tainted input. If there is no input validation in the application, these tainted data are processed as is by the `strcpy()` function, which could lead to erroneous behavior of the application.

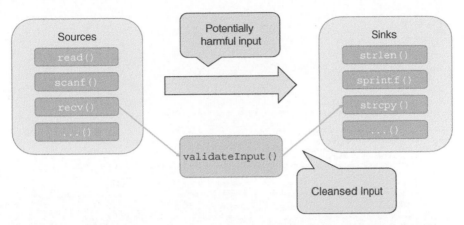

Figure 5.1 Example of data flow in an application from sources to sinks. Source: Adapted from [3]. Portions Copyright 2020 Synopsys, Inc. Used with permission. All rights reserved.

Furthermore, with a specifically crafted input message to the target software, an attacker may be able to successfully exploit a buffer overflow vulnerability and take full control of the application. Therefore, to prevent sinks from processing potentially harmful input, there should be some input validation performed, e.g. a function validateInput() that verifies that the input is of correct length, and does not contain any invalid characters or values. After the input has been validated, or cleansed by removing invalid characters, the input is provided to the sinks for correct processing, as shown in the figure. It is important that the static code analysis tool is able to recognize sources of taint functions in the code, where potentially harmful data may be input into the application. Moreover, it is important that the static code analysis tool also recognizes sinks for taint functions in the code, where the potentially harmful data may be processed in the application. Once all the sources and sinks have been identified, it is imperative that the static code analysis tool also recognizes any input validation functions in the code that cleanse the tainted data. If the static code analysis tool is not able to identify any input validation function for a specific source and sink, it will indicate the finding as a defect, specifying that tainted data from a source are reaching a sink. An example of a static code analysis tool identifying an SQL (Structured Query Language) injection vulnerability based on data-flow analysis where tainted data is processed by a sink is shown in Figure 5.2.

In the example shown in this figure, tainted data flow from the source to the sink, where an attacker may be able to provide arbitrary data as part of a request processed by the target application. This vulnerability may lead to an SQL injection attack [4], where an attacker is able to execute malicious SQL statements to, for example, bypass authentication or retrieve sensitive contents from a database.

Moreover, static code analysis tools can further analyze what the program flow of the software is when it is executed using so-called *control-flow analysis* [3]. As a result, using various security rules, the control-flow analysis can detect potentially dangerous operational sequences in the code. This is achieved by analyzing the control flow paths to detect whether a set of instructions is executed in a particular order. For example, control-flow analysis can help identify time-of-check-to-time-of-use issues [5] and uninitiated variables. Examples of control-flow analysis rules are "opening and closing a resource (e.g. FileInputStream)"

```
⊷ ⌗ ▣   ActivityDaoImpl.java
     import org.springframework.stereotype.Repository;
11
12  @Repository
13  public class ActivityDaoImpl implements ActivityDao {
14
15        @Autowired
16        private JdbcTemplate jdbcTemplate;
17
18        @Override
  4. taint_path_param: Parameter number receives the tainted data.
19        public List<Transaction> findTransactionsByCashAccountNumber(final String number) {
  ◈ CID 81579 (#1 of 1): SQL injection (SQLI)
  5. sql_taint: Insecure concatenation of a SQL statement. The value number is tainted.
  ♀ Perform one of the following to guard against SQL string injection attacks with JDBC.
       •  Refactor the JDBC code to use the PreparedStatement API instead of Statement.
       •  Add a positional parameter to the SQL statement using ?.
       •  Bind the tainted value to the parameter using the setString method: PreparedStatement.setString(1, number).
     More information
20        String sql = "SELECT * FROM transaction WHERE number = '" + number + "'";
21
  6. sql_sink: Passing the tainted value sql to the SQL API.
  org.springframework.jdbc.core.JdbcTemplate.query(java.lang.String, org.springframework.jdbc.core.RowMapper) may allow an attacker to inject SQL.
22        List<Transaction> customers = jdbcTemplate.query(sql, BeanPropertyRowMapper.newInstance(Transaction.class));
23        return customers;
24    }
25
```

Figure 5.2 Data-flow analysis identifying an SQL injection vulnerability. Source: Adapted from [3]. Portions Copyright 2020 Synopsys, Inc. Used with permission. All rights reserved.

and "validating and invalidating a session ID at logout." Figure 5.3 shows an example of a static code analysis tool identifying a resource leak based on control-flow analysis. Specifically, the control-flow analysis rule "opening and closing a resource" is triggered in this example since a resource in the code is not closed after being opened. A resource leak could negatively influence the available limited resources such as memory, storage and processing power, and may allow an attacker to cause denial of service by causing the allocation of such resources without their release.

Since using static code analysis for identifying weaknesses and vulnerabilities in software in the automotive industry is similar to other industries, we will not discuss this topic in further detail. Instead, since there are specific and relevant coding guidelines used in the automotive industry such as MISRA and AUTOSAR coding guidelines, often applied to the development of safety-relevant systems, we will do a deep-dive into the second topic on using static code analysis to check the code for compliance to these coding guidelines. It is crucial that an organization uses a static code analysis tool which provides a broad coverage of the various coding guidelines required for the specific development project, e.g. MISRA C/C++ and AUTOSAR C++. The rest of this chapter focuses on the challenges and solutions for automotive organizations using static code analysis tools to check whether their software is conforming with the MISRA and AUTOSAR coding guidelines.

Finally, as a side-note, for an organization to get the most value out of the static code analysis tools and run the tools in an automated fashion as part of the development process, it is imperative to ensure that such tools can easily integrate with other existing tools and systems used in the development lifecycle. Examples of such other tools and systems include automation tools, e.g. Jenkins [6], source code management systems, e.g. Git [7], and bug tracking systems, e.g. Jira [8]. Besides considering the technical aspects of integration, there are some additional considerations to keep in mind to ensure efficient use of the static code analysis tools in large development teams. For instance, it is important to consider how to enable roll-out of the specific static code analysis tools, including enablement

```
═  ✕  ■    PropertiesManager.java
49        }
50
51        public String getProperty(String key, String defaultValue) {
52              Properties props = new Properties();
53              InputStream is = null;
54              try {
   1. Condition isExternalFile, taking true branch.
55                    if (isExternalFile) {
   2. new_resource: new java.io.FileInputStream(file) creates a new resource.
   3. var_assign: Assigning: is = resource returned from new java.io.FileInputStream(file).
56                          is = new FileInputStream(file);
   4. Falling through to end of if statement.
57                    } else {
58                          is = this.getClass().getClassLoader().getResourceAsStream(propertiesFileName);
59                    }
   5. noescape: Resource is is not closed or saved in load.
60                    props.load(is);
   ◇  CID 85323: REC: RuntimeException capture (FB.REC_CATCH_EXCEPTION) [select issue]
   6. Falling through to end of try statement.
61              } catch (Exception e) {
62              }
63
   ◇  CID 59441: Resource leak (RESOURCE_LEAK) [select issue]
   ┌─────────────────────────────────────────────────────────────────────────┐
   │ ◇  CID 89195 (#1 of 1): Resource leak (RESOURCE_LEAK)                      │
   │ 7. leaked_resource: Variable is going out of scope leaks the resource it refers to. │
   └─────────────────────────────────────────────────────────────────────────┘
64              return props.getProperty(key, defaultValue);
65        }
66
67        public int getProperty(String key, int defaultValue) {
68              Properties props = new Properties();
69              InputStream is = null;
```

Figure 5.3 Control-flow analysis identifying a resource leak. Source: Adapted from [3]. Portions Copyright 2020 Synopsys, Inc. Used with permission. All rights reserved.

material to be shared with developers. For example, an organization may need to prepare user guides to help developers in different teams with different objectives: the static code analysis tools may be configured differently for security-oriented teams vs. safety-oriented teams. Moreover, to allow large development teams to use such tools efficiently, it is suggested to ensure that an appropriate IT infrastructure is prepared and available to allow for scalability and high-performance usage. As development teams grow, the need for static code analysis to run more often as part of automation in the development process, as well as being able to support larger volumes of software, increases. Therefore, it is necessary to consider whether to run static code analysis tools on high-spec computers on-premise at the organizations' sites or run such tools in the cloud for more flexibility, scalability, and performance.

The main points of this chapter are:

- We provide a brief introduction to MISRA and AUTOSAR coding guidelines used in automotive software development.
- We review an example of using MISRA guidelines checkers in static code analysis tools and discuss common challenges for MISRA and AUTOSAR.
- We present suggestions for a solution regarding the previously mentioned challenges for MISRA and AUTOSAR.

5.1 Introduction to MISRA and AUTOSAR Coding Guidelines

Owing to strict requirements on safety, quality, and security, automotive software development is often required to follow MISRA and AUTOSAR coding guidelines as indicated in standards such as ISO 26262 [9] and ISO/SAE 21434 [10]. This section gives an introduction to MISRA and AUTOSAR coding guidelines.

MISRA started in the early 1990s as a project for the UK government's "SafeIT" program, which focused on industries with safety-related electronic systems. The MISRA project was responsible for developing guidelines for embedded software in road vehicle electronic systems and, as an outcome of the project, in 1994, a document called "Development guidelines for vehicle based software" was published. After the official MISRA project ended, the MISRA members continued to work together informally and developed the MISRA C coding guidelines, which is a subset of the C programming language. The MISRA C coding guidelines have since become the de facto standard for embedded C programming in a majority of safety-related industries such as the automotive, aerospace, medical devices, and railway industries [11].

There have been several editions of the MISRA C coding guidelines released over the years [12]. The first edition of MISRA C coding guidelines was released in 1998, and the document is called "Guidelines for the Use of the C Language in Vehicle Based Software" and is officially known as MISRA-C:1998. It defines 127 coding rules, of which 93 are *required* and 34 are *advisory*. To claim conformance to MISRA C, the software shall comply with the required rules unless subject to a deviation, and the advisory rules are recommended but not mandatory. It is worth noting that rules being classified as advisory does not mean that an organization can ignore these rules but that the rules should be followed as far as is reasonably practical.

An update resulting in the second edition of the MISRA C coding guidelines, called "Guidelines for the Use of the C Language in Critical Systems," was released in 2004. This document is also known as MISRA-C:2004, and includes a number of different refinements and additions to the rules. The MISRA-C:2004 defines 142 rules of which 122 are required and 20 are advisory.

The guidelines were further updated and a third edition of the MISRA C coding guidelines was released in 2012, also called "Guidelines for the Use of the C Language in Critical Systems" and better known as MISRA-C:2012. This document defines 159 *guidelines*, of which 143 are rules and 16 directives. Out of the 143 rules, 10 are mandatory, 101 are required and 32 are advisory. New for the MISRA-C:2012 is the *mandatory* classification. Mandatory rules shall always be complied with and deviations are not permitted. Out of the 16 directives, nine are required and seven advisory. It is worth noting that with the MISRA-C:2012, a new category of guidelines called *directives* was introduced. A directive is a guideline that is not defined with reference to the source code alone but may also apply to requirements on processes, documentation, or functional requirements. Static code analysis tools may be able to assist in checking compliance but additional information, such as design documents or other documentation on processes or requirements, may be needed to perform the check for the directives. However, from a compliance perspective, there is no distinction between rules and directives [13].

For the *rules*, which are defined as guidelines for which compliance is dependent entirely on the source code and not on any design considerations or external documentation, it is in general possible to use static code analysis tools to verify whether the code complies with the individual rules. However, there are some rules for which an answer to the question "Does the code comply with this rule?" cannot be provided in all circumstances. Therefore, all the mandatory, required, and advisory rules are classified into *decidable* and *undecidable* categories. Please note that since the directives require additional information besides source code, the classifications *decidable* and *undecidable* are only applicable to the rules and not the directives. A rule that is decidable means that it is always possible to answer the question of whether the code complies with the rule with an unequivocal "Yes" or "No." Decidable rules are effective since it is always possible to verify compliance to the standard of these rules, granted that the static code analysis tool used is bug-free and configured correctly. A rule that is undecidable means that a static code analysis tool cannot guarantee to provide a "Yes" or "No" answer to the compliance question in every situation. There may be some situations where the static code analysis tool can provide a "Yes" or a "No" answer to undecidable rules, but in other situations compliance is uncertain. For example, a rule is likely undecidable if it depends on runtime properties in order to detect violations, such as the value that an object holds. This value may be set in a different function and by performing a system-wide check it may be possible to examine the behavior of that different function. However, a static code analysis tool cannot guarantee the unequivocal answer to the question "Does the code comply with this rule?" for this undecidable rule example. The analysis tool may be able to provide a "Yes" or "No" answer depending on the nature of the code or only report "Possibly," based on examining the behavior of relevant functions [13].

Please also note that as the C programming language evolved over time, there are new standards released for the C language itself. The MISRA coding guidelines are also updated to support the new standards of the C language. While MISRA-C:1998 and MISRA-C:2004 support the C90 version of the C language, MISRA-C:2012 provides additional coverage and also supports the C99 version of the C language [14]. Furthermore, in 2020, there was an update to MISRA-C:2012 called "MISRA C:2012 – Amendment 2: Updates for ISO/IEC 9899:2011 core functionality," which added support for the C11 version of the C language to the rules and directives [15].

Moreover, in 2016, an update in the form of an amendment called "MISRA C:2012 – Amendment 1: Additional security guidelines for MISRA C:2012" was published [16]. This document includes 14 new guidelines focusing on security, whereof 13 are rules and one is a directive. Out of the 13 rules, six are mandatory and seven are required. The single added directive is required.

To provide an idea of what rules can be verified using static code analysis tools, an example of the rules from MISRA C:2012 including Amendment 1 supported by a static code analysis tool called Coverity is presented in Table 5.1 and explained as follows [17].

As shown in the table, there are a total of 173 guidelines defined in MISRA C:2012 including Amendment 1, of which Coverity supports 167 of the guidelines. Thus, the static code analysis tool has a coverage rate of 96.5% for all the guidelines. As mentioned, the guidelines are divided into three categories: mandatory, required, and advisory, and also classified as decidable or undecidable. As can be seen in the table, the tool supports all 119 decidable

Table 5.1 Example of MISRA C:2012 rule coverage by Coverity static code analysis tool. Source: Data from [17].

	Decidable		Undecidable		Subtotal		Percentage coverage (%)
	Supported	All	Supported	All	Supported	All	
Mandatory	5	5	11	11	16	16	100
Required	86	86	27	32	113	118	95.8
Advisory	28	28	10	11	38	39	97.4
All	119	119	48	54	167	173	96.5

guidelines. The tool also supports 48 out of the 54 undecidable guidelines. The six remaining guidelines are not statically verifiable and are therefore not supported.

Besides the above-mentioned coding guidelines for the C programing language, since C++ is also commonly used in the development of safety-critical software, MISRA published a C++ coding guidelines document in 2008 called "Guidelines for the Use of the C++ Language in Critical Systems" [18]. This document is also known as MISRA-C++:2008. It defines 228 rules, of which 198 are required, 18 advisory, and 12 document. A new classification for MISRA-C++:2008 is *document*. The document rules are mandatory if the related feature is used and requires the developer to document the usage of the feature formally. The MISRA-C++:2008 supports the C++03 version of the C++ programming language.

As well as the MISRA coding guidelines documents described above, MISRA has also published documents to provide guidance to help organizations understand and achieve MISRA compliance [12]. One document, called "MISRA Compliance 2016: Achieving compliance with MISRA coding guidelines," was released in 2016 and is also known as MISRA Compliance:2016. A revised version of this document, called "MISRA Compliance 2020: Achieving compliance with MISRA coding guidelines," was released in 2020. This document is also known as MISRA Compliance:2020. The MISRA compliance document provides a framework to help organizations claim compliance with MISRA coding guidelines. In particular, it provides guidance on a robust and structured process for deviations, including a mechanism for establishing pre-approved permits to help streamline the deviation process. Additionally, the document provides an example deviation record highlighting the type of information that should be provided, including a detailed description and justification for the deviation. The MISRA compliance document is relevant to both the MISRA C and MISRA C++ coding guidelines for achieving compliance [13].

As briefly mentioned, C++ is becoming more commonly used in the development of safety-critical software. While MISRA has published a number of different coding guidelines for C and C++ for safety-critical software development, AUTOSAR published a coding guideline for C++ first in 2017 called "Guidelines for the use of the C++14 language in critical and safety-related systems" as an update to the MISRA-C++:2008 document. AUTOSAR [19] is a worldwide development partnership consisting of 280+ car manufacturers, suppliers, and other companies from the electronics, semiconductor, and software industries.

Figure 5.4 Simplified logical view of layers within an ECU.

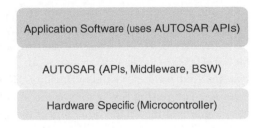

The main goal for AUTOSAR is to standardize the software architecture of ECUs (electronic control units)". This has several benefits, for example it increases the reuse and exchangeability of software modules between OEMs (original equipment manufacturers) and suppliers, and allows for the usage of standardized application protocol interfaces (APIs), middleware, and basic software (BSW). A simplified logical view of a typical automotive system or ECU is illustrated in Figure 5.4. It contains a hardware-specific microcontroller for the ECU at the lower layer, a middle layer based on AUTOSAR software, including supported APIs, middleware, and BSW, and specific application software tailored for the specific ECU at the higher layer. The application software contains functionality and logic that may be unique to the ECU; however, the application software uses standardized AUTOSAR APIs to communicate with the lower layers. This means that the application software developer can focus on developing the unique functionality and logic for the ECU, and does not need to develop the functions or features to, for example, send messages on the CAN (controller area network) bus or to perform cryptographic operations. These functions and features are provided by the lower layers through standardized APIs which the application software can simply use. Thus, this standardized software architecture defined by AUTOSAR is extremely beneficial for automotive software developers.

To better understand the development and progress of the AUTOSAR platform it is useful to be aware of the type of automotive systems used in vehicles. An overview of typical automotive systems is shown in Figure 5.5, including some common differences between such systems [20].

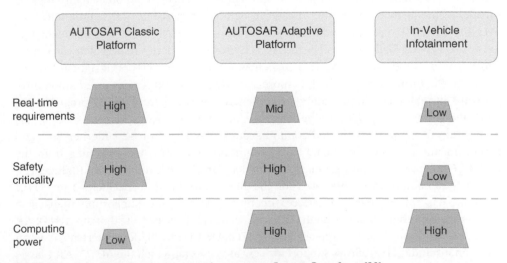

Figure 5.5 Overview of typical automotive systems. Source: Data from [20].

On the left-hand side of the figure are ECUs with small microcontrollers, responsible for certain specific and limited functionality in a vehicle, e.g. engine or brakes. For these systems, the AUTOSAR Classic Platform is suitable. On a simplified and relative scale, the AUTOSAR Classic Platform supports systems with *high* real-time requirements, and systems that have *high* safety-criticality. However, as mentioned these systems typically have *low* computing power due to the small microcontrollers and limited functionality they are providing. On the other end of the spectrum, on the right-hand side of the figure, are large, high-performance IT-based systems providing various functionalities, such as an in-vehicle infotainment system. These systems may be based on Automotive Grade Linux [21], GENIVI [22], or Android [23]. Since these systems focus more on providing a greater user experience and typically do not handle safety-critical functions, both real-time requirements and safety-criticality are *low*. In contrast, since the systems are closer to traditional IT systems than low-level embedded devices, computing power is *high*, which allows for running entire operating systems and various processing-heavy functions such as media streaming. As can be seen in the figure, there was a gap between these two extremes which has since been filled by the AUTOSAR Adaptive Platform. This gap mainly occurred due to increased requirements for performance, flexibility, and connectivity, and upcoming changes to the E/E (electrical/electronic) architecture including centralization, domain controllers and high-performance vehicle computers, where neither the AUTOSAR Classic Platform nor the in-vehicle infotainment systems would be suitable. The AUTOSAR Adaptive Platform may be used for systems providing ADAS (advanced driver assistance systems), autonomous driving functionality, and V2X (vehicle-to-X) communication. These systems have *mid* real-time requirements (i.e. slightly lower than the real-time requirements for the AUTOSAR Classic Platform but much higher than in-vehicle infotainment systems), *high* safety-criticality, and *high* computing power.

The following provides some more background on the need for the AUTOSAR Adaptive Platform and the major changes involved. Due to the advancements of connected and autonomous vehicles, which provide features that require more advanced coding, especially, to handle more complex functionalities – such as automated driving, AI (artificial intelligence) computing, image recognition processing, V2X communication, over-the-air (OTA) updates, and media streaming – AUTOSAR decided to make changes to the AUTOSAR Platform. Besides the AUTOSAR Classic Platform, of which version 1.0 was released in 2005, AUTOSAR released a new edition of the AUTOSAR standard, called Adaptive Platform, in 2017, which is more suitable and useful for advanced automotive software development. Major differences include switching from the C programming language to the C++ programming language, adopting an object-oriented style of programming, using service-oriented communication, e.g. based on IP (Internet Protocol) communication rather than signal-based communication on CAN, switching from the OSEK (Offene Systeme und deren Schnittstellen für die Elektronik in Kraftfahrzeugen [Open Systems and their Interfaces for the Electronics in Motor Vehicles]) to POSIX (Portable Operating System Interface) operating system, and supporting updateable software and configurations through OTA approaches [24]. Please note that the AUTOSAR Adaptive Platform does not replace the AUTOSAR Classic Platform, instead it is an additional standard that allows support for new use cases for which the AUTOSAR Classic

Platform is not suitable. It is expected that AUTOSAR will continue to maintain both the AUTOSAR Classic Platform and Adaptive Platform in the future [25].

With the AUTOSAR Adaptive Platform leading the way for C++ being used more prevalently for software development of safety-critical software, it is imperative that developers can follow an appropriate coding guideline to avoid common mistakes, which also allows organizations to get assurance that their developers are writing safer and more secure code.

Some history of the C++ programming language is given as follows to provide some insight on the emergence of the AUTOSAR C++14 coding guidelines. In 1998, the C++98 programming language standard was released, which was followed in 2003 by the release of the C++03 standard. As briefly mentioned previously, in 2008, MISRA published the MISRA C++:2008 coding guidelines, which covers the C++03 version of the programming language. Moreover, in 2011, the C++11 standard was released, followed by the C++14 version of the programming language released in 2014 [24]. In 2017, AUTOSAR released the AUTOSAR Adaptive Platform; however, at this time there were no appropriate coding standards for safety-critical systems supporting C++11 or C++14 available. The MISRA C++:2008 only covers the C++03 version and does not include considerations for the improvements made to the C++ language in versions C++11 and C++14. Moreover, MISRA C++:2008 was not fully appropriate for the AUTOSAR Adaptive Platform since it completely disallows dynamic memory, standard libraries are not fully covered, and security is not considered. Therefore, AUTOSAR made updates to the MISRA C++:2008 document by analyzing which MISRA rules are obsolete and removing them, reviewing the existing rules and making improvements, and adding several new rules. As a result, AUTOSAR created and initially published in 2017 a coding guideline called "Guidelines for the use of the C++14 language in critical and safety-related systems" as an update of MISRA C++:2008, covering the C++11 and C++14 versions of the programming language. Furthermore, updates to the AUTOSAR Adaptive Platform were made on a regular basis, twice a year, and, in conjunction with the updates to the platform, the AUTOSAR C++ 14 guidelines were updated accordingly. For example, in March 2017, the AUTOSAR Adaptive Platform 17-03 was released and, accordingly, the initial version of the AUTOSAR C++ 14 coding guidelines 17-03 were released. Correspondingly, in October 2017, the AUTOSAR Adaptive Platform 17-10 and AUTOSAR C++ 14 coding guidelines 17-10 were released. In March 2018, the AUTOSAR Adaptive Platform 18-03 and AUTOSAR C++ 14 coding guidelines 18-03 were released. Then, in October 2018, the AUTOSAR Adaptive Platform 18-10 and corresponding AUTOSAR C++ 14 coding guidelines 18-10 were released. The updated coding guidelines contain, for example, improvements to existing rules or additions of new rules. Therefore, when an organization is following the AUTOSAR C++ 14 coding guidelines in their software development, it is imperative to know which version of the guidelines to use. Specifically, when using static code analysis tools to detect violations of the rules specified in the coding guidelines, it is crucial to know which versions of the AUTOSAR C++ 14 coding guidelines the tools support to ensure that no added or modified rules are missed.

The latest version of the AUTOSAR C++14 coding guidelines available at the time of writing this book is AUTOSAR C++ 14 coding guidelines 19-03. The AUTOSAR C++14 coding guideline follows a similar rule classification as MISRA C++:2008, namely *required* and *advisory* rules. The required rules are mandatory requirements on the code.

For an organization to claim that C++ code is conforming to the AUTOSAR C++ 14 coding guidelines, the organization must fulfill all the required rules. A formal deviation must be declared if a required rule is not fulfilled. The advisory rules are recommended but not mandatory to be fulfilled, unlike the required rules. However, the advisory rules should normally be followed as far as reasonably practical. A formal deviation is not necessary if an advisory rule is not fulfilled, but may be declared if it is considered appropriate [26]. There is a total of 397 rules, of which 363 are required rules and 34 are advisory rules. To provide some background on the rules in the AUTOSAR C++ 14 coding guidelines document, around 150 rules come from the MISRA C++:2008, and around 130 rules are based on other C++ standards such as the C++ Core Guidelines [27], and Joint Strike Fighter C++ (JSF C++) [28]. The remaining around 120 rules are based on research or other literature or resources for coding best practices. Furthermore, the rules are classified into three categories according to enforcement by static analysis:

- Automated
- Partially automated
- Non-automated

The *automated* category includes rules that are automatically enforceable by means of static analysis. The *partially automated* category covers rules that can be supported by static code analysis, e.g. by heuristic or by covering some error scenarios, as a support for a manual code review. Finally, the *non-automated* category contains rules where static analysis cannot provide any reasonable support by a static code analysis and they require other means, e.g. manual code review or other tools [26].

An example of rules supported by a static code analysis tool, called Coverity, is shown in Table 5.2 and is described as follows [29]. As shown in the table, there are 329 automated rules of which Coverity supports 326. Thus, the static code analysis tool has a coverage rate of 99% for the automated rules. For partially automated rules, there are 22 rules of which Coverity supports 20 rules, thus a coverage rate of 91%. Finally, there are 46 non-automated rules, of which Coverity supports 14. Although non-automated rules are not typically easily checked by static code analysis tools, Coverity has a coverage rate of 30%. Overall, Coverity has a 91% coverage rate of all the AUTOSAR C++ 14 coding guidelines, including checkers to support 360 out of the total 397 rules.

Please note that the example of supported rules by a certain static code analysis tool is based on a snapshot in time. Generally, as the coding guidelines are updated to include more

Table 5.2 Example of AUTOSAR rule coverage by Coverity static code analysis tool. Source: Data from [29].

Automation type	Supported	Unsupported	All	Percentage coverage (%)
Automated	326	3	329	99
Partially automated	20	2	22	91
Non-automated	14	32	46	30
All	360	37	397	91

rules and as static code analysis tools are further improved to add support for additional rules over time, the coverage rate will certainly change.

As shown in above example, most of the rules are enforceable by static code analysis. In practice, a static code analysis tool that claims full compliance to the AUTOSAR C++ 14 coding guidelines shall fully check all rules that are enforceable by static analysis, i.e. the rules in the automated category, and all the rules that are partially enforceable by static analysis, i.e. the rules in the partially automated category, to the extent that is possible. It is important to note that not all rules are enforceable by static analysis, although static code analysis may provide some assistance for such rules; therefore, compliance to rules that are not enforceable by static code analysis, i.e. the rules in the non-automated category, may require other means of manual activities such as reviews and analyses.

As discussed in this section, there are static code analysis tools that can help organizations with checking their code for compliance to MISRA and AUTOSAR coding guidelines. However, it is imperative to be aware of the coverage of the guidelines that such tools provide. In general, while some coding guidelines can be checked with simple static code analysis technology, to achieve greater coverage of the guidelines it is crucial that the static code analysis tool used supports data-flow analysis and control-flow analysis to be able to reach deeper into the application and determine whether there is a violation [30]. It is also important to consider that there are rules that are not statically verifiable and therefore cannot be checked using static code analysis tools. Consequently, it is suggested that organizations should definitely use static code analysis tools to check appropriate guidelines that are statically verifiable; however, organizations must also be aware and consider how to handle the rules that are not covered by tools. For instance, an organization shall use a *guideline enforcement plan*, e.g. in the form of a matrix to provide an overview of how compliance with the guidelines is to be checked. The plan could show for each guideline which tools or manual activities are used to check for compliance as shown in Figure 5.6 [13].

Finally, it is worth noting that although there are other relevant coding standards often used in the automotive industry, such as CERT C [31] and CERT C++ [32], they are not specific to the automotive industry and therefore not discussed in further detail.

5.2 Problem Statement: MISRA and AUTOSAR Challenges

This section discusses common challenges automotive organizations are facing regarding MISRA and AUTOSAR coding guidelines.

Considering especially safety and security implications in automotive systems, there may be requirements for the software of an automotive system to be compliant with MISRA or AUTOSAR coding guidelines. However, the automotive system in question may be a complex system containing several layers of different software including own-developed code, third-party developed code, commercial software, and open-source software. It is imperative for an organization to consider how to handle the different types of software that may be included in the target system. For own-developed code, the developers in the organization can be instructed to follow the MISRA or AUTOSAR coding guidelines during the development of the software. For third-party developed code, the requirements passed to the third-party company developing the software could specify that the MISRA or AUTOSAR

Guideline	Compilers		Analysis tools		Manual review
	'A'	'B'	'A'	'B'	
Dir 1.1					Procedure X
Dir 2.1	No errors	No errors			
...					
Rule 4.1			Message 38		
Rule 4.2				Warning 97	
Rule 5.1	Warning 347				
...					
Rule 12.1				Message 79	
Rule 12.2			Message 432		Procedure Y
Rule 12.3			Message 103		
Rule 12.4				Message 27	
...					

Figure 5.6 Example of a guideline enforcement plan matrix. Source: [13]. Reproduced with permission from HORIBA MIRA Limited.

coding guidelines shall be followed during the development as a requirement. In contrast, for commercial software and open-source software, unless there is a strict requirement in the development process at the organizations developing the software to follow MISRA or AUTOSAR coding guidelines, it is unlikely that the commercial software and open-source software is conforming with the MISRA or AUTOSAR coding guidelines.

With more software used in automotive systems, this situation of including commercial software and open-source software is becoming more common. As mentioned, there may be requirements for the entire software on the automotive system to be conformant with the MISRA or AUTOSAR coding guidelines; however, some included software components may not have been developed following the MISRA or AUTOSAR coding guidelines, and therefore require careful consideration.

Considering the situation described above, there are two main common challenges automotive organizations are facing regarding MISRA and AUTOSAR coding guidelines [24]:

- Undefined workflow for handling MISRA and AUTOSAR coding guidelines.
- Running MISRA and AUTOSAR coding guidelines checkers on entire codebases generates a large number of findings.

These two challenges are described in more detail as follows. First, in many situations at organizations there is no specific defined workflow on how to handle MISRA and AUTOSAR coding guidelines and deviations. There is also often no defined workflow on determining what software components to scan and how to prioritize the coding guidelines. If there is no defined workflow on how to handle the MISRA or AUTOSAR coding guidelines and deviations, how to decide which software components to scan, and how to prioritize which guidelines to use, it means that an organization may simply enable all the coding guidelines checkers in the static code analysis tool for the entire codebase when scanning an automotive system. As a result, for example, a non-safety critical open-source software may be scanned with all the same coding guidelines as a safety-critical software component, and there is no difference in the priority of the findings, which makes it challenging for an organization to determine which findings to tackle first. A typical impact of an organization having no defined workflow for handling MISRA and AUTOSAR coding guidelines is that the entire codebase for the automotive system is scanned resulting in the generation of a large number of findings, which leads to the second challenge. The large number of findings is often caused by the fact that software components *not developed* according to the MISRA or AUTOSAR coding guidelines are included in the scan in the same manner as software components that *have been developed* following the MISRA or AUTOSAR coding guidelines. For example, besides the fully controlled in-house developed code, which may have been developed according to the MISRA or AUTOSAR coding guidelines, the entire codebase for an automotive system may comprise software that are out-of-control of the organization, such as third-party developed code, auto-generated code, legacy code, commercial software, and open-source software, which may not comply with the MISRA or AUTOSAR coding guidelines. Running the checkers for MISRA and AUTOSAR coding guidelines for these types of software typically generates a large number of irrelevant findings. The impact is that organizations require enormous efforts to handle the large number of findings resulting from scanning these types of software. These undesirable efforts include reviewing the findings, prioritizing the findings, deciding how to handle each finding, and finally either fixing the software to comply with the coding guidelines or creating deviation reports on guidelines that cannot be fulfilled.

This chapter presents an example to highlight the situation where software used in automotive systems contains, for example, commercial software and open-source software; however, the included software components have not been developed following the MISRA or AUTOSAR coding guidelines. In particular, the example focuses on a scenario where an open-source software component is included as part of a larger automotive system that has a requirement to comply with the MISRA coding guidelines. This example is used to illustrate the challenges and also to discuss the solutions presented in Section 5.3. As briefly mentioned, not all MISRA guidelines are statically verifiable and where applicable other approaches such as manual reviews are required; however, for this example, the focus is on using static code analysis tools to perform checks on the software to verify whether it fulfills the MISRA coding guidelines. Moreover, the results from the static code analysis scan are used to further discuss the challenges.

This example is based on an open-source lightweight cryptographic library specifically targeting embedded systems due to its size, speed, and feature set. The open-source software is a well-known library used to secure over two billion applications and devices. Let us imagine a scenario where a developer includes this particular library as a part of a larger automotive software. Let us also assume that there is a requirement for the entire target software to be compliant with the MISRA C guidelines. When scanning the entire codebase of the software including the cryptographic library, the static code analysis tool with the MISRA C checkers generates a large number of findings. In particular, for the cryptographic

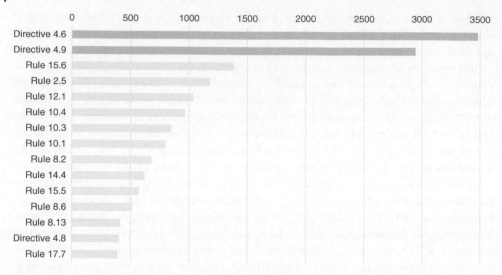

Figure 5.7 Top 15 MISRA C:2012 guidelines generating findings in a cryptographic library. Source: Based on [33].

library in question, there are over 34 000 findings in just 150 000 lines of code [33]. Assuming that it takes about five minutes to triage each finding, it requires more than 2800 man-hours to triage all the 34 000 findings. During triage, the person in charge analyzes and reviews each finding and classifies the finding as, for example, a bug, false positive, or intentional code. Just this activity takes more than 2800 man-hours. After triage, the owners of the findings would need to address the issues, e.g. fix the software to comply with the MISRA guidelines, or leave the issue as is and justify the violation by creating a MISRA deviation report, which of course would require additional time.

As described in Section 5.1, MISRA C:2012 has a total of 159 guidelines, of which 143 are rules and 16 directives. It is important to note that the 34 000 findings for the embedded library are not spread uniformly across all 159 guidelines. Instead, about half of the findings are concentrated on 15 guidelines, as can be seen in Figure 5.7 [33].

Moreover, the top two guidelines (generating about 6400 out of the 34 000 findings) are regarding two directives: Directive 4.6 and Directive 4.9 [14] described below.

- Directive 4.6: typedefs that indicate size and signedness should be used in place of the basic numerical types.
- Directive 4.9: A function should be used in preference to a function-like macro where they are interchangeable.

Both of these directives are categorized as *advisory* in the MISRA C guidelines. The MISRA C guidelines state that advisory guidelines are recommendations; please note that this does not mean that they should be ignored but should be followed as far as reasonably practical.

What this example is highlighting is that a relatively small open-source software component can generate a large number of findings. The findings may also not be uniformly spread across all the guidelines but instead be concentrated to a few of the guidelines. Therefore, before an organization dedicates too much time triaging the large number of findings, it is important for the organization to consider which MISRA guidelines are relevant for which parts of the software. Is it really necessary for an organization to consider, for example, some of the advisory guidelines, e.g. Directive 4.6 and Directive 4.9 from the above example, for a certain part of the software, in this case the cryptographic library? Is it possible for the organization to consider reducing the priority for some of the guidelines? The approaches to address these challenges are presented in more detail in the next section.

It is worth noting that this example was just focusing on the findings for a small cryptographic library for embedded systems with a size of 150 000 lines of code. Please note that this is typically just one small component of a larger automotive system with potentially millions of lines of code.

Please also note that there may be other challenges when using static code analysis tools such as generating false positives in the results, i.e. the tools indicate that there is an issue in the code when in fact there is not. Reviewing and determining false positives can be a time-consuming task for an organization. Other challenges include scalability and performance issues that can occur as new additions are made to the development teams, static code analysis tools are run more often, and increasingly larger codebases are used. Moreover, it is important to consider that a static code analysis tool is just a tool, and that an organization must recognize the limitations and consider other aspects of the development process to ensure secure software development. This includes, for example, training developers on relevant coding guidelines, following best practices for secure software development, and performing manual code and design reviews in situations where the use of a static code analysis tool is not applicable.

5.3 Solution: Workflow for Code Segmentation, Guideline Policies, and Deviation Management

This section presents a solution to address the challenges discussed in the previous section, namely undefined workflow for handling MISRA and AUTOSAR coding guidelines and the large number of findings resulting from the coding guidelines scans.

The solution is based on a workflow that helps organizations systematically handle MISRA and AUTOSAR coding guidelines, and consequently are able to manage fewer findings in a prioritized manner [24].

The following statements sum up the challenges this solution is addressing: since there is often no defined workflow for managing MISRA and AUTOSAR coding guidelines in an organization, entire codebases are scanned with all the guidelines checkers enabled, resulting in a large number of findings which may include many low priority and irrelevant findings. Managing and reviewing the large number of findings is not practical, therefore there is a need for a solution that allows an organization to prioritize and reduce the number of findings to manage.

The following workflow focuses on code segmentation, guideline policies, and deviation management to address the challenges, and contains six steps.

- Step 1: Segment the codebase into different categories/components based on risk.
- Step 2: Specify guideline policies (set of guidelines to apply) depending on risk categories.

- Step 3: Perform the scan and plan the approach for prioritization of findings.
- Step 4: Prioritize findings based on the risk categories and guideline policies and determine how to handle each finding, e.g. fix or leave as deviation.
- Step 5: Follow a defined deviation management process, including approval steps.
- Step 6: Report on MISRA or AUTOSAR coding guidelines compliance including deviations.

Finally, it is suggested to apply a technical solution to help implement the workflow where applicable. Each step is described in more detail in the following.

5.3.1 Step 1: Segment the Codebase into Different Categories/Components Based on Risk

Step 1 involves segmenting the entire codebase into different categories and components based on the risk. This step may require multiple activities such as reviewing design documents, inspecting the code, performing threat analysis and risk assessment (TARA) [10], and performing hazard analysis and risk assessment (HARA) [9] of the target software. The general idea is to determine what type of software components are included in the entire codebase based on the reviews and inspections, and using the risk assessments as a basis to determine the security and/or safety criticality of software components. An example of the results from this step is shown in Figure 5.8 to illustrate the different types of components included in the entire codebase.

This simplified example includes just eight different components in order to explain the point of the first step of segmenting the codebase. In reality, there may be many more components that can be identified in a real project. In this example, there are three in-house developed components: safety-critical component (Component 1 in the figure), security-critical component (Component 2), and non-safety/security critical component (Component 3). Another type of component contains auto-generated code (Component 4).

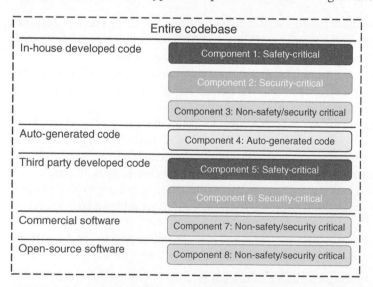

Figure 5.8 Example of different types of software components included in the codebase. Source: Based on [24].

Other types of components include third-party developed code, which is developed by a third-party developer where one component is safety critical (Component 5) and the other component is security critical (Component 6). An additional type is commercial software where a non-safety/security critical component is provided by a software vendor (Component 7). Finally, there is an open-source software component type which is a non-safety/security critical component (Component 8). To recap, as presented in the figure, the first step is for an organization to segment the codebase and identify the different included software components and determine the respective security and/or safety criticality of the software components.

5.3.2 Step 2: Specify Guideline Policies (Set of Guidelines to Apply) Depending on Risk Categories

In Step 2, the automotive organizations should specify guideline policies, i.e. the set of coding guidelines to apply depending on risk categories. These policies are defined by determining which coding guidelines are appropriate to use for which risk categories. A few examples are discussed below; however, the actual guideline policies would need to be investigated and defined by the automotive organizations. Based on the results from Step 1, different guideline policies are defined for the different software component types as depicted in Figure 5.9.

For example, for the safety-critical components (Component 1 and Component 5), an organization may define a "Guideline Policy 1" that states that all the MISRA and AUTOSAR coding guidelines should apply. Furthermore, for security-critical components (Component 2 and Component 6), the organization could create a "Guideline Policy 2" where the focus is on the 14 new guidelines added in the "MISRA C:2012 – Amendment 1: Additional security guidelines for MISRA C:2012" and maybe some other selected MISRA or AUTOSAR coding guidelines that are relevant from a security point of view

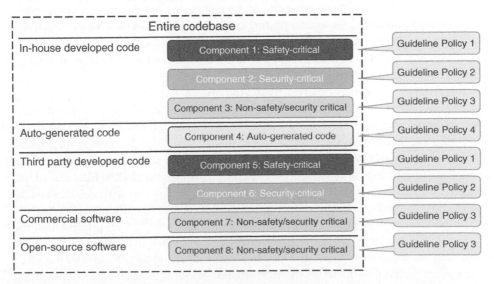

Figure 5.9 Example of different guideline policies mapped to the different types of software components included in the codebase. Source: Based on [24].

as well as selected CERT guidelines. Additionally, for the non-safety/security critical components (Component 3, Component 7, and Component 8), the organization may create a "Guideline Policy 3" with a limited set of selected coding guidelines from the MISRA or AUTOSAR coding guidelines or may even not include any of the MISRA or AUTOSAR coding guidelines. Moreover, for auto-generated code (Component 4), the organization may define a "Guideline Policy 4" containing a small set of selected guidelines from the MISRA or AUTOSAR coding guidelines that may be relevant to auto-generated code or the policy may exclude auto-generated code from any MISRA or AUTOSAR coding guidelines.

It is imperative that an organization uses careful consideration when defining the guideline policies for the different component types and risk categories to be able to include appropriate coding guidelines for the different policies. Please note that the policies should be reviewed periodically based on the findings results from the static code analysis scans with the MISRA or AUTOSAR checkers enabled to ensure that the policies are appropriate.

5.3.3 Step 3: Perform the Scan and Plan the Approach for Prioritization of Findings

In Step 3, the organization performs the static code analysis scan with the corresponding MISRA or AUTOSAR checkers enabled according to the guideline policies defined in Step 2. This means that different software components in the code will be scanned with different sets of guidelines enabled. For instance, a safety-critical component may be scanned with all the MISRA or AUTOSAR guidelines enabled whereas an open-source software component or a component based on auto-generated code may be excluded from the scan since no relevant coding guidelines are defined in the corresponding policy or scanned only with a few checkers enabled based on the guidelines defined in the corresponding policy. In this step, it is also important to plan the approach for prioritization of the findings. For example, even if an open-source software component or an auto-generated code component is scanned and generates several findings, it is possible to assign a lower priority to those findings compared with the findings from a safety-critical component, and thus the low-priority findings could initially be filtered out. This concept for prioritization of findings is illustrated in Figure 5.10.

Starting from the left-hand side in the figure, the MISRA or AUTOSAR scan of the target software generates a large number of findings, indicated by the differently colored small circles. As mentioned before, typically a scan results in too many findings, making it difficult for an organization to understand where to start analyzing and which findings to tackle. However, by following this workflow and based on the code segmentation and the guideline policies in Steps 1 and 2, it is possible for an organization to first filter out all the findings related to, for example, open-source software and auto-generated code. This results in fewer findings that an organization can start focusing on. Additionally, based on the policies, it is possible to filter out low-priority findings so that only the high-priority findings are shown in the results. This filtering allows an organization to initially focus its resources on handling the top-priority findings. Once the high-priority findings have been handled, the organization can then focus on the next-highest priority findings. This approach for prioritization is planned during Step 3 and is then executed in Step 4.

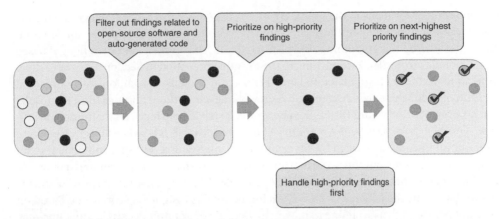

Figure 5.10 Concept for prioritization of findings to allow organizations to focus on high-priority findings first. Source: Based on [24].

5.3.4 Step 4: Prioritize Findings Based on the Risk Categories and Guideline Policies and Determine How to Handle Each Finding, e.g. Fix or Leave as Deviation

Continuing from Step 3, in Step 4 the organization prioritizes the findings based on the risk categories and guidelines and determines how to handle each finding. To assist in determining how to handle each finding, the findings are filtered based on priority as previously discussed. Figure 5.11 provides an overview to better understand the steps involved in this activity.

This activity is explained in more detail as follows. Starting from the left-hand side in the figure, the MISRA or AUTOSAR scan generates a large number of findings. These findings are filtered in a three-part process: *blocker*, *priority scoring*, and *high-pass filter*. The first part is a *blocker*, which basically filters out findings based on certain guidelines or software

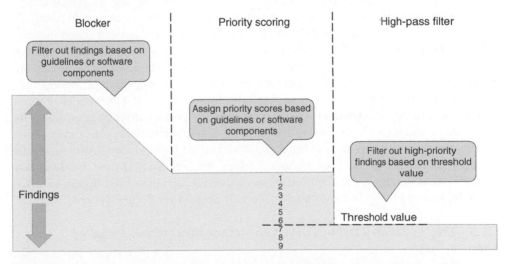

Figure 5.11 Overview of the three-part process for filtering findings. Source: Based on [24].

components (or locations in the source code). For example, an organization may determine that it will not handle any findings generated by a certain guideline, and therefore all findings generated by this guideline could be filtered out. The blocker can be configured based on the policies from Step 2. Returning to the example presented in Section 5.2, where there were about 6400 findings related to Directive 6.4 and Directive 6.9, an organization could use a blocker for these two directives, which would exclude these findings from the results that an organization would further review as a first step to help focus on high-priority findings. Another example is, when scanning a larger codebase, it is possible to use a blocker to filter out all findings generated by, for example, an open-source software component or an auto-generated code component so that an organization can focus on the findings generated by components containing in-house developed code. The second part is the *priority scoring* where, based on the policies in Step 2, each guideline is assigned a score value based on the importance of that guideline to the organization. For example, a certain guideline may have a higher priority than other guidelines and is therefore assigned a higher score, which means that the organization will tackle those corresponding findings with a higher priority. Alternatively, scores can be assigned to components or locations in the source code. For instance, the exact same guideline may receive a higher score if a finding is detected in an in-house developed component compared with the same guideline triggering a finding in an open-source software component or an auto-generated code component. In this approach, it is possible to, for example, assign score values from one through nine to allow for finer granularity when prioritizing findings. For example, while a certain guideline in a safety-critical in-house developed component may be assigned a score value of nine, the same guideline in a non-safety critical in-house developed component may be assigned a score value of five, and further the same guideline in non-safety critical commercial software may be assigned a score value of three, and finally the same guideline in a non-safety critical open-source software component may be assigned a score value of one. Please note that these score values are simply examples but give an idea of how an organization can use the priority scoring to help focus on high-priority findings first. Finally, the last part is the *high-pass filter*, where an organization can set a threshold value to filter out only high-priority findings. For example, an organization could set a threshold value of seven, which would exclude all the lower score findings initially and result in only showing a small number of high-priority findings. These findings could include, for example, findings from high-priority guidelines and findings from high-priority software components based on the scoring values set in the priority scoring part. Based on this smaller number of high-priority findings, an organization can start analyzing each finding to determine how to handle it. For instance, if it is a high-priority finding in an own-developed component, an organization can determine to fix it. Another example is a high-priority finding in an auto-generated code component which an organization may determine to leave as a deviation. As high-priority findings – in this example with score values of seven through nine – are handled over time, meaning that the software is maturing, the organization can reduce the high-pass filter threshold to, for example, a score value of five and can then focus on the next-level highest priority findings.

5.3.5 Step 5: Follow a Defined Deviation Management Process, Including Approval Steps

The organization should follow a defined deviation management process in Step 5 based on the findings in Step 4 that are left as deviations. It is worth noting that the AUTOSAR C++

14 coding guidelines do not explicitly define a deviation management process; however, since the AUTOSAR C++ 14 coding guidelines are seen as an update to the MISRA coding guidelines, a similar approach for a deviation management process described for MISRA coding guidelines compliance [13] could be followed.

Please note that the entire workflow presented in this section focuses on the MISRA and AUTOSAR guidelines that are statically verifiable, which is a majority of the guidelines, and therefore allows an organization to use a static code analysis tool to scan the code for violations. A systematic defined deviation management process should be followed to handle any resulting violations from the static code analysis tool scan that the organization decides to leave as deviations. It is important to note that there are also a few MISRA and AUTOSAR guidelines that are not statically verifiable and therefore require an organization to employ manual activities such as design reviews or code reviews. It is imperative that an organization also includes the MISRA and AUTOSAR guidelines that are not statically verifiable in the defined deviation management process. This means that any deviations resulting from the manual activities should be handled accordingly in the deviation management process.

As part of this process, every coding guideline violation should be documented with accompanying information in a *deviation record*. The deviation record should contain, among other things, the guideline being violated, a description of the circumstances in which a violation is acceptable, and the reason why the deviation is required. The deviation record may also contain the location of the violation, e.g. the file name and line number. An example of a deviation record for MISRA is shown in Figure 5.12.

Moreover, it is imperative that there is a defined approval process for deviations so that it is clear who can raise the deviations and create deviation records, and who will review and approve the deviation records. Finally, it is crucial that staff involved in the approval of deviations receive appropriate training and have the relevant skills and experience.

Furthermore, it is worth noting that over the years there have been several deviations that are consistent with well-known use cases that commonly occur in software. Therefore,

Project	F10_BCM		
Deviation ID	D_00102	**Status**	Approved
Permit	Permit / Example / C:2012 / R.10.6.A.1		
Rule 10.6	The value of a composite expression shall not be assigned to an object with wider essential type		
Use-case	The value of a composite expression is assigned to an object of wider essential type to avoid sub-optimal compiler code generation		
Reason	Code Quality (Time behavior)	**Scope**	Project
Tracing tags	D_00102_1 to D_00102_10		
Raised by	E C Unwin	**Approved by**	D B Stevens
	Signature		*Signature*
Position	Software Team Leader	**Position**	Engineering Director
Date	14-Mar-2015	**Date**	12-Apr-2015

Figure 5.12 Example deviation record for MISRA. Source: [13]. Reproduced with permission from HORIBA MIRA Limited.

during a scan of a new software, a number of violations may be identified in the code; however, many of those violations may conform to use cases that have been identified in the past. As a result, to reduce the effort required for documenting the deviations, it is possible for an organization to refer to approved deviation use cases as defined in a *deviation permit*. A deviation permit defines a use case under which a violation may be justified and specifies the documentation and process requirements that must be supplied in the deviation record. For example, MISRA publishes a set of public deviation permits that cover guidelines where violations can be reasonably justified [13].

5.3.6 Step 6: Report on MISRA or AUTOSAR Coding Guidelines Compliance Including Deviations

Finally, in Step 6, the organization provides a report on MISRA or AUTOSAR coding guidelines compliance including any identified deviations and required documentation.

As part of the documentation, an organization shall produce a *guideline compliance summary* which records the final compliance level claimed for the project. This summary contains an entry for each guideline with its corresponding level of compliance. There are four levels of compliance that may be claimed for a guideline [13]:

- Compliant
- Deviations
- Violations
- Disapplied

Compliant specifies that there are no violations of the guideline within the project. The meaning of *Deviations* is that there are violations of the guideline within the project which are supported by deviations. In contrast, *Violations* means that there are violations of the guideline within the project which are *not* supported by deviations. Last, *Disapplied* is defined as no checks have been made for compliance with the guideline. The compliance level that may be declared for each guideline depends on its respective guideline category. Table 5.3 presents an overview of the different levels of compliance related to the MISRA categories [13].

As shown in the table, *mandatory* guidelines must be compliant, *required* guidelines can be claimed as compliant or deviations, and *advisory* guidelines can be claimed to any of the four levels as compliant, deviations, violations, or disapplied.

Based on the four levels of compliance, an example of a guideline compliance summary table is presented in Table 5.4, where for each guideline a certain level of compliance is

Table 5.3 Compliance levels mapped to MISRA categories. Source: [13]. Reproduced with permission from HORIBA MIRA Limited.

MISRA category	Compliance levels that may be claimed within the guideline compliance summary
Mandatory	Compliant
Required	Compliant Deviations
Advisory	Compliant Deviations Violations Disapplied

Table 5.4 Example of guideline compliance summary. Source: [13]. Reproduced with permission from HORIBA MIRA Limited.

Guideline	MISRA category	Compliance
Directive 1.1	Required	Compliant
Directive 2.1	Required	Deviations
	...	
Rule 4.1	Required	Deviations
Rule 4.2	Advisory	Disapplied
Rule 5.1	Required	Compliant
	...	
Rule 12.1	Advisory	Compliant
Rule 12.2	Required	Deviations
Rule 12.3	Advisory	Violations
Rule 12.4	Advisory	Deviations

claimed. This table helps an organization get a clear overview of the compliance level claimed for every guideline.

Finally, as part of the project delivery, the following artifacts, among others, shall be made available to support a claim of compliance with the guidelines [13]:

- Guideline enforcement plan.
- Guideline compliance summary.
- Deviation permits.
- Deviation records.

These artifacts help an organization to demonstrate that compliance has been enforced. The *guideline enforcement plan* shows how compliance with the guidelines is to be checked, e.g. by which tools, and therefore any related evidence from such tools can be used to show that the guidelines checks have been performed. The *guideline compliance summary* provides an overview declaring the level of compliance that is claimed. Details of approved *deviation permits* that are used are included for any frequently encountered use cases that require deviations. Last, *deviation records* used to support and justify the presence of violations to the coding guidelines are included.

An organization shall be able to provide these above-mentioned documents that can be used as evidence to claim compliance with the coding guidelines.

5.4 Chapter Summary

This chapter discussed the usage of static code analysis tools in the automotive industry, focusing on their applicability to automotive-related coding standards such as MISRA and AUTOSAR coding guidelines. First, a brief general introduction to static code analysis tools is provided explaining how such tools can be used to identify weaknesses and vulnerabilities in the code early during development. These tools use built-in knowledge about defects and weaknesses and use various techniques such as data-flow analysis and control-flow analysis to identify common coding issues in the software without running the application. Since the approach of using static code analysis tools to find weaknesses and vulnerabilities in software is similar to other industries, this chapter instead provides a deeper discussion on using static code analysis tools for checking compliance to the MISRA and AUTOSAR coding guidelines, which are often used in the automotive industry. An introduction providing some background on the MISRA and AUTOSAR coding guidelines is first given to better understand the type of guidelines included in the coding standards. Next, common challenges that automotive organizations are facing regarding MISRA and AUTOSAR coding guidelines are discussed. The challenges presented include undefined workflow for handling MISRA and AUTOSAR coding guidelines, and the fact that running MISRA and AUTOSAR coding guidelines checkers on entire codebases generates a large number of findings. This is explained in more detailed as follows: since some automotive systems are complex systems that may contain software from multiple sources including in-house developed code, third-party developed code, auto-generated code, commercial software, and open-source software, then simply enabling MISRA or AUTOSAR coding guidelines checkers on the entire codebase is not practical since it will result in potentially millions of findings. To illustrate this challenge, results from scanning an open-source software cryptographic library with the MISRA C:2012 guidelines checkers enabled is presented. The MISRA scan generates 34 000 findings in 150 000 lines of code. It is important to note that this cryptographic library is just a smaller component included in a larger system. Therefore, it is imperative for an organization to consider how to handle the different types of software that may be included in the target system. To address the challenges, a workflow that helps organizations systematically handle MISRA and AUTOSAR coding guidelines is presented. This workflow allows organizations to manage fewer findings in a prioritized manner. The workflow consists of six steps, where an organization can first segment the codebase into different categories based on risk, specify policies for the respective risk categories, perform the MISRA or AUTOSAR coding guidelines scan and plan the approach for prioritization, prioritize the findings based on the risk categories and determine how to handle each finding, follow a defined deviation management process for deviations, and finally report on the MISRA or AUTOSAR coding guidelines compliance including deviations. By following a defined workflow process for handling MISRA and AUTOSAR coding guidelines, including an approach to segment codebases and defining guideline policies, it allows automotive organizations to overcome common challenges, and to prioritize and manage the most relevant and critical findings first.

References

1 MITRE (2020). CWE common weakness enumeration. https://cwe.mitre.org (accessed 30 July 2020).
2 SANS (2020). CWE/SANS TOP 25 most dangerous software errors. https://www.sans .org/top25-software-errors (accessed 30 July 2020).

3 Synopsys (2020). Why static application security testing (SAST) tools aren't just glorified grep.

4 OWASP (2020). SQL injection. https://owasp.org/www-community/attacks/SQL_Injection (accessed 30 July 2020).

5 MITRE (2020). CWE-367: time-of-check time-of-use (TOCTOU) race condition. https://cwe.mitre.org/data/definitions/367.html (accessed 30 July 2020).

6 Jenkins (2020). Jenkins build great things at any scale. https://www.jenkins.io (accessed 30 July 2020).

7 Git (2020). Git is a free and open source distributed version control system. https://git-scm.com (accessed 30 July 2020).

8 Atlassian (2020). Jira software. https://www.atlassian.com/software/jira (accessed 30 July 2020).

9 International Organization for Standardization (ISO) (2018). *ISO 26262-1:2018 – road vehicles — functional safety*. Geneva, Switzerland: ISO.

10 International Organization for Standardization (ISO)/Society of Automotive Engineers (SAE) International (2020). *ISO/SAE DIS 21434 – road vehicles — cybersecurity engineering*. Geneva, Switzerland: ISO and USA: SAE International.

11 MISRA (2020). A brief history of MISRA. www.misra.org.uk/MISRAHome/AbriefhistoryofMISRA/tabid/69/Default.aspx (accessed 30 July 2020).

12 MISRA (2020). MISRA publications. www.misra.org.uk/Publications/tabid/57/Default.aspx (accessed 30 July 2020).

13 MISRA (2020). MISRA compliance:2020 – achieving compliance with MISRA coding guidelines.

14 MISRA (2013). MISRA C:2012 guidelines for the use of the C language in critical systems.

15 MISRA (2020). MISRA C:2012 Amendment 2 – updates for ISO/IEC 9899:2011 core functionality.

16 MISRA (2016). MISRA C:2012 Amendment 1 – additional security guidelines for MISRA C:2012.

17 Synopsys (2019). Coverity support for MISRA coding standards.

18 MISRA (2020). MISRA C++. www.misra.org.uk/Activities/MISRAC/tabid/171/Default.aspx (accessed 30 July 2020).

19 AUTOSAR (2020). The standardized software framework for intelligent mobility. https://www.autosar.org (accessed 30 July 2020).

20 Reichart, G. (2019). AUTOSAR adaptive platform - a standardized software platform for intelligent vehicles with functional safety and data integrity. *ELIV Europe*, Bonn, Germany.

21 Automotive Grade Linux (2020). What is automotive grade Linux?. https://www.automotivelinux.org (accessed 30 July 2020).

22 GENIVI (2020). Beyond Linux IVI and into the connected vehicle. https://www.genivi.org (accessed 30 July 2020).

23 Android (2020). What is android automotive? https://source.android.com/devices/automotive/start/what_automotive. (accessed 30 July 2020).

24 Oka, D. K. (2020). The future of AUTOSAR and how to handle AUTOSAR coding guidelines. https://www.brighttalk.com/webcast/13983/414011/autosar (Webinar 17 June 2020).

25 Staron, M. (2017). *Automotive Software Architectures: An Introduction*. Cham, Switzerland: Springer International Publishing AG.

26 AUTOSAR (2019). Guidelines for the use of the C++14 language in critical and safety-related systems.

27 Stroustrup, B. and Sutter, H. (2020). C++ core guidelines. http://isocpp.github.io/CppCoreGuidelines/CppCoreGuidelines (accessed 30 July 2020).

28 Lockheed Martin Corporation (2005). JSF C++ – joint strike fighter air vehicle C++ coding standards.

29 Synopsys (2019). Coverity support for AUTOSAR coding standards.

30 Bagnara, R., Bagnara, A., and Hill, P. M. (2018). The MISRA C coding standard and its role in the development and analysis of safety- and security-critical embedded software. *International Static Analysis Symposium (SAS)*, Freiburg, Germany.

31 SEI (2016). CERT C coding standard – rules for developing safe, reliable, and secure systems.

32 SEI (2016). CERT C++ coding standard – rules for developing safe, reliable, and secure systems in C++.

33 Oka, D. K. (2018). Strategies and global trends for security in the automotive software development lifecycle. Presentation in *Next-Generation High-Speed In-Vehicle Network Reliability Technology* at the Aichi Science and Technology Foundation, Nagoya, Japan.

6

Software Composition Analysis in the Automotive Industry

SCIENTIA POTENTIA EST

As briefly described in Section 4.2.2, software composition analysis tools are primarily used to scan software to detect included open-source software components and to identify corresponding known vulnerabilities and license information associated with the identified components. Armed with this information, automotive organizations can determine the risks of including certain open-source software components in automotive software.

Open-source software has become increasingly prevalent in the past few decades across multiple industries. Open-source software components are included in numerous applications for mobile phones, they make up large parts of web browsers, do the heavy lifting in backend servers, and also now provide various functionality in automotive systems. Open-source software has several benefits, such as enabling rapid innovation, reducing costs for non-competitive technologies, and allowing organizations to focus more on developing new products and services. Other industries have already benefited from these advantages. For example, the Internet infrastructure completely changed in the late 1990s and early 2000s due to the usage of open-source software. One of the most well-known open-source software projects is Linux, which is an operating system powering a large number of backend servers and running on many embedded devices today. Linux is a great example that demonstrates the power of open-source software that helped drive the change of the Internet infrastructure. In the 1990s, Linux replaced proprietary systems in several production environments and, as a result, the Internet infrastructure become more open. Consequently, it became easier and cheaper to build websites and manage contents online. This was the beginning for a whole new breed of websites, systems, and tools providing new services and solutions online. For instance, search engines, shopping sites, video content sites, and other business tools quickly emerged on the Internet. As open-source software transformed the Internet, open-source software will surely transform the automotive industry in a similar manner. There are already several cases where open-source software has successfully been employed in the automotive industry, especially for systems such as infotainment systems, telematics units, and mobile apps. For example, in the summer of 2017, Toyota launched its first vehicle with an infotainment system based on Automotive Grade Linux [1]. Interestingly, open-source software will not be limited to only these types of systems but it will affect the entire eco-system of the car. That is, open-source

Building Secure Cars: Assuring the Automotive Software Development Lifecycle, First Edition. Dennis Kengo Oka.
© 2021 John Wiley & Sons Ltd. Published 2021 by John Wiley & Sons Ltd.

software will further drive innovation in all aspects of the four major automotive trends, commonly represented by the acronym CASE: *Connectivity*, *Autonomous*, *Shared and services*, and *Electric*. This will lead to the enablement of several new business models and solutions improving overall user experiences in the automotive industry similar to the transformation we experienced in the Internet infrastructure.

A recent report called "2020 Open Source Security and Risk Analysis" [2], which analyzes the use of open-source software in different industries, shows that codebases in the category to which the automotive industry belongs contain on average 69% open-source software. This category also includes aerospace, aviation, logistics, and transportation. For comparison, industry categories with the highest open-source software usage are "Internet & Software Infrastructure" with 83%, and "Internet of Things" with 82%. In the "2019 Open Source Security and Risk Analysis" report [3] released a year earlier, the category the automotive industry belongs to indicated, on average, 37% open-source software and was one of the categories with the lowest percentages of open-source software usage. It is possible to imagine that, in particular, the trends for connectivity and a growing eco-system for the automotive industry are major drivers for increased usage of open-source software. There are also several ongoing automotive-specific open-source software projects. One such example is Automotive Grade Linux [4] which is a collaborative open-source project that brings together auto manufacturers, suppliers, and technology companies to accelerate the development and adoption of a fully open software stack for the connected car. Another example is the Open Automotive Alliance where technology and automotive companies are working on adapting the Android platform to cars [5]. Moreover, GENIVI is an alliance of OEMs (original equipment manufacturers), automotive suppliers, software and services companies, and semiconductor companies, who together are focusing on the adoption of open-source in-vehicle infotainment software for the connected car [6].

Although the use of open-source software brings many benefits, it is equally important to consider the risks associated with open-source software, including *security risks*, *license compliance risks*, and *operational risks*. It is important to note that open-source software is like any other software and may include vulnerabilities that are exploitable. Thus, there are *security risks* with using open-source software. The following example, based on the Tesla hack presented by security researchers at Black Hat in 2017, is given to illustrate the security risks with open-source software. Eventually, the security researchers were able to send arbitrary CAN (controller area network) messages on the in-vehicle network to cause disruption to the brakes and steering as a result of this attack. However, the initial steps that allowed this attack were caused by vulnerabilities in open-source software. First, the security researchers exploited two vulnerabilities in the open-source software-based web browser on the infotainment system in the Tesla, which was using an old version of QtWebkit, containing a vulnerability in the JSArray::sort() function, and a known vulnerability with the CVE (Common Vulnerabilities and Exposures) identifier, CVE-2011-3928. As a result, the security researchers gained a remote shell with browser privileges. In the next step, they exploited another known vulnerability (CVE-2013-6282) in the open-source software operating system, namely the Linux kernel, which was using an old version of 2.6.36. Consequently, the security researchers successfully escalated the privilege level and gained access to a remote root shell. By exploiting vulnerabilities in open-source software, the security researchers were able to successfully gain entry to the vehicle remotely, and, as the next step, managed to gain access to the Gateway ECU (electronic control unit). As mentioned above, they were then able to inject CAN messages through the Gateway ECU to the rest of the in-vehicle network and cause disruption to the brakes and steering [7].

Moreover, open-source software are associated with various license types and conditions that define how the open-source software are allowed to be used, and therefore automotive organizations need to carefully consider *license compliance risks*. For example, some license types are very permissive and allow the open-source software to be used freely, e.g. the MIT (Massachusetts Institute of Technology) license [8], whereas other license types, e.g. GPLv2 (GNU General Public License version 2) [9], are more restrictive and have strong copyleft requirements, i.e. when distributing derived works, the source code of the codebase where the open-source software is used must be released under the same license conditions. Since the license conditions are not directly related to security this topic is not discussed further in detail, however it is imperative for an automotive organization to be aware and comply with the open-source software license conditions.

Furthermore, there are *operational risks* that could affect security when using open-source software. There exist many different open-source software projects, some which are actively maintained and updated by the open-source software community, and others where development may have stopped, or the projects have become obsolete. For automotive organizations it is important to understand the operational risks when selecting a certain open-source software to be used in a vehicle. Vehicles can be active in the field for 10–15 years and thus organizations must have an understanding of how well the selected open-source software will be maintained during this period of time. For example, some active open-source software projects may provide regular updates including bug fixes and added functionality. In contrast, other projects may have just a few active developers, or there may be long inactive periods between updates and releases, and therefore the software may not be updated in a timely manner. As a result, if a critical issue is found in this particular open-source software, the developers may not be able to patch the software quickly. Alternatively, if there is a need to support new functionality in the future, e.g. support for new cryptographic algorithms, the open-source software may not be updated to include such functionality if the project is no longer being actively maintained.

Finally, it is important to understand the concept of *software decay*. Generally for any software, one can assume that, over time, new vulnerabilities are detected in the existing code. For instance, there are more people reviewing the code, and security researchers find new attacks and vulnerability patterns. Therefore, a software that contains no known vulnerabilities at a certain point in time could, after a few years, potentially contain a large number of vulnerabilities because new vulnerabilities have been discovered in the included open-source software components. A practical example of software decay in a software package is depicted in Figure 6.1. This particular software package was compiled in April 2008 and at that time there were 22 CVEs, i.e. known vulnerabilities, associated with it. Over the years, a large number of new vulnerabilities in software components included in this software package were identified. In October 2015, the exact same (unpatched) software package now contained 582 CVEs, of which 74 CVEs have a Common Vulnerability Scoring System (CVSS) rating of 10 which is a "Critical" severity rating.

Consequently, software decay is something automotive organizations need to carefully consider since vehicles are typically active in the field for a long time. Moreover, since the

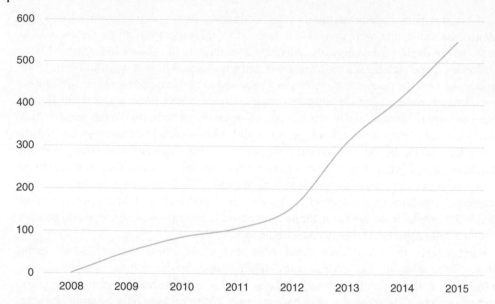

Figure 6.1 Software degrades over time with more than 500 vulnerabilities detected over seven years in a particular software package Source: Data from [10].

automotive development cycles traditionally span several years, the risk of including out-dated software in the final product is high. This topic is out of scope for this chapter but it is useful to mention that solutions to address these issues include cybersecurity monitoring and vulnerability management to detect and analyze new vulnerabilities, and incident response and software over-the-air update capabilities to patch vulnerable vehicles in the field. This topic is discussed in more detail in Chapter 12.

With a complex supply chain spanning multiple software suppliers and a large software codebase comprising more than 100 million lines of code for a vehicle, it is crucial for automotive organizations to have a clear view of which software is included and what the associated risks are. Software composition analysis tools provide organizations with a detailed view of the included open-source software components and the corresponding risks. Armed with this information, organizations should follow best practices to manage the associated risks.

The main points of this chapter are:

- We provide an overview of the current state of software composition analysis and discuss how such solutions can be applied in the automotive supply chain to improve software security.
- We review specific results from an analysis of several automotive software packages and discuss the associated risks of the identified open-source components and known vulnerabilities.
- We suggest best practices for managing open-source software risks across the automotive supply chain.

More details regarding software composition analysis in the automotive industry can be found in References [10–12].

6.1 Software Composition Analysis: Benefits and Usage Scenarios

As mentioned in the previous section, the automotive industry comprises a complex software supply chain, where multiple tiers of suppliers provide various layers of software, such as lower layer drivers, middleware, operating systems, and higher layer application software, which are finally integrated and run on top of the automotive system. To this end, it is important to ensure a proper level of quality and security of the various software components included in the supply chain. This is commonly achieved through *software signoff*. That is, when a software is handed over, both the producing party and the receiving party must have an agreed understanding of the expected software quality and security. The software does not have to be perfect but it should conform to a level within a certain tolerance. This is achieved by verifying and testing the software on both the producing and receiving sides. Since the focus of this chapter is on the use of open-source software and the associated risks, the producing side should first list all included open-source software components and their respective version numbers. The receiving side should then verify that only approved open-source software components are included in the delivered software package. This verification is an integral step in managing a software supply chain and can be achieved by creating and using a software bill of materials (SBOM). Software composition analysis tools can be used to help automate the process of generating SBOMs. Automotive organizations typically conduct software composition analysis during the software development phase as part of a secure software development lifecycle.

There are two approaches to software composition analysis: *source code analysis* and *binary analysis*. Each approach has its advantages and disadvantages. The first approach, *source code analysis* takes as input the source code, and analyzes and identifies included open-source software components, vulnerabilities, license compliance, and operational risks. A dashboard showing example results from a source code software composition analysis tool called Black Duck [13] is shown in Figure 6.2.

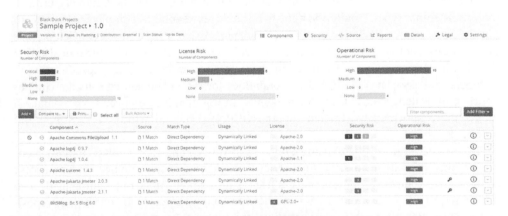

Figure 6.2 Dashboard showing example results from a source code software composition analysis tool. Source: synopsys.com. Portions Copyright 2020 Synopsys, Inc. Used with permission. All rights reserved.

The top section of the dashboard shows three bars which indicate the risks for the respective category. The left-hand side contains the *Security Risk*, describing how many components include critical, high, medium, and low risk vulnerabilities. The information regarding the vulnerabilities is based on the National Institute of Standards and Technology (NIST) National Vulnerability Database (NVD) [15] and Black Duck's own KnowledgeBase vulnerability database. The middle bars illustrate the *License Risk* in terms of license compliance risks and the right-hand bars show the *Operational Risk*. The operational risks indicate how well maintained an open-source project is. The tool gathers this information by monitoring the open-source community activities on, for example, how many active developers exist, and how often code is committed to the project. The operational risks provide an automotive organization valuable input and can be used as a criteria when selecting which open-source software components are allowed to be included in a software package. For example, projects that are not well-maintained have inherent risks including outdated software, newly discovered vulnerabilities not fixed in a timely manner, and new features not added in the future.

The benefits with source code analysis is that since it has access to the source code repository, it can scan source code files and package manager configuration files directly, and is therefore more accurate in identifying included open-source software components and respective version numbers. The disadvantage, however, is that it only works on source code so if only a binary file is available, it is not possible to use the source code analysis approach.

Instead, the second approach, *binary analysis*, can be used in this case since it only requires the binary of the software as input. Using various techniques, it breaks down the binary file, extracts and analyzes its contents and identifies included open-source software components and known vulnerabilities, license types and other potential risk issues. A dashboard showing example results from a binary software composition analysis tool called Black Duck Binary Analysis, formerly known as Protecode SC Binary Analysis [16], is shown in Figure 6.3.

The dashboard in the figure depicts three circles that show the following information. The left-hand circle presents the number of open-source software *Components* identified in the scanned binary and indicates how many of those components are vulnerable. The middle circle gives an overview of the type of *Vulnerabilities* identified, namely, critical, major, and minor types. Finally, the right-hand circle represents any compliance issues with *Licenses*, e.g. whether included license types are permissive or have strong copyleft properties. Although not shown in the figure, to provide more details to a user, the tool also lists the identified open-source software components in the dashboard. The respective version numbers and associated identified vulnerabilities for each open-source software component are indicated in the list. The vulnerability information is referenced from a database that contains information extracted from the NIST NVD, including the CVE identifiers and severity levels.

There are several benefits to using a binary software composition analysis tool. As mentioned, only software in binary form is required as input so there is no need to have access to the source code. The analysis process itself is fast, simple and can be automated since it only requires a binary and there is no need to configure access to source code repositories. Thus, this approach is very beneficial for automotive organizations who consume software and may not have access to the source code. The disadvantage is that since only

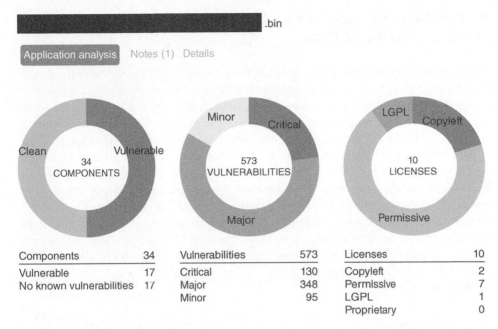

Figure 6.3 Dashboard showing example results from a binary software composition analysis tool. Source: synopsys.com. Portions Copyright 2020 Synopsys, Inc. Used with permission. All rights reserved.

the binary is used for analysis, the accuracy of identified components and versions may be lower compared with the first approach based on source code analysis.

Therefore, a hybrid solution of using both source code and binary approaches is appropriate. Automotive organizations that have access to source code, should use the first approach of conducting source code software composition analysis. In the case where the organizations do not have access to the source code and only have access to binaries, they should use the second approach of conducting binary software composition analysis.

Regardless of the approach, the software composition analysis tools can easily generate SBOMs, which can be used during the software signoff process. These tools can also help combat software decay proactively by automatically providing alerts on newly discovered vulnerabilities of previously scanned software. Consider an example where a certain automotive software package is scanned by a software composition analysis tool and at the time there are no known vulnerabilities included and the automotive software is released to the field; however, sometime in the future a critical vulnerability for one of the included open-source software components is detected. For an automotive organization to properly manage the risk, the software composition analysis tool can provide an alert to the organization that a new vulnerability has been detected in an open-source software component included in the previously released software package. The organization can then take immediate action to manage the situation based on information contained in the alert.

It is worth noting that the output results generated from the software composition analysis tools can be used to establish a common understanding of the security risks and support software signoff between the producing and receiving sides in the software supply chain.

6.2 Problem Statement: Analysis of Automotive Software Open-Source Software Risks

To better understand the open-source software related security risks in the current automotive landscape, this section discusses actual results from a previously conducted analysis on automotive software open-source software risks [10–12]. These results are not based on an exhaustive study but rather presents an overview of common open-source software related security risks. The analysis includes 14 automotive-related software from the connected car use case which contain open-source software. Target software includes both in-vehicle infotainment software and mobile apps. Since the source code for the target software are not publicly available, the above-mentioned binary analysis approach was taken. The binaries for these types of software packages are often publicly available on the Internet to allow for customers to perform updates themselves. Due to the nature of the results, specific details from the analysis of the software packages are not disclosed. Instead, the results are summarized to provide a better overview of commonly included open-source software components and to focus on highlighting common themes rather than to discuss specific results of individual software packages.

6.2.1 Analysis Results

Table 6.1 presents a summary of the results. The table includes the top five vulnerable open-source components and the respective number of critical vulnerabilities. Critical vulnerabilities are defined as vulnerabilities where the associated CVE has a CVSS score of 7 or higher.

The open-source software component name and its description are given in the first and second columns in Table 6.1. The third column indicates how common the open-source software component is by showing how many of the 14 analyzed software packages the corresponding open-source software component is included in. The fourth column presents the number of unique critical vulnerabilities (i.e. CVEs) associated with the identified open-source software components, respectively.

Please note that the table only provides an overview. Further details for each of the top five vulnerable open-source software components are given as follows.

Table 6.1 Overview of top five vulnerable open-source software components Source: Data from [12].

Open-source software	Description	Included in software (14)	No. of critical vulnerabilities
zlib	Library for data compression	12	3
libpng	Library for handling PNG images	8	11
openssl	Crypto library for secure communications	5	21
curl	Library for transferring data	5	12
Linux kernel	Operating system	3	162

6.2.1.1 zlib

zlib is a general purpose, lossless open-source data compression library for use on virtually any computer hardware and operating system. The latest stable release at the time of writing is zlib 1.2.11 from January 2017 [17].

A software package released in 2015 include a zlib library from 2002 (zlib 1.1.4). At the time the software package was released, this open-source software component was 13 years old and had a critical vulnerability that was discovered in 2003 (CVE-2003-0107), 12 years before the software package was released.

6.2.1.2 libpng

libpng is a platform-independent open-source library for handling PNG (portable network graphics) images and has been widely used for more than 23 years. libpng is dependent on zlib for data compression and decompression routines. The latest stable release at the time of writing is libpng 1.6.37 from April 2019 [18].

Software packages released in 2017 include old versions of libpng from 2004 (libpng 1.2.8). At the time the software packages were released, the 12-year-old open-source library contained, among others, a more than 10-year-old critical vulnerability discovered already in 2006 (CVE-2006-3334).

6.2.1.3 OpenSSL

OpenSSL is a general-purpose open-source cryptographic library that provides a robust, commercial-grade and full-featured toolkit for the TLS (transport layer security) and SSL (secure sockets layer) protocols. The latest stable release at the time of writing is OpenSSL 1.1.1g from April 2020 [19].

Software packages released in 2017 include a 7-year old version of the crypto library OpenSSL released in 2010 (openssl-0.9.8m). This version of OpenSSL includes several critical vulnerabilities detected as early as in 2010 (CVE-2010-4252, CVE-2010-0742, CVE-2010-3864). As a side note, even though it is not considered a critical vulnerability, this version of OpenSSL is vulnerable to the well-known POODLE (Padding Oracle On Downgraded Legacy Encryption) attack, which was discovered in 2014 (CVE-2014-3566) [20].

6.2.1.4 curl

curl is an open-source command line tool and library for transferring data with URLs (uniform resource locators) and supports myriad network protocols, including FTP (file transfer protocol), HTTP (hypertext transfer protocol), HTTPS (hypertext transfer protocol secure), MQTT (message queuing telemetry transport), SMB (server message block), SMTP (simple mail transfer protocol), etc. The latest stable release at the time of writing is curl 7.71.1 from July 2020 [21].

A software package released in October 2017 includes a fairly recent version of curl released only eight months earlier, in February 2017 (curl 7.53.1). In contrast to the above examples, where outdated and vulnerable open-source software components are included in the released software packages, a fairly recent version of the open-source software is included which did not contain any critical vulnerabilities at the time the software package was released; however, three critical vulnerabilities (CVE-2017-8816, CVE-2017-8817, CVE-2018-1000120) were discovered in just five months after the software package was released.

6.2.1.5 Linux Kernel

The Linux kernel is a free and open-source monolithic, modular, Unix-like operating system kernel. It is used on a wide variety of computing systems including embedded devices, mobile devices, personal computers, servers, etc. The latest stable release at the time of writing is Linux kernel 5.8 from August 2020 [22].

The software packages with the Linux kernel contain more than 162 critical vulnerabilities. There are too many critical vulnerabilities to discuss in this chapter but, to give an example, there is one included critical vulnerability worth mentioning: CVE-2017-1000251 [23], which is the Blueborne vulnerability discovered in September 2017 [24]. If exploited, an attacker is able to remotely – over Bluetooth – execute arbitrary code on the device where the vulnerable software is running. It was estimated that over 5.3 billion devices were impacted by Blueborne at the time the vulnerability was discovered and a year later, in September 2018, an estimated 2 billion devices were still vulnerable [25].

6.2.2 Discussion

Overall, the results show that all 14 analyzed software packages contain vulnerable open-source software components with critical vulnerabilities. Although the sample set is small, this indicates that it is not only some specific software packages that contain vulnerable open-source software components but instead the use of vulnerable open-source software components is prevalent among all of the analyzed software packages.

In the following, we will briefly discuss a few points regarding the results in more detail. First, there are multiple software packages that include outdated open-source software components that are several years old, e.g. zlib, libpng, and OpenSSL in the examples above. It is important to note that these old open-source software components contain vulnerabilities that had been fixed in newer versions that were available when the software packages were released. It is also worth noting that many of these open-source software components are regularly updated. Why outdated and vulnerable open-source software components were included in the software packages when newer fixed versions of the same open-source software components were available is unclear, but it is a concern that automotive organizations should be aware of.

Second, even if recent, in this case a few months old, versions of open-source software components are used, or, at the time of the release of the software package, there are no known critical vulnerabilities in the included open-source software components, e.g. curl in the example above, it is crucial to consider that new vulnerabilities are continuously discovered as discussed earlier in this chapter regarding software decay. The above example with curl also highlights this phenomenon with three new critical vulnerabilities discovered in just five months after release of the software package.

Please note that the purpose of this analysis is *not* to provide full coverage of all types of automotive software but rather to give an overview of how software composition analysis tools can be used by automotive organizations, what type of results the tools provide and what the common challenges are. The results presented are based on a small set of software in the automotive industry; however, there are similarities to the results found in a published "State of Software Composition" report [26], which includes a larger range of applications. More than 128 000 applications from various industries have been analyzed and are covered in this report. The top 10 vulnerable open-source software components presented in the report include the Linux kernel, curl, OpenSSL, and libpng. Additionally, although it is not in the top 10 list, it is worth noting that zlib is in 15th place. These are the same top five vulnerable open-source components identified in the automotive software analysis presented in this chapter.

It is also worth noting that a survey report on the cybersecurity posture in the automotive industry called "Securing the Modern Vehicle: A Study of Automotive Industry Cybersecurity Practices" [27], released in 2019, highlights the use of insecure and outdated open-source software as one of the primary factors causing vulnerabilities in automotive systems. This echoes the results from the analysis presented in this chapter where multiple open-source software components included in automotive software contain several known critical vulnerabilities. Moreover, many of these open-source software components were already several years old, even though newer versions of the components existed, when they were included in the released software packages. More information about the automotive survey report is provided in Section 1.3.

With the trend of using more open-source software in the automotive industry, the need to establish practices for managing open-source software risks becomes greater, including the need for automotive organizations to use software composition analysis tools as part of the software development lifecycle and for establishing practices for software signoff, explained in further detail in the next section.

6.3 Solution: Countermeasures on Process and Technical Levels

Since software is developed and integrated by multiple organizations in a complex supply chain in the automotive industry, both producing and receiving parties need to collaborate and have an agreed understanding on how to manage open-source software security risks. Several best practices, inspired by [2, 3, 28, 29], which can be adopted by automotive organizations as a basis to manage open-source software risks across the automotive supply chain are presented as follows:

- Fully inventory open-source software.
- Use appropriate software composition analysis approaches.
- Map open-source software to known security vulnerabilities.
- Identify license, quality, and security risks.
- Create and enforce open-source software risk policies.
- Continuously monitor for new security threats.
- Define and follow processes for addressing vulnerabilities in open-source software.

These activities are explained in further detail in the following sections.

6.3.1 Fully Inventory Open-Source Software

It is crucial for an automotive organization to have a clear understanding of what software components are used in the organizations' products and software packages. To this end, generating full and accurate SBOMs, including all open-source software components and their respective versions, is required for all relevant products and software packages.

Performing these activities of inventorying software requires changes to the organizational processes. To provide guidance to organizations, a task force within the NTIA (National Telecommunications and Information Administration) of the United States Department of Commerce is working on software transparency to promote SBOM both as a concept and for practical deployment, including building awareness and providing information on strategies, how to identify and name components, how to share SBOMs, and how to automate SBOM in production and use [30]. Moreover, the OpenChain WG (working group) has developed a new standard that was published in December 2020 called ISO/IEC 5230 [31] to help guide organizations in the supply chain with license compliance and to provide software transparency between the providing parties and the receiving parties which would assist in inventorying the usage of open-source software. Thus, automotive organizations can take advantage of these guidance documentations to help define internal processes to inventory open-source software.

6.3.2 Use Appropriate Software Composition Analysis Approaches

It is worth noting that creating and maintaining SBOMs manually could be a daunting task that is both time-consuming and error prone. Therefore, the recommendation is to use software composition analysis tools. An SBOM generated by a software composition analysis tool can provide more comprehensive information, including specific version information, dependencies, and libraries that those dependencies are linked to. As presented in Section 6.1, there are two approaches for software composition analysis: source code analysis and binary analysis. Automotive organizations should use the appropriate approaches based on the access to the relevant software.

For example, automotive organizations who develop their own software and have access to the source code should conduct source code software composition analysis. If the developed software is provided as a binary to a receiving party, the generated SBOM should be provided together with the binary to the receiving party to indicate the included open-source software components. In contrast, automotive organizations who have access only to binaries should conduct binary software composition analysis. In addition, they should request their suppliers who provide the binaries to also provide the corresponding SBOM. This allows the receiving organization to compare the contents of the received SBOM to the results from their own binary analysis to ensure that there are no discrepancies and no hidden open-source software components included. The analysis reports from the software composition analysis tools could then be used to support software signoff between the producing and receiving parties in the software supply chain.

6.3.3 Map Open-Source Software to Known Security Vulnerabilities

Based on the inventory of used open-source software components, automotive organizations should use vulnerability information sources – such as the NIST NVD and other applicable vulnerability information databases, which provide information on publicly disclosed vulnerabilities – and map the vulnerabilities to the included open-source software components. In particular, it is important to investigate whether there exist newer versions of the used open-source software components that have been patched against the known vulnerabilities. Automotive organizations can benefit from using software composition analysis tools that can be used to perform this type of vulnerability mapping automatically.

While performing mapping of open-source software to known security vulnerabilities, it is important to know that the number of known vulnerabilities reported yearly has steadily been increasing over the past years. For example, NVD listed 6400 new vulnerabilities in 2016 and 14 700 new vulnerabilities in 2017. There were also other reports stating that over 20 000 new vulnerabilities were detected in 2017, which includes more than 5000 vulnerabilities not listed in NVD. These numbers represent all known new vulnerabilities in both commercial and open-source software. For open-source software specifically, there were over 4800 vulnerabilities detected in 2017 [29]. This trend continued in 2018 with more than 16 500 new vulnerabilities listed in NVD, including over 7000 vulnerabilities detected in open-source software. In total, over 50 000 open-source vulnerabilities have been reported in the past 20 years [3].

While NVD is a great source for vulnerabilities, it is worth noting that there can be a time lag between the time a vulnerability is first made public until it is published in NVD. Some research reports an average of 27 days between the time a vulnerability is first disclosed until it is included as an entry in NVD [32]. During this time window, attackers who are aware of the vulnerability could try to exploit vulnerable systems before organizations are made aware of the vulnerability through NVD. Moreover, due to the format of the NVD records it is, in some cases, unclear which versions of the software are affected by a certain CVE. Therefore, while NVD provides valuable information, it is useful for automotive organizations to consider using multiple sources for vulnerability information to ensure faster up-to-date relevant information, including full details on vulnerable versions of open-source software components.

6.3.4 Identify License, Quality, and Security Risks

Even though license compliance is not directly related to security, it can have huge legal implications and therefore it is imperative that automotive organizations comply with the licenses for the included open-source software components in software packages that are released. For example, an organization needs to determine which license types and conditions for the open-source software components are acceptable to meet the organization's software distribution and license requirements. Using the SBOM, it is then possible to review the license types for the included open-source software components to ensure that only the acceptable license types are used. However, if there are any open-source software components whose associated licenses do not comply with the organization's license requirements, these need to be flagged and the organization should consider how to handle those situations.

With the understanding of the concept of software decay, it is important to know that the usage of open-source software components that are poorly maintained, e.g. not actively developed or not providing bug fixes in a timely manner, leads to quality and security risks.

Automotive organizations need to track and manage these types of risk. Thus, it is recommended that an organization establishes an automated process that tracks open-source software components and their licenses, known vulnerabilities and operational risks, and prioritizes issues based on severity. This type of information is valuable and could serve as criteria for organizations when determining which open-source software components are allowed to be included in a software package. Thus, an organization can create policies based on this information, as described further in the next section.

6.3.5 Create and Enforce Open-Source Software Risk Policies

Unfortunately, in several cases, many organizations lack proper documentation and enforcement of open-source policies to mitigate risks. Thus, at a minimum, automotive organizations should perform manual policy reviews. As software development becomes more automated using various tools, the management of open-source software policies should also become more automated and integrated into the tools.

For example, developers need to be educated on the managed use of open-source software. To this end, it may be useful for the organization to define a procedure on how to introduce, approve and document new open-source software components. This procedure helps to provide a systematic approach to control what type of open-source software enters the codebase and ensures that it complies with the organization's policies. Therefore, it is imperative that an organization first creates relevant policies for usage of open-source software regarding, for example, specifying acceptable open-source software components in whitelists, acceptable license types, acceptable number of known vulnerabilities, acceptable versions/age of the software components, etc. Additional criteria that could be considered are operational risks, such as how well-maintained an open-source software component is, based on, for example, how many active developers are contributing to the open-source software project or how often releases are made. A developer that requests including an open-source software component in their codebase can then follow this procedure. A flowchart of such a simplified example procedure is given in Figure 6.4.

Just to give an indication of the risks of using old open-source software components, in 2018, 43% of codebases in various industries surveyed in a report [3] contained open-source software vulnerabilities older than 10 years. In 2019, the situation seems to have generally improved, since only 19% of the surveyed codebases contained open-source software vulnerabilities older than 10 years [2]. However, the fact that more than 10-year-old vulnerabilities even exist in the codebases means that either open-source software components with *known vulnerabilities* were introduced into the codebase sometime in the past 10 years or the open-source software components were introduced into the codebases more than 10 years ago with *no known vulnerabilities* at the time. For the former, there is a need to create and enforce open-source software risk policies as described in this section, and for the latter, there is a need to continuously monitor for new threats and vulnerabilities as described in the next section.

6.3.6 Continuously Monitor for New Security Threats and Vulnerabilities

In the past few years, more than 5000–7000 new open-source software vulnerabilities have been discovered yearly. Although it is essential for automotive organizations to verify that

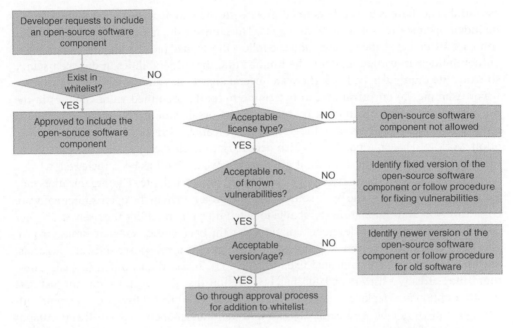

Figure 6.4 Example flowchart for procedure enforcing open-source software risk policies.

vulnerable open-source software components are not included in automotive software before release, it is equally important to monitor such automotive software after release, for as long as the software is being used. Thus, automotive organizations must establish processes to allow for continuously monitoring for new threats and vulnerabilities that are relevant to their software. It is imperative to note that monitoring is a continuous cybersecurity activity that needs to occur not only the during product development phases but also after release during the operations and maintenance phases, as explained in more detail in Section 2.3.12.

Once a new threat or a vulnerability has been detected, the organization should follow an established process for how to handle those situations. For example, the process could include performing a vulnerability analysis to understand the potential attack paths, how feasible it is to exploit the specific vulnerability in the open-source software component, and how exploiting the vulnerability may potentially affect the rest of the automotive system and vehicle. As a result, the organization can determine the risk of the affected software and consider appropriate countermeasures, including leaving the software as is or fixing the vulnerability. Since vehicles may be active in the field for 10–15 years, it is crucial that relevant automotive software is continuously monitored for new security threats and vulnerabilities during the lifetime of the vehicle.

6.3.7 Define and Follow Processes for Addressing Vulnerabilities in Open-Source Software

Automotive organizations should define a process for how to fix issues detected in open-source software. Since more automotive software contain open-source software, it is essential that there is a clearly defined process for how to address vulnerabilities in the included open-source software components. Thus, once vulnerabilities in an open-source software are detected, the organization can follow the defined process for how to handle the vulnerabilities. In particular, if it is determined that the vulnerabilities in the open-source software are required to be fixed, there are several approaches and steps that can be taken.

For example, an organization can determine to fix the identified vulnerabilities in the open-source software component internally in the organization. This requires assigning appropriate team members from the development team to perform the necessary remediation work to develop a patch. It is also necessary to track the progress of the activities, including tracking the status of what is being reviewed, what has been reviewed, what is being fixed, what has been fixed, what is planned to be fixed, etc. The organization may also provide the patch to the open-source software project to help the open-source software community. If an organization is not able to patch the vulnerabilities themselves, another approach is to request the developers maintaining the open-source software project to provide a fix. Depending on how well-maintained the specific open-source software project is, the time it takes to for an updated fixed version to be released may differ. In some cases, there may already exist an updated patched version that the organization can just use. Another option is to replace the affected vulnerable open-source software component with another non-vulnerable and perhaps more well-maintained open-source software component that provides the same functionality. Finally, one last option is to replace the vulnerable open-source software component with in-house developed code that the organization would then maintain. Each situation for new vulnerabilities detected in open-source software may be different and therefore it is important that the organizations in advance define and update when necessary the processes for addressing vulnerabilities in open-source software.

6.3.8 How to Get Started

This section briefly introduces four steps describing how an organization can get started with managing open-source software risks considering the previously described best practices.

These steps are illustrated in Figure 6.5 and explained as follows:

(1) Plan the necessary activities.
(2) Create required documents for processes and policies.
(3) Start a pilot project by applying the processes and policies.
(4) Roll out the processes and policies in the organization.

In Step 1, the organization first needs to understand the current state of open-source software management, including existing processes, policies, and approaches for using open-source software. The organization also needs to consider the target state of how the organization should be managing open-source software risks. Finally, it is recommended that a plan is created that will take the organization from the current state to the target state, including defining timelines and teams to be involved in the necessary activities, and the type of deliverables that should be produced, such as process and policy documents, tool integrations guidelines, and milestones such as pilot projects. Step 2 then proceeds

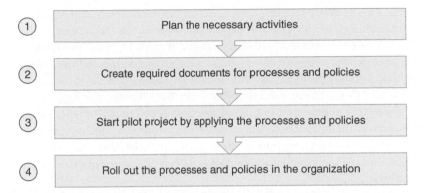

Figure 6.5 Steps describing how to get started managing open-source software risks.

with the organization creating the required documents for the internal processes and policies. Examples of processes include approval processes for the usage of new open-source software components in projects, processes for creating SBOMs and identifying known vulnerabilities, processes for continuously monitoring for new security threats and vulnerabilities, and processes for addressing vulnerabilities in open-source software. For the policies, it is imperative to define the criteria for acceptable open-source software components including license types, the number of known vulnerabilities, version/age, etc. Next, Step 3 is for the organization to start applying the processes and policies to a pilot project in a small team for better control. This step involves following the defined processes and policies and applying the tool integrations guidelines to, for example, inventory the used open-source software in the project by using a software composition analysis tool to create SBOMs, and determining which open-source software components are allowed to be included. It is of utmost importance that feedback regarding the processes and policies is collected during the pilot project. Finally, in Step 4, the organization takes the collected feedback from the pilot project and makes necessary adjustments to the internal process and policy documents and tool integration guidelines. These processes and policies are then rolled out in the organization to all relevant teams. The organization also establishes the necessary tool environments defined in the tool integration guidelines for managing open-source software risks. Lastly, it is imperative for the organization to continuously collect feedback and improve the internal processes and policies over time as needed.

6.4 Chapter Summary

This chapter gave an introduction to the usage of open-source software components in automotive software and discussed various considerations regarding the associated risks. Further, this chapter provided some background on software composition analysis tools and described how the two approaches, namely source code analysis and binary analysis, can be used by automotive organizations to improve software security in the supply chain. For example, the producing side and the receiving side of software should both perform software composition analysis to have a better understanding of the included open-source software components and the related security risks. Actual results from an analysis of 14 automotive software packages are reviewed to get an overview of the challenges in the current automotive software landscape. The results indicate that all 14 software packages contain vulnerable open-source software components with critical vulnerabilities. More interesting is that some software packages include several-years-old open-source software components that contain critical vulnerabilities that have been known for more than 10 years. Another interesting observation is that, at the time a certain software package was released, one specific included open-source software component did not contain any critical vulnerabilities; however, within a span of five months after the software package was released, three new critical vulnerabilities had been discovered in that specific open-source software component.

The use of open-source software in the automotive industry will continue to increase and therefore it is crucial for automotive organizations to employ best practices to address open-source software risks in the automotive supply chain. Best practices include making use of SBOMs to have clear inventory of which open-source software components and versions are included in the software packages and identifying known vulnerabilities associated with the included open-source software components. Moreover, it is necessary for automotive organizations to establish processes and policies for managing open-source software risks, including approval processes for including new open-source software components in projects, policies defining the criteria for acceptable open-source software components, processes for continuously monitoring for new security threats and vulnerabilities, and processes for addressing vulnerabilities in open-source software. Considering the increasing software sizes in modern vehicles and a complex supply chain consisting of multiple levels of suppliers, it becomes even more crucial for OEMs and suppliers to coordinate and have a common understanding of what open-source software components are included in the software and what the associated risks are. As with other industries, the increased usage of open-source software will surely transform the automotive industry and become a driving force for innovation for new products and services in the broader automotive eco-system.

References

1 Automotive Grade Linux (2017) Automotive Grade Linux Platform Debuts on the 2018 Toyota Camry. https://www.automotivelinux.org/announcements/automotive-grade-linux-platform-debuts-on-the-2018-toyota-camry (accessed 7 May 2018).

2 Synopsys (2020). 2020 Open source security and risk analysis. Synopsys.

3 Synopsys (2019). 2019 Open source security and risk analysis. Synopsys.

4 Automotive Grade Linux (2020). What is automotive grade Linux? https://www.automotivelinux.org (accessed 30 July 2020).

5 Open Automotive Alliance (2015). Introducing the open automotive alliance. https://www.openautoalliance.net (accessed 6 May 2018).

6 GENIVI (2020). Beyond Linux IVI and into the connected vehicle. https://www.genivi.org (accessed 30 July 2020).

7 Nie, S., Liu, L., and Du, Y. (2017). Free-fall: hacking tesla from wireless to CAN Bus. *Black Hat USA*, Las Vegas, NV, USA.

8 Open Source Initiative (2020). The MIT license. https://choosealicense.com/licenses/mit/ (accessed 30 July 2020).

9 GNU (2020). GNU general public license v2.0. https://choosealicense.com/licenses/gpl-2.0 (accessed 30 July 2020).

10 Oka, D.K. (2018). An analysis of open-source software risks in the automotive industry. *escar Asia*, Tokyo, Japan.

11 Oka, D.K. and Gay, C. (2018). What are the risks with open-source software in your car? *BSides Tokyo*, Tokyo, Japan

12 Oka, D.K. and Gay, C. (2019). Open-source software in your car – what can go wrong? *Symposium on Cryptography and Information Security (SCIS)*, Biwako, Japan.

13 Synopsys (2020). Black duck software composition analysis. https://www.synopsys.com/software-integrity/security-testing/software-composition-analysis.html. (accessed 30 July 2020).

14 Synopsys (2017). Scan nirvana: hub detect for all native build and CI tools. https://www.synopsys.com/blogs/software-security/hub-detect-native-build-ci-tools (accessed 30 July 2020).

15 NIST (2020). National vulnerability database. https://nvd.nist.gov (accessed 30 July 2020).

16 Synopsys (2018). Protecode SC binary analysis. https://www.synopsys.com/content/dam/synopsys/sig-assets/datasheets/protecode-binary-analysis.pdf (accessed 30 July 2020).

17 zlib (2017). https://zlib.net (accessed 30 July 2020).

18 libpng (2019). http://www.libpng.org/pub/png/libpng.html (accessed 30 July 2020).

19 OpenSSL (2020). https://www.openssl.org (accessed 30 July 2020).

20 NIST (2014). National vulnerability database – CVE-2014-3566. https://nvd.nist.gov/vuln/detail/CVE-2014-3566 (accessed 30 July 2020).

21 curl (2020). https://curl.haxx.se (accessed 30 July 2020).

22 The Linux Kernel Archives (2020). https://www.kernel.org (accessed 30 July 2020).

23 NIST (2017). National vulnerability database – CVE-2017-1000251. https://nvd.nist.gov/vuln/detail/CVE-2017-1000251 (accessed 30 July 2020).

24 Androidcentral (2017). Let's talk about Blueborne the latest Bluetooth vulnerability. https://www.androidcentral.com/lets-talk-about-blueborne-latest-bluetooth-vulnerability (accessed 6 May 2018).

25 Armis (2018). Blueborne: one year later. https://www.armis.com/resources/iot-security-blog/blueborne-one-year-later (accessed 30 July 2020).

26 Synopsys (2017). State of software composition 2017.

27 Ponemon Institute – SAE International and Synopsys (2019). Securing the modern vehicle: a study of automotive industry cybersecurity practices. Synopsys, Inc. and SAE International.

28 Synopsys (2018). Managing and securing open source software in the automotive industry.

29 Synopsys (2018). 2018 Open source security and risk analysis.

30 NTIA (2020). NTIA software component transparency. https://www.ntia.doc.gov/SoftwareTransparency (accessed 30 July 2020).

31 International Organization for Standardization (ISO)/International Electrotechnical Commission (IEC) (2020). *ISO/IEC 5230:2020 – information technology – OpenChain specification*. Geneva, Switzerland: ISO.

32 NopSec (2018). 2018 State of vulnerability risk management report.

7

Overview of Automotive Security Testing Approaches

THE MORE YOU TEST, THE MORE YOU WILL FIND

This chapter explores practical security testing approaches in more detail, based on the approaches briefly described in Section 4.2.3. Applying static code analysis tools and software composition tools, described in more detail in Chapters 5 and 6, respectively, during the software development phase helps to identify and reduce vulnerabilities in the software code early; however, there may be some weaknesses and vulnerabilities that these tools are not able to detect and therefore the next step in the product development typically involves security testing.

Functional testing in the automotive industry has been around for years, whereas security testing in the automotive industry is still in its infancy. Although, lately, there is more focus on security testing as part of the development process, there are many different approaches for embedded security evaluations, including *theoretical security analyses*, *practical security testing*, and *verifiable security verification*, as shown in Figure 7.1 [1].

This chapter first gives a brief introduction to the different types of embedded security evaluation approaches and discusses the respective advantages and disadvantages. It is a generally accepted understanding that the earlier the security evaluation and testing is performed in the development lifecycle, the less costly and time-consuming it is to fix identified weaknesses and vulnerabilities. Moreover, it may not be possible to address some weaknesses and vulnerabilities if they are detected too late in the development lifecycle since a countermeasure may require a complete redesign of the system.

Theoretical security analyses come in various flavors, including cybersecurity requirements review, security design review, and threat analysis and risk assessment (TARA). Specifically, the ISO/SAE DIS 21434 standard [2] specifies requirements for a TARA. It is worth noting that TARAs can be conducted during different phases in the development lifecycle, including the concept phase, product development, and operations and maintenance phases. During the concept phase, TARAs can be performed based on the initial description and requirements of the target system. In this step, the security evaluation helps to define the security goals and security requirements that can then further be used for the product requirements and design. This allows an organization to establish a strong security foundation in the product early on. TARAs can be conducted again during product development to

Building Secure Cars: Assuring the Automotive Software Development Lifecycle, First Edition. Dennis Kengo Oka.
© 2021 John Wiley & Sons Ltd. Published 2021 by John Wiley & Sons Ltd.

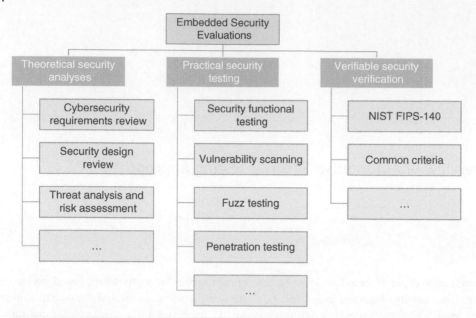

Figure 7.1 Overview of embedded security evaluation approaches. Source: Based on [1].

identify any new threats and risks based on the specific design and implementation chosen. Finally, during operations and maintenance phases, TARAs can be performed to detect any new threats and risks that arise due to new attack methods and tools being developed and new security research results released over time. Once a TARA has been performed for one product, subsequent TARAs for the next iteration of product development can often reuse results from the previous TARA and can therefore be done very efficiently. While a TARA is beneficial to understand threats and risks against a target system, it is a theoretical approach, and without actually performing practical testing it is very difficult to give indications of actual implementation flaws and exploitable vulnerabilities.

On the other hand, *practical security testing* can only be performed once an implementation of the target system is available, e.g. on a prototype system or a production system. It should be noted that while practical security testing can identify actual weaknesses, implementation flaws, and exploitable vulnerabilities on the target system, there are limitations to what countermeasures can be applied depending on how late in the development stage the system is. Design changes and hardware changes are typically not possible. If there is enough time, larger software changes may be achievable, but if it is very close to production, only minor software changes may be possible. Therefore, as important as practical security testing is, it cannot replace a strong foundation of security principles including security-by-design and following a defined security engineering process. It is worth noting that practical security testing is useful to get an understanding of what an outside attacker is able to do to a target system. It can help find implementation flaws that can be exploitable by attackers and also help to provide an estimate on the actual difficulty of a certain attack on the target system. Moreover, practical security testing can uncover unspecified functionality or discrepancies to specifications or security goals in the implementation of the target system. Consequently, practical security testing helps to build trust in the soundness of the implementation.

In general, practical security testing comprises at least four different testing methodologies: *security functional testing, vulnerability scanning, fuzz testing*, and *penetration testing*. A brief introduction is given below and more details about each test approach is given in Section 7.1. The first test approach, *security functional testing*, focuses on testing all security-related functions on the target system for correct behavior and robustness. This is similar to the typical functional testing performed on automotive systems, with the difference that the focus is on security-related functions, e.g. an authentication mechanism. Thorough security functional testing can uncover common implementation flaws, unspecified functionality, or discrepancies to the specification in the implementation due to, for example, misinterpretation of the specification. These types of issues can lead to weaknesses in the security function that may allow an attacker to abuse or bypass that certain security feature or function. The second testing method, *vulnerability scanning*, typically tests the target system for known vulnerabilities and, in some cases, also tries to detect unknown vulnerabilities by trying patterns with known weaknesses. The third test approach, *fuzz testing*, goes further to broaden the testing to uncover unknown vulnerabilities and weaknesses by sending systematically malformed input and observing the target system for unknown potentially security-critical behavior. Fuzz testing can be performed using various approaches, including black-box, gray-box and white-box fuzz testing. Finally, the fourth test methodology, *penetration testing*, focuses on testing the system as a whole, including both software and hardware, specifically to see how well the security goals specified for the target system hold up. While the previously mentioned three practical security testing methods can often by performed using automated tools, penetration testing typically requires a skilled and experienced "human security tester," often referred to as a penetration tester. The penetration tester acts like a real attacker and tries to exploit the vulnerabilities typically identified using the previous testing approaches with the objective of breaking the security goals of the target system. It should be noted that practical security testing, especially fuzz testing and penetration testing, cannot give any assertion on completeness. These test methods are often performed time-boxed, i.e. it is determined in advance how much time should be allocated to perform the tests, and once the time has passed the test finishes. Depending on how much time and resources are used for this type of testing, there is a risk that it may miss larger systematic flaws in the target system. Therefore, an organization cannot rely on just focusing on practical security testing but also needs to complement the practical security testing with theoretical security analyses to identify missing critical security requirements, larger system design flaws, and additional attack paths.

Although *verifiable security verification* exists in other industries it is not yet that common in the automotive industry. For example, in the industrial control systems (ICS) industry, ISASecure has defined an EDSA (embedded device security assessment) certification program [3] for component security assurance including practical security testing in terms of communication robustness testing and network stress testing. These components are used to build industrial control systems defined by the IEC 62443-4-2 standard [4]. There are several recognized EDSA certified tools that can be used in the development process to prepare for ISASecure certifications [5, 6].

In the banking industry, EMVCo certification [7] covers a security evaluation process that evaluates the general security performance characteristics and the suitability of the use for smart card-related products and IC (integrated circuit) chip-based tokens. The purpose of this evaluation is to assess whether the security features provided by the chip-based product have been appropriately implemented. This evaluation involves practical testing in terms of penetration testing, which investigates the interaction between the chip, operating system, and application to determine whether sensitive information, secret data, and payment assets are adequately protected by the final chip product.

Moreover, not really specific to any industry but more regarding general information technology and computer security certification, there is the international standard ISO/IEC 15408 Common Criteria for Information Technology Security Evaluation (CC) [8]. The CC standard defines seven different *Evaluation Assurance Levels* (EALs) where each level has a specific set of assurance requirements that the *Target of Evaluation* (TOE) must meet in order to achieve that level. These requirements typically include design documentation, design analysis, functional testing, and penetration testing. The higher EALs contain more requirements demanding more detailed documentation, analysis and testing, and therefore achieving a higher EAL is typically more costly and time-consuming. For example, EAL1 indicates that the TOE has been "functionally tested," which means that there is confidence in the correct operation of the system but threats against security may not have been considered. On the other hand, EAL7 is defined as "formally verified design and tested" and is applicable for TOEs used in extremely high-risk situations where this high level of assurance is required. A commonly used EAL is EAL4 which indicates "methodically designed, tested and reviewed." Operating systems that provide conventional, user-based security features are typically EAL4 certified, and examples include AIX (Advanced Interactive eXecutive), Oracle Linux, Solaris, and Windows 7. In some cases, the evaluation is augmented to include additional assurance requirements, which is often indicated by adding a plus sign (e.g. EAL4+). As part of CC, Protection Profiles (PP) are documents used to define a generic security target. The PP includes, for example, threats, security objectives, assumptions, security functional requirements, and security assurance requirements. In the automotive industry, CC has commonly not been used; however, one of the early examples from 2010 of CC in the automotive industry is a PP for a digital tachograph [9]. As mentioned in Chapter 3, odometer fraud attacks led to various new hardware-based security solutions. To provide security assurance, the PP for the digital tachograph provides, among other requirements, for data integrity, data authenticity, and cryptographic support to prevent recorded and stored data from unauthorized manipulation. A more recent example from 2019 is a PP for a V2X (vehicle-to-X) HSM (hardware security module) developed by the CAR 2 CAR Communication Consortium [10]. This PP covers various topics such as random number generation, key management, digital signature generation, and encryption and decryption. Recently, NXP Semiconductors was the first to receive a CC EAL4+ certification for a standalone automotive-qualified Secure Element for V2X applications that is compliant with this V2X HSM PP [11].

Furthermore, the NIST (National Institute of Standards and Technology) CSRC (Computer Security Resource Center) publishes security standards called the Federal Information Processing Standards (FIPS). One example is FIPS 140-2 which is a U.S. government standard used to approve cryptographic modules under the cryptographic module validation program (CMVP) [12]. As the FIPS 140-2 standard has grown in popularity, it has been adopted by other organizations and industries since the certification helps to prove the functionality and effectiveness of the cryptographic modules implemented. The FIPS 140-2 [13] specifies security requirements that need to be satisfied by a cryptographic module and is often used in automotive HSMs (cf. Chapter 3). FIPS 140-2 has been superseded by FIPS 140-3 [14], and testing of cryptographic modules against FIPS 140-2 will end in September 2021.

Although there is no specific security certification standard in the automotive industry for the software development process at this time, the ISO/SAE DIS 21434 describes *Cybersecurity Assurance Levels* (CALs) which can be used to help provide assurance that the assets of a component are adequately protected against relevant threat scenarios. A CAL can be used to specify a set of assurance requirements that can affect the requirements, design and testing. Multiple levels of CALs can be defined, and for each increasing CAL the corresponding requirements indicate an increase in the assurance of the component. For instance, a lower CAL may require only developer testing, however a higher-level CAL may require the component to be independently tested and reviewed. A higher-level CAL may also indicate that a broader coverage of testing is required, e.g. performing fuzz testing for longer periods of time and conducting deeper penetration testing.

Although several embedded security evaluation approaches exist, the focus of the remainder of this chapter is on practical security testing, and particularly doing a deep-dive on fuzz testing.

The main points of this chapter are:

- We provide an overview of practical security testing for automotive systems focusing on security functional testing, vulnerability scanning, fuzz testing, and penetration testing.
- We give insights into establishing a framework for security testing to allow for systematic and efficient testing based on defined processes, test tools, and test approaches.
- We do a deep-dive on fuzz testing for automotive systems and discuss the parts required in a fuzz testing environment, including the fuzz engine, injector, and monitor.

More details about automotive security testing approaches can be found in Reference [1].

7.1 Practical Security Testing

Following an in-depth security evaluations approach for automotive systems is necessary to identify potential security weaknesses and address them before attackers can exploit these weaknesses in the field and cause real financial, safety, operational, or privacy damage. The ISO/SAE DIS 21434 standard highlights both the importance of theoretical security evaluation in terms of TARAs as well as practical security testing as part of verification and validation, including mentions of vulnerability scanning, fuzz testing, and penetration testing.

As described before, theoretical security evaluations are extremely useful since they can identify many issues early and therefore allow an automotive organization to apply appropriate countermeasures early. However, even if a system is theoretically sound it may contain implementation flaws, configuration mistakes or physical weaknesses. For example, the random seed used in an authentication function may be designed to receive the random value from a hardware register; however, during the booting process, that particular register has no entropy and therefore, even though the seed should be random, a constant value is always returned. Theoretically the design may be sound but such an issue is easily discovered during a practical test, which emphasizes the importance of such tests.

As briefly mentioned in the previous section, there are multiple categories of practical security testing approaches based on the testing methodologies. Typically, what is common for all the different types of testing is that they require some time and effort; the difference between the testing approaches is how much time and effort can be allocated based on budget, schedule and resources.

As shown in Figure 7.2, examples of testing approaches range from simple security functional testing and vulnerability scanning to more time-consuming and invasive testing approaches, such as hardware penetration testing, including decapsulating chips to recover secret data [1]. In between these two extremes are, for example, fuzz testing to detect unknown vulnerabilities and reverse-engineering of software to recover secret data or identify vulnerabilities. To achieve comprehensive results during practical security testing of an automotive system, it is useful to use a combination of different approaches based on the risks of the target system and the time, effort, and budget available for the testing. Using multiple approaches broadens the scope of the testing and allows one to better identify vulnerabilities and weaknesses that might have been missed in the theoretical evaluation.

More details for each practical security testing category are given in the next sections. It is worth noting that practical security testing typically requires a human tester using various automated and semi-automated tools to perform the testing. It is possible to automate some activities to a higher degree, whereas some other activities require more manual work. For each testing approach, the tester needs access to the actual software and hardware of the target system, and the necessary peripherals to ensure that the target system is functional, e.g. power supply and, in some cases, network communication, including restbus

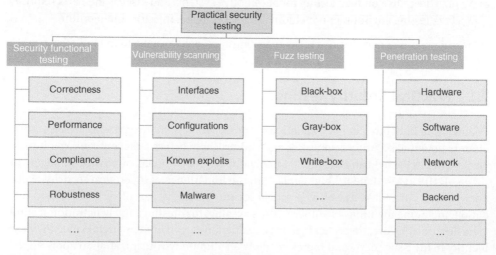

Figure 7.2 Overview of practical security testing approaches based on testing methodologies. Source: Based on [1].

simulation. Moreover, in some instances, special hardware and software tools are required, such as JTAG (Joint Test Action Group) debuggers, logic analyzers, network communication devices, reverse-engineering tools, and other "hacking" tools. Additionally, for security functional testing, the specification of the system is required.

7.1.1 Security Functional Testing

Security functionality is similar to any other functionality on the target system and therefore it needs to be functionally tested. *Security functional testing* should be performed to test the implementation of security functionality on the target system, i.e. the security-related functions. Similar to classic functional testing, security functional testing can unearth implementation errors, discrepancies to the specification and unspecified functionality. The main difference from traditional functional testing is that the identified issues may have an impact on the security of the target system since they are related to security functionality. Security functional testing focuses mainly on testing security functionality on the target system to detect any issues with *correctness*, *performance*, *compliance*, and *robustness*. For example, security functional testing helps to verify that the target system does not behave in an unexpected manner, i.e. ensuring *correctness* in the sense that the system correctly behaves according to the specification; any other behavior would be deemed unexpected. Furthermore, some security functions, e.g. that are also related to safety, have strict requirements on *performance*. Therefore, it is equally important to test the performance of, for instance, often computationally-intense security algorithms to identify potential bottlenecks that might affect the overall security performance and functionality. Moreover, the target system should be tested to verify *compliance* to specifications and standards of the implemented security functionality, e.g. encryption algorithms and authentication protocols. Additionally, the algorithms are not only tested for correct behavior per the specification but also for *robustness*. Consequently, the successful outcome of security functional testing gives confidence in dependable security functionality and that a functional weakness does not create any exploitable security vulnerabilities.

To address the increasing security threats targeting vehicles, automotive organizations are adding more security countermeasures and security solutions in their vehicles. Example countermeasures include securing remote interfaces and securing in-vehicle communication. Remote interfaces are typically secured using authentication mechanisms and firewalls. On the other hand, in-vehicle communication is often secured by separating the in-vehicle network into different domains and using one or more gateways that route traffic between the domains based on predefined rules. Additionally, the AUTOSAR (AUTomotive Open System ARchitecture) SecOC (secure onboard communication) specification [15] provides data authenticity on in-vehicle messages such as CAN (controller area network) messages by adding a MAC (message authentication code). These types of security measures can be used to effectively combat security threats if designed using state-of-the-art guidelines and following security principles and best practices for development. It is worth noting however that security solutions typically add complexity to the relevant automotive systems, which could introduce new issues that go undetected if the security solutions are not tested thoroughly. As an example, if the routing functionality on a gateway is incorrectly implemented or misconfigured and therefore does not behave as specified, it could lead to serious consequences. In such a case, safety-related CAN messages may be routed by mistake from external CAN networks to internal CAN networks which could allow an attacker to control steering or brakes from, for example, a compromised in-vehicle infotainment system.

Most security solutions are based on cryptography and therefore testing such solutions also involves testing the implementation of the corresponding cryptographic algorithms. Security functional testing of the cryptographic algorithms typically is performed by testing the target implementations against official test vectors (if available) or independent implementations. The target implementations of cryptographic algorithms may contain specific corner cases that could lead to security vulnerabilities, e.g. subtle flaws in numeric implementations that trigger only in one of four billion random cases. To detect such issues, the corner cases must be tested with specifically constructed test vectors and by running lengthy tests. Often developers of the cryptographic algorithms conduct these types of functional tests to ensure that the implementation is correct and robust. While testing the implementation of the cryptographic algorithms against test vectors provides confidence that the implementation is correct, the implementation of the algorithms is only part of the security solution. It is equally important to test the usage of the algorithms in the security solution on the target system. This type of testing includes verifying that the algorithms are configured according to specification and are provisioned with the correct data and keys. The AUTOSAR SecOC is used as an example to explain this in more detail.

SecOC specifies that MACs can be included in the payload of CAN messages to protect data integrity and authenticity of the contents in the CAN messages. The following approach in SecOC is typically used: a MAC is calculated over a concatenation of the message and a freshness value using a cryptographic algorithm and a shared secret key.

The transmitting electronic control unit (ECU) calculates, for example using the Advanced Encryption Standard (AES) cryptographic algorithm and a secret shared key, a MAC over a concatenation of the message data and a freshness value. The CAN message including the typically truncated MAC is then sent to the receiving ECU. The receiving ECU verifies the integrity and authenticity of the message data by using the same cryptographic algorithm, shared key, and freshness value to calculate the MAC of the received data and compare it with the included MAC. If it is a match, the receiving ECU can be assured that the received message data has not been tampered with, and can continue to process the message contents. In contrast, if it is a mismatch, i.e. the MAC is invalid, the receiving ECU ignores the message. Besides performing security functional testing of the implementation of the cryptographic algorithm AES used for generation and verification of MACs, it is also imperative to conduct security functional testing of the MAC generation and verification implementation. For instance, if the MAC generation function is faulty on the transmitting ECU (even though the AES implementation is correct), the receiving ECU will never be able to correctly verify the MACs and be able to process the received messages. On the other hand, if the MAC verification function is faulty on the receiving ECU, the receiving ECU may interpret all received MACs as invalid and ignore all messages, or the receiving ECU may by mistake interpret invalid MACs as valid and therefore incorrectly accept tampered message contents. Thus, the entire functionality of the security-related function SecOC must be carefully tested.

Moreover, many modern cryptographic schemes and implementations of security-related functions rely on secure random number generators. Random number generators can be implemented in software or hardware, e.g. automotive HSMs typically provide a true random number generator (TRNG) to be able to generate key material and random numbers used in cryptographic schemes. More details about automotive HSMs can be found in Chapter 3. It is required to perform extensive statistical testing to be able to gain confidence in the randomness of the random number generator implementations.

With more security solutions being developed and deployed in vehicles, including SecOC, authentication protocols for external communication such as V2X communication, secure ECU flashing protocols, and theft protection mechanisms, it is imperative that these security-related solutions go through proper security functional testing to verify the correctness and robustness of such solutions.

Additional details about security functional testing for automotive systems are described in [16].

7.1.2 Vulnerability Scanning

The second type of practical security testing is *vulnerability scanning*. Vulnerability scanning is a test approach that is very common in the IT industry. It typically tests the target system for already known common security vulnerabilities and configurations with known weaknesses based on information in a continuously updated database. Additionally, some vulnerability scanning includes testing known attack patterns on the target system to detect unknown vulnerabilities.

In contrast to vulnerability scanning in the IT industry where the target systems are usually hosts in an enterprise network, the target systems for automotive vulnerability scanning are typically embedded devices such as ECUs in the in-vehicle network. Traditionally, there are three steps involved in the vulnerability scanning activity:

(1) information gathering,
(2) identification of vulnerabilities,
(3) reporting.

In the first step, relevant information about the target systems is gathered, e.g. identifying which ECUs exist in a full vehicle test, identifying which network protocols and software are applicable for testing, and identifying which software applications and services are running on the ECUs. The second step encompasses identifying vulnerabilities using different techniques, e.g. using static application security testing (SAST) tools, software composition analysis (SCA) tools, and dynamic application security testing (DAST) tools, based on available information. This step involves either correlating information gathered in the first step with information from vulnerability databases to identify known vulnerabilities or using automated tools to test for known attack patterns to detect unknown vulnerabilities. The last step is to prepare a report on the identified vulnerabilities, and include an evaluation of the associated risk for each vulnerability so that the relevant organization can properly handle the vulnerabilities.

Three variations of vulnerability scanning for automotive systems are presented as follows. The first example focuses on the software/firmware of the target system. Using a combination of SAST, SCA, and DAST tools to scan and test the target system it is possible to detect, e.g. buffer overflow or heap overflow vulnerabilities. Depending on the type of scan, the target software must be available in either source code or as a binary. Please note that the results from scanning source code may differ from scanning binaries. The reason is that the compilation process may introduce security vulnerabilities, e.g. by removing security checks during the optimization step or through faulty compilers. Consequently, it is important to carefully examine the compiler settings to reduce the risk of new vulnerabilities being introduced.

The second example involves scanning the target system for open ports and interfaces, and additionally identifying accessible services running on these interfaces. Relevant network protocols for some automotive systems include classical IT interfaces such as IP (Internet Protocol) communication over Ethernet, Wi-Fi, Bluetooth, and cellular network communication. Using existing vulnerability scanning tools available in the IT industry, it is possible to scan these interfaces over IP to identify vulnerabilities. It is highly recommended to perform scans of these interfaces on automotive systems because, generally, large volumes of software for operating systems, network communication stacks, applications and libraries from the IT industry are reused, which may be vulnerable. There already exist databases with known vulnerabilities that can be used to easily perform automated scans of such software and interfaces. Additionally, vulnerability scanning can be used to find open ports and services available on the target system. For example, a scan can include performing a port scan and identifying listening network ports or executing a service discovery scan on Bluetooth to detect available Bluetooth services. Then, based on the open ports and available services, it is possible to use DAST tools to test common attack patterns on these available services to uncover unknown vulnerabilities. Please note that these classical IT interfaces are highly susceptible to be targeted in real attacks since attackers are commonly more familiar with these interfaces and, in general, there are more attack tools available for attackers to use to target these interfaces. Besides the IT interfaces available on some systems, most automotive systems use standardized automotive network communication protocols such as CAN and UDS (Unified Diagnostic Services). Similar to a Bluetooth services scan, it is possible to use an automated scan tool to identify diagnostic services available over UDS on a target system. Diagnostic services are an important target for testing since the features offered by such services are often highly sought after by attackers. Such features often include functionality for configuration and debugging, specifically being able to read or write data to the target system.

The third example of vulnerability scanning focuses on analyzing the configuration of the target system. There may be certain critical functions on the target system that require authentication prior to allowing the functions to be executed, e.g. reprogramming of the ECU or running certain diagnostics tests. Using UDS, it is possible to protect access to such critical functionality by ensuring that authentication using the UDS Security Access service has been performed first. However, a faulty implementation or incorrect configuration may allow access to such critical functionality without authentication or authorization. By running automated tests using various combinations of sequences to try to access this protected functionality it may be possible to detect cases where such functionality is accessible without authentication. Furthermore, during the Security Access authentication, a random value called seed, which is used as the challenge in the challenge–response authentication protocol, is generated on the target system. Using an automated scan tool it is possible to test the entropy of numerous seed values generated on the target system over time to detect any weaknesses in the seed generation. A simple example result is that the same seed is always used or, for example, 10 different hard-coded seeds are continuously reused instead of the seed being completely randomly generated. Moreover, to prevent brute-force attacks on the Security Access authentication mechanism, there is often a time delay imposed for successive authentication attempts after, for example, three failed attempts. Using an automated tool it is possible to detect vulnerabilities in the implementation by trying multiple successive authentication attempts to detect any issues in the time delay countermeasure.

Vulnerability scanning is an efficient and extremely useful approach to test the target system, especially against known attacks using vulnerability databases and unknown attacks using known attack patterns. For some interfaces it may be possible to use existing vulnerability scanning tools from the IT industry; however, for some automotive-specific interfaces and protocols there may not exist any relevant vulnerability scanning tools and, instead, it is possible for automotive organizations to write some scripts or develop some simple tools to perform the scanning and testing, e.g. a script that does UDS services scanning.

Please note that for backend infrastructures of the connected car, traditional IT-based vulnerability scanning methods can be used, and they are therefore not covered in this chapter.

7.1.3 Fuzz Testing

The third type of practical security testing is *fuzz testing*, also known as fuzzing. While vulnerability scanning may be useful for finding some unknown vulnerabilities based on known attack patterns, fuzz testing goes further to uncover unknown vulnerabilities in the implementation by sending systematically malformed input to the target system and observing it for any unexpected and potentially security-critical behavior.

Fuzzing is a common test technique that has been used for decades in the IT industry to test software applications and network stacks. The idea is that, as a result of sending unexpected, invalid, or random input to the target system, it will react in an unexpected manner, which can be analyzed to identify new vulnerabilities. Examples of abnormal behavior include the target system hanging or "freezing," executing unexpected functions, and providing unspecified output. Fuzz testing is extremely powerful and useful as it can find many software vulnerabilities. If the software behaves erratically or crashes, it is possible to investigate further to understand the root cause and consequently fix the issue. It is best practice to perform fuzz testing as a systematic step in the software development lifecycle to find and remove software vulnerabilities. Since fuzzing is a technique often used by real attackers, if the developed software is left untested when it is released, attackers would most likely be able to easily detect software vulnerabilities using fuzzing and correspondingly be able to develop exploits. Therefore, to stay ahead of attackers, it is crucial that automotive organizations adopt fuzz testing as early in the development cycle as possible to reduce potential software vulnerabilities.

Although the information from a published "State of Fuzzing" report [17] is a bit dated, the report indicates that the top protocols targeted for fuzz testing in the automotive industry include IP, CAN, Wi-Fi, Bluetooth, MQTT (message queuing telemetry transport), and file formats such as mp3, jpg, png, and mp4. Fuzz testing of these network communication protocols and file formats focuses on identifying unknown vulnerabilities in the implementations of parsers and application code in the automotive software. Common target systems include ECUs and in-vehicle infotainment systems.

While fuzzing as a test technique for automotive systems has gained popularity in the past few years, it is still not as commonly used as in the IT industry, where there already exist several fuzz testing solutions applicable for traditional IT systems and protocols. Modern vehicles have many similarities to traditional IT networks, in the sense that the ECUs can be seen as nodes, running different types of software, and are interconnected over various network types such as CAN, CAN-FD (controller area network flexible data-rate) and Ethernet. There may also be one or more gateways responsible for routing traffic between different domains in the in-vehicle network. Although there are similarities in the network structure, the communication patterns on automotive network protocols such as CAN and CAN-FD are very different from traditional IT network protocols. As an example, in the IT industry, many network protocols, such as HTTP (hypertext transfer protocol), use a specifically defined request–reply format, and therefore it is relatively simple for the fuzz testing tool to generate relevant fuzzed messages, send the fuzzed messages to the target system and finally observe the corresponding replies to the fuzzed requests. For example, the Open Web Application Security Project (OWASP) has defined a testing guide which includes fuzz testing of HTTP [18]. In contrast, many ECUs may only receive and process certain CAN messages without sending any responses on the CAN bus. Instead, the ECUs may change some internal behavior or control some external peripheral as a result of the received CAN message. Consequently, it is not that easy to detect abnormal behavior on ECUs compared with detecting an erroneous reply on the same communication channel, as in the case of IT networks. An example solution that bridges this gap between IT and automotive systems by adding additional monitoring capabilities (besides the CAN bus) to allow proper fuzz testing of ECUs can be found in [19]. This topic is also covered in more detail in Chapter 8.

In recent years, there has been a trend to move toward Ethernet-based communication in the in-vehicle network. Using Automotive Ethernet-based communication has several impacts on the network architecture and communication patterns. For example, protocols such as SOME/IP (Scalable service-Oriented MiddlewarE over IP) [20], which provide service-based communications, have more similarities to classical IP-based network communication found in the IT industry. Moreover, more traditional high-performance IT-based systems are more commonly used in modern vehicles such as in-vehicle infotainment systems based on Linux or Android, which typically have support for Wi-Fi and Bluetooth communication. Fuzz testing the software implementation of these communication protocols on an in-vehicle infotainment system is virtually the same as fuzz testing any other IT system that implements these protocols. Thus, the long experiences of performing fuzz testing in the IT industry will surely be beneficial for conducting fuzz testing of such protocols in the automotive industry.

More details about fuzz testing can be found in Section 7.3.

7.1.4 Penetration Testing

The fourth type of practical security testing is *penetration testing*, also known as pentesting. During penetration testing, the purpose is to test the security of the target system in its entirety, including software and hardware, often as a validation step against the security goals of the target system. One major difference from the previously described test types is that penetration testing cannot be done by simply using automated tools but requires an experienced and skilled "human security tester," a pentester, who mimics a real attacker. The pentester finds vulnerabilities typically using a combination of the previously mentioned test approaches and then tries to exploit the vulnerabilities using various techniques based on years of "hacking experience."

Automotive penetration testing is mainly motivated by either IP (intellectual property) protection, protection of safety-related functionality or security-related functionality. Examples of mechanisms that are often targeted for penetration testing are theft protection, component protection, odometer tampering protection, feature activation, safety functionality including unauthorized control of engine, steering and brakes, and security functionality including secure boot, secure communication, secure software update, tampering or extraction of cryptographic keys, unauthorized access to protected functions, etc.

There are different scopes of testing depending on what the focus of the testing is. For instance, performing penetration testing on a single ECU allows one to go deeper into specific hardware and software interfaces and functions on the target system. Performing testing on a system of ECUs consisting of multiple hardware and software components allows one to perform system-level testing where the target system is mostly behaving as it would in a real situation, to better understand what the impacts of a system-level compromise would look like. Full vehicle testing includes multiple interfaces on the vehicle and included automotive systems, and allows one to perform testing to better understand an entire attack chain, from how an attacker can gain entry to the vehicle through various communication interfaces to how an attacker can move laterally within the vehicle once one system has been breached to finally how an attacker can gain access to and compromise a specific target system.

As well as performing penetration testing on the actual vehicle and ECUs, considering that the *connected car* use case introduces new attack vectors in the larger eco-system that is part of the connected car, there is also an increased demand to perform penetration testing on externally accessible systems such as automotive backend systems and mobile apps that connect to the vehicle or backend.

In addition, besides penetration testing that typically focuses on the technical aspects of the target system, it is important for automotive organizations to also consider testing their organizational processes through, for example, email or phone-based social engineering attacks, and physical facility exploitation, e.g. unauthorized entries to secure facilities including office buildings and factories. This type of security assessment is commonly known as red teaming [21].

Typically, all penetration tests follow a similar pattern. The first step is *reconnaissance* where the pentester is gathering information about the target system, including finding available physical interfaces, determining hardware components and connections on the PCB (printed circuit board), identifying software and services running on the target system, and locating any other useful information such as manuals or specifications or other documents that can be obtained online. This step includes manual activities such as physically inspecting the hardware board and finding relevant hardware component specifications, as well as automated approaches using tools and scripts to perform scanning of the target system to detect open ports and available services.

The next step is *finding a vulnerability or weakness* in the target system. Using the information gathered in the first step, the pentester starts testing different interfaces. For example, for hardware pentesting, local physical interfaces such as serial ports, JTAG, USB, and hardware components such as external memory modules, are often in the focus area. The pentester may be able uncover unlocked debug interfaces, detect undocumented debug access, identify missing or misconfigured secure boot, and find insecure firmware update mechanisms. Besides physical hardware interfaces, the pentester examines the external communication interfaces on the target system, such as CAN bus, Ethernet, Wi-Fi, and Bluetooth. For instance, previous work has shown how it is possible to test and perform attacks over CAN [22]. In addition, if included in the scope of the penetration test, the pentester also analyzes the backend systems for vulnerabilities and configuration mistakes. There are various methods and techniques that can be used for this step, including what is described in previous sections including vulnerability scanning and fuzz testing.

Once one or more vulnerabilities or weaknesses have been identified, the next step involves finding ways to *exploit the identified vulnerabilities or weaknesses*. In this step, the pentester tries to break the security goals, for instance, bypassing authentication to gain access to protected functionality, extract secret information or take control of the target system. For hardware attacks, the pentester may be able to perform side-channel analysis to extract cryptographic keys [23], or perform glitching attacks to bypass authentication such as UDS Security Access [24]. More advanced testing methods include invasive attacks that typically require expensive test equipment; however, recently, more affordable test methods have been made public [25]. The invasive attacks focus on IC decapsulation and require etching open chip packages and accessing the actual silicon die. Once the package is decapped, by exposing the die to UV (ultraviolet) light it is possible to change the contents by flipping the bits. For example, there might be a code protect (CP) flag enabled which prevents external programmers through, for example, JTAG, from accessing flash memory unless the device is erased first. By exposing the die to UV light, the configuration bits including the CP flag can be reset. This attack allows unlocking a locked chip and extracting its firmware [25]. For software attacks, the pentester typically writes attack scripts, develops exploits, or reuses existing exploits for known vulnerabilities to attack the identified vulnerabilities and weaknesses in the target system. A pentester may also be able to chain certain attacks together to first gain remote entry to the vehicle, bypass protection mechanisms on in-vehicle systems, to finally gain access a specific ECU on the in-vehicle network. For instance, a vulnerability in the Bluetooth network stack or in the web browser on the in-vehicle infotainment system could first be exploited to gain remote access to the vehicle. With the gained access, the pentester can abuse update functionality to flash a malicious software to the target system to bypass protection mechanisms, and finally be able to send arbitrary messages on the CAN bus to access unauthorized functionality on a specific ECU [26, 27].

There are generally three accepted approaches for penetration testing: *black box*, *white box*, and *gray box*. Each approach is explained in more detail as follows. A *black-box* penetration test is typically conducted in a similar fashion to how a real attack in the wild would be conducted. The pentester does not have access to any non-public information and thus the situation simulates what a real attacker can do to the target system with access to the same limited information. The advantage is that a black-box penetration test gives an idea of what a real attacker could do; however, the disadvantage is that since the penetration test is time-bound and the pentester would typically spend much time on, for example, reverse-engineering tasks when such information is typically available in the automotive organization, valuable time is lost. The result is that deeper issues may be left uncovered and certain security functionality untested since the pentester was not able to break a first-line defense mechanism. A real attacker may be able to circumvent the first-line defense mechanism at some point because the real attacker is not time-bound and has more resources than the black-box pentester or because new state-of-the-art test tools have become available. This allows the real attacker to explore untested functionality and identify issues in unchartered territory.

In contrast, for a *white-box* approach, the pentester is typically given all necessary information and documentation, including hardware specifications, proprietary communication protocol specifications, design documents, and source code. A white-box penetration test is useful to uncover deeper issues in the target system and avoids any unnecessary waste of time for pentesters to gather information, e.g. reverse-engineering a proprietary communication protocol, if such information is already available. Thus, a white-box test can be performed more efficiently targeting specific weaknesses and vulnerabilities in the target system. However, it is not a realistic scenario since a real attacker would, in most cases, not have access to all the relevant non-public information, and therefore this does not give a reliable estimate of attack difficulty and the likelihood of what a real attacker could do.

Finally, in the middle ground between black-box and white-box approaches is the *gray-box* approach. In a gray-box penetration test, the pentester is provided with partial useful information regarding specific systems that are especially in focus, or information that is semi-public, i.e. typically only available to certain restricted groups, such as repair manuals and information obtainable from diagnostics tools that are available to dealer workshops. In some cases, a step-wise approach is suitable where the pentester receives more information or access after showing how a certain security mechanism may be bypassed or how a vulnerability may be exploited without actually having to fully develop and perform the attack. An example is showing a viable and realistic approach of how it is possible to brute-force an authentication key to gain access, and instead of wasting time to actually brute-force the key, the key can be provided by the automotive organization so that the pentester can use the allocated time more wisely to identify deeper issues once the authentication stage is passed. The advantage of this approach is that it optimizes the ratio between test efficiency and realism.

7.2 Frameworks for Security Testing

Besides the different categories of testing mentioned in Sections 7.1.1–7.1.4, rather than considering these as independent test activities, there are different approaches to establishing frameworks for security testing. Security testing frameworks allow automotive organizations to achieve more systematic and efficient testing using defined processes, test tools, and approaches.

One example is establishing a cybersecurity test lab that incorporates a security testing framework [28]. In this framework, there are seven layers defined in the testing model including: functional testing, source code scan, information scan, library scan, fuzz testing, penetration test, and limitation test. This type of test model allows for defined processes, test tools, and approaches to be used in security testing. Moreover, there are seven areas that are in the focus for security testing, which helps the automotive organization to define the type of target systems for testing. The seven focus areas are: system test (mobile apps, backend systems), code test (source code, libraries), hardware test (microcontroller, SoC [system-on-chip]), in-vehicle network test (CAN, Ethernet), wireless network test (Wi-Fi, Bluetooth, cellular), autonomous perceptual test (lidar, camera, radar), and functional test (test automation).

It is also useful for automotive organizations to consider various environments for testing. For example, some parts of the testing require only software, which means that testing can start as soon as the needed functionality has been developed and is available. Other testing may require both software and hardware, which means that testing can only start once hardware for the target system is available, which is typically in the later stages of the development lifecycle. Moreover, an automotive organization can perform testing in a static environment or in a dynamic environment [28]. In the static environment, the target system could be software only, a standalone ECU, a system of ECUs or a full vehicle. No additional input is provided to the target system to simulate different conditions; instead, the target system is "static." Therefore, while it is extremely easy to start testing since the target system is in a static environment, it is also important to note that because the target system is in a static environment certain functionality or test scenarios may not be covered. For instance, how would a vehicle behave if a message with a certain attack pattern is sent while the vehicle is driving? This type of testing is not included since the vehicle is in a static environment. However, to test the vehicle under varied circumstances requires a dynamic environment, where various inputs are provided to the target system to simulate different conditions. The target system needs to be able to operate in the dynamic environment and therefore typically requires a system of ECUs or a full vehicle to be effective. The external input in the environment includes, for example, network communication from other systems or vehicles as well as camera and sensor data input. The purpose is to make sure that the target system is in a realistic environment when the security testing occurs, to observe how the target system behaves as a result of the testing in the realistic environment. For example, during fuzz testing it may be possible to detect unexpected behavior on a target system in a vehicle that is driving or simulated to be driving and observe how the unexpected behavior affects the vehicle itself or affects other vehicles in a realistic environment.

Another example of a framework describes testing on different levels, including component level and vehicle level [29]. The purpose of this framework is for automotive organizations to follow a systematic approach for testing and analyzing security of automotive systems. There are two types of test approaches described: generic and specific. The generic tests are vehicle-independent and cover common areas and standard features available on all vehicles and systems. These tests are generally easy to execute and applicable to many systems. Examples include CAN flooding attacks, baud rate attacks, and diagnostics attacks. For CAN flooding attacks, the CAN bus is flooded with a large number of CAN messages injected with high frequency, which may cause denial of service if such messages are not handled properly. For baud rate attacks, the attacking device or ECU is configured to transmit with a baud rate different from the other ECUs connected to the CAN bus, which may cause denial of service. For diagnostics attacks, the target system is accessed with diagnostics commands to, for example, disable normal CAN communication, perform ECU reset, or initiate ECU reprogramming, which may lead to changing the normal behavior of the target system. On the other hand, the specific tests are vehicle-dependent and focus on a specific cyber-physical system which is not defined by standard features. As a result, the specific test cases cannot be made generalized and would not be applicable to other target systems or vehicles. In comparison with the generic tests that can be performed using a black-box approach, the specific tests require more time for preparation and would benefit from a white-box approach, where information regarding the E/E (electrical/electronic) architecture, the ECU hardware interfaces and communication signals and messages are provided. The steps to define and execute specific tests are as follows:

(1) analyze the target system (ECUs, messages and signals);
(2) define the goal of the attack, e.g. prevent the system's activation;
(3) identify the signals to be overwritten;
(4) identify existing protections, e.g. rolling counter, checksum;
(5) define a strategy to bypass protection;
(6) implement the attack.

Another framework specifically targets in-vehicle CAN networks to allow for systematic pentesting [30]. This framework is based on considerations from NIST SP-800-115 [31] and OSSTMM (Open Source Security Testing Methodology Manual) [32], which both define penetration testing and security evaluation methodologies. Some common steps in these methodologies are related to the planning, discovery, and attack phases. The in-vehicle CAN network pentesting framework proposes a systematic approach to help pentesters follow the necessary steps and to assist in using suitable tools and methods. Following this approach allows automotive organizations to save time and ensure that no vital steps are missed. The pentesting framework focuses mostly on providing details for the discovery and attack phases specific to in-vehicle CAN networks, meaning that the planning phase can be conducted according to NIST SP-800-115 or OSSTMM. The framework gives several examples of attack trees, which describe the different paths that can be taken to achieve a certain attack goal. For example, to achieve the attack goal of reverse-engineering CAN IDs, a pentester can perform the following three steps: sniff and record transmitted CAN messages on the bus, analyze the recorded CAN messages, and identify the behavior of the transmitted CAN messages. Each of these steps can be further achieved by performing some sub-steps. For instance, sniffing and recording CAN messages requires preparing the necessary hardware and software tools, and then connecting to the CAN bus. Another more comprehensive example is achieving the attack goal of exploiting UDS commands. This attack tree is illustrated in Figure 7.3. To be able to exploit UDS commands, which is the attack goal indicated at the top of the attack tree in the figure, requires performing UDS addresses mapping, scanning UDS services, executing UDS commands, and bypassing Security Access. These activities may be achieved in different independent ways as indicated by an OR branch, or in some cases require a combination of different activities as indicated by an AND branch in Figure 7.3.

Please note that the attack tree is incomplete but rather serves to provide an idea on how automotive organizations can create such trees. Some steps may not be applicable based on

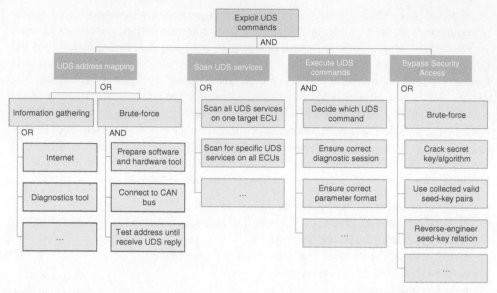

Figure 7.3 Example attack tree for exploiting UDS commands. Source: Based on [30].

the target system and other steps may need to be added. By utilizing this framework, it is possible for an organization to write scripts or use tools to perform the various testing steps and activities. It would also be possible to automate several steps, e.g. the output from a previous test can be used as input to a different tool in the next test. For instance, based on the activities in Figure 7.3, one tool could be used to brute-force the UDS address mapping and once it has identified the relevant UDS address of the target ECU, it could pass the UDS address onto the next tool, which then performs the UDS services scanning for that UDS address. Next, once the UDS service scan has completed, it would provide the list of identified UDS services to the next tool, which then tries to automatically execute some UDS commands for those UDS services. If Security Access is required for a particular UDS service, it would launch a separate tool that automatically tries to break Security Access. Thus, by using this framework in a systematic manner, these four steps in the attack tree can be automated and chained together using various scripts and tools.

Besides in-vehicle network communication, Bluetooth in automotive systems is also a common test target. Previous work [33] has shown that multiple Bluetooth-enabled automotive systems contain inherent weaknesses such as using fixed PINs and are always in discoverable mode. The results from such work indicate that these systems are susceptible to attackers connecting to them by either guessing the fixed PIN, which is often 0000 or 1234, or simply by sending a pairing request. To properly test Bluetooth for such weaknesses and vulnerabilities, there is a framework that allows pentesters to follow a systematic approach for evaluating automotive Bluetooth systems [34]. More specifically, the framework describes the process including performing threat modeling, creating attack trees, and performing penetration testing. A prototype tool written in Python using the Linux Bluetooth stack Bluez was developed. The tool is semi-automated and follows the various steps specified in the attack tree, including connecting to the target system and trying to compromise the pairing mechanism, as long as all necessary information is available.

Moreover, besides security testing frameworks for the vehicle and in-vehicle systems as mentioned above, there is also the notion of a testing framework for the connected car infrastructure [35]. This framework focuses more on a security assessment of vehicle services, provided by a managed infrastructure and over various vehicle communication channels. The managed infrastructure encompasses the automotive company applications center, third party applications center, trusted network, untrusted network, and Internet backbone. The vehicle communication channels include communication between the vehicle and the managed infrastructure, the vehicle and mobile devices, and the vehicle and other vehicles. Examples of services that this framework cover are remote vehicle diagnostics, remote software download, multimedia streaming, Internet browsing and exchange of information between vehicles and the infrastructure. Using the framework allows automotive organizations to assess the security in the connected car infrastructure and, as a result, to identify potential weaknesses in services for the connected car.

7.3 Focus on Fuzz Testing

Although there are several test approaches, as described in the previous sections, the focus of this chapter is on *fuzz testing* since it is one of the techniques that is most efficient in identifying new vulnerabilities and can be performed in an automated fashion. It is also typically the first technique used by attackers to find new vulnerabilities on a target system. Therefore, it is important that automotive organizations perform fuzz testing on their own products first, before the products are released and attackers are able to use fuzzing as part of their attack arsenal, in order to have some confidence that their products are robust enough to be able to resist a certain level of fuzzing. In general, fuzz testing is applicable to any target system and therefore is a great complement to conventional testing methodologies. Fuzz testing has already been briefly explained in Sections 2.3.9 and 7.1.3. Moreover, performing a TARA of the target system helps the organization to identify high-risk interfaces of the target system, e.g. supported wireless protocols that allow the organization to focus fuzz testing on those interfaces.

A fuzz testing environment generally comprises three main parts as follows. First, the fuzz testing tool contains a *fuzz engine* that is responsible for generating fuzzed contents, which will serve as input to the target system, also known as the system under test (SUT). The second part is the *injector*, which handles delivery of the fuzzed contents generated by the fuzz engine to the SUT. The injector may be different for different protocols and interfaces. The third part is the *monitor*, which is responsible for observing the SUT and detecting unexpected behavior. Obviously, the SUT would be an additional part that is required to successfully be able to perform fuzz testing in this environment; however, the SUT itself is not part of the fundamental fuzz testing environment and is therefore not counted. A simplified overview showing the concept of the fuzz testing environment is presented in Figure 7.4. It shows the three main parts and includes the SUT for illustrative purposes. The three parts can typically be implemented independently, allowing for flexibility and interaction with other test systems. Rather than considering that a single standalone fuzz testing tool can accommodate all target systems, it is important to consider a fuzz testing framework where the different parts of the fuzz testing environment are constructed accordingly to support

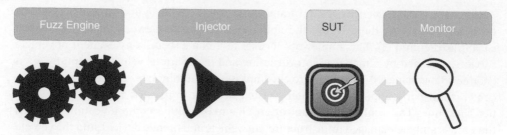

Figure 7.4 Concept of the fuzz testing environment consisting of fuzz engine, injector and monitor. Source: Openclipart. Creative Commons Zero 1.0 License.

specific characteristics of the target system. For example, the fuzz engine is provided by a fuzz testing tool running on a PC, a separate hardware tool, e.g. a certain communication device for the target protocol, is used as the injector, and a third separate tool, e.g. a debugger, is used as the monitor. The following sections describe these three parts in more detail.

7.3.1 Fuzz Engine

The quality of fuzzing largely depends on the engine responsible for the creation of malformed messages that are sent to the target system to provoke failures. Therefore, the techniques used in the fuzz engine to generate such messages are extremely important. Previous work has described various methods and techniques for fuzz testing [36–39] and, as a general point, when it comes to generating useful fuzzed contents there are often two characteristics that need to be considered. The first characteristic is the fundamental mechanism to generate data and inject anomalies, and the second characteristic is how well the fuzz engine understands the underlying target protocol, specifications, and message structure.

For the first characteristic of the fuzz engine, there are typically three approaches that can be taken, or three types of fuzz engines: *dumb*, *mutation-based*, and *generation-based* or *model-based*, as briefly introduced in Section 2.3.9. To recapitulate, the first type is a simple, *dumb* fuzzer where the fuzz engine is not aware of the input structure and just generates random data. This could also include injecting simple anomalies such as overflow anomalies by adding a long string of "A"s at the end of a message. This approach is simple and easy to get started with, and there are some merits in testing the target system with random data of random length to test robustness and input validation; however, it is limited in reaching deeper areas of the target system and unable to navigate through complex protocols. The second approach is a *mutation-based* fuzz engine. This type requires specific seed inputs, e.g. valid files or communication protocol logs. For instance, to fuzz test the image library libpng, a set of valid PNG (portable network graphics) files would be used as seed input to the mutation-based fuzz engine. The fuzz engine then generates fuzzed data by modifying or "mutating" the seed data. More specifically, the fuzz engine will flip random bits of the valid seed data to generate semi-valid variants of the seed data. The mutation-based technique requires little preparation; only valid files or communication logs need to be provided, and the fuzzed messages can reach fairly deep into the message processing on the target system since most of the contents are correct based on valid data. However, how well the target system can be tested depends on completeness of the seed inputs and the technique used for mutating the valid files. The third type is a *generation-based* or *model-based* fuzzer. This approach is based on creating models that define the message structure to be fuzzed for the target system and then the fuzzed data is generated from scratch based on the fields specified in the message structure. This approach requires more preparation since it needs to understand the specifics of the target message format. However, it offers extensive coverage since it is able to generate all relevant types of messages and is able to inject various anomalies in the right context for the model. For example, if the model contains a text field, the fuzz engine can inject text-based anomalies, e.g. overflow of whitespaces and tabs, positive and negative integers, or non-printable ASCII (American Standard Code for Information Interchange) characters. On the other hand, if the model contains a binary field, the fuzz engine can inject binary-based anomalies, e.g. binary terminators, bit-flip anomalies, or overflow or underflow of the binary field. For broader coverage of testing the target system, a combination of anomalies in different fields of the message can be used. Both mutation-based and generation-based fuzzing techniques are effective since they generate semi-valid data, ranging from very close to valid data, e.g. single bit flip, to farther away, e.g. multiple combinations of anomalies. Since fuzz testing is about testing corner cases, it is common to test several messages with minor deviations consecutively to achieve better coverage of the target system.

Besides the first characteristic for a fuzz engine, which includes the three types for generating fuzzed data, the second characteristic defines how well the fuzz engine is aware of the input message structure. This characteristic plays an important role in allowing the fuzzed data to reach deeper into the message processing of the target system. For example, if fuzzed data are not "valid enough" according to the input message structure, they will be rejected directly by the parser and will not be able to reach the main target application code. There are two types presented here: a *static fuzzer* and a *block-based fuzzer*. The first type, a *static fuzzer*, simply generates fuzzed messages based on one of the previously mentioned three approaches for fuzzed data generation. However, the generated fuzzed data may not be properly aligned to the input message structure. For instance, there may be a cyclic redundancy check (CRC) field in the message structure. The CRC field is an error-detecting checksum code used to provide data integrity of the message during transmission. If parts of the message have been fuzzed, it is likely that the checksum calculation of the message does not match the CRC value, and therefore the message will be rejected by the parser. The second type, a *block-based fuzzer*, overcomes this challenge by having full understanding of the fields, or *blocks*, in the message format, and based on the fuzzed data is able to update each block accordingly to ensure consistency. For instance, using the same CRC example from above, after a fuzzed message has been generated, a block-based fuzzer is able to recalculate a correct checksum value based on the fuzzed data and update the CRC field in the fuzzed message. With the correct CRC value, the fuzzed message is then able to successfully go past the parser and reach deeper into the message processing of the target system.

Besides understanding the fields or blocks in the message format, which allows the fuzz engine to generate valid malformed contents for a *single message*, it is also necessary to consider how the fuzz engine can handle *statefulness* to be able to successfully fuzz a *consecutive set of messages* in one protocol run. Regarding statefulness, the fuzz engine recognizes the context of a certain message together with the previous sequence of messages to better allow for detecting unknown behavior. Please note that the messages can be fuzzed individually as "single messages," or each message can be considered as a part of a longer message sequence, where each message could be swapped, dropped, or injected in arbitrary places in the protocol run. As a result of performing fuzz testing based on message sequences, it may be possible to detect invalid state transitions on the target system and bypass certain checks to reach deeper logic within the application code on the target system. For example, in the UDS Security Access [40] authentication protocol, typically when a seed request message (0x27 0x01) is sent to the target system, it correspondingly responds with a seed value (0x67 0x01 0xXX 0xXX 0xXX 0xXX), where "x" represents a hexadecimal value, and then the target system is expecting a key value response as the next incoming message (0x27 0x02 0xXX 0xXX 0xXX 0xXX), as illustrated in Figure 7.5.

It is worth noting that it is possible to fuzz the message sequence, e.g. instead of sending the key value response (0x27 0x02 0xXX 0xXX 0xXX 0xXX), the seed request message (0x27 0x01) is repeatedly sent to the target system. Alternatively, prior to sending a seed request message, the key value response (0x27 0x02 0xXX 0xXX 0xXX 0xXX) is sent with random data without first receiving an initial seed value message. This type of testing may uncover invalid state transitions where it may be possible to bypass the authentication. Additionally, besides reordering messages in the sequence, the individual messages could be fuzzed such that fuzzed seed request messages or fuzzed key value messages are repeatedly sent.

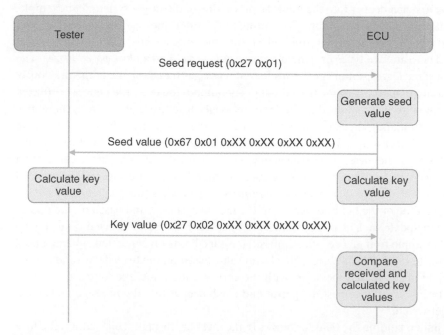

Figure 7.5 Example sequence of exchanged messages for UDS Security Access authentication. Source: Based on [40].

Some other examples of statefulness include the following. Continuing with the Security Access example above, some diagnostic services are only allowed to be used after Security Access has successfully been passed. Typically changing from the default diagnostic session to the programming session, which allows reprogramming of the ECU, requires Security Access. While testing if such protected services can be accessed without Security Access is useful, considering statefulness it is also necessary to ensure that Security Access has passed first before performing fuzz testing of such services. Otherwise those fuzzed messages are instantly discarded by the initial check in the protected services since the target ECU is not in the correct state. Thus, the fuzzed messages would not reach the actual logic responsible for processing such messages.

Moreover, for security purposes, some critical in-vehicle network messages use AUTOSAR SecOC to provide data integrity and authenticity, which is explained in more detail in Section 7.1.1. While functional testing of such security solutions is necessary, performing fuzz testing of the same solutions is equally important. Since SecOC uses, for example, a MAC to protect each message, it is important to consider statefulness when fuzz testing so that the correct MACs are generated based on the fuzzed contents. To generate correct MACs based on fuzzed contents requires the fuzzer to keep track of the sequence of messages and to know the freshness value used. This allows for fuzz testing to successfully pass the MAC verification function on the target system and allows the fuzzed contents to reach deeper into target application code responsible for the message processing part. Obviously, fuzz testing can also target the MAC verification function itself, e.g. by sending correct data with a fuzzed MAC or sending fuzzed data with a fuzzed MAC to test the robustness of the MAC verification function.

Furthermore, since the CAN bus only supports up to eight bytes payload in CAN frames, to be able to support larger payloads, ISO 15765-2 [41], also known as ISO-TP (transport layer), defines a method of segmenting longer messages into multiple frames. As a result, payloads of up to 4095 bytes in one message split into multiple frames can be sent. These frames use metadata, including for example sequence numbers, to be able to reassemble the complete message at the receiver side. Thus, to be able to successfully generate consecutive fuzzed frames, it is necessary to know the sequence numbers expected by the target system so that the complete fuzzed message can be reassembled properly.

As described above, it is important to be aware that there are different types of fuzzing techniques that can be applied since the fuzz engine plays a major role in how successful and efficient the fuzz testing will be. Fuzz testing in the automotive industry will mostly benefit from using a generation-based fuzzer since it is the most efficient and useful approach. This type of fuzzer is also known as an intelligent fuzzer since it has an understanding of the protocols and specifications that it is generating fuzzed input for. This is an extremely crucial characteristic especially for automotive fuzz testing since it is often required to know the specific formats and sequences used by automotive protocols to be able to effectively generate malformed messages. For situations where proprietary protocols are used and specifications are not available, and therefore it is not possible to create a model for generating fuzzed messages, a mutation-based fuzzing approach is suitable. Using valid proprietary communication data or file formats as a basis to "mutate" or generate fuzzed messages is an efficient and valid approach. In both cases, block-based fuzzing is considered a prerequisite. This is important to ensure that certain fields of the input are generated correctly, e.g. length fields or checksum and CRC fields, so that the fuzzed messages reach deeper areas in the target code and are processed by the application to be tested rather than being discarded at an initial check, e.g. by a simple length check or checksum check. A generation-based block-based fuzzer is considered in the automotive fuzz testing environment examples presented in Chapters 8, 9, and 10.

7.3.2 Injector

Using the injector, the fuzzed data generated by the fuzz engine is provided to the target system using the required input method. There are different injectors that can be used based on the type of input to the target system. The input also defines the different target types for fuzzing, e.g. *protocol fuzzing*, *file format fuzzing*, and *API* (application programming interface) *fuzzing*. Each type is described in more detail below.

The first type is *protocol fuzzing*, where fuzzed messages are sent over a communication protocol. Communication protocols are used to send messages between different systems. Delivering the fuzzed contents to the target system over a certain protocol typically requires specific hardware communication devices. Not only do the hardware communication devices need to be able to communicate over the fuzzed protocol but they also need to allow sending malformed and out-of-specification messages. Please note that not all hardware communication devices allow sending malformed messages, as some hardware communication devices will autocorrect the lower layers of the protocol or will not allow sending a faulty frame. Therefore, it is required to use hardware communication devices that allow the fuzz testing tool to have full control of the messages that are sent, including the lower layers of the protocol. Generally, fuzz testing tools provide a list of compatible hardware communication devices that are able to send malformed messages over the specific protocols.

ECUs in the in-vehicle network use automotive network protocols such as CAN, CAN-FD, and Automotive Ethernet, to communicate with each other. Communication messages range from safety-critical and security-critical messages, such as brake signals, to non-safety, non-security critical messages, such as signals to open a window. Fuzzing ECUs over the automotive network protocols is important to be able to detect potential vulnerabilities and test the robustness of the automotive systems. To be able to inject fuzzed messages onto the automotive network buses typically requires specific hardware communication devices. For example, a CAN or Ethernet communication device [42, 43] can be used to deliver fuzzed contents for the automotive protocol generated by the fuzz engine on a PC onto the CAN or Ethernet buses over USB and finally reach the target system, an ECU on the automotive network bus.

Moreover, systems with wireless external communication interfaces, such as in-vehicle infotainment systems, telematics units, and V2X communication systems, increase the attack surface and therefore should be considered for fuzz testing. Relevant protocols include various Bluetooth communication layers and profiles such as L2CAP, RFCOMM, SDP, A2DP, HFP, and SMP, Wi-Fi lower layer communication such as IEEE 802.11 Media Access Control, IEEE 802.2 Logical Link Control, and WPA (Wi-Fi protected access), and additional wireless communication layers including 5G and V2X communication. Moreover, considering the upper layers in the communication stack as well as the connected car use case, including communication with backend systems, the following protocols are also often considered for fuzz testing: IPv4, IPv6, TCP, UDP, DHCP, TLS, MQTT, and HTTP. Since external-facing wireless communication protocols and interfaces are remotely accessible, they are typically the first entry point for attackers. Therefore, it is crucial for automotive organizations to perform fuzz testing of such protocols before product release in order to identify unknown vulnerabilities in the implementation of the communication stacks and relevant applications. To be able to inject messages for the different wireless communication protocols typically requires different hardware communication devices. For instance, protocol fuzzing over Wi-Fi or Bluetooth requires the fuzz testing tool to use a Wi-Fi or Bluetooth dongle as the injector to be able to send the fuzzed messages to the target system over those wireless communication protocols. Correspondingly, for 5G and V2X protocol fuzzing, although a more comprehensive setup may be required for such wireless network communication, fuzz testing requires hardware communication devices that allow sending fuzzed messages over those wireless protocols. For example, base station simulator tools [44] can be used as the injector for fuzz testing target systems over cellular networks. As a side note, software-defined radios (SDRs) have emerged in recent years to allow for more flexibility in wireless communication, where parts traditionally built in hardware can be implemented in software, meaning that SDRs could be considered as flexible and suitable options to be used as injectors for fuzz testing of various wireless protocols [45, 46]. It is also worth noting that, rather than using hardware communication devices as injectors, it may be possible to perform fuzz testing in virtual environments. For instance, it has been shown that it is possible to perform fuzz testing of virtual ECUs by sending fuzzed CAN messages over a virtual bus [47]. While the usage of such virtual environments overcomes the need for physical hardware communication devices, it is important to note that it is not possible to test the lower layers of the communication protocols since they are virtualized.

Examples of protocol fuzzing are explained in Chapter 8, with the focus on automotive network protocols, and Chapter 9, with the focus on protocols for in-vehicle infotainment systems.

The next type, which is *file format fuzzing*, focuses on generating fuzzed files and providing them as inputs to the target system. There are two main goals for file format fuzzing:

(1) to test the file parser layer that handles the input, e.g. file format constraints, structure, field sizes, flags, input validation function etc.
(2) to test the application layer deeper in the message processing, e.g. attacks targeting the internals of the program in the target system

A common test target for file format fuzzing is the in-vehicle infotainment system, which typically supports a number of different file formats. Examples of common fuzzable file formats include image file formats such as jpg and png, audio file formats such as mp3 and ogg, and video file formats such as mp4. Other examples include archive file formats such as zip files, which are often used for map updates or software updates. These types of files are often supported by in-vehicle infotainment systems and, as a typical use case, can be provided by a user using, for example, a USB memory stick. This means that a malicious user or an attacker has full control of the input and could, through file format fuzzing, identify potential exploitable vulnerabilities and, as a result, provide specially crafted files to exploit said vulnerabilities. Additionally, considering the connected car scenario, for communication with backend systems, typical file formats targeted for fuzz testing include X.509 certificates, JSON (JavaScript object notation) files, and XML (extensible markup language) files. To be able to inject fuzzed files to the target system may require different injectors based on the target system. For example, for the in-vehicle infotainment system, the injector is typically a USB memory stick. For backend systems, the injector is the communication protocol with the backend system in question, e.g. providing fuzzed X.509 certificates in the certificate exchange in the TLS (transport layer security) communication, or embedding fuzzed JSON or XML files in HTTP communication.

Chapter 10 gives more details about file format fuzzing in general and in particular explains how to automate file fuzzing over USB for in-vehicle infotainment systems.

Finally, the third type is *API fuzzing* and is explained as follows. Rather than generating fuzzed input and providing it to the target system through its input channels, e.g. supported communication protocols or file formats, it is also possible to generate fuzzed contents and provide directly to the individual functions within the target application. This is generally known as API fuzzing. This approach gains flexibility and speed since it allows the fuzz testing to target specific API functions within the application, which are typically associated with certain libraries. It is important to note though that while the API fuzzer tries to identify unexpected behavior it still needs to stay within the usage prescribed by the API. The reason is that simply calling random API functions with fuzzed data may cause the target library to crash; however, these crashes are not interesting because they are not from a valid usage of the library. An example is explained as follows. There may be some API functions that need to be called in a certain order, e.g. allocate and initialize some memory, then prepare the format of the data to be written, and then finally write the data to the allocated memory. If the third API function to write data to allocated memory is randomly called first with some fuzzed data, it will crash because memory has not been allocated yet due to the incorrect calling order of the API function and not due to the fuzzed data provided through the API. Thus, the crash is not caused by an exploitable vulnerability but rather due to incorrect usage of the API during testing. This incorrect calling order of the API function would not be reachable through the application behavior and therefore would not be relevant. Consequently, to achieve effective results from API fuzzing requires a certain understanding of the API functions [48–50].

API fuzzing is an interesting area, and although currently API fuzzing is commonly targeting web application APIs, e.g. REST (representational state transfer) APIs [51, 52], and there is not much support for automotive API fuzzing, there exist several possibilities to expand API fuzzing to also support automotive systems where such fuzzing would be useful. However, since there is limited information presently available, this topic will not be discussed further at this point.

7.3.3 Monitor

The third part of the fuzz testing environment is the monitor. It is crucial that the target system is monitored for unexpected behavior caused by the fuzzed input provided to it in order to detect potential vulnerabilities on the target system. Monitoring can be performed using various techniques of *instrumentation*, where the target system's execution or performance is measured.

As mentioned in the previous section, the focus is on protocol fuzzing and file format fuzzing for automotive systems. Starting with protocol fuzzing, one of the simplest methods for monitoring is *in-band instrumentation*, where the protocol being fuzzed is monitored. This approach works exceptionally well for communication protocols that have a well-defined request-reply structure. Hence, the reply from the target system to a fuzzed request can be observed to determine if there are any exceptions based on what the expected response should be according to the specification. One example is the famous Heartbleed bug (CVE-2014-0160) [53] in the OpenSSL implementation of the TLS/DTLS (datagram transport layer security) heartbeat extension, which does not do proper input validation on the incoming request. When sending a malformed request to a vulnerable OpenSSL implementation, it replies with a much larger response than is expected [54]. The Heartbleed bug poses a serious threat since it could be exploited to extract various secret data, such as encryption keys, or personal or financial details, from the server where the vulnerable OpenSSL is used. Thus, by monitoring the protocol being fuzzed, in this case, the TLS protocol, it is possible to detect abnormalities in the replies.

As mentioned, in-band instrumentation works well for network communication protocols using a well-defined request–reply format, and is therefore suitable as a monitoring approach for fuzz testing network protocols, such as Wi-Fi, Bluetooth, Ethernet, IPv4, IPv6, TCP, DHCP, TLS, MQTT, and HTTP. However, some communication protocols do not follow a strict request–reply structure, e.g. CAN messages are typically sent by a transmitting ECU, and received and consumed by the receiving ECU without providing any replies. Therefore, when fuzzing over such protocols, where the target system does not provide any responses to the fuzzed messages, using simple in-band instrumentation is not effective since it does not yield any information on how the target system behaves. Instead, for such protocols, a different means of instrumentation is required. One approach is to do some advanced in-band instrumentation, where the protocol being fuzzed is still being monitored; however, besides the fuzzed messages sent to the target system, additional valid messages are sent to the target system. For example, valid messages could be sent after each fuzzed message. Even though the fuzzed messages yield no responses, the valid messages are in the request–reply format and therefore can serve to determine whether the target system provides correct replies to these valid requests. These replies can help determine if the target system behaves correctly, e.g. whether the target system is still alive or how fast the target system responds to certain messages. For instance, this approach is useful when fuzzing CAN messages where there are no responses to the fuzzed messages from the target ECU. Specifically, by sending a valid diagnostics message, which is in the request–reply format, after each fuzzed CAN message it is possible to observe whether the target ECU provides a valid response to the diagnostics message. For instance, sending an UDS Extended Diagnostics Session request (`0x10 0x03`) or a UDS Tester Present message (`0x3E`) and observing the responses would help in determining whether the target ECU is alive.

Besides in-band instrumentation, for some target systems and protocols, *external instrumentation* may be necessary. External instrumentation may also be required for file format fuzzing to observe how the target system reacts to processing the fuzzed files. External instrumentation encompasses monitoring the target system using external means besides the protocol or interface being fuzzed. For example, for embedded ECUs with limited hardware interfaces, it is necessary to consider how to monitor the behavior of the target ECU.

It may be possible to use debug ports on the target ECU to monitor the internal status of the target system, including monitoring the execution and memory of the ECU [55]. Moreover, it is possible to use hardware-in the-loop (HIL) systems to monitor output signals from the target ECU [19, 56, 57]. More details about using HIL systems for external instrumentation when fuzzing automotive systems can be found in Chapter 8. For target systems, e.g. in-vehicle infotainment systems and telematics units, running a rich operating system, such as Linux, it is possible to use Agents, which are small pieces of code, running on the target system, to monitor the behavior of system processes and memory usage to detect abnormalities [58, 59]. This approach is suitable both for protocol fuzzing, e.g. over Wi-Fi and Bluetooth, and file format fuzzing, e.g. mp3 and mp4 files, to observe how the network stack, media parsers, and relevant applications behave due to fuzzed input. Chapter 9 describes in more detail how to use external instrumentation based on Agents when fuzz testing target systems running rich operating systems. Additionally, for target systems with a display, e.g. in-vehicle infotainment systems, it is feasible to use external instrumentation by visually inspecting the display. For example, it is possible to use cameras or other visual recognition techniques to detect unexpected behavior on the target system. This approach of external instrumentation based on visual recognition when fuzz testing target systems with displays is discussed further in Chapter 10.

One important aspect for fuzz testing is *code coverage*. Code coverage helps to understand which portions of the code have been executed based on the fuzzed messages. For a pure black-box fuzz testing approach, it is typically not possible to have these insights into the target system to know exactly what code has been tested. However, using certain monitoring features and following a white-box approach, it is possible to track the progress of what parts of the code have been tested. For a target ECU, the white-box approach requires access to the debug port of the microcontroller and the source code of the target system. While these resources may not always be available, a white-box approach allows one to directly inspect inside the microcontroller and therefore get more information for monitoring. Understanding the code coverage helps to gauge the value and usefulness of fuzz testing. An example of using the debug port on an automotive microcontroller to determine code coverage of fuzz testing over CAN is explained in detail in Reference [55]. By using hardware breakpoints on instruction addresses it is possible to trace and record the instructions and portions of code that were executed during fuzz testing. Consequently, it allows one to know which parts of the code were tested or not tested. For example, based on processing a fuzzed message, if there is a branch in the code, the monitoring function reads the instruction pointer address of the microcontroller, and determines which branch is taken. As a result, the monitoring function can provide a list of instruction memory blocks that have been executed as well as which fuzz test cases triggered the execution of those blocks. It also gives insight on which instruction blocks or which parts of the code have not been tested yet, which helps to determine if further fuzz testing is required.

Another important aspect is *feedback-based fuzzing* or *coverage-guided fuzzing* [60, 61]. It is built on the previously mentioned code coverage aspect. One can consider cases where various input validation or authentication mechanisms are preventing fuzzed messages from reaching the application code on the target system. Based on which parts of the code is tested during a fuzz test, the monitoring function can provide feedback to the fuzz engine on what type of fuzzed input should be generated next to reach deeper into the message processing on the target system. This approach is applicable to both the generation of individual fuzzed messages as well as to stateful fuzzing [62]. Specifically, an automotive example is if the code for certain functions on a target ECU is not reached during fuzz testing over CAN, then feedback can be provided to the fuzz engine to be instructed to use different CAN IDs or subfunction IDs. Additionally, if the code for a certain critical function is not reached during fuzz testing, one can imagine that the critical function can only be executed after successfully passing the UDS Security Access authentication function. Thus, feedback can be provided to the fuzz engine to change the message sequence to, first, successfully pass Security Access before the fuzz testing tool sends the fuzzed messages targeting the particular critical function. Ultimately, the goal is to achieve a higher degree of code coverage and reach more portions of the code on the target system. While feedback-based fuzzing or coverage-guided fuzzing is more prevalent in the IT industry, it is interesting to consider how such techniques may be applied when fuzz testing automotive systems.

Although not typically included in the monitoring activities themselves, it is worth noting that the monitoring technique used for external instrumentation often also allows one to provide various inputs to a target system to put it into different testable states. One important aspect of fuzz testing that is sometimes overlooked is to ensure that the target system is put into appropriate testable states. It is important to note that a target system may behave differently based on the same received fuzzed messages while in different testable states. Therefore, the monitoring environment can often play dual roles where, on the one hand, it monitors the target system and, on the other hand, it provides the necessary input to the target system to enable different testable states. An example is the HIL system described above, which is used to monitor output signals from the target ECU. The same HIL system can also provide input signals to the target ECU to enable various testable states. For example, input signals can enable different conditions for the target ECU such as engine off or on, different vehicle speed values, different gear position values, different wheel angles, etc. It is worth noting that some application code in the ECU may only execute under certain circumstances, e.g. a certain automatic park function only executes if the engine is on, speed is less than 7 km/h, and gear position is in reverse [63]. Therefore, for fuzzed messages to reach deep into the specific message processing often requires external instrumentation to provide the necessary input to the target system to enable these testable states.

Finally, the main goal of the monitoring function is to detect unexpected behavior on the target system. If any such unexpected behavior is detected, the monitor could instruct the fuzz engine to repeat the previously sent fuzzed messages to try to reproduce the issue in order to verify that it is a deterministic and systematic issue. Moreover, some monitors may be run asynchronously, meaning that there are multiple fuzzed messages processed by the target system before the target system is monitored to detect any abnormal behavior. This approach makes it more difficult to determine which fuzzed message actually caused the abnormal behavior. To overcome this challenge, the monitor can instruct the fuzz engine to resend some of the previously sent fuzzed messages and repeatedly monitor the target system to narrow down the actual fuzzed message that causes the abnormal behavior. Although the monitor is able to detect unexpected behavior in an automated fashion, in the end, the fuzzed messages causing unexpected behavior must be analyzed by an expert to determine whether it leads to exploitable vulnerabilities or weaknesses in the target system. Examples of such vulnerabilities or weaknesses include insufficient input validation, resource exhaustion, authentication bypass, and undocumented functionality on the target system, e.g. debug access.

7.4 Chapter Summary

This chapter presented an overview of practical security testing in the automotive industry. There are several different types of practical security testing methodologies including security functional testing, vulnerability scanning, fuzz testing, and penetration testing. Security functional testing focuses on providing assurance that specific security functions on automotive systems have been implemented correctly. Examples of test targets include the MAC generation and MAC verification functions for secure in-vehicle communication specified by AUTOSAR SecOC, as well as implementations of cryptographic algorithms and random number generation functions. Vulnerability scanning tests the target system for known security vulnerabilities and known weaknesses, and unknown vulnerabilities based on known attack patterns using information from a database. Common focus areas include testing authentication mechanisms such as UDS Security Access. Fuzz testing goes further to use sophisticated techniques to detect unknown vulnerabilities by providing malformed input to the target system and observing the system for any unexpected behavior. Finally, penetration testing focuses on testing the security of the target system in its entirety, including software and hardware. One major difference compared with the previous mentioned test methods is that penetration testing cannot be performed solely with automated tools but requires a "human security tester" who acts like a real attacker. Rather than performing different practical security testing haphazardly, it is imperative for automotive organizations to establish testing frameworks to allow for systematic and efficient testing using defined processes, test tools, and approaches. Moreover, since fuzz testing is one of the most powerful and efficient approaches of identifying unknown vulnerabilities and can be run in an automated fashion, this chapter presents a deep-dive into fuzz testing. Fuzzing is also a common technique employed by real attackers to find new vulnerabilities in released products, therefore it is crucial that automotive organizations perform fuzz testing on their own products before release, to have some confidence that their products are robust enough to be able to resist a certain level of fuzzing by attackers.

A fuzz testing environment typically consists of three parts: fuzz engine, injector, and monitor. The fuzz engine is responsible for generating fuzzed contents. These fuzzed contents are malformed messages where some parts of the message are replaced, added, or removed to include anomalies. Next, the injector delivers the generated fuzzed data to the target system. For automotive target systems, there are different injectors, e.g. network communication devices for protocol fuzzing, and USB memory sticks for file format fuzzing. Finally, one crucial aspect for automotive systems fuzzing is to monitor the target system for unexpected behavior. The monitor can be based on in-band instrumentation, where the same protocol that is being fuzzed is observed, or external instrumentation, where separate means for monitoring the target system is used, including, for example, debug interfaces, Agents running on the target system, and HIL systems.

References

1 Bayer, S., Enderle, T., Oka, D.K., and Wolf, M. (2015). Security crash test – practical security evaluations of automotive onboard it components. *Automotive – Safety & Security 2015*, Stuttgart, Germany.

2 International Organization for Standardization (ISO)/Society of Automotive Engineers (SAE) International (2020). *ISO/SAE DIS 21434 – road vehicles – cybersecurity engineering*. Geneva, Switzerland: ISO and USA: SAE International.

3 ISASecure (2019). IEC 62443 – EDSA certification. https://www.isasecure.org/en-US/Certification/IEC-62443-EDSA-Certification (accessed 30 July 2020).

4 International Electrotechnical Commission (IEC) (2019). *IEC 62443-4-2:2019 – security for industrial automation and control systems*. IEC.

5 ISASecure (2017). Synopsys defensics X Test tool updated for use in latest version of the ISASecure cybersecurity certification program. https://www.isasecure.org/en-US/News-Events/Synopsys-Defensics-X-Test-tool-updated-for-use-in (accessed 30 July 2020).

6 ISASecure (2015). Beyond security's beSTORM receives recognition as communication robustness testing tool for use in ISASecure cybersecurity certification program. https://www.isasecure.org/en-US/News-Events/Beyond-Security-s-beSTORM%C2%AE-receives-recognition-as (accessed 30 July 2020).

7 EMVCo (2020). Certification processes. https://www.emvco.com/processes-forms/certification (accessed 30 July 2020).

8 International Organization for Standardization (ISO)/International Electrotechnical Commission (IEC) (2009). *ISO/IEC 15408-1:2009 – information technology – security techniques – evaluation criteria for IT security*. Geneva, Switzerland: ISO.

9 Common Criteria (2010). Common criteria protection profile – digital tachograph – vehicle unit (VU PP).

10 CAR 2 CAR Communication Consortium (2019). Protection profile V2X hardware security module.

11 NXP Semiconductors (2020). NXP first to receive common criteria certification for standalone V2X secure element. https://media.nxp.com/news-releases/news-release-details/nxp-first-receive-common-criteria-certification-standalone-v2x (accessed 30 July 2020).

12 NIST CSRC (2020). CMVP – cryptographic module validation program. https://csrc.nist.gov/projects/cryptographic-module-validation-program (accessed 5 November 2020).

13 NIST CSRC (2001). FIPS 140-2 – security requirements for cryptographic modules. https://csrc.nist.gov/publications/detail/fips/140/2/final (accessed 30 July 2020).

14 NIST CSRC (2019). FIPS 140-3 – security requirements for cryptographic modules. https://csrc.nist.gov/publications/detail/fips/140/3/final (accessed 30 July 2020).

15 AUTOSAR (2017). Specification of secure onboard communication.

16 Oka, D.K., Wittmann, J., Bayer, S, and Gay, C. (2017). Security functional testing of automotive ECUs: verifying the correct implementation of security features. *Symposium on Cryptography and Information Security (SCIS)*, Naha, Japan.

17 Synopsys (2017). State of fuzzing 2017.

18 OWASP (2020). WSTG – latest – fuzz vectors. https://owasp.org/www-project-web-security-testing-guide/latest/6-Appendix/C-Fuzz_Vectors (accessed 30 July 2020).

19 Oka, D.K., Yvard, A., Bayer, S., and Kreuzinger, T. (2016). Enabling cyber security testing of automotive ECUs by adding monitoring capabilities. *escar Europe*, Munich, Germany.

20 AUTOSAR (2016). SOME/IP protocol specification.

21 Synopsys (2020). What is red teaming?. https://www.synopsys.com/glossary/what-is-red-teaming.html (accessed 30 July 2020).

22 Nilsson, D.K. and Larson, U.E. (2008). Simulated attacks on CAN buses: vehicle virus. *Fifth IASTED International Conference on Communication Systems and Networks (AsiaCSN)*, Langkawi, Malaysia.

23 NewAE Technology (2017). V3:tutorial A5 breaking AES-256 Bootloader. https://wiki.newae.com/V3:Tutorial_A5_Breaking_AES-256_Bootloader (accessed 5 November 2020).

24 Milburn, A., Timmers, N., Wiersma, N. et al. (2018). There will be glitches: extracting and analyzing automotive firmware efficiently. *Black Hat USA*, Las Vegas, NV, USA.

25 Duo (2018). Microcontroller firmware recovery using invasive analysis. https://duo.com/labs/research/microcontroller-firmware-recovery-using-invasive-analysis (accessed 30 July 2020).

26 Tencent Keen Security Lab (2020). Tencent keen security lab: experimental security assessment on lexus cars. https://keenlab.tencent.com/en/2020/03/30/Tencent-Keen-Security-Lab-Experimental-Security-Assessment-on-Lexus-Cars/ (accessed 30 July 2020).

27 Nie, S., Liu, L., and Du, Y. (2017). Free-fall: hacking tesla from wireless to CAN bus. *Black Hat USA*, Las Vegas, NV, USA.

28 Chen, B. (2019). Security development by China FAW Group. *escar Asia*, Tokyo, Japan.

29 Bragaglia, E., Nesci, W., and Senni, C. (2017). A framework for vehicle penetration tests. *escar USA*. Ypsilanti, MI, USA.

30 Bayer, S., Hirata, K., and Oka, D.K. (2016). Towards a systematic pentesting framework for in-vehicular CAN networks. *escar Europe*, Munich, Germany.

31 National Institute of Standards and Technology (2008). Technical guide to information security testing and assessment. NIST SP-800-115.

32 ISECOM (2010). OSSTMM 3 – the open source security testing methodology manual.

33 Oka, D.K., Furue, T., Langenhop, L., and Nishimura, T. (2014). Survey of vehicle IoT bluetooth devices. *IEEE 7th International Conference on Service-Oriented Computing and Applications (SOCA)*, Matsue, Japan.

34 Cheah, M., Shaikh, S.A., Haas, O.C.L., and Ruddle, A.R. (2017). Towards a systematic security evaluation of the automotive Bluetooth interface. *Vehicular Communications* 9: 8–18.

35 Kleberger, P., Javaheri, A., Olovsson, T., and Jonsson, E. (2011). A framework for assessing the security of the connected car infrastructure. *International Conference on Systems and Networks Communications (ICSNC)*, Barcelona, Spain.

36 Shapiro, R., Bratus, S., Rogers, E., and Smith, S. (2011). Identifying vulnerabilities in SCADA systems via fuzz-testing. *International Conference on Critical Infrastructure Protection (ICCIP)*, Hanover, NH, USA.

37 Aitel, D. (2002). The advantages of block-based protocol analysis for security testing. https://www.immunitysec.com/downloads/advantages_of_block_based_analysis.html (accessed 30 July 2020).

38 Burns, B., Killion, D., Beauchesne, N. et al. (2007). *Security Power Tools*. Sebastopol, CA: O'Reilly.

39 Bayer, S. and Ptok, A. (2015). Don't fuss about fuzzing: fuzzing controllers in vehicular networks. *escar Europe*, Cologne, Germany.

40 International Organization for Standardization (ISO) (2013). *ISO 14229-1:2013 – Road vehicles – Unified Diagnostic Services (UDS)*. Geneva, Switzerland: ISO.

41 International Organization for Standardization (ISO) (2016). *ISO 15765-2:2016 – road vehicles — diagnostic communication over controller area network (DoCAN)*. Geneva, Switzerland: ISO.

42 Peak System (2020). PCAN-USB – CAN interface for USB. https://www.peak-system .com/PCAN-USB.199.0.html?&L=1 (accessed 30 July 2020).

43 Vector (2020). VN5610A/VN5640 – powerful and multifunctional USB network interfaces for automotive ethernet and CAN FD. https://www.vector.com/int/en/products/ products-a-z/hardware/network-interfaces/vn56xx (accessed 30 July 2020).

44 Anritsu (2020). Signalling tester (base station simulator) – MD8475B. https://www .anritsu.com/en-us/test-measurement/products/md8475b (accessed 30 July 2020).

45 Knight, M. (2018). Designing RF fuzzing tools to expose PHY layer vulnerabilities. *GNU Radio Conference*, Henderson, NV, USA.

46 Hond, B. (2011). Fuzzing the GSM protocol. Master thesis. Radboud University Nijmegen.

47 Oka, D.K. (2020). Fuzz testing virtual ECUs as part of the continuous security testing process. *SAE International Journal of Transportation Cybersecurity and Privacy* 2 (2): 159–168. https://doi.org/10.4271/11-02-02-0014.

48 Zeller, A., Gopinath, R., Bohme, M. et al. (2019). Fuzzing APIs. The Fuzzing Book, Saarland University.

49 Regehr, J. (2015). API fuzzing vs. file fuzzing: a cautionary tale. https://blog.regehr.org/ archives/1269 (accessed 30 July 2020).

50 Fuzzit (2019). Discovering CVE-2019-13504 CVE-2019-13503 and the importance of API fuzzing. https://fuzzit.dev/2019/07/11/discovering-cve-2019-13504-cve-2019-13503-and-the-importance-of-api-fuzzing (accessed 30 July 2020).

51 Atlidakis, V., Godefroid, P., and Polishchuk, M. (2019). RESTler: stateful REST API fuzzing. *IEEE/ACM 41st International Conference on Software Engineering (ICSE)*, Montreal, Canada.

52 Tinfoil Security (2020). APIs scanned the way they should be. https://www .tinfoilsecurity.com/solutions/api-scanner (accessed 30 July 2020).

53 NIST (2014). National vulnerability database - CVE-2014-0160. https://nvd.nist.gov/vuln/ detail/CVE-2014-0160 (accessed 30 July 2020).

54 Synopsys (2016). Podcast: Rauli Kaksonen on discovering heartbleed. https://www .synopsys.com/blogs/software-security/podcast-rauli-kaksonen-on-discovering-heartbleed (accessed 30 July 2020).

55 Hirata, K., Oka, D.K., and Vuillaume, C. (2016). Using monitoring capabilities to improve fuzz testing over CAN: memory checking and code coverage. *Symposium on Cryptography and Information Security (SCIS)*, Kumamoto, Japan.

56 Oka, D.K., Bayer, S., Kreuzinger, T., and Gay, C. (2017). How to enable cyber security testing of automotive ECUs by adding monitoring capabilities. *Symposium on Cryptography and Information Security (SCIS)*, Naha, Japan.

57 Oka, D.K., Fujikura, T., and Kurachi, R. (2018). Shift left: fuzzing earlier in the automotive software development lifecycle using HIL systems. *escar Europe*, Brussels, Belgium.

58 Kuipers, R. and Oka, D.K. (2019). Improving fuzz testing of infotainment systems and telematics units using agent instrumentation. *escar USA*, Ypsilanti, MI, USA.

59 Oka, D.K. and Kuipers, R. (2019). Efficient and effective fuzz testing of automotive Linux systems using agent instrumentation. *Automotive Linux Summit*, Tokyo, Japan.

60 Manes, V., Han, H., Han, C. et al. (2019). The art, science, and engineering of fuzzing: a survey. *IEEE Transactions on Software Engineering*.

61 ClusterFuzz (2020). Coverage guided vs blackbox fuzzing. https://google.github.io/ clusterfuzz/reference/coverage-guided-vs-blackbox (accessed 30 July 2020).

62 DeMott, J.D., Enbody, R.J., and Punch, W.F. (2007). Revolutionizing the field of grey-box attack surface testing with evolutionary fuzzing. *Black Hat USA*, Las Vegas, NV, USA.

63 Miller, C. and Valasek, C. (2013). Adventures in automotive networks and control units. *Defcon*, Las Vegas, NV, USA.

8

Automating Fuzz Testing of In-Vehicle Systems by Integrating with Automotive Test Tools

ONE PLUS ONE EQUALS THREE

This chapter presents an approach for improving and automating fuzz testing of in-vehicle systems by integrating with automotive test tools. As described in Section 7.3, a fuzz testing environment requires three parts: fuzz engine, injector, and monitor. This chapter focuses mostly on the third part, namely the monitor, and how existing automotive test tools at an automotive organization can be reused to provide monitoring capabilities to improve and automate fuzz testing. Please note that in this fuzz testing environment, the automotive test tools are responsible for providing *external instrumentation*, explained in more detail in Section 7.3.3. Briefly explained, external instrumentation means that the target system is monitored using external means besides the protocol or interface being fuzzed in order to detect exceptions on the target system.

To realize advanced functionality, such as autonomous driving, modern vehicles contain larger software codebases and more complex software solutions running on automotive systems or electronic control units (ECUs). With increasing connectivity, cyber threats targeting vehicles are becoming more prevalent. If there are vulnerabilities in the software on automotive systems, attackers may potentially be able to exploit such vulnerabilities and abuse various vehicle functionality to cause safety damage, including taking control of the steering or disabling the brakes. To assure safe and secure execution of such functionality, cybersecurity needs to be considered in all steps of the automotive software development lifecycle as mentioned in Chapter 2. Moreover, for advanced vehicle functionality, more functional testing and security testing, including fuzz testing, which are described in more detail in Chapter 7, are required during the software development lifecycle. Fuzz testing is an efficient and powerful testing technique to detect unknown vulnerabilities in especially newly developed code. More details about fuzz testing in general are given in Section 7.3.

As introduced in Chapter 7, there exist a number of readily available fuzz testing solutions for traditional IT systems and protocols. However, fuzz testing ECUs communicating over automotive network protocols such as CAN (controller area network) or CAN-FD (controller area network flexible data-rate) brings new challenges. For example, there is often no easy way to determine how the target ECU reacted to a certain fuzzed message.

Building Secure Cars: Assuring the Automotive Software Development Lifecycle, First Edition. Dennis Kengo Oka.
© 2021 John Wiley & Sons Ltd. Published 2021 by John Wiley & Sons Ltd.

In the IT world, many network protocols such as HTTP (hypertext transfer protocol) use a request–reply format, which makes it easy for a fuzz testing tool to generate a fuzzed request message and observe the reply from the target system to determine whether there are any exceptions. However, ECUs communicating over CAN or CAN-FD do not typically follow a specific request-reply format. Instead, the ECUs often only receive and process certain CAN messages without sending any corresponding replies on the CAN bus. Due to these inherent differences between IT and automotive network protocols, there is a need for external instrumentation provided by automotive test tools to monitor other aspects of the target system besides the CAN communication.

This chapter presents in detail a fuzz testing solution where the monitor part comprises an automotive test tool such as a hardware-in-the-loop (HIL) system. The integration of a fuzz testing tool with an automotive test tool provides several advantages. First, it allows reuse of an existing test environment, typically used for functional testing at an automotive organization, which also provides the added benefit that fuzz testing can be built into the functional testing workflow and therefore it is possible to *shift left* in the automotive software development lifecycle to allow finding and fixing issues earlier in the development. Second, it allows one to put the ECU that is being tested, also known as the system under test (SUT), in various testable states by providing the necessary input, e.g. restbus simulation or analog or digital signals to the SUT. Third, it allows one to properly observe the SUT for exceptions in its behavior, using various monitoring techniques, such as internal ECU state and analog or digital output signals from the SUT. Last, it allows one to automate the entire test process in such a manner that the automotive test tool controls the fuzz testing tool and the SUT. For example, if there is an exception detected on the SUT, the automotive test tool can reset the SUT back into a testable state and instruct the fuzz testing tool to either repeat the previous fuzzed messages to verify that the issue is reproduceable or continue testing with the next round of fuzzed messages.

Two variants of a test environment comprising a fuzz testing tool integrated with an automotive test tool are presented. The first setup, described in more detail in Section 8.3.1, is a test environment consisting of a fuzz testing tool, an SUT, and a HIL system. The fuzz testing tool sends fuzzed messages over an automotive network such as CAN or CAN-FD to the SUT, and the HIL system performs external instrumentation by measuring and monitoring various values from the SUT to detect any abnormal ECU behavior. This setup is more of a white-box approach where the HIL system needs to be configured in advance on what is considered correct vs. abnormal behavior of the target system. The second setup, presented in more detail in Section 8.3.2, is a test environment consisting of a fuzz testing tool, an SUT, a reference system which is a duplicate system that is identical to the SUT, and a HIL system. Similarly, the fuzz testing tool sends fuzzed messages over an automotive network such as CAN or CAN-FD to the SUT, and the HIL system performs external instrumentation by measuring and monitoring various values from both the SUT and the reference system and comparing the values to detect any abnormal ECU behavior. This setup is more of a black-box approach, where the HIL system does not need to know what is considered correct behavior but instead identifies exceptions by comparing the behavior of the fuzzed SUT to the reference system. If there are any differences in behavior, it can be determined that the fuzzed messages caused this abnormal behavior.

By shifting left and performing fuzz testing earlier in the automotive software development lifecycle by integrating with automotive test tools, it is possible for an automotive organization to remedy software vulnerabilities before the ECU software is released and used in production.

The main points of this chapter are the following.

- We provide an overview of automotive test tools with the focus on HIL systems that are typically used for functional testing of automotive systems.
- We discuss the common challenges of fuzzing automotive systems such as testing on standalone systems, lack of appropriate input to the target system and inability to properly monitor the target system for unexpected behavior.
- To overcome these challenges, we present a solution based on integrating a fuzz testing tool with an automotive test tool to improve and automate fuzz testing of automotive systems.

More details about improving and automating fuzz testing of automotive systems by integrating with automotive test tools are found in References [1–3].

8.1   Overview of HIL Systems

This section gives an introduction to how automotive test tools, with the focus on HIL systems, are used in the automotive software development lifecycle. Figure 8.1 shows a simplified automotive software development process based on the ASPICE (Automotive Software Process Improvement and Capability dEtermination) V-model [4].

HIL systems are typically used for functional testing of automotive systems. As depicted in Figure 8.1, functional testing occurs after implementation, generally once developed functionality is available for testing. It is typically the first form of testing before any other type of testing – such as security testing, including vulnerability scanning, fuzz testing and penetration testing – occurs.

There are numerous automotive HIL testing systems. The following gives a general overview of what such systems are and how they are used [5–8]. The main purpose of HIL systems is to help automotive organizations conduct functional testing of ECUs during the early phases of ECU development. This type of testing is generally known as

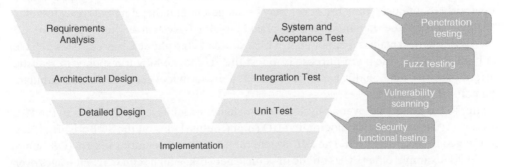

Figure 8.1   Simplified automotive software development process.

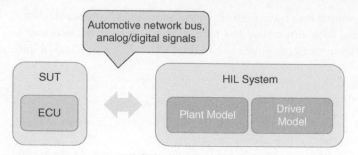

Figure 8.2 Generic overview of a HIL system test environment.

quality assurance (QA) testing, which helps to provide quality assurance of the developed functionality. Using HIL systems it is possible to perform testing of specific ECU functions and diagnostics functionality on ECUs in a simulated environment. The simulated environment provides the benefit of running comprehensive and reproducible tests of the SUT in various testable states. Because a simulated environment is used, it is possible to cover myriad test cases and test states, including test states that typically would endanger a driver or a vehicle. One can imagine testing the anti-lock braking system (ABS) functionality of a brake ECU during dangerous weather conditions such as icy or wet roads. Performing real tests on real roads would endanger the driver; however, using a HIL system it is possible to perform such testing in the comfort and safety of a test lab. A generic overview of a HIL system test environment is given in Figure 8.2.

The main features and functionalities of a HIL system test environment are as follows. The SUT is the real ECU under development, e.g. a prototype ECU, that is the target for testing. In a finished state, the ECU would be fitted in a vehicle, connected to other ECUs over in-vehicle network buses and potentially connected to various sensors and actuators to control physical aspects of the vehicle, e.g. fuel injection in the engine or opening a window. Examples of ECUs encompass more complex systems such as engine, transmission, and brake ECUs to more simple systems such as a door ECU, responsible for door lock and window control. To test the functionality of the ECU would normally require other ECUs in the vehicle to be functional and provide the appropriate input to the SUT, as well as require the physical peripherals such as an engine or a headlamp to which the SUT is connected via sensors and actuators. The typical challenges with such testing are that testing occurs late in the development lifecycle, since other ECUs and hardware peripherals are required and, as previously mentioned, some test states may be dangerous and therefore not easily testable.

To overcome these challenges, it is possible to use a HIL system as shown in Figure 8.2. The HIL system contains a plant model, which simulates the physical aspects of the vehicle and environment. The main purpose is to test the SUT to see how it responds to realistic virtual stimuli. Additionally, based on the SUT, a driver model could be used to simulate the behavior of a driver.

The SUT is connected over a physical in-vehicle network bus, e.g. a CAN bus to the HIL system. Additionally, the analog/digital I/O (input/output) pins on the SUT are physically connected to the HIL system. The HIL system runs a real-time operating system (OS) simulating, for example, other ECUs on the in-vehicle network, which send CAN messages over the physical CAN bus to the SUT. This is commonly known as *restbus simulation*, where the necessary in-vehicle network communication is simulated to ensure the SUT functions properly. Examples of such simulated CAN messages include wheel speeds and steering angle to an ABS brake ECU to test that the stability control is working properly. Moreover, the HIL system simulates various analog or digital inputs typically provided by sensors from virtual peripherals and provides such inputs to the SUT over the physical I/O pins connections. An example is the "ignition on" signal to an engine ECU, which is typically provided by a sensor once the key in the ignition is turned to start the vehicle. It is not only the HIL system providing input to the SUT, but also – in the opposite direction – the SUT provides input to the plant model in the HIL system. For example, the SUT sends CAN messages that are processed by the simulated ECUs in the HIL system. One example is a CAN message containing relevant data from an engine ECU SUT that is processed by a simulated transmission ECU in the HIL system to determine when to shift gears. Additionally, the SUT provides input to the plant model in the HIL system over analog or digital I/O pins. That is, the SUT provides analog or digital output to control an actuator, e.g. turn on or turn off a headlamp or lock or unlock a door. These analog or digital signals are interpreted by virtual peripherals in the plant model to perform the simulated behavior. To perform functional testing to verify the correct behavior of an SUT, e.g. that the SUT controls an actuator properly, it is necessary for the HIL system to measure these output signals from the SUT.

The HIL system test environment has a modular approach where simulated ECUs and peripherals can be gradually replaced with real ECUs and peripherals when available. For example, the test environment can contain a combination of real ECUs and real peripherals in addition to the virtual ECUs and virtual peripherals, as shown in Figure 8.3. In the end, it is imperative that the HIL system allows one to perform functional testing of the SUT in an environment which is, for all intents and purposes, no different from the real vehicle environment in which the SUT finally will be running.

Moreover, it is worth noting again that the HIL system test environment allows one to put the SUT in a larger number of testable states based on different input signals provided by the virtual ECUs and virtual peripherals in the HIL system, which allows for more automated and efficient testing. Thus, this test environment contributes to a larger test scope

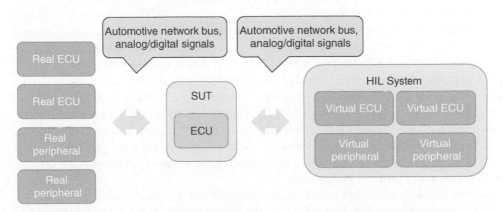

Figure 8.3 HIL system test environment with a combination of real and virtual ECUs and peripherals.

and improved quality of testing compared with performing testing in a standalone environment with just the SUT itself, which limits the number of testable states, or in a real vehicle, which occurs late in the develop lifecycle and can endanger the driver or have limited testable states. Thus, this test approach leads to cost and time savings.

In terms of the organizational structure within an automotive organization, HIL systems are typically used by QA teams, separate from the development teams, to test the functionality of ECUs in simulated environments. Moreover, security testing, including fuzz testing, is often performed by separate teams, namely security teams, who typically do not have access to HIL systems and instead often perform testing on standalone ECUs. This leads to several challenges that are presented in the next section.

8.2 Problem Statement: SUT Requires External Input and Monitoring

The focus is on testing in-vehicle automotive systems for robustness and detecting unexpected behavior on the SUT through fuzz testing. The unexpected behavior could be an indication of exploitable vulnerabilities in the SUT and therefore it is imperative for automotive organizations to perform fuzz testing as a systematic part of the software development lifecycle. However, there are numerous challenges regarding fuzz testing and detecting unexpected behavior on the SUT that are explained as follows. There are technical challenges due to the fact that ECUs and automotive network protocols have some inherent behavior that complicates the process of performing fuzz testing of such systems. Additionally, there are organizational challenges since fuzz testing is typically performed by security teams, who normally do not have access to HIL systems and instead perform fuzz testing on standalone ECUs, which often leads to inefficiencies and coverage issues.

First, from a technical standpoint, there are two main challenges by just sending fuzzed messages on the automotive network bus to the SUT and observing responses on the same bus from the SUT, which is typically how many fuzz testing tools work. As briefly mentioned in Section 8.1, testing an ECU typically requires putting the SUT in different testable states by providing various inputs to the SUT over the automotive network protocol, or providing electrical signals over analog or digital interfaces. If the SUT is not put in the correct testable states, the fuzzed messages may not reach the target application code. An example target is a specific function on the ECU that is only executable if certain other in-vehicle network messages are sent on the bus to the SUT. Specifically, one example is an automatic park function which requires in-vehicle network messages containing certain values, such as vehicle speed less than 7 km/h, and gear position in reverse [9] being sent to the SUT to allow the function to execute. These messages would typically be sent from other ECUs on the in-vehicle network. Therefore, to properly fuzz test the implementation of that function and to make sure the fuzzed messages reach the target application code requires that the SUT is put in the correct testable state by simulating the required vehicle speed and gear position messages from the HIL system.

Besides automotive network messages to enable different testable states on the SUT, some SUTs may also require certain analog or digital input signals to the ECU. For instance, to fuzz test the DoIP (Diagnostic communication over Internet Protocol) implementation requires putting the SUT in a state that allows DoIP functionality by enabling the DoIP activation line with a certain voltage on the DoIP activation pin [10].

Thus, the *first main technical challenge* is that lack of appropriate input to the SUT leads to not being able to put the SUT in correct testable states. If the SUT is not put in these testable states, there is a risk that large portions of the target software code go untested since the criteria to execute those functions are not fulfilled. Thus, a fuzz testing tool that simply generates and sends fuzzed messages over the automotive network bus may not be able to reach deeper areas of the message processing on the SUT.

The *second main technical challenge* is that, in many cases, ECUs on the in-vehicle network only receive and process messages without sending any replies on the automotive network bus such as CAN and CAN-FD. This is in contrast to how many IT protocols typically operate, such as the HTTP protocol where there are defined formats for responding to specific requests. For example, an SUT may only receive messages with certain values for the steering wheel angle or accelerator pedal position over the automotive network and process those values internally in various functions on the SUT. The results of those functions may lead to changing an internal state on the SUT or generating some output on the analog or digital interfaces. Regardless, there is no response on the automotive network bus based on the processing of the fuzzed messages. Thus, if an SUT only receives and processes fuzzed messages without sending any replies it is difficult to observe the behavior of the SUT by just monitoring the fuzzed protocol to detect any exceptions based on the fuzzed messages. Therefore, simply using a fuzz testing tool to send fuzzed messages to an SUT and just observing the same protocol being fuzzed may not allow one to properly capture unexpected behavior on the SUT. The SUT may be changing internal states or sending output signals to actuators to control various vehicle functionality such as turn on or off lights or lock or unlock doors. These activities are not visible on the automotive network bus as is, and may therefore lead to an incorrect assumption about the behavior of the SUT that it is more robust than it actually is and that it does not contain any vulnerabilities. To be able to detect these types of exceptions it may be possible to monitor the behavior of the ECU by physically measuring various analog/digital signals on the SUT. However, a challenge is that it may be unclear which analog/digital signals to monitor and what values to inspect to properly be able to determine whether there is an exception on the SUT.

Besides the technical challenges there are also three organizational-related challenges discussed here. The *first organizational challenge* is that fuzz testing typically occurs late in the development lifecycle and often lacks a proper test environment. Fuzz testing is generally performed by security teams at an organization or by external third party security teams after QA teams have finished the functional testing of the SUT. The purpose for fuzz testing the target system often covers both security testing and robustness testing. The focus for security testing is to uncover unknown vulnerabilities that could be exploited by attackers to cause serious safety or security impacts, whereas the focus for robustness testing is to ensure that the target system is able to survive being bombarded by a plethora of malformed input without any negative impact on performance, availability, and functionality. Since security teams typically do not have the same test environments as QA teams, they are often performing fuzz testing of the target system in a standalone environment. This restricted environment leads to the technical challenges mentioned above about lack of input to the SUT to put the target system in appropriate testable states, and the inability to properly detect exceptions on the SUT. There may be a few exceptions that can be detected in this restricted test environment which need to be analyzed and potentially fixed by the relevant development teams. However, since fuzz testing occurs late in the software development lifecycle and often as one of the last activities before product release, it is generally a challenge to be able to assign resources from the software development team to fix the identified issues in a timely manner since there may not be enough time before the final release. Thus, to sum up, the challenge is that fuzz testing occurs late in the development lifecycle and security teams performing fuzz testing lack proper test environments.

The *second organizational-related challenge* is regarding manual "fuzz testing" activities performed by QA teams. QA teams typically use HIL systems to perform functional testing of ECUs. As mentioned previously, HIL systems provide the required input, i.e. analog/digital signals, to the SUT to allow for testing of the SUT, and are able to monitor the SUT for exceptions. QA teams would typically define a large number of functional test cases related to the functionality on the SUT to test that the SUT functions properly. Additionally, the QA teams would define a few misuse cases or corner cases to verify that the SUT behaves correctly and is able to withstand some incorrect input. These misuse cases could be considered a simple form of fuzz test cases. Examples include messages where certain values exceed the acceptable defined values, and valid messages sent in out-of-order sequences. A common approach is that QA teams manually define the misuse cases, which is a cumbersome and time-consuming task. In other words, QA teams often perform some limited manual "fuzz testing." Although some of these misuse cases may be able to detect some exceptions in certain ECU functionality, there is typically not a deep focus on detecting software vulnerabilities, faulty implementations, or back doors, including hidden functionality on the SUT. Due to the time constraints to meet strict deadlines in automotive development, it is a challenge to ensure that enough misuse cases are defined by the QA teams and that the quality and coverage of the misuse cases are acceptable.

Furthermore, the *third organizational challenge* is regarding the process on how to define which target systems and protocols should be fuzzed and how much fuzz testing is required. For example, an automotive organization needs to define and follow a process for how to decide which target systems and which interfaces should be fuzzed and to what extent. In many cases fuzz testing occurs as a test activity performed by security teams without following any systematic process. This leads to some products going through more rigorous fuzz testing than other products. Generally speaking, high-risk target systems and high-risk interfaces should have a higher focus on fuzz testing. However, without following an established process, the challenge for an organization is that it may be difficult to ensure that high-risk products are properly tested using the appropriate level of fuzz testing. It may also lead to fuzz testing activities being misaligned where low-risk products receive more fuzz testing, relatively, than high-risk products. As a result, this gives the organization a false impression that the high-risk products are more secure and robust than they actually may be.

8.3   Solution: Integrating Fuzz Testing Tools with HIL Systems

This section discusses solutions to address the organizational and technical challenges presented in Section 8.2. To recap, there are three organizational-related challenges and two technical challenges. The organizational-related challenges are:

- fuzz testing often occurs late in the development lifecycle and often lacks a proper test environment,

- misuse cases, or in other words manual "fuzz testing," defined by QA teams is cumbersome and time-consuming, and
- lack of an established process for fuzz testing makes it harder to define what to fuzz and how much.

The two technical challenges for fuzz testing in-vehicle systems are:

- lack of additional input to SUT leads to not being able to put the SUT in correct testable states, and
- lack of monitoring capabilities leads to not being able to properly detect exceptions on the SUT.

Each of these challenges above are addressed by discussing appropriate solutions to overcome the challenges. To address the organizational-related challenges, changes to the workflow process are first described. Additionally, to address the technical challenges, two different test environments are presented that can be used to support different situations when fuzz testing in-vehicle systems.

To address the organizational-related challenges, it is required that the automotive organization establishes a workflow that includes the necessary activities for automated and effective fuzz testing. To address the first challenge of fuzz testing occurring late in the development lifecycle requires a change in the workflow process to move fuzz testing from being a separate activity performed by security teams occurring after functional testing to becoming a part of the functional testing activity. This *shift left* change is illustrated in Figure 8.4. The purpose of this approach is to perform fuzz testing as a natural step during the functional testing.

By shifting left in the V-model, fuzz testing occurs earlier in the automotive software development lifecycle, which allows an organization more time to handle any issues and exceptions found. Consequently, development teams would have more time to perform a deeper analysis to identify the root causes and fix the issues. By performing fuzz testing as part of QA activities, it also addresses the first challenge that fuzz testing lacks a proper test environment. During ECU development, QA teams typically perform functional testing using HIL systems. The HIL systems provide the necessary input signals to the ECUs to

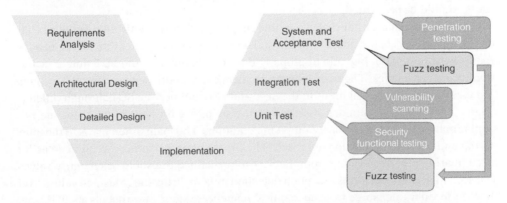

Figure 8.4 Shifting the fuzz testing activity left in the automotive software development process.

allow testing of the SUT in various states. QA teams are able to reuse their existing test environments, e.g. HIL systems, to also perform fuzz testing on the SUT in this environment. Because fuzz testing is then performed on the SUT in the "functional testing" test environment, the HIL system is able to provide the necessary input signals to the SUT to put it into various states that need to be tested. Moreover, the fuzz testing tool can be interconnected with the HIL system so that fuzz testing of the various states can be automated. Thus, a better test coverage of the target system can be achieved. This approach is preferable since it saves cost and time compared with security teams acquiring their own expensive test environments and requiring additional time to configure the test environments correctly. The use of a proper test environment also addresses the technical challenges described in more detail below. Moreover, moving the fuzz testing activity into the functional testing workflow also addresses the second challenge. That is, QA teams can use automated fuzz testing tools to automatically generate myriad malformed messages, or in other words "misuse cases," rather than performing the cumbersome activity of manually defining a limited set of misuse cases. This approach has the advantages of saving time and providing a greater test coverage due to the larger set of automatically generated misuse cases.

To address the third organizational-related challenge of lacking an established process for fuzz testing to help define what to fuzz and how much, it is suggested that automotive organizations establish a process where TARAs (threat analysis and risk analysis) are first performed on the target systems during the concept phase and the results used to define the level of fuzz testing required for the identified high-risk interfaces. As a result of performing a TARA, high-risk protocols and interfaces are identified. The TARA should be performed according to the defined activities steps in ISO/SAE DIS 21434 [11]. Section 2.3.3 provides a brief introduction to the TARA activity. Based on the TARA results it would then be possible for an organization to define how much fuzz testing should be performed for each of the high-risk interfaces identified. Section 2.4 briefly presents an example based on a combined approach of using Cybersecurity Assurance Levels (CALs) from ISO/SAE DIS 21434 and a Fuzz Testing Maturity Model [12] to define the level of fuzz testing required for the identified high-risk protocols. Therefore, it is imperative for an organization to establish a process where, for example, TARAs are first performed and the results from the TARAs focusing on high-risk interfaces are assigned CALs, where each CALs then defines how much fuzz testing should be performed.

Besides the organizational challenges, this chapter also addresses the two technical challenges, namely, not being able to put the SUT in proper testable states due to lack of additional input and not being able to properly detect exceptions on the SUT due to lack of monitoring capabilities. The two technical challenges are addressed by using HIL systems that can provide additional input to the SUT and also monitor the SUT through different means. Two different solutions based on HIL systems are presented which operate in a similar manner but are suitable for different conditions. The main difference is in the monitoring and exception detection approach. The first solution performs exception detection by comparing measured values from the SUT to predefined threshold or reference values. The second solution performs exception detection by comparing the measured values from the SUT to values measured from an identical reference system. More details about the two solutions are presented below.

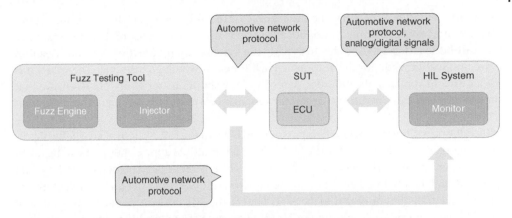

Figure 8.5 Overview of fuzz testing environment using a HIL system.

First, the common parts for the two solutions are described and then the differences in monitoring functionality are explained. The general setup of the test environment is illustrated in Figure 8.5 and presented as follows. There are three main components: *Fuzz Testing Tool*, *SUT*, and *HIL System*. The *Fuzz Testing Tool* contains the fuzz engine and injector to generate and send fuzzed messages over the automotive network protocol, e.g. CAN, to the SUT. The *SUT* is the target ECU for the fuzz testing and receives and processes the fuzzed messages from the Fuzz Testing Tool. The *HIL System* provides various input signals to the SUT, and also monitors and measures numerous values from the SUT to observe the ECU behavior based on its processing of the fuzzed messages. There are different methods that can be applied for monitoring the behavior of the target ECU. The HIL System can, for example, measure analog/digital output signals from the SUT as well as monitor the automotive network communication bus such as the CAN bus to observe messages sent to and from the SUT.

First, to enable the correct states of the SUT to allow fuzz testing to reach deeper in the message processing on the SUT and achieve better code coverage, the HIL System generates and provides the necessary analog/digital signals and automotive network communication to the SUT. For example, the SUT may require restbus simulation, i.e. communication from other ECUs to enable the correct states on the SUT. The restbus simulation can be realized by virtual ECUs running on the HIL System, which are generating and sending the necessary automotive network communication messages to the SUT. Moreover, it is possible to define several different test runs where the HIL System puts the SUT into various states while performing fuzz testing. A few examples are as follows: Test Run 1: ignition is Off, gear position is Park, vehicle speed is 0; Test Run 2: ignition is On, gear position is Reverse, vehicle speed is 5; Test Run 3: ignition is On, gear position is Drive, vehicle speed is 50, and so on. For the different test runs, the SUT may behave differently based on the input signals and the conditions. Remember that some ECU functionality may only be accessible if certain conditions are fulfilled. One example is the automatic park function mentioned earlier, which only executes if ignition is on, speed is less than 7 km/h, and gear position is in reverse [9]. To successfully fuzz test this function requires performing fuzz testing in Test Run 2. The same fuzzed messages in Test Run 1 and Test Run 3 would be rejected by the input validation function since the criteria for the automatic park function are not fulfilled. While testing the input validation function is still useful to ensure that only messages that fulfill the criteria will be able to execute the automatic park function, without Test Run 2 the application code for the automatic park function would go untested. Therefore, it is imperative to consider the different states the SUT should be tested in and to ensure that the HIL System can provide the necessary signals to perform fuzz testing in these different test runs.

Besides providing the necessary input to the SUT from the HIL System, it is equally important to consider how to monitor the SUT. There are multiple approaches that can be taken regarding monitoring the behavior of the SUT. As briefly mentioned before, the HIL System can monitor the analog/digital output signals from the SUT and the automotive network communication bus connected to the SUT. That is, the HIL System connects physically and directly using wires and cables to the I/O pins on the SUT to be able to measure the analog/digital output signals. Additionally, the HIL System physically connects to the same automotive network bus, e.g. CAN bus, as the SUT. This is a general setup that should be similar to the functional testing environment normally used for the SUT.

The first fuzz testing solution is based on this general setup and shows how analog/digital signals from the SUT as well as the CAN communication can be monitored during fuzz testing. While the SUT is subjected to fuzzed messages, all the measured and monitored values are compared with predefined reference or threshold values to detect exceptions on the SUT [1]. This solution is described in more detail in Section 8.3.1.

The second fuzz testing solution is based on the HIL System monitoring and comparing two identical target systems that are operated in parallel to detect any exceptions. One of the target systems is the SUT that processes the fuzzed messages, and the other target system is a reference system that does not receive any of the fuzzed messages. The HIL System then compares the behaviors of both target systems to detect if there is any effect of the fuzzed messages on the SUT [3]. This approach of using duplicate target systems makes exception detection fairly easy since it avoids the need to define a number of different reference and threshold values in advance. These reference and threshold values would typically be used for comparison with the measured values as in the first solution. However, for the second solution, the measured values from the SUT are compared with measured values from the duplicate target system acting as a reference system. The second solution extends the general setup and shows how analog/digital signals from two target systems as well as the CAN communication can be monitored and compared during fuzz testing. This solution is described in more detail in Section 8.3.2.

For additional references, there are more examples of monitoring approaches and they are described as follows. These approaches would be applicable to both solutions presented above. The first example is to directly *monitor the memory* of the ECU using debug port access. Using such access through, for example, an ETK interface [13] on an ECU, it is possible to read the runtime memory of the ECU. As a result, it is possible to monitor specific values in predefined memory addresses of the SUT while performing fuzz testing of the SUT. By comparing the monitored values to reference values, it is possible to detect any discrepancies. These reference values can be predefined or can be read from a duplicate target system. Thus, this monitoring approach is able to detect if any important variables or specific values, e.g. controller states, in memory are overwritten due to processing of the fuzzed messages.

Thus, it may be possible to detect buffer overflow vulnerabilities using this monitoring approach. The debug port access is typically closed on production ECUs and therefore fuzz testing using this approach should be performed earlier in the development lifecycle.

Another example is an approach based on visual monitoring of the SUT [14]. For example, if the output from the SUT is used to display something or is shown using indicators, e.g. the SUT controls an instrument cluster, it is possible for the HIL System to perform *visual monitoring*. As an example, the HIL System can use a video camera to record the instrument cluster and compare visual cues of the instrument cluster in the video stream to specific reference patterns. It would then be possible to detect contradicting patterns, such as the Gear position indicator displaying both Park and Drive at the same time. Reusing, for example, conditions from functional testing on correct behavior to define parameters for the visual cues in the HIL System, it would be possible to detect such exceptions automatically. Moreover, it is also possible to use a duplicate target system and perform a visual comparison between the SUT and the reference system to detect any discrepancies in an automated fashion.

8.3.1 White-Box Approach for Fuzz Testing Using HIL System

This section presents a setup for a fuzz testing environment using a HIL system and is based on Reference [1]. In particular, the solution shows how analog/digital signals from the SUT as well as the automotive network communication can be monitored to identify exceptions on the SUT during fuzz testing. This test setup is based on a *white-box approach* for fuzz testing using a HIL system and is illustrated in Figure 8.6. The numbers in the figure indicate the procedure steps and are explained by the swimlane diagram in Figure 8.7.

As mentioned before, there are three main parts: *Fuzz Testing Tool*, *SUT*, and *HIL System*. These parts provide the basis for fuzz testing of the SUT, putting the SUT into different testable states and monitoring the SUT. However, there are two additional components that are required to properly perform fuzz testing. These components are called the *Comparison Module* and *Feedback Loop*. The *Comparison Module* is running on the HIL System and

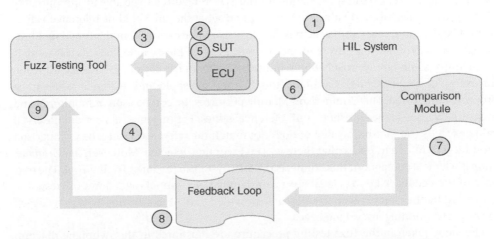

Figure 8.6 White-box approach for fuzz testing using a HIL system Source: Based on [1].

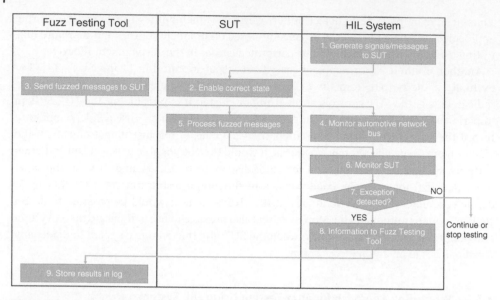

Figure 8.7 Swimlane diagram of the white-box approach fuzz testing procedure showing the interaction between the different parts.

uses the measured and monitored values from the SUT to determine whether there is unexpected behavior on the SUT based on processing the fuzzed messages. There are different methods that can be used for detecting exceptions on the SUT. For example, it is possible to compare the monitored and measured values to certain predefined *threshold* or *reference values*. Examples of *threshold values* are specific voltage values on the analog output pins, frequencies in how fast certain values in analog/digital outputs can change, and how often certain messages can be sent on the CAN bus. Examples of *reference values* are controller states in memory, certain security-critical values in memory such as checksums and parameters, and specific CAN IDs that should be sent periodically by the SUT on the CAN bus. Typically, access to the specification for the SUT is required to be able to appropriately identify which signals and values to monitor and what the threshold or reference values should be. In some cases, it may be possible to reuse information from the functional testing test cases to define the threshold and reference values. Please note that this test setup is following a white-box approach where information about the correct ECU behavior from, for example, specifications, is available to allow the threshold and reference values to be properly configured. The Comparison Module performs the comparison of monitored and measured values to the threshold and reference values. For instance, if a certain observed value exceeds the threshold value or does not match the reference value, the Comparison Module generates a response that there was an exception detected. Moreover, the *Feedback Loop* is a logical component that connects the HIL System to the Fuzz Testing Tool. The purpose of the Feedback Loop is to create a communication channel that allows the response generated by the Comparison Module to be provided to the Fuzz Testing Tool as feedback to the corresponding fuzzed messages.

The steps taken in the fuzz testing procedure are illustrated in the swimlane diagram shown in Figure 8.7. Each step in the procedure is numbered accordingly. Moreover, the same numbers are used in Figure 8.6 to visually indicate where each step in the procedure takes place in the test environment.

The procedure in Figure 8.7 is described as follows. First, the HIL System generates the analog/digital signals and relevant automotive network messages, e.g. CAN bus messages, to the SUT to enable the correct state for fuzz testing in Step 1. Based on these input signals, the SUT enables the correct state for testing in Step 2. In Step 3, the Fuzz Testing Tool transmits the fuzzed messages over the automotive network communication bus to the SUT. The HIL System also monitors this communication bus in Step 4 so that it knows what fuzzed messages are sent to the SUT in Step 3. Next, in Step 5, the SUT processes the fuzzed messages sent by the Fuzz Testing Tool. The HIL System uses various monitoring capabilities to monitor the SUT in Step 6, e.g. measuring the analog/digital output signals on the SUT. The Comparison Module then compares the monitored and measured values to predefined threshold or reference values and determines whether there is an exception detected or not in Step 7. That is, if an observed value exceeds the threshold value or is not a match to the reference value, the Comparison Module determines that an exception has occurred. This step contains a conditional branch where if no exception is detected, the testing procedure then continues or stops depending on the current progress of the test run. If a certain number of test cases have been executed or fuzz testing has progressed over a certain time, and consequently no more testing is required, the test procedure will stop. If that is not the case, the test run will continue with the next fuzzed message. If in Step 7, an exception is detected, the Comparison Module provides additional information about the exception, e.g. what the measured and monitored values were at the time of the exception as well as what the corresponding threshold and reference values are, over the Feedback Loop to the Fuzz Testing Tool in Step 8. Last, in Step 9, the Fuzz Testing Tool stores the relevant information received from the HIL System in a log file for the corresponding fuzz test case.

The purpose with the additional information passed through the Feedback Loop is to gain a better understanding of which fuzzed messages caused what type of abnormal behavior. For instance, the feedback may include which fuzzed messages were received by the SUT when the exception occurred, the current state, e.g. the test state of the SUT, what the exception was, i.e. which specific monitored values exceeded the threshold values or did not match the reference values, as well as what the corresponding threshold/reference values are. The feedback received by the Fuzz Testing Tool may also be displayed in a warning or error screen to the user to indicate that an exception occurred. This type of information would also be extremely useful for the ECU software developers to help analyze and better understand the root cause of the issues. It would also help to determine whether the exceptions could lead to any potential security issues, and in such cases the developers should use the feedback information to help remedy the security issues.

8.3.1.1 Example Test Setup Using an Engine ECU

This section gives a detailed description of an example test setup using an engine ECU as the SUT and is based on Reference [1]. First, the normal use case and the test environment typically used for functional testing of the engine ECU is presented to understand how the system would typically work. Then, by adding the Fuzz Testing Tool, Comparison Module and Feedback Loop, an example setup for this fuzz testing environment for the same system is presented in Section 8.3.1.2.

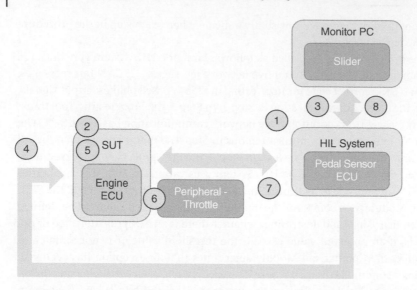

Figure 8.8 Overview of the test setup for the normal use case of Engine ECU Source: Based on [1].

The test setup for the normal use case is depicted in Figure 8.8. Please note that this use case has been simplified for illustrative purposes. There are four main parts: the *Monitor PC*, the physical *Engine ECU*, which is used as the SUT, a physical *throttle peripheral*, and the *HIL System*. The *Monitor PC* and the *HIL System* are connected over Ethernet. The *Engine ECU* and the HIL System are connected over a CAN bus and analog/digital I/O pins. Additionally, the Engine ECU is physically connected over analog/digital pins to the *throttle peripheral*, which opens and closes based on the electrical output signals from the Engine ECU.

The normal use case is described as follows. A virtual ECU running on the HIL System called the Pedal Sensor ECU senses the accelerator pedal angle, which is a value defined by a slider on the Monitor PC, and sends the value over the CAN bus to the Engine ECU. The Engine ECU processes the CAN message and, based on the accelerator pedal angle value, it provides a digital output to adjust the PWM (pulse-width modulation) frequency of the throttle.

The numbers in the figure indicate the procedure steps and are explained as follows. In Step 1, the HIL System provides the necessary analog/digital signals and automotive network messages to the Engine ECU to enable the correct state for testing. Based on the input signals from the HIL System, the Engine ECU enables the correct state for testing in Step 2. In Step 3, the Monitor PC, which is connected over Ethernet to the HIL System, controls the accelerator pedal position. In a graphical interface on the Monitor PC, there is a slider that simulates the pedal position which can be moved in real-time during testing to simulate the driver pressing the accelerator pedal. The Pedal Sensor ECU, which is a virtual ECU running on the HIL System, detects the pedal position by continuously monitoring the slider position on the Monitor PC. The pedal position is a value between 0 and 120 and is limited by the physical maximum angle of a real pedal. This pedal position value is sent from the Pedal Sensor ECU on the HIL System to the Engine ECU over the CAN bus using the CAN ID 0x350 in Step 4. Next, in Step 5, the Engine ECU processes the received CAN messages. The Engine ECU knows that the first byte of the message using CAN ID 0x350 indicates the pedal position value. This byte should normally be between 0x00 and 0x78, which is the same as the maximum decimal value 120. Based on the received value, the Engine ECU controls the throttle by providing signals to update the PWM frequency in Step 6. Part of the logic in the Engine ECU multiplies the received value in the CAN message by 10, resulting in a value between 0 and 1200 Hz, before providing the output signals to control the throttle. Then, in Step 7, the analog/digital output signals from the Engine ECU are measured by the HIL System. These values can help identify whether the Engine ECU is properly functioning and correctly controlling the throttle. Last, in Step 8, the measured values from the SUT are displayed in a graphical interface on the Monitor PC to help visualize the comparison of the measured values to the threshold values. The PWM frequency output by the SUT during the typical use case measured by the HIL System and displayed in the Monitor PC graphical interface is shown in Figure 8.10 later. During normal behavior, the pedal angle value is physically limited to 120, which is the maximum physical pedal angle represented by the maximum position value of the slider in the top of the figure. The corresponding measured PWM frequency value based on the pedal angle is below the threshold value indicated by the thick horizontal line in the middle of the graph in the bottom part of the figure.

Let's imagine there is a weakness or a software development mistake in the Engine ECU. For example, the Engine ECU does not verify whether the first byte value received in the CAN message with CAN ID 0x350 exceeds the value of 0x78. If the Pedal Sensor ECU is correctly implemented it should only be able to send CAN messages with byte values between 0x00 and 0x78 for CAN ID 0x350, and therefore an incorrect assumption that the Engine ECU would not have to consider any other values might have been made. However, an attacker-controlled ECU or device may be able to send arbitrary CAN messages, including values exceeding 0x78 in the first byte of messages with CAN ID 0x350.

Therefore, to illustrate how a fuzz testing setup can be used to detect these types of software mistakes or weaknesses, there is an intentional software mistake included on the Engine ECU in this experiment. Thus, the Engine ECU does not verify whether the first byte in the CAN ID 0x350 messages exceeds the value of 0x78.

8.3.1.2 Fuzz Testing Setup for the Engine ECU
The complete fuzz testing environment for the Engine ECU is depicted in Figure 8.9. There are seven main parts, of which four are the same from the normal use case and functional test environment, namely, the *Monitor PC*, the physical *Engine ECU* which acts as the SUT, a physical *throttle peripheral*, and the *HIL System*. However, please note that the Pedal Sensor ECU which was a virtual ECU running on the HIL System in the previous setup is not present in the fuzz testing environment as it is not required. Please also note that the peripheral connected to the SUT, in this case the throttle connected to the Engine ECU, is optional but useful to visually inspect the behavior of the SUT. The three new parts are the *Fuzz Testing Tool*, *Comparison Module*, and *Feedback Loop*. The *Fuzz Testing Tool* is connected over CAN to the SUT and will play the role of "faulty" Pedal Sensor ECU generating malformed messages. The same CAN bus is also connected to the HIL System. Moreover, the *Comparison Module* is a software module running on the HIL System. It specifically compares the

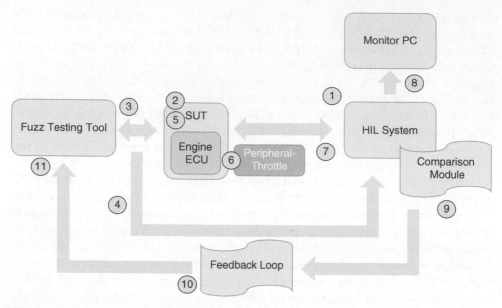

Figure 8.9 Fuzz testing environment for the Engine ECU Source: Based on [1].

measured PWM signal values that are output from the SUT to control the throttle and compares with threshold values to determine whether there is any abnormal behavior on the SUT based on processing the fuzzed messages. Finally, the *Feedback Loop* is implemented as a communication channel over Ethernet between the HIL System and the Fuzz Testing Tool and is used to provide feedback about exceptions to the Fuzz Testing Tool, where the information is stored in a log.

The numbers in the figure indicate the procedure steps and are explained as follows. In Step 1, the HIL System provides the required input signals to the SUT which enables the correct states for testing in Step 2. Then, the Fuzz Testing Tool generates and sends fuzzed CAN messages to the SUT in Step 3. The fuzzed messages are using the same CAN ID (0x350) as the Pedal Sensor ECU to specifically target the logic in the SUT that handles the processing of messages from the Pedal Sensor ECU. The purpose is to see how the SUT behaves based on these malformed input messages generated by the Fuzz Testing Tool. In the fuzzed CAN messages, the first byte could be of any value between 0x00 and 0xFF. In Step 4, the HIL System monitors the same CAN bus connected to the SUT and the Fuzz Testing Tool and therefore also receives the fuzzed CAN messages from the Fuzz Testing Tool. The HIL System does not process the messages but rather just records them in a log file. The purpose is to later be able to match which fuzzed CAN message caused a certain behavior on the SUT. Next, the SUT processes the fuzzed messages in Step 5. Since the fuzzed messages use the same CAN ID as the Pedal Sensor ECU, the SUT processes the messages in the same manner as if the real Pedal Sensor ECU had sent the messages. Based on processing the messages, the SUT changes the value of the PWM frequency according to the value in the first byte, which normally should be between 0x00 and 0x78 as previously explained. However, the fuzzed messages may contain a value up to 0xFF in the first byte. Therefore, a message with a value higher than 0x78 will cause the SUT to change the PWM frequency to a value that

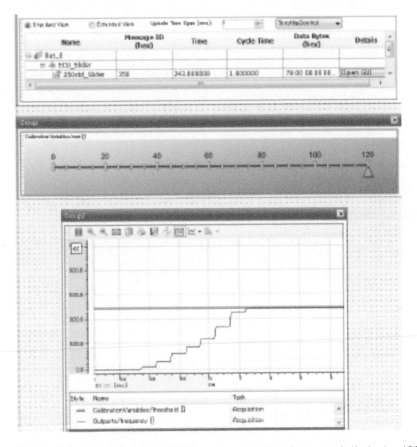

Figure 8.10 Normal Engine ECU behavior where PWM frequency is limited to 1200 Hz (thick horizontal line). Sources: [2, 15]. Reproduced with permission from IEICE, ESCRYPT GmbH, ETAS GmbH.

exceeds the typical maximum value. Then, in Step 6, similar to the normal use case, the SUT controls the throttle by outputting signals to adjust the PWM frequency. If the SUT receives a message with a value higher than 0x78, it will control the throttle to move in an abnormal way since it exceeds the typical maximum value for normal behavior. It is possible to visibly observe the abnormal throttle behavior. At the same time, in Step 7, the HIL System measures the PWM output signals sent from the SUT to the throttle. In Step 8, the Monitor PC, which provides a graphical interface to the HIL System, helps to visualize the monitoring capabilities and displays the comparison of measured values to threshold values. Please note that the Monitor PC is not an essential part of the fuzz testing environment but is useful to help understand how the measurements and comparison of measured signals work. Similar to Figure 8.10 which shows the measured signals during the normal use case, Figure 8.11 shows the PWM frequency output by the SUT measured by the HIL System during fuzz testing. As can be understood from the graphical representation of the PWM frequency signal, some measured values exceed the threshold value indicated by the thick horizontal line in the middle of the graph in the bottom part of the figure. Next, in Step 9, the Comparison

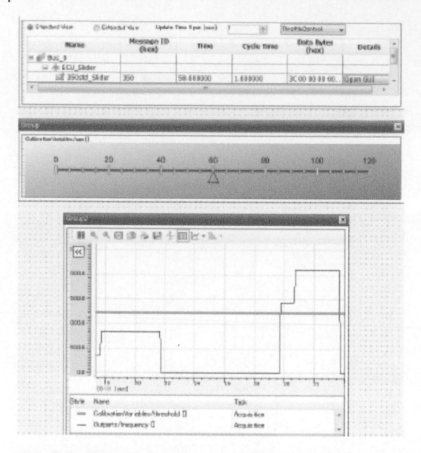

Figure 8.11 Effect of Engine ECU processing fuzzed message causing abnormal behavior where PWM frequency exceeds 1200 Hz (thick horizontal line). Sources: [2, 15]. Reproduced with permission from IEICE, ESCRYPT GmbH, ETAS GmbH.

Module compares the measured values to threshold values to detect any invalid values exceeding the maximum allowed values. In this case, a threshold value of a maximum of 1200 Hz for the PWM signal is defined. Please note that threshold values or reference values would need to be individually defined in advance based on the specific behavior and characteristics of the SUT. For example, it may be possible to use ECU specifications or test cases defined in the functional testing to help identify the threshold and reference values for fuzz testing. In this case, we know that the SUT should receive a value between 0 and 120 from the Pedal Sensor ECU and multiply the received value by 10 and therefore output a value between 0 and 1200 Hz to the throttle. One can imagine that this type of information is defined in the ECU specifications. Therefore, the PWM value should not exceed 1200 Hz. Thus, 1200 Hz is used as the threshold value as indicated by the thick horizontal lines in Figures 8.10 and 8.11. If the Comparison Module detects that a certain measured signal exceeds the threshold value, it determines that an exception has occurred. In such a case, in Step 10, feedback about the exception is provided to the Fuzz Testing Tool over the Feedback Loop. In this setup, information about the exception is provided in a syslog message.

The syslog message contains which fuzzed CAN message caused the exception, which is determined by the HIL System logging the CAN messages in Step 4, the measured PWM frequency, which is determined by measuring the signals in Step 7, and the threshold frequency, which is predefined in the Comparison Module and used in Step 9. This feedback is logged in the Fuzz Testing Tool in Step 11 and can later be used by developers to reproduce and analyze the issue in order to help identify the root cause and fix the issue.

8.3.1.3 Fuzz Testing Setup Considerations

One important consideration about this fuzz testing environment is how to configure the Comparison Module used in Step 9 in Figure 8.9. The Comparison Module plays an integral role in detecting exceptions on the SUT. If the Comparison Module is not adequately configured, there is a risk that several abnormal behaviors on the SUT go undetected. Therefore, it is imperative to have a clear idea on how to configure the Comparison Module. Moreover, configuring the Comparison Module may be a time-consuming task depending on the complexity of the SUT. There are various approaches that can be taken to automate or reduce the required workload that should be considered. For instance, it may be possible to reuse test specifications and configurations with already correctly defined threshold and reference values from the functional testing activity. Furthermore, to reduce the time and cost to build specific fuzz testing environments targeting each SUT, considerations on how to make the test environment general should be made. The idea is to build upon existing test environments that are already used for functional testing, similar to what is shown in Figure 8.8, and then add the corresponding parts needed for fuzz testing as illustrated in Figure 8.9, in order to reuse as much as possible of existing test environments. Although many parts of the test environment can be reused, the Comparison Module needs to be uniquely configured for the specific SUT. It is worthwhile investigating how to establish a process on how to reuse any configuration from the functional testing activity for the fuzz testing activity. Moreover, it is important to consider how to verify the configuration of the Comparison Module to ensure trust in the test results. For the sake of comparison, it is possible to consider that the configuration of the Comparison Module is similar to the configuration of an intrusion detection system. Both of these systems monitor certain functionality or the behavior of a target, and typically compare the monitored behavior with some types of rules or configuration of normal or acceptable behavior. If there is a mismatch, in both the Comparison Module and the intrusion detection case, there is an exception detected. It is important to note that, in both cases, the system is only as good as the detection rules or the configuration that has been defined. Therefore, since the Comparison Module plays an integral part of this solution, careful consideration must be taken when defining the configuration to ensure that exceptions and abnormal behavior can be detected.

Using this fuzz testing setup with a HIL System to monitor the behavior of the SUT, it is possible to detect software mistakes on the ECU that can cause abnormal behavior of the ECU functionality and the peripherals that the ECU controls based on processing certain received fuzzed CAN messages. In many cases, the abnormal behavior is not detectable over the CAN bus. Therefore, without the additional monitoring capabilities provided by the HIL System, it would not be possible to detect these issues. It is important to note that software vulnerabilities that can lead to abnormal ECU behavior, especially that can cause abnormal behavior of the peripherals that the ECU controls, could have serious consequences including impacts on safety. An example is a software mistake on an airbag ECU where a certain fuzzed CAN message may trigger the airbag functionality. If the airbag is triggered at an unexpected time it may cause physical damage to the driver or passenger. Therefore, conducting fuzz testing of these ECUs in a proper fuzz testing environment where such exceptions can be detected is imperative.

Furthermore, this fuzz testing environment may also be used to allow *feedback-based fuzzing*, as briefly introduced in Section 7.3.3. Feedback-based fuzzing is an approach where, based on which parts of the software are tested during a fuzz test, the monitoring function provides feedback to the fuzz engine on what type of fuzzed input should be generated next to be able to reach deeper into the message processing on the target system. In the presented fuzz test environment in Figure 8.9, the Feedback Loop can be used to provide this type of feedback to the Fuzz Testing Tool. To achieve feedback-based fuzzing, the Fuzz Testing Tool needs to know how to adjust its parameters for generating and sending the next fuzzed messages. This type of configuration must be done in advance and, in some cases, may need to be specific to the SUT. However, this is an area that requires further exploration and there may also be possibilities to use machine learning to effectively achieve feedback-based fuzzing. Based on the detected ECU behavior from previous fuzzed messages and feedback from the HIL System, the goal is for the Fuzz Testing Tool to generate fuzzed messages more effectively to achieve better code coverage, i.e. achieving a greater coverage of code on the SUT that is executed based on the fuzzed messages. Consider the following example scenario. Initially, the Fuzz Testing Tool sends a number of fuzzed messages with random CAN IDs to the SUT. The HIL System detects some exceptions on the SUT based on the processing of messages for one specific CAN ID and provides the feedback to the Fuzz Testing Tool through the Feedback Loop. Based on this feedback, the Fuzz Testing Tool adjusts its parameters to focus testing on that specific CAN ID. That is, the Fuzz Testing Tool generates a number of fuzzed messages with fuzzed data in the payload but with a fixed CAN ID. As a result, the HIL System may be able to detect exceptions on the SUT based on processing fuzzed payloads for the specific CAN ID. Since fuzz testing is now targeted on that specific CAN ID, any exceptions found by this fuzz testing approach would be found much faster than if the fuzz testing would not use any feedback from the SUT to adjust its parameters.

8.3.2 Black-Box Approach for Fuzz Testing Using HIL System

This section presents a setup for a fuzz testing environment based on a HIL system monitoring two identical target systems operated in parallel, based on Reference [3]. This setup overcomes the major challenge with the previously presented fuzz testing setup in Section 8.3.1, which is how to configure the Comparison Module in an efficient and effective manner. This test setup follows a *black-box approach* for fuzz testing using a HIL system and is illustrated in Figure 8.12. The numbers in the figure indicate the procedure steps and are explained by the swimlane diagram in Figure 8.13.

This test setup contains six main parts, of which five parts are similar to the test set up in Figure 8.6. Among the similar parts are the *Fuzz Testing Tool*, the *SUT*, the *HIL System*, the *Comparison Module*, and the *Feedback Loop*. The only new part is a *Reference System*, which is a duplicate of the SUT.

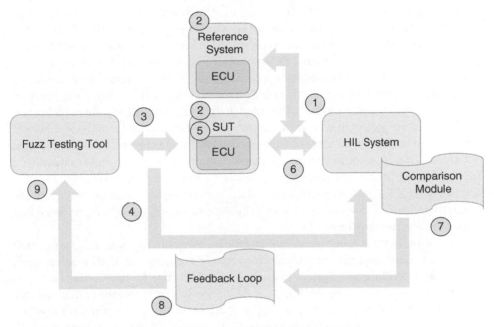

Figure 8.12 Black-box approach for fuzz testing using a HIL system.

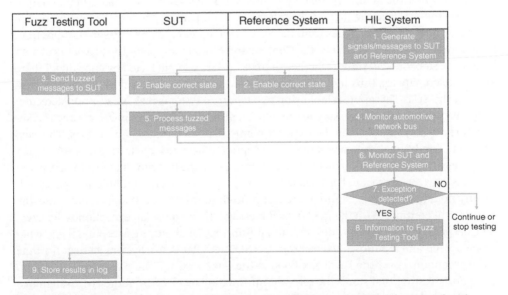

Figure 8.13 Swimlane diagram of the black-box approach fuzz testing procedure showing the interaction between the different parts Source: Adapted from [3]. © 2018 Nagoya University, © 2018 dSPACE, Portions Copyright 2018 Synopsys, Inc. Used with permission. All rights reserved.

This test approach also builds on reusing the existing functional test environment. In a black-box approach for fuzz testing, it may not be possible to define the threshold and reference values for the Comparison Module, as presented in Section 8.3.1, since the information or specification regarding the normal ECU behavior may not be available. In such a case, the test setup in Section 8.3.1 may not be applicable. Instead, the test setup presented in this section would be more suitable. The idea is that the two identical systems are operated in parallel, where one system is the SUT connected to the Fuzz Testing Tool, and the other system is the *Reference System* that is *not* connected to the Fuzz Testing Tool. The HIL System is connected to both the SUT and the Reference System and measures the analog/digital output signals as well as the automotive network communication from these systems.

The steps taken in the fuzz testing procedure are illustrated in the swimlane diagram shown in Figure 8.13. Each step in the procedure is numbered accordingly. Moreover, the same numbers are used in Figure 8.12 to visually indicate where each step in the procedure takes place in the test environment.

The procedure in the figure is described as follows. First, the HIL System generates the analog/digital signals and relevant automotive network messages, e.g. CAN bus messages, to the SUT and the Reference System to enable the correct state for fuzz testing in Step 1. Based on these input signals, the SUT and the Reference System enable the correct state for testing in Step 2. In Step 3, the Fuzz Testing Tool transmits the fuzzed messages over the automotive network communication bus to the SUT but not the Reference System. The HIL System also monitors this communication bus in Step 4 so that it knows what fuzzed messages are sent to the SUT in Step 3. Next, in Step 5, the SUT processes the fuzzed messages sent by the Fuzz Testing Tool. The HIL System uses various monitoring capabilities to monitor the SUT and the Reference System in Step 6, e.g. measuring the analog/digital output signals on the SUT and the Reference System. The Comparison Module then compares the monitored and measured values from the SUT to the monitored and measured values from the Reference System. Essentially, the Comparison Module compares the behaviors of both systems in Step 7 to determine whether there is an exception detected by checking if there are any discrepancies, thus indicating that there was an effect caused by the fuzzed messages on the SUT. This approach of using two identical systems makes exception detection fairly easy since it is not necessary to predefine a number of different reference and threshold values that typically would be used for comparison to the measured values. This step contains a conditional branch where, if no exception is detected, the testing procedure then continues or stops depending on the current progress of the test run. If a certain number of test cases have been executed or fuzz testing has progressed over a certain time, and consequently no more testing is required, the test procedure will stop. If that is not the case, the test run will continue with the next fuzzed message. If, in Step 7, an exception is detected, the Comparison Module provides additional information about the exception – e.g. what the measured and monitored values from the SUT and Reference System were at the time of the exception – over the Feedback Loop to the Fuzz Testing Tool in Step 8. Last, in Step 9, the Fuzz Testing Tool stores the relevant information received from the HIL System in a log file for the corresponding fuzz test case.

8.3.2.1 Example Target System Setup Using Engine and Body Control Modules

This section gives a detailed description of an example test setup using engine and body control modules as the SUT and is based on Reference [3]. The example test setup has been modified to align with the test setup described in Reference [1] for the sake of uniformity.

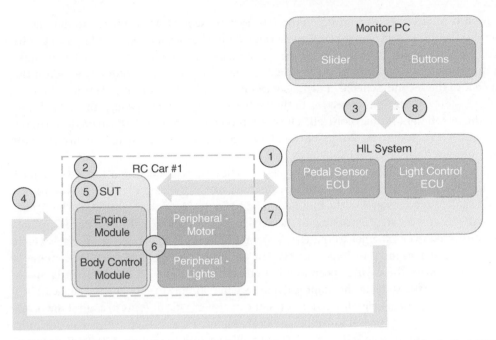

Figure 8.14 Overview of the test setup for the normal use case for the Engine and Body Control Modules.

The purpose of this test setup is to show how the target system typically works in a normal use case. First, the test setup for the normal use case is presented in this section and then the corresponding fuzz testing environment for this target system is presented in Section 8.3.2.2.

The test setup for the normal use case is illustrated in Figure 8.14. Please note that this use case has been simplified for illustrative purposes. There are four main parts: the SUT containing the *Engine and Body Control Modules*, physical *peripherals*, the *HIL System* and the *Monitor PC*.

In this example, rather than a real vehicle, to simulate a realistic environment for in-vehicle systems, components for a radio controlled (RC) car are used. The RC car has several functions, such as controls for motor and lights. The motor and lights are *peripherals* that are physical components controlled by the *Engine and Body Control Modules*, which are part of the SUT. The peripherals are connected over analog/digital signals to the Engine and Body Control Modules. In this case, the SUT and connected peripherals are part of RC Car #1. The Engine and Body Control Modules are based on RH850/F1L microcontrollers [16]. These microcontrollers are connected over a CAN bus. The Engine Module controls the motor, e.g. the speed of the RC car. The Body Control Module controls the lights, e.g. turns on and off the headlamps. The software on the microcontrollers is based on AUTOSAR [17] and is running TOPPERS/ATK2 [18] as the real-time OS, and the application code for the specific functionality to control the peripherals is implemented as AUTOSAR software components (SW-C) on top. CAN messages are used to control the functionality provided by the Engine and Body Control Modules. The Engine and Body Control Modules and the *HIL System* are connected over a CAN bus and analog/digital I/O pins. The *Monitor PC* and the HIL System are connected over Ethernet. Two examples of normal use cases are described as follows. In the first example, a Pedal Sensor ECU, which is a virtual ECU running on the HIL System, sends CAN messages to the Engine Module with the accelerator pedal angle value defined by a slider on the Monitor PC. The Engine Module processes the CAN messages and, based on the values received, it provides a digital output to adjust the PWM signal to control the motor accordingly to adjust the speed. In the second example, a Light Control ECU, which is a virtual ECU running on the HIL System, sends CAN messages to the Body Control Module to adjust the lights based on the on/off light settings controlled by buttons on the Monitor PC. Based on the contents of the CAN messages, the Body Control Module provides electrical signals to turn on or off the relevant lights, e.g. the headlamps.

The numbers in Figure 8.14 indicate the procedure steps for operation and are explained as follows. In Step 1, the HIL System provides the necessary analog/digital signals and automotive network messages to the Engine and Body Control Modules on the SUT. The signals enable the correct state for testing of the SUT in Step 2. In Step 3, the Monitor PC, which is connected over Ethernet to the HIL System, provides a graphical user interface which allows a tester to input various controls. For example, the graphical interface contains a slider to control the engine speed and buttons to turn on and off the different lights. A tester can use the slider in the graphical interface in real-time to simulate the behavior of a driver pressing the accelerator pedal. A tester can also use the buttons to control the headlamps, blinkers, fog lamps, tail lamps, and brake lamps. Then, in Step 4, based on the input from the Monitor PC, the HIL System accordingly transmits the appropriate CAN messages to the Engine and Body Control Modules. CAN ID 0x130 is used for messages to send the accelerator pedal angle value, and are received by the Engine Module. CAN ID 0x120 is used for messages to control the lights, and are received by the Body Control Module. This message contains the values for all the lights, e.g. headlamps, blinkers, fog lamps, tail lamps, and brake lamps, indicated by the respective bit positions of the message. The Engine and Body Control Modules process the received CAN messages in Step 5. Based on the values of the received CAN messages, the Engine and Body Control Modules generate the appropriate electrical signals to control the respective peripherals in Step 6. Next, in Step 7, the HIL System measures the output signals from the Engine and Body Control Modules. Last, in Step 8, the Monitor PC shows the measured values from the Engine and Body Control Modules in a graphical interface on the Monitor PC. The values displayed in the Monitor PC can help verify the correct functionality of the Engine and Body Control Modules.

We can imagine similar weaknesses or software development mistakes on the Engine and Body Control Modules as presented in Section 8.3.1.1. That is, proper input validation is not performed on the values of the received CAN messages. For the Engine Module, for example, a value indicating the accelerator pedal position that exceeds a maximum value may cause abnormal behavior. For the Body Control Module, for example, which lights to turn on and off may be indicated by the values at different bit positions in a CAN message. Subsequently, a message with invalid values for which lights to turn on or off – for instance, values set on reserved bits – may cause abnormal behavior on the Body Control Module. Additionally, let's imagine that there is some hidden functionality or perhaps a debug or maintenance function that in this case turns on or off all the lights. Even though the Pedal Sensor ECU and Light Control ECU may be implemented correctly and would not send any invalid messages to the Engine and Body Control Modules, an attacker-controlled device on the CAN bus may be able to send arbitrary CAN messages and could therefore potentially exploit software development mistakes or trigger hidden functionality.

Thus, to show how a fuzz testing setup can be used to detect these types of software mistakes or weaknesses, an assumption is made that input validation is missing and a hidden function is included on the Engine and Body Control Modules.

8.3.2.2 Fuzz Testing Setup Using Duplicate Engine and Body Control Modules

The complete fuzz testing environment for the duplicate Engine and Body Control Modules setup is shown in Figure 8.15. This test setup contains nine main parts, of which four are the same as the normal use case setup in Figure 8.14. The parts that are the same are the target system *Engine and Body Control Modules*, which play the role of the SUT, the corresponding physical *peripherals*, the *HIL System* and the *Monitor PC*. The new parts are the *Fuzz Testing Tool*, the duplicate target system, namely the Reference System, consisting of identical *Engine and Body Control Modules*, corresponding physical *peripherals*, *Comparison Module*, and *Feedback Loop*. Please note that the different *peripherals* are optional, since the electrical output signals are monitored by the HIL System, but could be useful for comparison between the two systems to visually inspect any abnormal behavior. Thus, in this case, RC Car #2 is used as the Reference System. The Reference System is connected over a separate CAN bus to the HIL System, where it can receive correct CAN messages from the Pedal Sensor ECU and the Light Control ECU. The Reference System only receives correct CAN messages and no fuzzed messages, which means that the Reference System should behave correctly, and hence can be used as a *reference system*. The SUT also receives the same correct CAN messages from the Pedal Sensor ECU and the Light Control ECU as the Reference System. Thus, without any fuzzed messages the behavior of the SUT and the Reference System should be identical. It is important to note that the *Fuzz Testing Tool* is connected over a CAN bus to the SUT but *not* the Reference System. This CAN bus is also connected to

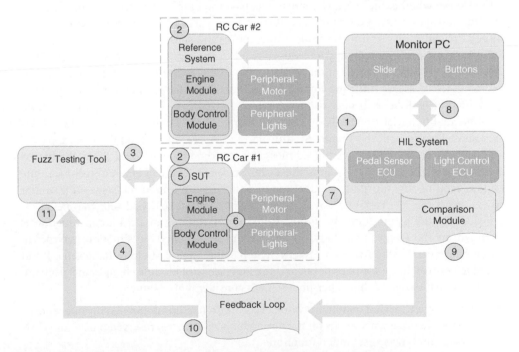

Figure 8.15 Fuzz testing environment for the Engine and Body Control Modules.

the HIL System. The Fuzz Testing Tool will generate and send fuzzed messages, including invalid variants of the messages that typically would only be sent by the Pedal Sensor ECU and Light Control ECU to the SUT. Thus, the SUT receives a combination of both valid CAN messages from the Pedal Sensor ECU and the Light Control ECU as well as fuzzed messages from the Fuzz Testing Tool. Both the electrical signals output from the SUT's Engine and Body Control Modules and the electrical signals output from the Reference System's *Engine and Body Control Modules* are measured by the HIL System. Moreover, a software module called the *Comparison Module* is running on the HIL System. It is responsible for comparing the measured electrical signal values that are output from the SUT with the measured values from the Reference System to detect if there is any abnormal behavior on the SUT based on processing the fuzzed messages. As the last part, the *Feedback Loop* is realized as a communication channel over Ethernet between the HIL System and the Fuzz Testing Tool. This communication channel is used to provide feedback about any exceptions detected by the HIL System to the Fuzz Testing Tool.

The procedure steps for this fuzz testing environment are indicated by the numbers in Figure 8.15 and are described as follows. First, in Step 1, the HIL System provides the required input signals to both the SUT and the Reference System to enable the correct states for testing. These input signals also include relevant CAN messages from the Pedal Sensor ECU and Light Control ECU. Based on the input signals, the SUT and the Reference System enable the correct states for testing in Step 2. In Step 3, the Fuzz Testing Tool generates and sends fuzzed CAN messages to the SUT. The fuzzed messages use the same CAN IDs (0x120 and 0x130) as the Pedal Sensor ECU and Light Control ECU with the purpose of targeting the logic in the SUT that handles the processing of these messages that normally are sent from the real Pedal Sensor ECU and Light Control ECU. The goal is to observe whether there is any abnormal behavior on the SUT based on processing the invalid messages generated by the Fuzz Testing Tool. These fuzzed messages may contain values exceeding maximum threshold values or invalid settings based on the values on the wrong bit positions of the CAN message. Next, in Step 4, the HIL System monitors the same CAN bus connected to the SUT and the Fuzz Testing Tool and thus receives the fuzzed CAN messages from the Fuzz Testing Tool. These fuzzed messages are stored in a log file and will be used later to match which fuzzed CAN message may have caused an abnormal behavior on the SUT. Then, in Step 5, the SUT processes the fuzzed CAN messages. That is, both the Engine Module and the Body Control Module that are part of the SUT process the respective fuzzed messages based on the CAN IDs. Since the fuzzed messages use the same CAN ID as the Pedal Sensor ECU and Light Control ECU, the Engine Module and the Body Control Module process the fuzzed messages in a similar fashion as if the real Pedal Sensor ECU and Light Control ECU had sent the messages. Considering the assumption that input validation is missing and a hidden function is included on the Engine and Body Control Modules the following situation may occur. Based on processing the fuzzed messages in Step 5, the Engine Module changes the PWM signal to control the motor peripheral, and the Body Control Module changes the electrical signals to turn on/off the lights peripheral. Let's consider two examples:

(1) a fuzzed message that contains a value exceeding a maximum threshold value, and
(2) a fuzzed message with values on the wrong bit positions, e.g. reserved bits, of the CAN message that triggers a hidden function.

Therefore, based on processing such fuzzed messages, the SUT generates electrical signals to erroneously control the peripherals. In Step 6, similar to the normal use case, if the fuzzed messages cause the SUT to generate output signals, the SUT controls the corresponding peripherals by outputting electrical signals to adjust the PWM signal to the motor or adjust the lights to turn on/off. Please note that in Step 5, while the SUT and the Reference System receive valid messages from the Pedal Sensor ECU and Light Control ECU, and the respective Engine and Body Control Modules behave identically and accordingly, only invalid messages are sent from the Fuzz Testing Tool to the SUT so any difference in the behavior between the peripherals connected to the SUT and the peripherals connected to the Reference System is considered abnormal. In this case, it is therefore possible to visually observe the abnormal behavior of the SUT by observing the behavior of the motor or the lights. Please note that since the peripherals are optional in this test setup, this visual observation step is just an additional example of how it is possible to detect exceptions. Then, in Step 7, the HIL System measures the output signals from the SUT provided to the peripherals. Equally important is that the HIL System measures the output signals from the Reference System sent to control its peripherals. In Step 8, the measured values on the HIL System are visually represented in a graphical interface shown on the Monitor PC. Please note that the visual comparison on the Monitor PC is optional in this fuzz testing environment; however, it helps to understand and verify the comparison of the measured values from the SUT to the measured values from the Reference System. The measured values from the SUT and from the Reference System are then compared by the Comparison Module in Step 9. Different from the solution presented in Section 8.3.1.2, the Comparison Module does not use any predefined threshold or reference values, but instead it uses values measured live from the Reference System for the comparison. In this case, considering the two examples described above, the Comparison Module is able to detect abnormal behavior on the SUT. Please note again that only invalid messages are generated by the Fuzz Testing Tool and sent to the SUT. Therefore, in principle, the SUT should not control the peripherals based on any messages from the Fuzz Testing Tool. If the SUT controls a peripheral in a different manner from the Reference System, it means that there was an exception. In the first example, a fuzzed message with an invalid value exceeding a threshold value is sent to the SUT. In this example, the fuzzed message causes the Engine Module to generate electrical signals to control the motor peripheral. Thus, the motor peripheral connected to the SUT behaves differently from the motor peripheral connected to the Reference System, and the Comparison Module is able to detect the difference and determine that there was an exception. In the second example, a certain fuzzed message with invalid settings based on the values in wrong bit positions of the CAN message triggers a hidden function on the Body Control Module. The hidden function is a maintenance function that generates the appropriate electrical signals to control the lights peripheral to turn on/off all lights. Hence, the lights peripheral connected to the SUT behaves differently from the lights peripheral connected to the Reference System, and therefore the Comparison Module is able to detect the difference and identify that there was an exception. Thus, if the Comparison Module detects any mismatches between the measured signals from the SUT and the Reference System, it determines that an exception has occurred. As a result, in Step 10, feedback about the exception is provided to the Fuzz Testing Tool over the Feedback Loop. In this test setup, information about the exception is provided in a syslog message.

The syslog message contains which fuzzed CAN message caused the exception, which is identified by logging the CAN messages in the HIL System in Step 4, and the measured electrical signal values both from the SUT and the Reference System, which are determined by measuring the signals in Step 7. This feedback is then logged in the Fuzz Testing Tool in Step 11 and can later be used by developers to reproduce and analyze the issue in order to help identify the root cause and fix the issue.

Please note that to simulate realistic test scenarios, the HIL System may generate different test states by providing appropriate CAN messages to both the SUT and the Reference System in Step 1. For example, one can consider a driver model on the HIL System that follows a certain test pattern by accelerating, and turning on and off various lights. These types of test patterns may already be used during functional testing and could often be reused. In order to achieve a broad coverage of fuzz testing, it would be useful to replay these different test scenarios using the driver model in Step 1 to verify that the different fuzzed messages processed during different test states do not cause any abnormal behavior. During these test patterns, normal behavior on both the SUT and the Reference System would generate output signals to control the peripherals. The behaviors of the peripherals connected to the SUT and the Reference System would be synchronized and identical. However, if a fuzzed message causes abnormal behavior, the peripherals connected to the SUT would behave differently from the peripherals connected to the Reference System. Thus, the Comparison Module on the HIL System would be able to detect such exceptions caused by fuzzed messages during these different test patterns.

An example implementation of this type of fuzz testing environment is shown in Figure 8.16.

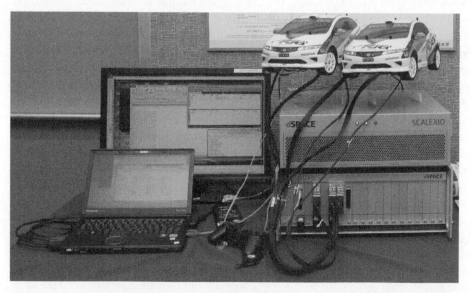

Figure 8.16 Example implementation of a fuzz testing environment with duplicate target systems. Source: Adapted from [3]. © 2018 Nagoya University, © 2018 dSPACE, Portions Copyright 2018 Synopsys, Inc. Used with permission. All rights reserved.

8.3.2.3 Fuzz Testing Setup Considerations

This fuzz testing setup using duplicate target systems allows for easy exception detection; however, one challenge is that it requires two target systems to be available during testing. In some cases, there may be limitations in an organization on how many test targets are available and therefore this approach may not be suitable. It may also incur additional costs if two target systems must be prepared for testing. Another challenge is that the two target systems need to be synchronized during testing. Since measurements are taken from both systems and compared, it is imperative that both systems behave in the same manner during normal behavior. If one system enters a different state, e.g. goes into sleep mode, the measurements from both systems would not match and the test setup could incorrectly report that there are exceptions. Thus, it is important to consider how to ensure that both systems stay synchronized during the fuzz testing.

Since two identical target systems are used in this fuzz testing setup it is possible to quickly get started with a black-box approach for testing. Because a black-box approach is taken, it is not necessary to have a deep understanding of the internal workings of the target system. Consequently, in contrast to the careful considerations that are needed to define exception detection logic for the Comparison Module discussed in Section 8.3.1.3, this fuzz testing setup does not require one to define any intricate exception detection logic. The reason is that because only invalid messages are generated by the Fuzz Testing Tool and transmitted to the SUT, any behavior on the SUT that differs from behavior on the Reference System can be determined to be an exception. Thus, this black-box approach allows for quickly getting started with fuzz testing of various target systems from simple systems to more complex systems without the need to define specific exception detection logic in advance, which is an advantage compared with the fuzz testing setup described in Section 8.3.1. Subsequently, this approach allows one to quickly detect abnormal behavior on the SUT caused by fuzzed messages.

Although the advantage of the black-box approach is that it allows quickly getting started with fuzz testing and detecting exceptions, it is possible to extend this approach to perform more in-depth testing and get a better understanding of failures by following a white-box approach. Based on knowledge about the SUT and the measured signals by the HIL System it is possible to define more advanced detection logic. This detection logic would not only indicate an exception that two measurements differ but could also help identify the failures related to that exception. For example, a certain type of exception for a specific signal could be related to an operation failure, such as the SUT hanging or freezing. Another type of exception could be related to incorrect control of a peripheral. With a better understanding of the related failures, it would allow developers to better prioritize which exceptions are more critical and should be investigated first. This information would also help developers in the analysis to better understand the underlying issues to allow for faster fixes. Compared with the black-box approach, the white-box approach requires more knowledge about the target system to define specific detection logic and therefore naturally takes more time to get started with fuzz testing. However, the results from the white-box approach gives more insight into particular failures on the SUT caused by the fuzzed messages and helps developers better understand the underlying root causes.

8.4 Chapter Summary

This chapter discussed approaches for improving and automating fuzz testing of in-vehicle systems by integrating with automotive test tools. Specifically, the focus is on fuzz testing setups using automotive test tools such as HIL systems. In general, the integrated fuzz testing environment comprises a Fuzz Testing Tool, the SUT, and a HIL System. The Fuzz Testing Tool provides fuzzed messages over an automotive network such as CAN or CAN-FD to the SUT. The HIL System is responsible for external instrumentation by measuring analog/digital signals from the SUT to determine whether there are exceptions in the ECU behavior based on processing the fuzzed messages. There are two approaches presented in detail, namely a white-box approach and a black-box approach. The white-box approach uses a Comparison Module on the HIL System to compare measured signals from the SUT to predefined threshold or reference values. Thus, the Comparison Module needs to be configured in advance based on, for example, ECU specifications on what is considered correct vs. abnormal behavior. In contrast, the black-box approach does not require any preconfiguration; however, a duplicate of the SUT called a Reference System is used instead. The HIL System measures electrical signals from both the SUT and the Reference System, and the Comparison Module performs the comparison of the measured values to detect any exceptions based on the fuzzed messages. In this case, the Comparison Module does not need to be configured in advance to know what is considered correct behavior; instead, it identifies abnormal behavior by any discrepancies between the fuzzed SUT and the "normal" Reference System. In both approaches, for any detected exceptions, the HIL System provides valuable information as feedback over the Feedback Loop to the Fuzz Testing Tool. Information includes, for example, which fuzzed message caused the exception, the measured values from the SUT, and the predefined or measured values from the Reference System. This type of feedback information can be used by ECU software developers to quickly analyze potential security vulnerabilities.

This type of fuzz testing setup where a fuzz testing tool is integrated with a HIL system provides multiple benefits. From a general perspective, since HIL systems are typically already used in the automotive software development lifecycle during functional testing, it would be possible to *shift left* and integrate fuzz testing as a natural step in the functional testing process. This allows reuse of the existing test equipment already available and used by the QA teams to reduce additional costs and improve efficiency. That is, rather than standalone security teams performing fuzz testing on isolated test environments, fuzz testing is performed as part of the functional testing workflow by QA teams. For example, after running thousands of tests during functional testing, it would be easy to automatically add a number of fuzz test cases at the end. These fuzz test cases would typically also cover the misuse cases. By integrating fuzz testing into the workflow, it would be easier to automatically run the fuzz test cases as part of the process. Performing fuzz testing earlier in the development lifecycle during QA testing, rather than during security testing which occurs after QA testing, allows for detection of exceptions earlier in the development lifecycle, which in turn allows development teams to work on software fixes at an earlier stage. Feedback including the identified exceptions and the corresponding fuzzed messages can be provided to the relevant development teams. The exceptions can then be analyzed early by the developers to understand what might have caused the misbehavior and appropriate fixes can be applied. Thus, this approach overcomes the challenge of security teams detecting these types of exceptions and issues later in the development lifecycle, where fixing such issues may be too costly.

Additional benefits include specific technical aspects such as the HIL system providing the necessary input signals to the SUT to enable various testable states, the HIL system monitoring the SUT through different means to detect exceptions, and the HIL system controlling the fuzz testing tool and SUT to automate the test process, e.g. resetting the SUT into a testable state and continuing fuzz testing after an exception is detected. As automotive systems contain more software and are responsible for more critical functionality within a vehicle, it is recommended to follow an approach that allows fuzz testing at an earlier stage in the development lifecycle.

References

1 Oka, D. K., Yvard, A., Bayer, S., and Kreuzinger, T. (2016). Enabling cyber security testing of automotive ECUs by adding monitoring capabilities. *escar Europe*, Munich, Germany.

2 Oka, D. K., Bayer, S., Kreuzinger, T., and Gay, C. (2017). How to enable cyber security testing of automotive ECUs by adding monitoring capabilities. *Symposium on Cryptography and Information Security (SCIS)*, Naha, Japan.

3 Oka, D. K., Fujikura, T., and Kurachi, R. (2018). Shift left: fuzzing earlier in the automotive software development lifecycle using HIL systems. *escar Europe*, Brussels, Belgium.

4 VDA QMC Working Group 13/Automotive SIG (2017). *Automotive SPICE Process Assessment/Reference Model Version 3.1*. VDA QMC Working Group 13/Automotive SIG.

5 ETAS (2020). Test and validation. https://www.etas.com/en/applications/applications_testing_validation.php (accessed 30 July 2020).

6 dSPACE (2020). HIL testing. https://www.dspace.com/en/pub/home/products/systems/ecutest.cfm (accessed 30 July 2020).

7 Vector (2020). Scalable and modular systems for efficient hil testing. https://www.vector.com/us/en/products/products-a-z/hardware/vt-system (accessed 30 July 2020).

8 National Instruments (2020). What is hardware-in-the-loop?. https://www.ni.com/en-us/innovations/white-papers/17/what-is-hardware-in-the-loop-.html (accessed 30 July 2020).

9 Miller, C. and Valasek, C. 2013. Adventures in automotive networks and control units. *Defcon*, Las Vegas, NV, USA.

10 International Organization for Standardization (ISO) (2016). *ISO 13400-3:2016 – road vehicles — diagnostic communication over internet protocol (DoIP)*. Geneva, Switzerland: ISO.

11 International Organization for Standardization (ISO)/Society of Automotive Engineers (SAE) International (2020). *ISO/SAE DIS 21434 – road vehicles — cybersecurity engineering*. Geneva, Switzerland: ISO and USA: SAE International.

12 Synopsys (2017). Fuzz testing maturity model.

13 ETAS (2020). ETK – ECU interface. https://www.etas.com/en/products/etk.php (accessed 30 July 2020).

14 dSPACE (2020). Testing electronic control units with an optical display. https://www.dspace.com/en/inc/home/products/systems/ecutest/configuration_examples/conf_examp_simulator_whth_opti.cfm (accessed 30 July 2020).

15 Bayer, S., Kreuzinger, T., Oka, D. K., and Wolf, M. (2016). Successful security tests using fuzzing and HiL test systems. ETAS white paper.

16 Renesas (2020). RH850/F1L. https://www.renesas.com/eu/en/products/microcontrollers-microprocessors/rh850/rh850f1x/rh850f1l.html (accessed 30 July 2020).

17 AUTOSAR (2020). The standardized software framework for intelligent mobility. https://www.autosar.org (accessed 30 July 2020).

18 TOPPERS Project (2020). TOPPERS/ATK2 (automotive kernel). https://www.toppers.jp/atk2.html (accessed 30 July 2020).

9

Improving Fuzz Testing Coverage by Using Agent Instrumentation

AUDI, VIDE, TACE

This chapter presents an approach for improving fuzz testing coverage by using *Agent instrumentation*. As described in Section 7.3, a fuzz testing environment contains three parts: fuzz engine, injector, and monitor. Similar to Chapter 8, the focus of this chapter is on the monitor part. The main difference is that the SUT (system under test) in Chapter 8 is a typical embedded ECU (electronic control unit) communicating over an automotive network such as controller area network (CAN) or controller area network flexible data-rate (CAN-FD), whereas the SUT considered in this chapter is a rich operating system (OS) embedded system such as an in-vehicle infotainment system or a telematics unit communicating over multiple different protocols including Wi-Fi and Bluetooth. Please note that the fuzz testing environment presented in this chapter is built on using Agents running on the SUT that are responsible for providing *external instrumentation*, which is explained in more detail in Section 7.3.3. To quickly recap, external instrumentation means that the SUT is monitored using external means besides the protocol or interface being fuzzed in order to detect exceptions on the SUT.

With the rapid development in areas of the connected car and autonomous driving, more complex software is being developed and used in vehicles. Moreover, since these vehicles contain communication interfaces to communicate with external entities outside of the vehicle, they have a larger attack surface and are also prone to receiving more erroneous or malformed input originating from external systems or the infrastructure that are out of the control of the vehicle manufacturer or automotive system manufacturer. Intentional attacks or unintentional malformed messages may cause vehicle systems to behave erratically, which may have an impact on robustness, safety, or security. Therefore, it is imperative that cybersecurity is considered in all relevant activities during the entire automotive software development lifecycle as described in Chapter 2. In addition, especially for complex systems that may affect safety and systems with external-facing network communication interfaces, it is important to have proper processes in place for security testing, including fuzz testing, which are described in more detail in Chapter 7. Fuzz testing is an effective and powerful testing technique used to identify unexpected behavior and unknown vulnerabilities in systems. More details about fuzz testing in general can be found in Section 7.3.

Building Secure Cars: Assuring the Automotive Software Development Lifecycle, First Edition. Dennis Kengo Oka.
© 2021 John Wiley & Sons Ltd. Published 2021 by John Wiley & Sons Ltd.

There exist several automated tools that can be used to perform fuzz testing of automotive systems in the sense that they support the relevant protocols over which to communicate with the SUT. However, there are often challenges to properly instrument the SUT to be able to detect exceptions on the SUT. Moreover, fuzz testing is often performed following a black-box approach where it may be difficult to gather appropriate information from the SUT to determine the underlying root causes for exceptions.

Lately, due to advancements in automotive systems development, it is possible to consider two types of categories for embedded systems in a vehicle. The first type is a traditional automotive embedded system, i.e. an in-vehicle ECU that typically is responsible for a certain set of limited functionality. There are generally different ECUs divided into different domains in a vehicle. For instance, engine ECU and transmission ECU in the powertrain domain, antilock brake system (ABS) ECU and electronic stability control (ESC) ECU in the chassis domain, and body control modules handling, for instance, lighting and door lock functionalities in the body domain. These systems typically have a small embedded codebase, are developed following a model-based development approach, and run on small dedicated automotive microcontrollers. The safety criticality can range from low to high depending on the system and the domain, where typically the powertrain and chassis domain contain more safety-critical ECUs. However, the security exposure is often low since these ECUs mainly communicate over in-vehicle networks without any direct external communication exposure. Obviously, considerations need to be taken where an attacker may be able to gain access to the in-vehicle network through some other means and, in such cases, may be able to directly target these ECUs. On the other hand, the second type of embedded systems is more similar to high-performance IT-based systems that may be responsible for a larger set of functionality. Examples of such systems are in-vehicle infotainment systems and telematics units. These systems typically have a larger codebase, running a rich OS, using open-source software libraries or based on open-source software platforms, may follow a more typical IT software development process, such as the agile software development methodology, and are running on more powerful multicore hardware architectures. For example, there are Linux-based solutions specifically targeting the automotive industry such as Automotive Grade Linux (AGL) [1] and GENIVI [2]. Safety criticality for these systems is typically low; however, security exposure is generally high since these systems contain a larger volume of software, often including open-source software, that may have been developed according to different software development methodologies than the strict automotive development practices and therefore may contain more bugs and vulnerabilities. Moreover, systems such as in-vehicle infotainment and telematics units provide external communication interfaces, which further increases the security exposure since attackers may be able to remotely target vulnerabilities in these systems.

For the first category of systems, fuzz testing typically occurs over automotive network protocols such as CAN and CAN-FD. ECUs communicating over CAN or CAN-FD do not typically follow a specific request–reply communication format that is common for many IT protocols, but instead ECUs often only receive and process certain CAN messages without sending any corresponding replies on the CAN bus. Therefore, to properly perform fuzz testing of such systems there is a need for external instrumentation to monitor the behavior of the ECU through other means besides the CAN communication. There are fuzz testing solutions for these embedded ECUs based on test environments using HIL (hardware-in-the-loop) systems to perform the external instrumentation [3–5]. External instrumentation is achieved by the HIL system measuring the analog/digital signals generated by the SUT. This integrated test environment allows for various approaches to detect exceptions on the SUT. The most important point is that this test setup is able to detect exceptions on the SUT that otherwise would be undetectable if only the fuzzed protocol was observed. One example is an ECU that is being fuzzed over the CAN bus that misbehaves based on the processing of fuzzed messages and erroneously generates electrical signals to control an external peripheral. It would not be possible to detect this type of exception if only the CAN bus is monitored. However, with the integrated test setup using a HIL system to perform external instrumentation of the SUT it is possible to detect such abnormal behavior. The challenges for fuzzing in-vehicle systems and corresponding solutions are presented in more detail in Chapter 8.

Instead, in this chapter, the focus is on fuzz testing of the second category of embedded systems, namely, embedded systems that run a rich OS and are more relevant to the connected car use case, such as in-vehicle infotainment systems and telematics units. This chapter presents a fuzz testing solution where the monitor part is based on the concept of an *Agent Instrumentation Framework* that allows for more efficient and accurate fuzz testing. In other words, external instrumentation is achieved by using additional means in the form of *Agents*, which are small pieces of code, running on the target system that allow to observe the SUT besides the protocol being fuzzed. There are several advantages of this test setup using the Agent Instrumentation Framework. First, the target embedded systems are typically based on a rich OS, such as Linux and Android [6, 7], providing a larger set of diverse functionality. By using Agents on the SUT that utilize appropriate functionality or tools provided by the OS it would be possible to gather information from the SUT to help determine whether there are any exceptions based on the processing of fuzzed messages. Thus, the Agents allow one to properly observe the SUT for exceptions in behavior using various monitoring techniques, such as monitoring the memory usage, CPU (central processing unit) usage, or specific states of certain processes, which are the instances of the relevant applications being executed. Moreover, the Agents can help automate the test process by providing instructions to the SUT and the fuzz testing tool. For example, if an exception is detected on the SUT, the Agent can reset the SUT back into the original testable state, e.g. by restarting the process that crashed, and instruct the fuzz testing tool to retransmit the same previously sent fuzzed messages to try to reproduce and verify the issue or continue testing with the next round of fuzzed messages. Last, the Agents can help provide more details about the identified abnormal behavior on the SUT and send back relevant information as feedback to the fuzz testing tool. This information could include the specific processes that were impacted by the fuzz testing and what the abnormal behavior was. This type of fuzz testing is closer to a white-box or gray-box approach where access to the internals of the SUT is required to be able to run the Agents on the SUT. Thus, rather than performing a pure black-box fuzz testing late in the development lifecycle by a separate security team, it is possible to *shift left* in the development process and perform this type of fuzz testing earlier in the development lifecycle conducted, for example, by development teams or quality assurance (QA) teams. Consequently, using the additional feedback captured by the Agents would help developers to analyze the underlying root causes and fix potential software vulnerabilities earlier in the software development lifecycle.

The main points of this chapter are:

- We provide an introduction to Agent instrumentation and explain how it can be used to improve fuzz testing, including how additional information can be collected on the SUT and used to determine whether there are exceptions.
- We discuss the challenges of fuzz testing rich OS embedded systems; in particular, we review a number of undetectable issues on the SUT.
- To overcome these challenges, we present a solution based on the Agent Instrumentation Framework and highlight some examples of exceptions that would not have been detected unless Agent instrumentation is used.

More details about improving fuzz testing of rich OS embedded systems such as in-vehicle infotainment systems and telematics units using Agent instrumentation are found in References [8, 9].

9.1 Introduction to Agent Instrumentation

This section gives an introduction to Agent instrumentation based on a solution presented in References [8, 9]. As illustrated in Figure 9.1, in a general fuzz testing setup, the monitor is responsible for detecting exceptions on the SUT. In the test setup presented in this chapter, external instrumentation is used for the monitor part. Specifically, external instrumentation is achieved by the use of Agent instrumentation as part of the Agent Instrumentation Framework. The goal of the Agent Instrumentation Framework is to provide the fuzz testing tool with detailed instrumentation data from the SUT during a fuzz testing session. This feedback data is then used to help determine whether a specific fuzz test case caused an exception on the SUT or not. Additionally, the information can be used later by developers during analysis to better understand the causes for any unintentional behavior.

As a general concept, the Agent Instrumentation Framework is modular and flexible to allow for supporting various different target systems. In this manner, it is possible to quickly adapt the necessary functions in the framework to match the target system. One of the main functions of the framework is provided by *Agents*, which are software modules running on the SUT. The primary purpose of an Agent is to perform a single instrumentation task on the SUT and provide the collected information to the fuzz testing tool. Please note that while the Agent Instrumentation Framework describes how Agents can be used, the framework does not specifically define or limit what Agents should do. Instead, the framework is flexible, to

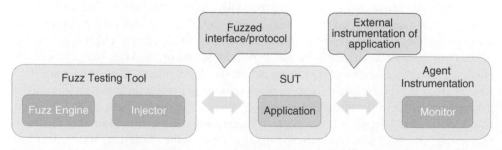

Figure 9.1 Overview of fuzz testing environment including Agent instrumentation.

allow developers and testers to define suitable Agents specifically for target systems they are testing. Obviously, there are common functions of the Agents that can be reused, but Agents can also be extended to particularly monitor a unique behavior of a certain SUT. Typically, an Agent measures or monitors a specific part of the SUT to be able to determine whether there are exceptions based on processing of fuzzed messages. Moreover, to help automate the fuzz testing process and to allow for more complex in-depth instrumentation, an Agent may also execute various functions before, during, or after fuzz test cases are provided to the SUT. Thus, an Agent may take some measurements before a fuzz test case, monitor the test case being processed and then take some other measurements after the fuzz test case has been executed, in order to better detect exceptions. An Agent may also assist in automating the test process by resetting the SUT into a testable state, e.g. by restarting the necessary services that may have crashed during a previous test run.

Furthermore, as a general notion, it is important to consider that an Agent should not perform more than a single instrumentation task. That is, if an Agent triggers an exception detection it is clear which data or which action caused the exception. Otherwise, if an Agent is responsible for collecting and measuring multiple data values that it uses to base its decision on whether there is an exception, further analysis is required by developers or testers, e.g. by reviewing log files to pinpoint exactly which data or action caused the exception. Moreover, all SUTs do not provide the same the functionality and data points that can be measured or monitored in the same way. Therefore, an overly complex Agent may contain functions to measure certain data that are not available on the SUT, or unnecessary functions in the Agent may be executed during each test case, which will slow down testing. If the Agent is overly complex, it may even be required to constantly modify the complex Agent to be compatible with different configurations and target systems. Therefore, as a rule of thumb, it is better to create several simple and single-tasked Agents and then select only the relevant Agents for the SUT from a larger pool of such Agents, than creating a few complex Agents that require constant reconfiguration for each SUT.

The framework is modular and designed to support launching and controlling multiple Agents with their own set of configurations simultaneously. As a result, it is possible for testers using this framework to configure multiple custom individual Agents and reuse the relevant custom Agents with different parameters on different SUTs to allow for more efficient and effective fuzz testing. More details about a fuzz testing solution based on the Agent Instrumentation Framework is described in Section 9.3.

9.2 Problem Statement: Undetectable Vulnerabilities

In recent years, there has been a trend for many automotive organizations to make fuzz testing a mandatory step in the software development process. While fuzz testing is relatively new in the automotive industry, fuzz testing as a test practice has been commonplace for several years in organizations in other industries, such as enterprise, and network and telecommunications industries. In such industries, fuzz testing is deeply integrated in the software development process and has proven to be an effective technique to quickly detect bugs and unknown vulnerabilities. The target systems in such industries are typically relatively easy to instrument, generally using *in-band instrumentation* where the same protocol being fuzzed is observed to detect exceptions. This approach is common when fuzzing typical IT and enterprise solutions, such as web services or communication libraries. Often, observing the same protocol being fuzzed is an effective approach, especially for protocols using a request–reply communication format such as HTTP (hypertext transfer protocol). Thus, a fuzz testing tool would send, for example, fuzzed HTTP requests to the target system and observe the HTTP responses to identify any unexpected behavior in the target system based on processing the fuzzed messages. One famous example identified by in-band instrumentation, which affected more than 600 000 Internet-connected systems, is the Heartbleed vulnerability (CVE-2014-0160 [11]) which was detected during fuzzing of the OpenSSL library. By observing the responses to fuzzed heartbeat request messages, it was possible to determine that there was an issue due to unexpected responses from the target system [12]. Further analysis of this issue led to the detection of this serious vulnerability where potentially sensitive data are leaked from the target system. Moreover, as part of in-band instrumentation, one common approach is to perform valid-case instrumentation, which means that a correct message, i.e. a valid case, is sent after one or several fuzzed messages to test whether the target system correctly responds to the valid message. Thus, due to common request–reply communication formats used in other industries, it is relatively easy to detect exceptions based on in-band instrumentation.

In contrast to many of these IT-based solutions, automotive systems are often more complex with various states and are interconnected with other systems, and therefore often not easy to instrument. Thus, one major challenge is that without proper instrumentation there are many unknown vulnerabilities and potential issues that would go undetected during fuzz testing. Without proper instrumentation, e.g. using HIL systems, when fuzz testing in-vehicle ECUs, numerous potential issues would go undetected. Further details about the challenges and relevant solutions for such scenarios are described in more detail in Chapter 8. Similarly, for rich OS automotive systems such as in-vehicle infotainment systems and telematics units, there are many potential issues that would go undetected if fuzz testing is conducted without proper instrumentation. This challenge is described in more detail as follows. Generally, when performing fuzz testing of a certain protocol or over a certain interface – for instance, conducting fuzz testing over Wi-Fi or Bluetooth on an in-vehicle infotainment system – instrumentation occurs over the same protocol being fuzzed. That is, only in-band instrumentation is used, meaning that only the protocol being fuzzed is monitored to determine whether there is any abnormal behavior on the SUT. Since only the protocol being fuzzed is observed, this limited instrumentation could result in a number of potential issues on the SUT being undetectable. Examples of such issues are indicated in Figure 9.2 and are explained in more detail as follows.

There are several examples of issues that can occur on the SUT but are undetectable over the protocol being fuzzed, including *memory leaks*, *core dumps*, and *zombie processes*. These examples are described as follows.

9.2.1 Memory Leaks

The first example of an issue that can go undetected during fuzz testing is *memory leaks* on the SUT. During the fuzz testing session, fuzzed messages are sent from the fuzz testing tool to the SUT over the protocol or interface being fuzzed. Please note that since the SUT is a rich-OS based system with, typically, a large number of applications running on top of it, there could be different target applications within the SUT based on the protocol

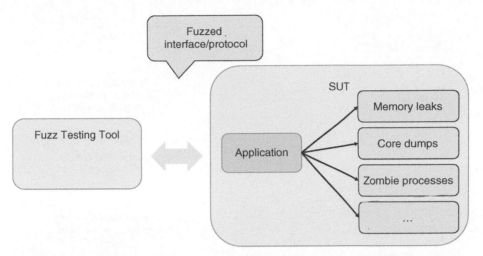

Figure 9.2 Examples of issues that are undetectable over the protocol being fuzzed. Source: Adapted from [10]. Portions Copyright 2020 Synopsys, Inc. Used with permission. All rights reserved.

being fuzzed. For example, there are lower layer communication stacks responsible for enabling communication over different interfaces, there are cryptographic libraries such as the previously mentioned OpenSSL, and upper-layer applications responsible for specific functionality, e.g. media players playing music or video files on the in-vehicle infotainment system. Consider the following example scenario. The target application within the SUT processes the fuzzed messages and if a request–reply communication format is used, correctly provides replies to the fuzzed requests. By just observing the protocol being fuzzed there is no indication of any issues and it would be determined that the fuzz test cases passed and that the SUT behaves correctly. However, in reality, there is a software bug in the application on the SUT that causes memory leaks when processing the fuzzed messages, a software bug that is undetectable over the fuzzed protocol. Although there are memory leaks on the SUT, the application still correctly processes the fuzzed messages and is able to provide correct responses to the fuzz testing tool. Nevertheless, if fuzz testing is performed over a long period of time with a certain type of fuzzed messages it may be possible to determine that there is an exception by just observing the protocol being fuzzed. For instance, it may be possible to detect abnormal behavior on the SUT due to a response being slower than expected or that a certain response to a fuzzed request is missing. Yet, if such an exception is identified, it would typically be extremely difficult to pinpoint what caused the unintended behavior. Generally, significant time would have to be invested to analyze all the previous messages exchanged over the fuzzed protocol to try to identify the root cause. On the other hand, if it is possible to use some external instrumentation to be able to detect the memory leak on the SUT directly after the first fuzzed message that causes the memory leak it would be a much more efficient test approach. Moreover, such external instrumentation would also serve to provide more detailed information to developers to better assist in identifying the root cause of the memory leak.

9.2.2 Core Dumps and Zombie Processes

The second example of issues that could be missed during fuzz testing is the case where the application on the SUT crashes but restarts quickly. That is, a certain fuzzed message over

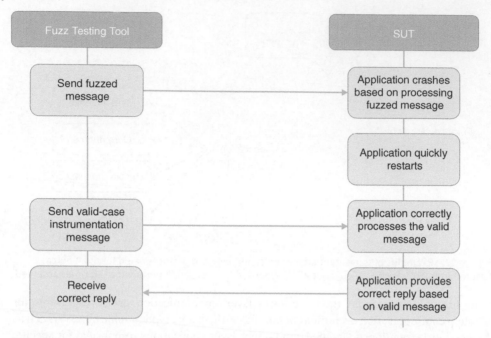

Figure 9.3 Example flow leading to issues being undetected during fuzz testing due to application restart.

the fuzzed protocol causes the application to crash. On the SUT, there may exist a watchdog functionality that monitors certain processes and detects whether a specific application has crashed and, in such a case, restarts the application. From a technical design viewpoint, this is a sound approach to preserve availability of the system such that even if certain functionality becomes unavailable for whatever reason there is a countermeasure to ensure that the functionality becomes available again as soon as possible. Thus, during fuzz testing, even though the application crashes due to processing a fuzzed message, it restarts quickly and by the time instrumentation over the communication protocol occurs, e.g. valid-case instrumentation, the application is back up and running and can correctly process the valid message and provide a valid response to the fuzz testing tool. Thus, the target application seems to be responding correctly and the exception, i.e. the application crash, is not properly detected. This scenario is illustrated in Figure 9.3.

From a functional standpoint and considering the availability properties of the SUT, this behavior may be acceptable to a user since, from the user's perspective, everything seems to be working. Even though the application might have crashed due to malformed input, since the application is restarted quickly, the crash is not noticeable to the user. However, the crashes may have long-term negative consequences on the SUT. For example, as a result of crashes triggered over a period of time, a number of *core dump* files may be generated, or multiple *zombie processes* may be spawned in the SUT. Eventually this behavior may lead to the entire system crashing, a specific application becoming unresponsive, or causing the SUT to behave erratically. Additionally, an attacker may be able to identify the type of fuzzed message that causes the application to crash and investigate the issue. Consequently, it may be possible for an attacker to identify an exploitable vulnerability and by crafting a specific message be able to exploit the vulnerability and execute arbitrary commands. Thus, as a result, an attacker could potentially exploit a vulnerability in an application responsible for Wi-Fi or Bluetooth communication to achieve remote code execution. An example of such an attack is described in Reference [13]. Since the vulnerable application will not crash but rather execute the attacker-controlled code, the watchdog will not detect any application crash and therefore not restart the application. Thus, the attacker would have full control of the execution on the SUT. Consequently, even though the approach of using a watchdog to detect and restart crashed applications is sound, it is important to be able to detect and analyze the reasons for such crashes on the SUT to identify any potential security weaknesses and vulnerabilities.

9.2.3 Considerations for Addressing Undetectable Vulnerabilities

Therefore, the above-mentioned example issues, among others, could lead to vulnerabilities and bugs going undetected when using only in-band instrumentation during fuzz testing of rich OS-based automotive systems. Most commonly, fuzz testing is considered a black-box approach when performed by security teams conducting standalone testing of the SUT. However, normally developers and QA testers have access to the internals of the SUT, including access to the OS, e.g. Linux or Android, and the corresponding applications. This access allows them to execute additional commands and scripts on the SUT during, for example, functional testing.

Therefore, by shifting left and performing fuzz testing earlier in the development lifecycle during development and QA testing, it would be possible to perform fuzz testing in a more gray/white-box approach to achieve more efficient and accurate fuzz testing. By utilizing this access to the internals of the SUT, it would be possible to run additional scripts on the SUT to help identify exceptions during fuzz testing. These scripts are part of the Agents and integral to the Agent Instrumentation Framework, where the Agents are placed on the SUT to assist with the instrumentation. This solution is presented in detail in the next section, Section 9.3.

9.3 Solution: Using Agents to Detect Undetectable Vulnerabilities

Ultimately, the main goal with fuzz testing is to detect exceptions and find unknown vulnerabilities on the SUT. To overcome the challenges presented in the previous section, this section presents a fuzz testing solution for rich OS automotive systems based on the Agent Instrumentation Framework introduced in Section 9.1. First, an overview of the test environment is given and the requirements for setting up the Agent Instrumentation Framework are discussed. Then, the different modes of operation of the framework are described. To better understand the type of exceptions that can be detected in this framework, a list of example Agents is presented. Last, some example results are shared to give an idea of actual findings that can be discovered through the use of the Agent Instrumentation Framework.

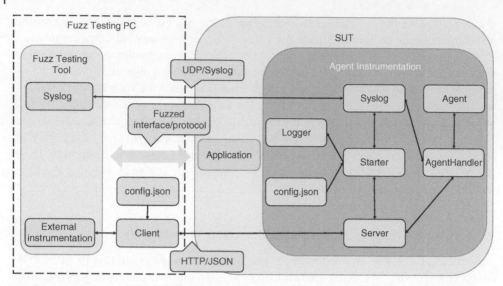

Figure 9.4 Overview of fuzz testing environment using the Agent Instrumentation Framework. Source: Adapted from [10]. Portions Copyright 2020 Synopsys, Inc. Used with permission. All rights reserved.

9.3.1 Overview of the Test Environment

An overview of the fuzz testing environment using the Agent Instrumentation Framework is illustrated in Figure 9.4. On the left-hand side is the Fuzz Testing PC, which contains the Fuzz Testing Tool, and on the right-hand side is the SUT, including the functionality to support Agent instrumentation.

An example implementation of the Agent Instrumentation Framework used as the basis in this chapter is written in the popular Python programming language [8]. Python is one of the most popular programming languages and is very commonly used in the developer community. Thus, it is possible for developers and testers to write and configure Agents with great flexibility, utilizing the large functionality offered by the vast set of available Python libraries.

There are a number of prerequisites for the test environment in order to enable the functionality required for the Agent Instrumentation Framework, explained as follows. First, on the Fuzz Testing Tool side, the following requirements need to be fulfilled. The Fuzz Testing Tool requires using an external instrumentation feature to be able to, for example, send requests to the Agents on the SUT. These requests typically include asking the Agents whether an exception was detected based on the SUT processing the fuzzed messages. The Agent Instrumentation Framework contains both client-side code that is required to be run on the Fuzz Testing PC and server-side code that is required to be run on the SUT. The client-side code uses a configuration file to help the Fuzz Testing Tool understand which Agents are currently active on the SUT, how to communicate with the Agents and so forth. In this example framework implementation, the client-code is written in Python, and therefore requires that the Fuzz Testing PC has the ability to execute Python scripts. Moreover, to communicate with the SUT, the client-side code contains communication functionality that is responsible for establishing a communication channel to the server-side code. Thus, to allow the communication channel to be established, the Fuzz Testing PC is required to have the ability to open a port to be able to communicate over HTTP with the SUT.

Furthermore, the SUT also has a number of requirements that need to be fulfilled. One of the prerequisites for the Agent Instrumentation Framework is to have access to the internals of the SUT since more advanced instrumentation is required. Thus, this test setup moves away from a black-box test approach to a more gray/white-box testing approach. The more white-box approach that is possible in terms of access to the internals and understanding of the execution of processes and functions on the SUT, the easier it is to configure relevant Agents to gather information and instrument the target applications. Thus, being able to use the Agents in their fullest capacity allows for better and more efficient fuzz testing.

There are typically various approaches for developers and testers to gain access to a rich OS SUT, e.g. shell access to allow execution of custom code. Examples include remote communication over built-in wireless communication interfaces, such as Wi-Fi or Bluetooth, serial communication, Ethernet communication or using USB-to-Ethernet converters where supported by USB ports. Describing the details on how to establish a communication channel to the SUT is out of the scope of this chapter; however, from a white-box perspective, it should be a fairly trivial task for the involved developers or testers.

Similarly to the client-side code being executed on the Fuzz Testing PC, the server-side code of the Agent Instrumentation Framework needs to be executed on the SUT. Therefore, the SUT first requires a writeable filesystem to allow storing the necessary server-side code, including the communication functionality, configuration files, and Agents. Moreover, to allow the Agents to properly collect information from the SUT during fuzz testing, the SUT requires a writeable filesystem or a writeable secondary storage accessible from the SUT to store the files that are generated or updated during the processing of the fuzzed messages including core dump files and log files. Furthermore, the SUT requires the necessary execution environment to launch the server-side code, including the Agents, namely the Python scripts in this case. The execution environment would normally consist of a programming language implementation, which in most cases is the interpreter or compiler. In this example Agent Instrumentation Framework setup, CPython, which is a reference implementation of the Python programming language, is used on the SUT. CPython is written in the C language and compiles the Python code in the Agent scripts into bytecode and then interprets the bytecode to execute the code on the SUT. Since CPython can be statically cross compiled it is possible to run this Agent Instrumentation Framework on virtually any embedded architecture. Finally, the server-side code contains communication functionality that allows for establishing a communication channel to the Fuzz Testing PC. This communication channel is used to provide feedback from the Agents based on the SUT processing the fuzzed messages to the Fuzz Testing PC. Therefore, for the SUT to be able to communicate with the client-code or the Fuzz Testing Tool on the Fuzz Testing PC, the SUT is required to have the ability to open a port to be able to communicate over HTTP or syslog with the Fuzz Testing PC.

9.3.2 Modes of Operation

The Agent Instrumentation Framework supports two main modes of operation: *synchronous mode* and *asynchronous mode*. The different modes have their own advantages and disadvantages. The difference between the modes are related to the configuration required on the Fuzz Testing Tool, how accurately the Agents are able to pinpoint a certain detected exception to a specific fuzz test case, and the speed of execution of the fuzz test run. While many Agents may support running in either mode, due to the differences and prerequisites for the different modes, some Agents may only support being executed in one of the modes to be fully functional. During a fuzz testing session, the Agent Instrumentation Framework needs to be configured to run in only one mode, and thus only Agents supporting that mode can be used during that test run. Once the fuzz testing session is over, it is possible to configure the Agent Instrumentation Framework to use a different mode for the next session and thus it is now possible to use the Agents that were not supported in the previously configured mode in the first test run.

The mode of operation is defined in the main configuration file: `config.json`. Additionally, the Agents to be used during the fuzz testing session and their configurations are also defined in the same file. This type of configuration file is used on both the Fuzz Testing PC and the SUT as shown in Figure 9.4. The tasks and actions taken on the Fuzz Testing PC and the SUT for the respective modes are described as follows.

9.3.2.1 Synchronous Mode

The main advantage with running the Agent Instrumentation Framework in *synchronous mode* is that it allows for the greatest control of the Agents executing on the SUT. However, the disadvantage is that it is much slower than running in asynchronous mode. Since the testing mode is synchronous, it is possible to allow Agents to perform various actions both *before* and *after* a specific fuzz test case is sent and processed by the SUT, which sometimes may be needed to allow automated testing and more advanced techniques for detecting exceptions and identifying unknown vulnerabilities.

First, on the SUT, the Starter script, `starter.py`, reads the configuration file, which in this case is configured to use synchronous mode. Based on this mode, the Starter script starts the processes for the communication functionality, namely the Server daemon, which listens to incoming requests from the Fuzz Testing PC.

On the Fuzz Testing PC, the Client `client.py` script and the `config.json` configuration file are prepared in advance. Specifically, the Agents to be used, and the IP (Internet Protocol) address and the port number pointing to the Server daemon process on the SUT are defined in the configuration file. The `client.py` script can be called at various times during the fuzz testing session to send information or commands to the Server daemon. Moreover, this communication channel can also be used for the Server on the SUT to provide feedback from the Agents back to the Client on the Fuzz Testing PC. Different arguments can be used for the `client.py` script depending on the functionality and requirements of the Agents that are configured to be used. The `client.py` script is invoked through a command line interface by the Fuzz Testing Tool. The following options are available for the `client.py` script to send information from the Fuzz Testing PC to the SUT:

- Before the test run (`python client.py -config config.json before_run`): contains information on all Agents to start, and their respective configuration. This is a requirement when running the framework in synchronous mode since it tells the Server to start the relevant Agents through the AgentHandler.

- Before sending a test case to the SUT (`python client.py -config config.json before_case`): can be used to put the SUT in a certain mode or perform certain actions before fuzzed messages are processed.
- To initiate the instrumentation process (`python client.py -config config.json instrumentation`): this argument requests the Agents on the SUT to perform instrumentation. Based on the collected information in a certain Agent, the Agent determines whether the test case passed or failed. This pass/fail verdict is then provided as feedback from the Agent to the Fuzz Testing Tool. Additionally, details about the measured values and the reasons for the pass/fail verdict can the provided as feedback. The Agents would typically be implemented with some logic to gather and analyze certain information on the SUT.
- After sending a test case to the SUT (`python client.py -config config.json after_case`): can be used to put the SUT back in the same state as it was before processing the fuzzed message or perform certain actions after the fuzzed messages are processed, e.g. copy relevant log files into a separate folder.
- When a test case has failed (`python client.py -config config.json instrumentation_fail`): if the instrumentation verdict is fail, this command can be used to restore the SUT back into a working testable state. For example, it could restart the target process on the SUT, kill any hanging or zombic processes, restart a virtual machine or respawn a docker container containing the SUT.
- After the test run (`python client.py -config config.json after_run`): where needed, this command could be used to stop all the Agents, reset the SUT to prepare it for the next test run or shut down the SUT.

Since the mode of operation is synchronous, basically the Agents are executed in-line with the fuzzing session, which means that actions taken before or after a test case, or as part of the instrumentation, will add overheads to the execution of each test case. Based on how complex the actions are for each Agent, the overhead to each test case could range from a small overhead to a very significant overhead. Thus, this total overhead will affect the speed of each test case and the overall time required for the fuzzing session. To address this concern, it is possible to apply different test strategies, e.g. initially only enable a smaller set of Agents and configure the Agents to focus on detecting higher-level exceptions. If an exception is detected, more Agents can be enabled, or the Agent configuration can be adjusted to be more precise to help narrow down the root cause of the detected exception to a single issue. Consequently, defining Agents to focus on specific tasks and be as minimal and concise as possible is essential to improve the overall effectiveness and reduce the time required for a fuzzing session.

9.3.2.2 Asynchronous Mode

The main advantage of running the Agent Instrumentation Framework in *asynchronous mode* is that the speed of execution during a fuzz testing session is much faster compared with the synchronous mode. However, the disadvantage is that it is not possible to tie a certain exception detected by an Agent on the SUT to a specific fuzz test case since the Agent only reports when a prespecified condition has been met. In addition, the asynchronous mode does not allow the fine granularity for Agents to define what actions should be performed before or after a test case since the Agents are unaware of when a test case starts or stops. Rather, the Agents are continuously running on the SUT and are polled periodically based on the time intervals in their configuration.

First, on the SUT, the Starter script, `starter.py`, reads the `config.json` configuration file, which in this case is configured to use asynchronous mode. Additionally, the configuration file specifies the IP address and the port number used by the Fuzz Testing PC to receive feedback, which occurs over the syslog protocol. A custom polling rate for the Agents can also be specified; however, by default, Agents are polled every 0.5 seconds. Based on this mode, the Starter script launches the configured Agents on the SUT through the AgentHandler.

On the Fuzz Testing PC, the Fuzz Testing Tool needs to be configured to run a syslog daemon to parse incoming syslog messages provided as feedback from the SUT. No additional configuration on the Fuzz Testing PC is required in asynchronous mode.

During the fuzz test session, while the Fuzz Testing Tool uninterruptedly and continuously sends fuzz test cases to the SUT, every configured Agent is polled at the predefined time interval to provide instrumentation data, which contains a pass or fail verdict and, optionally, additional information regarding the measured values and the reason for the pass/fail verdict. Since the instrumentation process is not occurring synchronized with the fuzz test cases provided by the Fuzz Testing Tool to the SUT, the Agents on the SUT, and in turn the Fuzz Testing Tool, cannot know specifically which test results are associated with which test cases. For instance, when an Agent is polled and detects an exception based on a prespecified condition, it will provide a fail verdict as feedback to the Fuzz Testing Tool. However, the Fuzz Testing Tool is unable to determine exactly which test case caused the exception since multiple fuzz test cases might have been sent and processed by the SUT between the time the Agent was previously polled and when the Agent was polled next, and detected the exception.

To summarize, the advantage of running the Agent Instrumentation Framework asynchronously is speed of execution, however with the loss of accuracy. Consider the following example of a buffer overflow bug on an in-vehicle infotainment system slowly leading to a measurable failure over a thousand test cases. Performing fuzz testing using the Agent Instrumentation Framework in asynchronous mode, the Agent would provide a fail verdict when the prespecified condition of the failure is fulfilled only when test case number 1000 is reached, that is, when the actual failure occurs. However, performing fuzz testing using the Agent Instrumentation Framework in synchronous mode would allow the Agent to detect exceptions at, for example, test case numbers 143, 376, and 1000, where the Agent is able to identify that test cases 143 and 376 indicate some sort of exception although not leading to a full failure yet.

9.3.2.3 Hybrid Approach

Depending on the SUT and type of instrumentation provided by Agents, it is possible to use test strategies following a hybrid approach based on a combination of both synchronous and asynchronous modes. Thus, fuzz testing can be performed initially using the Agent Instrumentation Framework in *asynchronous* mode to utilize the improved speed of execution and quickly detect exceptions. Once exceptions are observed, fuzz testing can be performed using the Agent Instrumentation Framework in *synchronous* mode to reproduce the previously detected exception. Using synchronous mode, information from the relevant Agent helps to better pinpoint the specific fuzz test case that causes the exception, and additional information collected by the Agent assists in identifying the root cause of the issue. Ultimately, a combination of both modes helps maximize the efficiency and effectiveness of the fuzz test run.

9.3.3 Examples of Agents

This section gives an introduction to a number of examples of Agents that can be used on the SUT. Please note that the Agent Instrumentation Framework is considered modular and therefore it is possible to virtually create any type of Agent ranging from more general Agents that would be suitable for multiple types of SUTs to extremely specific Agents that would be applicable only for a unique SUT or target application on an SUT.

As mentioned previously in Section 9.2, one common approach for in-band instrumentation is to perform valid-case instrumentation, which in many cases has limitations on what type of exceptions can be detected. Typically, the valid-case instrumentation involves sending a protocol-specific RFC (request for comments)-compliant sequence of messages to the SUT after one or several fuzz test cases have been processed by the target application in order to test whether the SUT responds accordingly. In some cases, basic ICMP (Internet Control Message Protocol) messages can be used to test whether the SUT is still alive after it has processed fuzzed messages. The Agents extend on this limited exception detection functionality and provide more insight into what is occurring on the SUT or the specific target applications on the SUT. In the following, a number of different Agents are presented that have been implemented in the Agent Instrumentation Framework and used to test numerous SUTs. These Agents provide additional monitoring capabilities to allow detection of the previously undetected issues explained in Section 9.2. In general, every Agent monitors a specific aspect of the SUT or target application and contains some logic to compare or use the monitored or measured information with some predefined conditions or criteria to determine whether there is an exception or not. Based on this exception detection logic, the Agent provides a pass or fail verdict through the Agent Instrumentation Framework to the Fuzz Testing PC.

9.3.3.1 AgentCoreDump

The AgentCoreDump Agent's task is to identify the existence of a core dump file. Normally, when a process crashes, a core dump file can be created by writing the current contents of RAM (random access memory) to a persistent storage. This file is typically used by developers to analyze the state of the process during the crash and can help to identify what may have caused the crash, e.g. any specific values used by the instruction pointer. When the Agent detects that a core dump file has been generated, it will flag it as an exception and safely copy the core dump file to a prespecified destination to prevent it from being overwritten. This exception causes the Agent to provide a fail verdict. Parameters regarding the Agent that can be configured in the `config.json` file include the file path on the SUT that the Agent should monitor for core dump files and the name of the core dump file that will be generated.

9.3.3.2 AgentLogTailer

The AgentLogTailer Agent's task is to monitor a log file during its lifetime. The Agent reads every new line written to the log file and compares the new line to a set of predefined keywords. If there is a match, it is assumed that there is an exception detected on the SUT and the Agent gives a fail verdict. The parameters for the Agent that can be configured in the `config.json` file are the file path and file name of the log file that is monitored and the set of keywords that are used for the comparison to detect whether there is a match.

9.3.3.3 AgentProcessMonitor

The AgentProcessMonitor Agent's task is to monitor the state of a process. This can be achieved in multiple ways. For example, the Agent could either start the target process and monitor it or attach itself to monitor an existing running process. The Agent observes whether the target process dies or is turned into a zombie process. If this occurs, the Agent flags it as an exception and gives a fail verdict. Additionally, the Agent can monitor the memory usage and CPU usage of the target process. Thus, if the target process usage exceeds a certain preconfigured memory or CPU limit, it is determined that an exception has occurred and the Agent gives a fail verdict. To reset the target application into a testable state after an exception has been detected, the Agent will kill the target process and restart it in the `instrumentation_fail` method. Parameters for this Agent that can be configured in the `config.json` file are, among others, the target process name, the memory and CPU threshold values, and the start delay in seconds before the process is respawned.

9.3.3.4 AgentPID

The AgentPID Agent's task is similar to the AgentProcessMonitor in that it also monitors the processes on the SUT; however, it allows for more options and advanced instrumentation. Therefore, this Agent can only be run in synchronous mode, otherwise it may generate false positives where it alerts that an exception has occurred even though there is no exception. This Agent contains two steps of execution. First, before each fuzz test case is sent by the Fuzz Testing Tool and processed on the SUT, a mapping of the preconfigured processes with their associated process identifiers (PIDs) and PIDs of their children is made. Then, the Fuzz Testing Tool sends the fuzz test case and the SUT processes it. After each test case, the second step of this Agent is executed. At this point, the same mapping between the predefined processes and their PIDs is performed again. The Agent then compares the mapping from *before* the fuzz test case was processed on the SUT to the mapping made *after* the test case. If a specific process died between the two points of measurements, its PID will not exist in the new mapping, and the Agent will indicate it as an exception. Additionally, if a process died but was quickly restarted and therefore issued a new PID, the new PID would exist in the new mapping in place of the old PID, and thus the Agent would detect the discrepancy and mark it as an exception. Please note that it is common practice in high-availability systems to use a process daemon watchdog to support monitoring and restarting of critical processes that have died. In both of the cases mentioned above, the original process has died and therefore the Agent issues a fail verdict. Additional information regarding which process that died and any relevant information may be provided as feedback to the Fuzz Testing PC. Parameters for this Agent that can be configured in the `config.json` file include the target processes to be monitored.

9.3.3.5 AgentAddressSanitizer

The AgentAddressSanitizer Agent's task is to identify memory addressability issues and memory leaks in the target software on the SUT. The logic of this Agent is built on the Google ASan framework [14]. This Agent allows detecting issues such as:

- Use after free (dangling pointer dereference)
- Heap buffer overflow
- Stack buffer overflow
- Global buffer overflow
- Use after return
- Use after scope
- Initialization order bugs
- Memory leaks

An important requirement to allow this Agent to function properly is that the target software has to be recompiled with additional compiler flags to correctly be able to utilize the functionality provided by the Google ASan framework. Similar to AgentPID, this Agent provides more advanced instrumentation and therefore can only run in synchronous mode. It is possible to execute this Agent using two different approaches. The first approach focuses on exclusively finding memory leaks. This approach requires the Agent to kill the target process after each and every fuzz test case and analyze the output generated by the Google ASan framework to identify any memory leaks causes by the fuzzed message. The Agent contains logic to automatically perform these actions, including setting up the environment for the next test case. In the second approach, the Agent focuses on finding all other memory addressability issues. In this case, the Agent configures the Google ASan framework using environment variables to kill the target process only if the ASan framework identifies any issues. Thus, unless the ASan framework detects any issues, the target process stays alive between fuzz test cases. Therefore, this approach of testing is faster than the approach for finding memory leaks since that approach requires the target process to be restarted after every fuzz test case. In both approaches, if the Agent detects any issues, a fail verdict is reported to the Fuzz Testing Tool. Additionally, crash traces and other detailed crash information is provided as feedback to the Fuzz Testing Tool.

9.3.3.6 AgentValgrind

The AgentValgrind Agent's task is similar to AgentAddressSanitizer in that it also identifies memory addressability issues and memory leaks in the target software on the SUT. The major differences are in the mode of operation and speed. While AgentAddressSanitizer uses the Google ASan framework, this Agent uses various checkers and profilers from the Valgrind project [15]. As mentioned, the AgentAddressSanitizer requires the source code of the target application to recompile the target software using flags to utilize the functionality provided by the Google ASan framework. However, in cases where the source code of the target application is not available, AgentValgrind can be used instead to achieve the same functionality. Thus, the advantage with this Agent is that there is no need to recompile the target software. Since this Agent is using the Valgrind project, which effectively emulates a hardware layer for the target application to run on, it is possible to perform testing on the target binary as is. However, the disadvantage is that performing testing of the target software on the emulated hardware layer is quite computational-heavy and adds a significant overhead to each test case. Thus, this Agent is not ideal from a performance point of view to run on an embedded target device with limited processing power, despite the Valgrind project providing native support for a wide range of architectures. If testing is not time-critical and there is no access to the source code of the target software, using this Agent would be a suitable approach to find memory addressability issues and memory leaks in the target software.

9.3.3.7 An Example config.json Configuration File

Figure 9.5 shows a simple example of a `config.json` configuration file. This example is configuring the Agent Instrumentation Framework to be used in synchronous mode as indicated by the "instrumentation_method" parameter and the keyword "external." On the SUT, the Starter script `start.py` starts the Server daemon to listen to port 1337. The SUT has already been configured to use the IP address 192.168.137.76 during the initial network configuration. The `client.py` script on the Fuzz Testing PC will to connect to the Server daemon running on the SUT at 192.168.137.76:1337, as configured using the "ip" and "port" parameters. A token is used to perform simple authentication to the Server daemon and in this case is using the value "SecretPassword." The configuration file indicates that the AgentPID Agent should be executed on the SUT before the start of the test run as indicated by the "before_run" parameter. The `client.py` script on the Fuzz Testing PC sends the configuration parameters to the Server daemon on the SUT. On the SUT, the AgentPID Agent is started through the AgentHandler with the configuration to monitor three target processes specified in the configuration file, namely, "/system/bin/mediaserver," "com.android.bluetooth," and "android.process.media." Please note that this is just a simple example showing how the Agent Instrumentation Framework can be configured as well as how to configure specific parameters for individual Agents.

```
 1  {
 2        "instrumentation_method": "external",
 3        "external": {
 4              "ip": "192.168.137.76",
 5              "port": 1337,
 6              "token": "SecretPassword"
 7        },
 8        "before_run": {
 9              "agents": {
10                    "pid_monitor": {
11                          "type": "AgentPID",
12                          "executables": [
13                                  "/system/bin/mediaserver",
14                                  "com.android.bluetooth",
15                                  "android.process.media"
16                          ]
17                    }
18              }
19        }
20  }
```

Figure 9.5 Simple example of a `config.json` configuration file. Source: Adapted from [10]. Portions Copyright 2020 Synopsys, Inc. Used with permission. All rights reserved.

9.3.4 Example Results from Agent Instrumentation

This section is based on Reference [8] and presents some example results from an implementation of a fuzz testing environment using the Agent Instrumentation Framework on various target systems and using different configurations of Agents. The purpose is to highlight some example results where Agents found unknown vulnerabilities that are otherwise undetectable if only in-band instrumentation is used (cf. Section 9.2).

The test bench setup for the fuzz testing environment using Agent Instrumentation Framework is illustrated in Figure 9.6.

The Fuzz Testing Tool used in this setup is Defensics [16] since it provides functionality to easily extend the instrumentation features, and thus would allow utilizing the Agents in the Agent Instrumentation Framework. A series of different in-vehicle infotainment systems, including original equipment manufacturer (OEM) and aftermarket solutions, running Android or Linux were used as the SUTs. Additionally, one of the SUTs was an extracted target software running entirely in an emulated environment. The test bench was configured to run the Agent Instrumentation Framework in synchronous mode since it allows for better control of the testing and SUTs. Moreover, some Agents that were used during the testing only support running in synchronous mode. The same test environment was used for all the fuzz testing of the different SUTs. Since the Agent Instrumentation Framework is run in synchronous mode, the Fuzz Testing Tool is required to be configured to call the `client.py` script with additional parameters at different times during the fuzz testing session, e.g. before the test run, before each test case, as instrumentation, and after each test case. Defensics is able to support this requirement by using a built-in feature called *external instrumentation*, which allows configuring the tool to run the `client.py` script at these different times during the fuzz testing session. The configuration for external instrumentation in Defensics is shown in Figure 9.7.

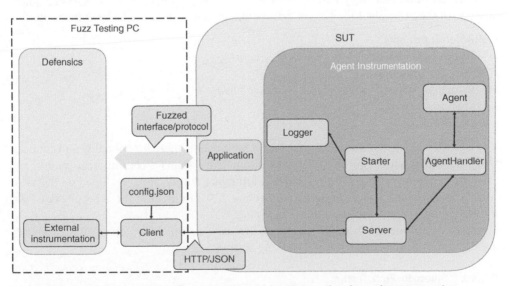

Figure 9.6 Test bench setup for the fuzz testing environment using Agent Instrumentation Framework. Source: Adapted from [10]. Portions Copyright 2020 Synopsys, Inc. Used with permission. All rights reserved.

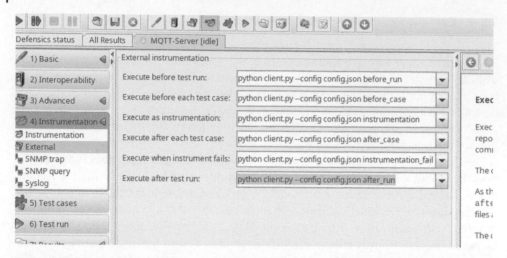

Figure 9.7 Configuration for external instrumentation in the Fuzz Testing Tool Defensics. Source: [10]. Portions Copyright 2020 Synopsys, Inc. Used with permission. All rights reserved.

The Agents to be run on the SUT and their individual configuration options are configured in the `config.json` configuration file stored on the Fuzz Testing PC. The configuration file also specifies the IP address and port number of the Server daemon running on the SUT, so that the `client.py` script knows where to send its requests to. An example configuration file is described in Section 9.3.3.7. The Agents most commonly used during the testing include AgentPID, since this agent requires no additional configuration or modification of the SUT and can easily detect issues with running processes, and the AgentAddressSanitizer and AgentValgrind to identify potential memory issues.

In-vehicle infotainment systems typically support a wide range of protocols. After a quick analysis of the SUTs, the following interfaces and protocols were the focus of the testing:

- Bluetooth protocols
- Wi-Fi (802.11) protocols
- Messaging protocols
- File format parsers (audio, video, and image files)
- CAN bus protocol
- Browser protocols

It is worth noting that due to advancements in providing more functionality and connectivity, the attack surface for these rich OS automotive systems is continuously increasing. Therefore, it is recommended to perform a full attack surface analysis based on a TARA (threat analysis and risk assessment, cf. Section 2.3.3) to identify the relevant high-risk interfaces and protocols to target for fuzz testing.

A few example results from fuzz testing of the above-mentioned interfaces and protocols are presented and discussed in the following sections.

9.3.4.1 Bluetooth Fuzz Testing

To perform Bluetooth fuzz testing, the SUT with Bluetooth functionality first needs to be configured in Defensics. There is a function in Defensics that allows for scanning and pairing with nearby Bluetooth devices and for configuring the relevant Bluetooth test suites. For Defensics to be able to successfully locate a Bluetooth-enabled SUT during a scan, the SUT first has to be put into discoverable mode, which may require some manual interaction on the SUT. The scan then returns a list of all Bluetooth-enabled devices in discoverable mode in the vicinity. Moreover, by using the service discovery function on the target device, it is possible to obtain further information about the supported services and profiles on the target. Next, this information can be imported automatically into Defensics and used to perform interoperability tests of sequences used by the supported protocols to verify what is actually supported by the target device. Finally, based on the results of the interoperability tests, suitable test cases for the target device are then generated.

Since the Bluetooth protocol is typically used to transfer payloads of data for various applications and often runs with low-level privileges – for instance, with root privileges on an in-vehicle infotainment system – Bluetooth is a desirable target for an attacker. A remote attacker has full control of the contents of the payload to be provided to the SUT, and if the payload successfully exploits a Bluetooth vulnerability, the attacker may be able to gain low-level privileges on the target system. For example, previous research shows that by exploiting a vulnerability in Bluetooth, an attacker is able to gain root privileges on an in-vehicle infotainment system [13]. Bluetooth is also used for various critical operations in and around the vehicle, such as unlocking doors or accessing certain vehicle information. Therefore, the Bluetooth-related processes and daemons are suitable candidates for the Agents to focus on.

A critical vulnerability identified using the Agent Instrumentation Framework, while testing in-vehicle infotainment systems, is described as follows. A single Bluetooth frame containing a buffer overflow anomaly caused the main Bluetooth kernel module to crash. It is possible to detect this exception using AgentPID, which monitors the `bluetoothd` daemon during the execution of the fuzz test case. It is noteworthy that the SUT has a daemon watchdog that quickly restarts the `bluetoothd` daemon process, and without the additional instrumentation provided by the Agent, this exception would have gone undetected.

The combination of the fuzzed message being of an overflow anomaly nature, and that it causes a core kernel module to crash is of major concern, since by adjusting the contents of the overflow message it may be possible to exploit the vulnerability and execute arbitrary code on the target system using the root privileges of the target process. In Figure 9.8, the relevant parts of the logs generated by AgentPID reporting a fail verdict are shown. Before the fuzz test case, the `bluetoothd` daemon is running with the PID 896 but after processing the fuzz test case, the PID is missing, indicating that the process crashed. Furthermore, it is not shown in the log but during the next fuzz test case, the `bluetoothd` daemon has restarted and has now been assigned a different PID. Thus, it is possible to infer that a Bluetooth daemon watchdog has restarted the `bluetoothd` daemon.

9.3.4.2 Wi-Fi Fuzz Testing

To perform Wi-Fi (802.11 protocol family) fuzz testing, the SUT needs to be configured in Defensics first. Defensics uses a Monitor WLAN (wireless local area network) Scan feature which automatically copies the required parameters to the corresponding settings fields in the test suite based on the selected target device. Generally, an in-vehicle infotainment system either allows creating hotspots so that users can connect to it, or the in-vehicle

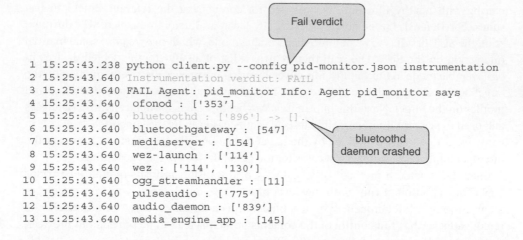

```
 1  15:25:43.238  python client.py --config pid-monitor.json instrumentation
 2  15:25:43.640  Instrumentation verdict: FAIL
 3  15:25:43.640  FAIL Agent: pid_monitor Info: Agent pid_monitor says
 4  15:25:43.640    ofonod : ['353']
 5  15:25:43.640    bluetoothd : ['896'] -> [].
 6  15:25:43.640    bluetoothgateway : [547]
 7  15:25:43.640    mediaserver : [154]
 8  15:25:43.640    wez-launch : ['114']
 9  15:25:43.640    wez : ['114', '130']
10  15:25:43.640    ogg_streamhandler : [11]
11  15:25:43.640    pulseaudio : ['775']
12  15:25:43.640    audio_daemon : ['839']
13  15:25:43.640    media_engine_app : [145]
```

Figure 9.8 Log excerpt showing that the bluetoothd daemon crashed. Source: Based on [8].

infotainment system can be configured to connect to an external access point. Finding vulnerabilities in the 802.11 implementation on these systems is also desirable for remote attackers since it potentially could give them access to other systems within the wireless network and, compared with Bluetooth, the wireless communication is often more reliable, has a higher transfer rate, thus allows for transferring larger payloads in less time, and is accessible from a longer distance.

A critical vulnerability on an in-vehicle infotainment system was identified during Wi-Fi fuzz testing using the Agent Instrumentation Framework. A single fuzzed frame containing a buffer overflow anomaly caused several kernel modules to crash. Often when communicating over Wi-Fi a connecting device needs to be authenticated, e.g. to be able to join a wireless network, a device needs to use the correct password or secret key. However, in this test case, the fuzzed frame is a non-authenticated frame, meaning that theoretically it could be sent by anyone without knowledge of the password or secret key needed to join the Wi-Fi network of the in-vehicle infotainment system. The combination of the fuzzed message being an anomaly of an overflow nature that causes core kernel modules to crash, and that the message is a non-authenticated frame, is of major concern. By adjusting the contents of the overflow message, it may be possible for an attacker to exploit the vulnerability and execute arbitrary code on the target system with the root privileges of the core kernel modules. Additionally, it would be possible to perform this attack without the need to first perform authentication to the Wi-Fi network of the in-vehicle infotainment system, thus the attack scope becomes extremely wide.

Similar to the Bluetooth example, a kernel watchdog restarts the affected kernel modules immediately without a noticeable drop in the wireless connectivity. Therefore, if only in-band instrumentation is used, it would not have been possible to detect this exception. Only by applying additional instrumentation measures provided by the Agent Instrumentation Framework is it possible to identify this exception.

A number of different Agents can be used to detect this exception. For example, if the functionality in the kernel is enabled so that the kernel modules generate a core dump

```
[  +0.000032] ------------[ cut here ]------------
[  +0.000019] WARNING: CPU: 3 PID: 912 at drivers/net/wireless/████████████████████████
[  +0.000002] Modules linked in: loop(O) ████████████████████████████████████████████████
████████████████████████████████████████████████████████████████████████████████████████
████████████████████████████████████████████████████████████████████████████████████████
████████████████████████
[  +0.000083] CPU: 3 PID: 912 Comm: ███████████ Tainted: G     U W O  ████████████████
[  +0.008363] task: edfbab40 task.stack: ecf66000
[  +0.005063] EIP: iwl_mvm_tx_mpdu+0x1a7/0x3d7 [iwlmvm]
[  +0.000003] EFLAGS: 00010286 CPU: 3
[  +0.000002] EAX: 0000001f EBX: ee75cde4 ECX: f4670344 EDX: f466ab4c
[  +0.000002] ESI: 00000002 EDI: 000001a0 EBP: ecf67bdc ESP: ecf67ba0
[  +0.000003] DS: 007b ES: 007b FS: 00d8 GS: 0000 SS: 0068
[  +0.000002] CR0: 80050033 CR2: a63de000 CR3: 2bcd8ec0 CR4: 001006f0
[  +0.000002] Call Trace:
[  +0.002741] iwl_mvm_tx_skb+0x5b/0x139 [iwlmvm]
[  +0.005071] iwl_mvm_mac_tx+0x9c/0x144 [iwlmvm]
[  +0.005068] ? iwl_mvm_stop_ap_ibss+0x12e/0x12e [iwlmvm]
[  +0.005952] ieee80211_tx_frags+0x17b/0x192 [mac80211]
 ...
```

Figure 9.9 Log excerpt showing Wi-Fi related kernel modules crashing. Source: Adapted from [10]. Portions Copyright 2020 Synopsys, Inc. Used with permission. All rights reserved.

when they crash, AgentCoreDump would be able to identify this exception. Similar to the Bluetooth example, it is possible to use AgentPID to monitor the relevant kernel processes and detect when they crash. Alternatively, AgentLogTailer can be used to detect this exception. It is first configured to tail syslog with the keywords "stack," "crash" and the relevant kernel module names. During Wi-Fi fuzz testing, when a relevant kernel module crashes, a stack trace with the associated information is generated in syslog and, consequently, the Agent indicates that an exception has occurred when it detects the keywords in syslog. An example of the syslog output when the kernel modules crash during fuzz testing is shown in Figure 9.9.

9.3.4.3 MQTT Fuzz Testing

There are various messaging protocols used in automotive systems. One such protocol is MQTT (message queuing telemetry transport) [17], which is a lightweight application layer protocol that has several advantages over traditional protocols due to its simplicity and lightweight nature. MQTT is a simple publish–subscribe network protocol that transports messages between devices. It typically runs over TCP/IP (Transmission Control Protocol/Internet Protocol), which provides ordered, lossless, and bi-directional connections. It is primarily designed for connections with remote locations where a small code footprint is required, or processing power or network bandwidth is limited. For example, a typical use case is for an embedded device to publish and subscribe to messages in the cloud. It is very efficient and suitable for such environments since it has minimal packet overhead compared with protocols such as HTTP.

MQTT was a target application on the SUT in the fuzz testing session. Since the source code for the MQTT broker used on the SUT was available, it was possible to use the AgentAddressSanitizer to test for memory addressability issues and memory leaks. In order to perform such testing, the MQTT broker was first recompiled with the additional compilation flags to enable the Google ASan framework. These flags allow the Agent to use environment variables while MQTT is executing the fuzzed messages to be able to detect exceptions.

During the fuzz testing of the SUT, the AgentAddressSanitizer identified a memory leak in the popular MQTT broker Mosquitto [18]. This vulnerability (CVE-2017-7654 [19]) was

mqtt .connect-disconnect .valid - 0x78EF0409DB41550B
Attack Modifier = 0 CVSS/BS = 9.3 (components)

MQTT CONNECT

000000	Fixed-Header	
000000	Type	
000000	CONNECT	4bit 0001
	Flags	4bit 0000
000001	Remaining-Length	. 1b
000002	Variable-Header	
000002	Protocol-Name	
000002	Length	.. 00 04
000004	Value	MQIT 4d 51 54 54
000008	Protocol-Level	. 04
000009	Connect-Flags	
000009	User-Name-Flag	1bit 0
	Password-Flag	1bit 0
	Will-Retain	1bit 0
	Will-QoS	2bit 00
	Will-Flag	1bit 0
	Clean-Session	1bit 1
	Reserved	1bit 0
00000a	Keep-Alive	.. 00 00
00000c	Payload	
00000c	Client-Identifier	
00000c	Length	.. 00 0f
00000e	Value	
00000e		MQTTServerSuite 4d 51 54 54 53 65 72 76 65 72 53 75 69 74 65
00001d	Will-Topic	()
00001d	Will-Message	()
00001d	User-Name	()
00001d	Password	()

Figure 9.10   Correct MQTT Connect message as defined by the RFC. Source: [10]. Portions Copyright 2020 Synopsys, Inc. Used with permission. All rights reserved.

reported and has since been fixed. Without additional instrumentation provided by the Agent Instrumentation Framework it would not have been possible to detect this type of issue.

The detailed steps for finding this issue are explained as follows. First, to understand the structure of MQTT messages, a correct MQTT Connect message, as defined by the RFC, is shown in Figure 9.10.

During fuzz testing, the AgentAddressSanitizer reported several failed test cases. After the failed test cases were reported, it continued execution and processed the subsequent fuzz test cases. The test cases that generated a fail verdict are based on the same anomaly, namely an underflow anomaly, where certain bytes of a message are removed before it is sent out as the fuzzed message to the SUT. An example fuzzed MQTT Connect message is depicted in Figure 9.11, where the Variable-Header has been fuzzed by removing the byte value for the Value field.

In each of the failed test cases, the underflow anomaly increased by one byte in each of the subsequent fuzzed messages. In total, five test cases for the MQTT Connect messages were identified as failed by the AgentAddressSanitizer as illustrated in Figure 9.12.

Using the Google ASan framework, the AgentAddressSanitizer is able to detect memory leaks in the MQTT target application. By analyzing the logs, it is possible to see that for each increased byte of the underflow anomaly in the fuzzed messages, the number of leaked bytes increased by one byte as well. An example of the trace showing the memory leak is found in Figure 9.13.

‹ #29 ›

Underflow of 12 -10 =2 octets
mqtt .connect-disconnect .connect .element - 0x7EEDAB2883649F1C
Attack Modifier = +25 CVSS/BS = 9.3 (components)
Underflow CWE-124 CWE-118

MQTT CONNECT [with anomaly]			
000000	Fixed-Header		
000000	Type		
000000	CONNECT		4bit 0001
	Flags		4bit 0000
000001	Remaining-Length		. 02
000002	Variable-Header		
000002	Protocol-Name		
000002	Length		.. 00 00
000004	Value		()

Figure 9.11 Fuzzed MQTT Connect message containing an underflow anomaly. Source: [10]. Portions Copyright 2020 Synopsys, Inc. Used with permission. All rights reserved.

test-group	index	status	input-octets	output-oct...	diagnosis	time	instrument...
mqtt.conn...	25	MQTT...	4	10485764	pass	2.060	1
mqtt.conn...	26			10485763	pass	1.179	1
mqtt.conn...	27			2	pass	0.861	1
mqtt.conn...	28			3	pass	0.809	1
mqtt.conn...	29			4	fail	0.995	2
mqtt.conn...	30			5	fail	0.938	2
mqtt.conn...	31			6	fail	0.862	2
mqtt.conn...	32			7	fail	0.867	2
mqtt.conn...	33			8	fail	0.871	2
mqtt.conn...	34			9	pass	0.851	1
mqtt.conn...	35			10	pass	0.170	1

Figure 9.12 Five failed test cases identified by the AgentAddressSanitizer. Source: [10]. Portions Copyright 2020 Synopsys, Inc. Used with permission. All rights reserved.

9.3.4.4 File Format Fuzz Testing

A common feature provided by in-vehicle infotainment systems is the ability to play rich media content. For instance, some simple systems only allow audio files to be played, but more advanced systems with large screens are also able to display video and image content. There are previous works showing that vulnerable media players on automotive systems can be exploited [20]. Since an attacker would typically have full control of the content provided to media players, if there is a vulnerability in the file format parser, an attacker may be able to specifically craft a certain message that would exploit said vulnerability and embed it in an attacker-controlled file. To this end, it is imperative for automotive organizations to perform file format fuzz testing to detect any potential vulnerabilities in their automotive systems.

File format fuzz testing can be performed on the target application to test how well the file format parsers can handle unexpected input. There are generally three steps involved to perform file format fuzzing:

(1) generate the fuzzed files using the *fuzz engine*;
(2) transport the fuzzed files as input to the target application using the *injector*;
(3) perform instrumentation to detect exceptions using the *monitor*.

```
21:34:37 TEST CASE #29
21:34:37 mqtt.connect-disconnect.connect.element: Underfloor of 12 -10 =2 octets
21:34:37 tcp 45264 --> localhost:1883 4 NTT CONNECT ANOMALY:
21:34:37 Receiving connack over tcp failed: expected (0b0010) but got ()
21:34:37 Instrumenting (1. round)...
21:34:37 /usr/bin/python2 /home/p0c/synopsys/aif/client.py --config/home/p0c/synopsys/aif/configs/mqtt-asan.json instrumentation
21:34:37 Instrumentation verdict: FAIL
21:34:37 FAIL Agent: memory_mqtt Info: Agent memory_mqtt says Memory leak found in /home/p0c/mosquitto/src/mosquitto:
21:34:37
21:34:37 ================================================================
21:34:37 ==20==ERROR: LeakSanitizer: detected memory leaks
21:34:37
21:34:37 Direct leak of 1 byte(s) in 1 object(s) allocated from:
21:34:37   #0 0x7f6af581ed99 in __interceptormalloc /build/gcc/src/gcc/libsanitizer/asan/asan_malloc_linux.cc:86
21:34:37   #1 0x56218adca9e3 in _mosquitto_malloc (/home/p0c/mosquitto/src/mosquitt0+0x3d9e3)
21:34:37   #2 0x56218ade0802 in _mosquitto_read_string (/home/p0c/mosquitto/src/mosquitto+0x53802)
21:34:37   #3 0x56218ade5d85 in mqtt3_handle_connect (/home/p0c/mosquitto/src/mosquitto+0x58d85)
21:34:37   #4 0x56218ade2e77 in mqtt3_packet_handle (/home/p0c/mosquitto/src/mosquitto+0x55e77)
21:34:37   #5 0x56218ade2b61 in _mosquitto_packet_read (/home/p0c/mosquitto/src/mosquitto+0x55b61)
21:34:37   #6 0x56218adca6b7 in loop_handle_reads_writes (/home/p0c/mosquitto/src/mosquitto+0x3d6b7)
21:34:37   #7 0x56218adc891c in mosquitto_main_loop (/home/p0c/mosquitto/src/mosquitto+0x3b91c)
21:34:37   #8 0x56218ada185c in main (/home/p0c/mosquitto/src/mosquitto+0x1485c)
21:34:37   #9 0x7f6af430606a in __libc_start_main (/usr/lib/libc.s0.6+0x2306a)
21:34:37
21:34:37 SUMMARY: AddressSanitizer: 1 byte(s) leaked in 1 allocation(s).
21:34:37
```

Figure 9.13 Excerpt trace showing the identified memory leak. Source: [10]. Portions Copyright 2020 Synopsys, Inc. Used with permission. All rights reserved.

The general steps to performing fuzz testing based on the fuzz engine, injector, and monitor are described in more detail in Section 7.3.

The three steps for file format fuzz testing are described in more details as follows. First, the *fuzz engine* generates the fuzzed versions of the media files. There are generally two approaches to generating the test cases for the fuzzed files: *mutation-based* fuzzing and *generation-based* fuzzing. A brief description of the two approaches used for file format fuzzing is presented as follows, and general descriptions including more details of the two approaches are given in Section 7.3.1. Please note that the approach of using dumb random fuzzing is not recommended as file formats typically follow a specification where different fields have certain meanings and therefore completely providing random content to the SUT would yield less efficient fuzz testing.

Regarding *mutation-based* fuzzing, sample files are given as input to a fuzz engine, which then continuously generates fuzzed versions of the original files. The anomalies used during mutation-based fuzzing are typically quite random in nature and do not follow any heuristics. Mutation-based fuzzing is useful if there is little or no information known about the original file structure. This approach allows for quick generation of fuzz test cases but may have a negative effect on the "test case to found issue" ratio over time. As the fuzz engine is not aware of the protocol semantics, any complexity embedded in the file itself will likely be broken during mutation. A common example of this effect is the absence of a correct checksum calculation or dynamic relationships between fields. The coverage of the fuzz test cases also depends on the quality of the original input.

Regarding *generation*-based fuzzing, the fuzz test cases are generated based on the description of the file format such as RFCs, documentation, etc. The first advantage is full coverage of the structure as all fields and elements are known by the fuzz engine. This allows for the generation of fuzz test cases covering the entire spectrum of the file format specification without the need for numerous valid sample files, which all combined contain all functionality. Second, as the fuzz engine fully understands the specification itself, the test cases themselves become more meaningful. Specific anomalies can be inserted into fields selected on type, length, functionality, and so on. More advanced anomalies can spawn over multiple fields and take the relation of elements within the file into account. For example, a correct checksum can be calculated of a field which now contains an anomaly. As the fuzzed file passes the parser's input validation checks based on the correct checksum, it is possible to reach deeper into the message processing of the target application implementation as the fuzz test cases still fully adhere to RFC definitions.

In this scenario, the generation-based fuzzing approach was followed during the file format fuzz testing. Defensics supports fuzzing of several different file formats, including common audio, video, and image formats. The file format test suites generate fuzzed versions of the files based on the full specifications of the file formats using the generation-based approach. Additionally, the target application on the SUT supports proprietary file formats. Therefore, the Defensics SDK (software development kit) [21], which allows for easy definition of file structures, was used to define the proprietary file format standards by using information from the proprietary file format specifications. If access to the proprietary file format specifications is not given, it is possible to use mutation-based fuzzing by providing sample files of valid proprietary files to the fuzz engine to generate the corresponding fuzzed files.

Regardless of the mutation-based (i.e. generating fuzzed files using a set of valid sample files as input) or generation-based (i.e. generating fuzzed files based on the file format definitions) approach, the fuzz engine produces fuzzed files that are typically stored on a disk on the Fuzz Testing PC.

The next step is the *injector*, which is responsible for transporting the fuzzed files to the target application. There are multiple ways to transport the fuzzed files to the SUT depending on what features are supported by the SUT. A manual approach based on a typical use case is to copy the fuzzed files from disk on the Fuzz Testing PC to a USB memory and then physically insert the USB memory to the USB port on the SUT. Alternatively, using remote network access to the SUT it may be possible to transfer fuzzed files over different protocols such as SCP (secure copy protocol) or FTP (file transfer protocol), and store the files locally on the SUT. Another option using remote network access to the SUT is to remotely mount on the SUT a directory where the fuzzed files are stored using, for example, NFS (network file system) or SMB (server message block). Further considerations regarding performance, network communication load, and how the fuzzed files can be provided as input to the target application need to be taken into consideration when determining the approach for the injector. More specifically, an approach on how to automate file format fuzzing over USB for automotive systems is provided in Chapter 10. It is worth noting that in order to test the media player playback functionality on the SUT, it may be required to create some logic that provides the fuzzed files as input to the target application and automatically plays the fuzz test cases.

The third and last step is the *monitor*, which performs the instrumentation of the target application. The instrumentation is based on the Agent Instrumentation Framework and utilizes the standard approach of using Agents. Thus, Agents deployed on the SUT can assess and determine whether there are any exceptions occurring in the target applications by processing the fuzzed files. As the fuzzed files containing the anomalies now reside on the SUT or are accessible on the SUT, there are several aspects that would need to be considered, depending on the SUT:

- If the target application can only read files off a USB memory, the Agent needs to reload the kernel module that mounted that medium. This causes a reread and allows the target application to "see" the fuzzed files. The assumption here is that the SUT runs some form of Linux.

- During the setup of the fuzz testing environment, it is important to determine which processes on the SUT are typically used to read the files. The Agent can then be configured to start those processes manually and provide the fuzzed files as input, e.g. launching a media player application with the fuzzed file as input. Additionally, those processes reading the files and other important processes can be simultaneously monitored using other Agents. For example, the AgentProcessMonitor can be used to determine if a certain process exceeds the allowed CPU or memory usage.

- Target processes which are monitored during the parsing of the fuzzed files can be monitored more extensively by the use of additional instrumentation enabled by recompiling the target software if access to the source code is available. For instance, using the AgentAddressSanitizer, it would be possible to detect memory addressability issues and memory leaks in the target applications.

9.3.5 Applicability and Automation

This section briefly discusses the applicability of the Agent Instrumentation Framework for use in fuzz testing environments and how to automate the fuzz testing process. When fuzzing communication protocol implementations and file format parsers on SUTs running a rich OS, the Agent Instrumentation Framework is an extremely useful solution. The benefits are that it is possible to detect several exception types and vulnerabilities that are undetectable otherwise, and that additional information about the exceptions can be provided to developers to assist in identifying the root causes. Shifting from a black-box approach to a more gray/white-box approach by allowing developers and testers access to the SUT to run the Agents on the SUT itself allows for the developers and testers to perform more efficient and effective fuzz testing.

To automate the fuzz testing process, there may be additional steps that need to be taken for the SUT. For example, it is possible to integrate the SUT with other devices or tools. One example is when the SUT crashes and prevents further testing. As external instrumentation, the Fuzz Testing PC can launch a script to restore the SUT back into a testable state. This script, which could be considered a local Agent running on the Fuzz Testing PC, could control the power supply unit connected to the SUT and power cycle the SUT. Furthermore, if required for continued testing, this local Agent could remotely access the SUT internals and copy necessary core dump files and log files to a secondary storage and then clean up or factory reset the SUT. Additionally, the SUT may require certain input to function properly, e.g. restbus simulation or analog/digital input to the SUT (described in more detail in Chapter 8). These types of inputs can be achieved using separate tools such as automotive network communication tools or HIL systems, which can be integrated with the Fuzz Testing PC and the Agent Instrumentation Framework. That is, before a test run or a test case is executed, the Agent Instrumentation Framework calls the local Agent to trigger the separate automotive test tools to provide the required inputs to the SUT to enable the correct states for testing. An overview of this example automated test setup, which expands on the general test setup in Figure 9.4 by including other devices and tools, is illustrated in Figure 9.14.

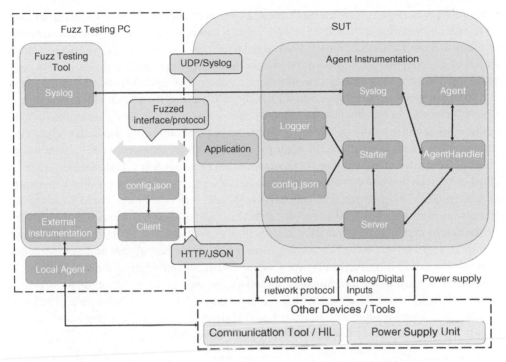

Figure 9.14 Example setup of an automated fuzz testing environment using Agent Instrumentation Framework.

Furthermore, it is possible to include additional instrumentation capabilities on the SUT such as debug capabilities. For example, by running a GDB (GNU Debugger) server [22] on the SUT and then running GDB on the Fuzz Testing PC with the parameters to remotely connect to the GDB server on the SUT, it is possible to remotely debug the target software during fuzz testing. Consequently, it would be possible to detect exceptions by analyzing, for example, register values and stack values which are collected using GDB that monitors specific processes on the SUT. Moreover, GDB can be used to pause the process and give control to the Agent to perform any specific task if required. Using more advanced Agents provides the advantages to improve fuzz testing by achieving higher detection rates, to collect relevant data for developers to further investigate and determine the root cause of underlying issues, and to allow for automation of the entire fuzz testing process.

9.4 Chapter Summary

This chapter presented the Agent Instrumentation Framework and explained how it can be used to improve fuzz testing of automotive systems running a rich OS, such as Linux and Android, providing more functionality. Moreover, several examples of Agents are introduced and explanations on how the Agents can be used to instrument the SUT in different ways that allow for more efficient and accurate fuzz testing are given. For instance, one or more Agents deployed on the SUT is used to collect additional information from the SUT. This information is then used to determine whether the recent fuzz test case caused an exception on the SUT. Moreover, if an Agent detects an exception, a fail verdict together with the collected information is provided from the SUT to the Fuzz Testing Tool and stored in the log file. This additional information serves to help developers identify the underlying root cause of any detected issues and allows them to address the potential vulnerabilities more efficiently. To demonstrate the effectiveness of the proposed Agent Instrumentation Framework, a test bench using the Agent Instrumentation Framework was built and used to perform fuzz testing of several SUTs. Multiple examples where issues on the SUTs would not have been detected unless the Agent Instrumentation Framework was used are highlighted. Finally, a discussion on how to automate the fuzz testing process by integrating the Agent Instrumentation Framework with other test tools and devices is given. The Agent Instrumentation Framework is well-suited for rich OS automotive systems, such as in-vehicle infotainment systems and telematics units, which provide suitable environments to allow Agents to run on the SUTs. The continued adoption of connected cars and autonomous vehicles is leading to software playing a major role in the automotive development process. Moreover, with the increasing awareness of cybersecurity in the automotive industry, the demands for automated fuzz testing for these types of systems will increase. The presented Agent Instrumentation Framework in this chapter can assist developers and testers to perform automated fuzz testing of such systems more effectively.

References

1 Automotive Grade Linux (2020). What is automotive grade Linux?. https://www .automotivelinux.org (accessed 30 July 2020).

2 GENIVI (2020). Beyond Linux IVI and into the connected vehicle. https://www.genivi .org (accessed 30 July 2020).

3 Oka, D. K., Yvard, A., Bayer, S., and Kreuzinger, T. (2016). Enabling cyber security testing of automotive ECUs by adding monitoring capabilities. *escar Europe*, Munich, Germany.

4 Oka, D. K., Bayer, S., Kreuzinger, T., and Gay, C. (2017). How to enable cyber security testing of automotive ECUs by adding monitoring capabilities. *Symposium on Cryptography and Information Security (SCIS)*, Naha, Japan.

5 Oka, D. K., Fujikura, T., and Kurachi, R. (2018). Shift left: fuzzing earlier in the automotive software development lifecycle using hil systems. *escar Europe*, Brussels, Belgium.

6 Open Automotive Alliance (2015). Introducing the open automotive alliance. https:// www.openautoalliance.net (accessed 30 July 2020).

7 Android (2020). What is android automotive?. https://source.android.com/devices/ automotive/start/what_automotive (accessed 30 July 2020).

8 Kuipers, R. and Oka, D. K. (2019). Improving fuzz testing of infotainment systems and telematics units using agent instrumentation. *escar USA*, Ypsilanti, MI, USA.

9 Oka, D. K. and Kuipers, R. (2019). Efficient and effective fuzz testing of automotive Linux systems using agent instrumentation. *Automotive Linux Summit*, Tokyo, Japan.

10 Kuipers, R. and Oka, D. K. (2020). Improving fuzz testing of infotainment systems and telematics units using agent instrumentation. Synopsys white paper.

11 NIST (2014). National vulnerability database – CVE-2014-0160. https://nvd.nist.gov/vuln/detail/CVE-2014-0160 (accessed 30 July 2020).

12 Synopsys (2020). The heartbleed bug. http://heartbleed.com (accessed 30 July 2020).

13 Tencent Keen Security Lab (2020). Tencent keen security lab: experimental security assessment on lexus cars. https://keenlab.tencent.com/en/2020/03/30/Tencent-Keen-Security-Lab-Experimental-Security-Assessment-on-Lexus-Cars/ (accessed 30 July 2020).

14 Google (2019). AddressSanitizer (ASan). https://github.com/google/sanitizers/wiki/AddressSanitizer (accessed 30 July 2020).

15 Valgrind Developers (2020). Valgrind. http://www.valgrind.org (accessed 30 July 2020).

16 Synopsys (2020). Defensics fuzz testing. https://www.synopsys.com/software-integrity/security-testing/fuzz-testing.html (accessed 30 July 2020).

17 MQTT (2020). MQTT: the standard for IoT messaging. https://mqtt.org (accessed 30 July 2020).

18 Mosquitto (2020). https://mosquitto.org/ (accessed 30 July 2020).

19 NIST (2018). National vulnerability database – CVE-2017-7654. https://nvd.nist.gov/vuln/detail/CVE-2017-7654 (accessed 30 July 2020).

20 Checkoway, S., McCoy, D., Kantor, B. et al. (2011). Comprehensive experimental analyses of automotive attack surfaces. *USENIX Security*, San Francisco, CA, USA.

21 Synopsys (2017). Fuzz testing software development kit (defensics SDK). https://www.synopsys.com/content/dam/synopsys/sig-assets/datasheets/fuzzing-software-development-kit.pdf (accessed 30 July 2020).

22 GDB Developers (2020). GDB: the GNU project debugger. https://www.gnu.org/software/gdb (accessed 30 July 2020).

10

Automating File Fuzzing over USB for Automotive Systems

MORE (AUTOMATION) IS LESS (MANUAL)

This chapter presents a method to perform automated file format fuzzing over USB by building a fuzz testing environment using emulated file systems. As described in Section 7.2, a fuzz testing environment contains three parts: fuzz engine, injector, and monitor. A brief introduction explaining these three parts, especially for file format fuzz testing, is given in Section 9.3.4.4. Figure 10.1 illustrates an example fuzz testing setup over USB which serves as the basis for this chapter. This chapter does a deep-dive on the injector part but will also briefly discuss the monitor part. Specifically, for the injector part a customized solution that allows for automated fuzz testing over USB is presented.

The SUT (system under test) considered in this chapter is similar to the SUT presented in Chapter 9, namely, an embedded device running a rich OS (operating system) such as Linux or Android. For example, there are Linux and Android-based systems specifically developed for the automotive industry such as AGL (Automotive Grade Linux) [1], GENIVI [2], and Android Automotive OS [3]. An example SUT is an in-vehicle infotainment system which is a typical automotive system that has a USB interface to allow for reading of user-provided files, including audio, video, and image files.

With the adoption of autonomous driving, it can be expected that vehicles will offer even more features for users to bring their own media files into the vehicle in order to help pass the time. However, media files have a long history of being a common attack vector. Given the large number of complicated formats available such as mp3, mp4, wma, jpg, png, avi, etc., that are typically supported, media files parsers are prone to bugs. For example, previous work has identified vulnerabilities in a media player parsing WMA (windows media audio) files on an in-vehicle infotainment system. By specifically crafting a WMA file containing exploit code, which is then played on the vulnerable media player, it is possible to send arbitrary CAN (controller area network) messages on the in-vehicle network to take control of the vehicle [4].

Additionally, besides media files, it is a common practice for manufacturers to allow users to download update files, e.g. map updates or program updates, provided by the official manufacturer websites, and store the updates files (often in archive file formats such as zip files or ISO files) on a USB memory that is then inserted into the in-vehicle infotainment

Building Secure Cars: Assuring the Automotive Software Development Lifecycle, First Edition. Dennis Kengo Oka.
© 2021 John Wiley & Sons Ltd. Published 2021 by John Wiley & Sons Ltd.

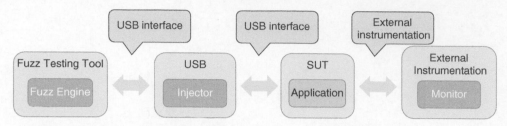

Figure 10.1 Overview of fuzz testing environment for testing over USB.

system to be updated. Thus, in many cases, the in-vehicle infotainment systems would contain zip file parsers or other file type parsers that also naturally become attack vectors.

It is also useful to note that a "State of Fuzzing" report [5] highlights that among the top protocols targeted for fuzz testing in the automotive industry are file formats such as mp3, jpg, png, and mp4, besides network communication protocols such as IP (Internet Protocol), CAN, Wi-Fi, Bluetooth, and MQTT (message queuing telemetry transport).

Depending on where in the development stage of the in-vehicle infotainment system fuzz testing occurs and by whom, e.g. by the tier 1 supplier during the development phase, or by the original equipment manufacturer (OEM) during integration with other systems, there are different approaches to testing that are possible. For instance, during development with access to the system internals it may be possible for a tier 1 supplier to run the in-vehicle infotainment system in a virtual machine using, for instance, QEMU (Quick EMUlator) [6] or KVM (Kernel-based Virtual Machine) [7] to perform fuzz testing of file parsers in a virtual environment. For an OEM, typically tests would be performed on the actual hardware of the in-vehicle infotainment system provided by the tier 1 supplier. Moreover, the OEM may not have access to additional information or internal functions known only by the tier 1 supplier. Regardless, the approach presented in this chapter would be applicable for both scenarios and might be slightly easier to set up in the virtual environment since no physical hardware is required.

The general approach contains two steps. First, relevant fuzzed files are generated by a Fuzz Testing Tool in advance and stored on a large-capacity storage medium, e.g. an external hard drive. Second, an Embedded Linux Board, in this case a BeagleBone Black, is used to emulate a filesystem as a USB storage, which contains a set of the pregenerated fuzzed files from the storage. The Embedded Linux Board acts as the injector and is physically connected over USB to the SUT. However, the physical cable is never unplugged, instead the Embedded Linux Board virtually plugs/unplugs the emulated USB storage to the SUT using custom software. For the virtual test environment, a similar setup can be used; however, the Embedded Linux Board and physical USB cable may not be needed since the custom software may be able to run in the virtual machine to virtually plug/unplug the emulated USB storage containing the fuzzed files.

The target application, e.g. a media parser on the SUT, processes the fuzzed files on the mounted emulated USB storage. If the media parser contains a bug or vulnerability, parsing the fuzzed file may cause an exception on the SUT, e.g. leading to the target application crashing or displaying something unexpected on the display on the SUT.

The main points of this chapter are:

- We provide some background on attacks using the USB interface and file parsers as an attack vector and highlight the need for file format fuzzing.
- We discuss the common challenges performing file format fuzzing over USB on automotive systems.
- To overcome these challenges, we present a solution based on using emulated filesystems to automate file format fuzzing.

This chapter is based on previous work on automating file fuzzing over USB and fuzzing the filesystem layer over USB [8, 9].

10.1 Need for File Format Fuzzing

Since the file input to the target system is often under the full control of the attacker, it is imperative that there is proper input validation performed before processing file contents and that the file parsers are robust to handle any malformed file formats. For example, an in-vehicle infotainment system providing a USB interface is susceptible to an attacker providing arbitrary files stored on a USB memory to be processed by target applications on the in-vehicle infotainment system.

A few examples of media parser vulnerabilities are presented first. These highlight the need for performing file format fuzz testing during development and testing to reduce the risk of such vulnerabilities being detected and exploited in production systems. Additionally, a couple of examples of how it is possible to abuse the update feature on an in-vehicle infotainment system through the USB interface and therefore change the functionality of the target system are also discussed.

Several vulnerabilities in a media parser for Android were identified using file format fuzzing [10]. Since media files typically contain binary streams of complex data, parsing of such data in different media parser components may cause memory corruption issues. In addition, since media players often support a large variety of codecs and formats and the fact that media playback does typically not require special permissions, media players are a lucrative attack vector for attackers. The famous Stagefright bug is the name given collectively to a set of bugs (including CVE-2015-1538 [11], CVE-2015-3824 [12], CVE-2015-3864 [13], and CVE-2015-6602 [14] among others) in the Android operating systems, specifically, in the multimedia framework library called libstagefright, which is responsible for media parsing in Android [15]. An example of how this vulnerability could be abused is an attacker providing a maliciously crafted media file, e.g. an mp4 file, which is played on the target's Android media player and as such exploits the vulnerability and executes the payload containing arbitrary commands.

In more detail, the *stagefright* command line interface is used to decode the malformed media files [10]. By providing a set of fuzzed media files, including mp4, mp3, mpg, and mkv, during fuzz testing, the stagefright command line interface decodes the inputted files and generates logs and highlights when the application crashes.

Another example of a vulnerability identified during fuzzing is in the libbpg library (CVE-2017-2575 [16]). This library is used for handling the BPG (better portable graphics) file format for digital images. It is a more compression-efficient alternative to the JPEG (Joint Photographic Experts Group) file format. The vulnerability appears when converting a malicious JPEG file to BPG and is caused by a NULL pointer dereference issue due to a missing check of the return value of a function malloc in the BPG encoder. Testing these types of media libraries with fuzzed input files, e.g. malformed JPEG files, allows identifying such issues.

Yet another example of a vulnerability type is described as follows. Interestingly, it is not in the media codec parser however rather in the subtitles file parser [17, 18]. By providing a maliciously crafted subtitles file to a vulnerable media player, this type of vulnerability can be exploited to execute arbitrary commands on the target system. An example of this type of vulnerability exists in the ParseJSS function in the popular media player VLC (CVE-2017-8311 [19] and CVE-2017-8313 [20]). The JSS (JACOsub script) file format is defined in Reference [21] and is a flexible subtitles format. It allows for some control by using directives which determine, for example, the subtitle's position, font, style, color and so on. These vulnerabilities were detected by providing invalid values for these directives using fuzzing, which then were parsed by the ParseJSS function.

Furthermore, some in-vehicle infotainment systems provide an update feature to allow updates to the software or map data to be made via the USB interface. There are various file formats used for these update files including zip files and ISO files. It has been shown that a maliciously crafted update file can bypass security verification checks [22]. By intelligently modifying the update file, it is possible to execute arbitrary commands during the update process, e.g. enabling remote access to the target system by starting an SSH (secure shell) service on the target system. Moreover, intentionally crafted updates files can provide additional functionality such as enabling hidden or disabled services, such as Wi-Fi and SSH [23]. Such services may have been disabled by the auto manufacturer in production systems since they were only used during the development stage, or certain services may have been disabled based on a region where the vehicle is sold. In both examples of modifying the update files, by crafting a specific update file taking into consideration the features of the target system, an attacker is able to run arbitrary commands on the target system and gain remote access to take full control of the target system.

While the update file examples showcase weaknesses that may be easier found during a design review or a penetration test of the target system, performing systematic file format fuzzing for these systems is also valuable. File format fuzzing of these types of update files allows testing of the security verification functions on update files and testing whether the target system is robust to handle modified, i.e. fuzzed, update files, without crashing or behaving erratically.

As a general concern, a simple attack targeting a USB interface could be performed by storing a maliciously crafted file on a USB memory stick, which a victim unsuspectedly inserts into a target in-vehicle infotainment system. More advanced attacks could be performed using small Embedded Linux Boards such as the PocketBeagle [24] which are easy to conceal and would be able to deploy more complex payloads to exploit vulnerabilities over USB. There also exist specific USB cables constructed with a malicious USB chip inside [25] that could launch attacks over the USB interface. These malicious USB cables could, for example, be introduced in the supply chain, where unsuspecting victims who plug the cables into their in-vehicle infotainment systems would trigger attacks over USB. Therefore, it is critical to thoroughly test USB interfaces and file parsers on automotive systems.

10.2 Problem Statement: Manual Process for File Format Fuzzing

The typical functionality of automotive systems with USB interfaces such as in-vehicle info-tainment systems is described as follows. Often, the target system only supports one USB device class: mass storage. The target system can mount different USB storage media, e.g. a USB memory, and can read the media files stored on it. The relevant media player on the target system then parses the media files read from the USB storage medium. Besides media files, the target system may support various update files for updating software on the target system in the form of zip files or ISO files among others. Often, file format fuzzing on automotive systems occurs on actual hardware. However, depending on the access to the internals of the target systems it may be possible to perform testing using software only, e.g. using virtual machines. This chapter focuses on the main challenges when performing testing on actual hardware and considering the cases where access to the internals of the target system such as source code may be limited. Therefore, the typical testing is following more of a black-box and gray-box approach. The solution presented in the next section chiefly addresses these challenges when testing on actual hardware, however the solution is also useful for software-only scenarios.

The typical test approach for file format fuzzing over USB on actual hardware is rather simple, however it requires several manual steps, which are described as follows and illustrated in the workflow in Figure 10.2.

In Step 1, the tester generates the fuzzed files using a Fuzz Testing Tool on a Fuzz Testing PC. Then, in Step 2, the tester copies the fuzzed files from the PC to a USB storage medium, e.g. a USB memory. Step 3 involves physically transferring the USB storage medium to the

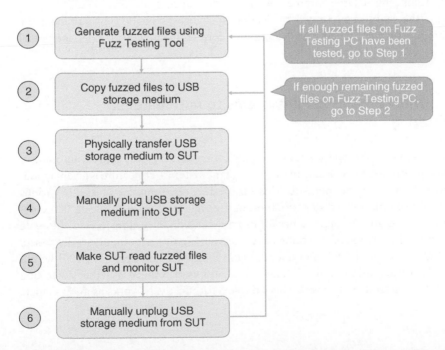

Figure 10.2 Workflow describing the steps involved in file format fuzzing over USB on actual hardware.

SUT, which may involve very short distances to longer distances depending on how close the Fuzz Testing PC is to the SUT. In Step 4, the tester manually plugs in the USB storage medium into the SUT. Please note that, depending on the SUT, there may be size restrictions on the USB storage medium, e.g. an SUT may only support up to 32 GB or 64 GB USB memory sticks. As an example, if there is 1000 GB worth of fuzzed files to test, it may require a tester to plug and unplug the USB memory 15–30 times. Moreover, depending on the SUT, in Step 5, the tester may be required to manually navigate through the menus on the SUT to launch the fuzzed files to be read from the USB storage medium. This navigation may require physical input through buttons on the target system or input through a touch screen. This step also requires the tester to verify the progress and wait for the SUT to process all the fuzzed files on the USB storage medium. Additionally, this step involves monitoring of the SUT to determine whether there are any exceptions based on reading the fuzzed files. In many cases, this may be a manual approach where the tester has to physically sit in front of the SUT and visually inspect the display to detect any abnormal behavior, e.g. warning messages displayed, application hanging or crashing, application restarting, or the system rebooting. Once the SUT has completed reading all the fuzzed files, in Step 6, the tester has to manually unplug the USB storage medium from the SUT and go back to Step 1 or Step 2, depending on how many fuzzed files were generated in Step 1. If there are enough fuzzed files already generated on the Fuzz Testing PC, the tester can go to directly Step 2 and copy the next set of fuzzed files to use in the testing. If all the fuzzed files on the Fuzz Testing PC have been used in testing the SUT already, the tester goes to Step 1 and generates more fuzzed files for the same or next file format type. This loop then continues with all the manual steps included and the physical actions required by the tester until the fuzz testing session is deemed finished.

Thus, these manual steps in the test process are time-consuming and error-prone due to manually managing a large number of fuzzed files during the fuzz testing session, and therefore the solution presented in Section 10.3 focuses on how to automate the above-mentioned process when performing file format fuzzing over USB on actual hardware.

10.3 Solution: Emulated Filesystems to Automate File Format Fuzzing

This section presents a solution for automating file format fuzzing over USB on automotive systems based on Reference [8]. First, an overview of the system architecture is given including the required system components for this fuzz testing environment. Next, the various requirements for automating the steps are thoroughly explained. An example implementation is then presented and the approaches for instrumentation, including how to automate the monitoring and detection of exceptions as well as automating user input, are discussed.

A simplified in-vehicle infotainment system consisting of a Raspberry Pi 2 [26] with a specific Kodi [27] distribution, shown in Figure 10.3, was used as the SUT in the fuzz testing environment for illustrative purposes. This sample SUT effectively works as an in-vehicle

Figure 10.3 Sample SUT of an in-vehicle infotainment system running on Raspberry Pi 2 with a specific Kodi distribution.

infotainment system, which allows touch-screen control and has the capability to playback various media files from a USB storage. Please note that the same fuzz testing environment was also used to perform fuzz testing on several actual automotive infotainment systems to validate that the solution is applicable for real systems.

Since the main focus is on *automation* of the file format fuzz testing over USB when testing actual hardware, this SUT is suitable as an example target system. It is worth noting that for software-only based fuzz testing, it would be possible to use virtualization and set up a fuzz testing environment by following similar steps for the solution for automation presented in this section; however, the implementation details for such a software-only based test environment are not discussed further.

10.3.1 System Architecture Overview

An overview of the system architecture is described as follows. The included system components in the fuzz testing environment for file format fuzzing of actual hardware target systems are described as:

- Fuzz Testing PC with Fuzz Testing Tool to generate the fuzzed files.
- A Storage Medium capable of storing a large volume of fuzzed files, e.g. an external hard drive, SD (secure digital) card or a fileserver/NAS (network-attached storage).

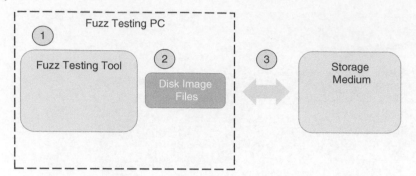

Figure 10.4 Prepare fuzzed files in phase one. Source: Adapted from [8]. Portions Copyright 2018 Synopsys, Inc. Used with permission. All rights reserved.

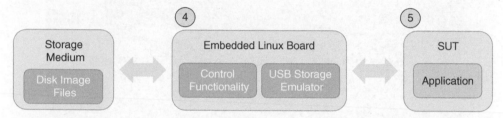

Figure 10.5 Automatically emulate filesystems as USB storage in phase two. Source: Adapted from [8]. Portions Copyright 2018 Synopsys, Inc. Used with permission. All rights reserved.

- An Embedded Linux Board with USB OTG (on-the-go) support and custom software to enable USB storage emulation and various control functionality for automation.
- SUT with USB interface and relevant target applications, e.g. media player to allow playback of media files.
- Other necessary accessories such as power supplies and USB cables to enable and connect the above-mentioned components.

There are two phases to enable automated file format fuzzing in this fuzz testing environment. The first phase is preparing the fuzzed files and is illustrated in Figure 10.4. The second phase is to automatically emulate filesystems as USB storage and is depicted in Figure 10.5. The numbers in the figures visually indicate where each step in the procedure takes place in the test environment.

First, in phase one, the following three steps are taken to prepare the fuzzed files as shown in Figure 10.4. These three steps involve three parts: *Fuzz Testing Tool*, *disk images files*, and *Storage Medium*. In Step 1, the *Fuzz Testing Tool* on the Fuzz Testing PC generates the relevant fuzzed files to be used for testing on the target system, e.g. a certain set of media files. The fuzzed files are then in Step 2 stored in *disk image files* which are later used to represent the contents of USB storage to the SUT. Next in Step 3, the disk image files are copied to the *Storage Medium*.

In the second phase, the following two steps continuing from the steps in phase one are taken to automatically emulate filesystems as USB storage as shown in Figure 10.5. These two steps involve three parts: *Storage Medium*, *Embedded Linux Board*, and *SUT*. In Step 4, custom software on the *Embedded Linux Board* reads a disk image file from the *Storage*

Medium and emulates a filesystem over USB containing the fuzzed files in the disk image file. Next, in Step 5, the emulated filesystem over USB is recognized as a USB storage by the *SUT* which then uses the appropriate target application to read the fuzzed files, e.g. a media player. Once the SUT has completed reading all the fuzzed files contained in one disk image file, the fuzz testing automatically proceeds with repeating Steps 4 and 5 by loading the next disk image file, emulating the corresponding filesystem, and the SUT reading the fuzzed files contained within the disk image file.

Further details on an example implementation based on References [8, 9] of phase one are described in Section 10.3.2 and of phase two in Section 10.3.3.

It is important to note that to fully automate file format fuzzing over USB, a certain level of external instrumentation to automate user input and to detect exceptions is also required, which is described in more detail in Sections 10.3.4 and 10.3.5.

10.3.2 Phase One Implementation Example: Prepare Fuzzed Files

An example implementation of the three steps from Figure 10.4 to prepare the fuzzed files is described as follows.

In Step 1 in Figure 10.4, Defensics [28] is used as the *Fuzz Testing Tool* as it supports the generation of a large number of different file formats. First, it is required to understand which file formats the target system supports and should be tested in order to generate the relevant fuzzed files. This information is often defined in requirements or may be available in, for example, the user manual. Moreover, it is recommended to perform a TARA (threat analysis and risk assessment, cf. Section 2.3.3) to better understand the risks associated with the target system and to identify the high-risk file formats to target for fuzz testing.

As a side-note and optional step, if it is unclear what file formats are supported on the target system or if there are concerns that there may be additional file formats that the target system supports but are not advertised, such hidden supported file formats may be uncovered using some form of exploration. During the exploration it is possible to use different tools to generate and convert a number of different file formats to potentially detect any file formats that are not advertised but supported. For example, for image files, the imagemagick library [29] could be used to convert one sample image to a number of different formats, including bmp, gif, jpg, png, ico, etc. Similarly, for audio and video files, the ffmpeg library [30] could be used to convert a sample video to a number of different formats, including avi, mp3, mp4, wav, wma, etc. Please note that when converting to audio files, only the audio is extracted and converted from the sample video file. All of these different file formats could then be loaded onto the SUT and tested to see whether there are relevant target applications on the SUT that can play or read the different file formats during this exploration step. If the SUT is able to play/read a specific file format that the SUT does not explicitly state that it supports, it can be determined that a hidden supported file format has been detected. In such a case, that file format should most likely also be included in the fuzz testing.

For common media file formats, it is possible to use generation-based fuzzing, which is described in more detail in Sections 7.3.1 and 9.3.4.4. Based on an understanding of the file format specification, various anomalies are inserted to generate files that are malformed but often structurally valid or close to valid. An example of generating fuzzed jpg files using the JPEG Test Suite in Defensics is shown in Figure 10.6 [8]. Running this test suite generates a large number of fuzzed jpg files on the Fuzz Testing PC.

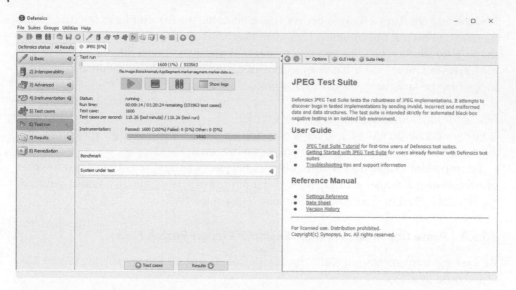

Figure 10.6 Generating fuzzed jpg files using the JPEG Test Suite in Defensics. Source: Adapted from [8]. Portions Copyright 2018 Synopsys, Inc. Used with permission. All rights reserved.

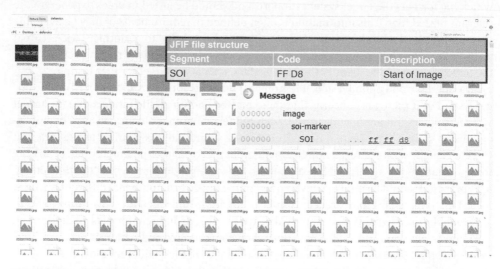

Figure 10.7 Generated fuzzed jpg files stored on the Fuzz Testing PC. Source: Adapted from [8]. Portions Copyright 2018 Synopsys, Inc. Used with permission. All rights reserved.

Figure 10.7 shows the fuzzed jpg files generated by Defensics stored on the Fuzz Testing PC. Examining the contents of a certain fuzzed jpg file shows that the SOI (start of image) marker has the invalid value of 0xFF 0xFF 0xD8. The correct value for SOI according to the JPEG specification is 0xFF 0xD8. Thus, this particular fuzzed file contains an additional 0xFF byte.

```
1  #  dd if=/dev/zero of=$DISKIMAGE bs=$BSVALUE count=$COUNT 2>/dev/null
2  #  mkfs.fat $DISKIMAGE >/dev/null
3  #  mount $DISKIMAGE $MOUNTPOINT
4  #  cp $FUZZEDFILESFOLDER/* $MOUNTPOINT
5  #  umount $MOUNTPOINT
```

Figure 10.8 Commands to create a disk image file on Linux.

If proprietary file formats are supported by the SUT, using generation-based fuzzing is generally not possible since the file format specification is not available. In this case, it is possible to use mutation-based fuzzing, which is described in more detail in Sections 7.3.1 and 9.3.4.4. The Fuzz Testing Tool takes a valid file in the proprietary file format as input and modifies, i.e. mutates, certain bits in the file to generate a number of different fuzzed files.

In Step 2 in Figure 10.4, the fuzzed files are stored in *disk image files*. One way to implement this step is to run some commands on a Linux system. For example, if the Fuzz Testing PC is running Linux, the following commands shown in Figure 10.8 can be executed in a script to create a disk image file and copy the fuzzed files into the disk image file. The $DISKIMAGE variable would contain the path and filename of the disk image, e.g. /tmp/JPG_0.img. The $BSVALUE variable is the blocksize that the dd command will read/write at one time. The $COUNT variable could be defined so that its value multiplied by the $BSVALUE equals, e.g. the maximum USB storage size supported by the SUT. The $MOUNTPOINT variable would point to a temporary mount point, e.g. /mnt/tmp. The $FUZZEDFILESFOLDER variable would point to the folder containing the fuzzed files, e.g. /tmp/fuzzedfiles.

The commands on the different lines are explained as follows. On Line 1, the dd command is used to create a disk image file from /dev/zero. It basically creates an empty disk image containing NULL (zero value) bytes. The size of the disk image is equal to the value of the $BSVALUE multiplied by the $COUNT. As an example, to create a 64 GB disk image emulating a 64 GB USB memory, the dd command can be used with the $BSVALUE set to 1 048 576 and $COUNT to 64 000. On Line 2, a filesystem is created on the disk image file. In this example, the mkfs.fat command is used to create a FAT filesystem. It is important to use a filesystem that is supported by the SUT. Based on the supported filesystems there are different commands that can be used such as mkfs.ext2, mkfs.ext3, mkfs.ext4, and mkfs.ntfs. Then, on Line 3, once a filesystem has been created on the disk image, the disk image is mounted to a certain mount point in the Linux system, i.e. it makes the filesystem in the disk image accessible and attaches it to the existing directory structure. At this point, the contents of the disk image is empty. Next, on Line 4, the fuzzed files that were generated in Step 1 are copied into the mounted filesystem. The contents of the mounted filesystem are the same contents that would be presented to the SUT as an emulated USB storage. Finally, on Line 5, after all the fuzzed files have been copied to the mounted filesystem, the filesystem is unmounted from the existing directory structure. The disk image now contains the fuzzed files that were previously generated. An example of such a disk image file of size 64 GB which contains fuzzed jpg files is shown in Figure 10.9.

Name ^	Date modified	Type	Size
JPG_0.img	7/28/2020 23:30	Disc Image File	65,536,000 KB

Figure 10.9   Created 64 GB disk image file which contains fuzzed jpg files.

Name ^	Date modified	Type	Size
JPG_0.img	7/28/2020 21:05	Disc Image File	8,192,000 KB
JPG_1.img	7/28/2020 21:15	Disc Image File	8,192,000 KB
JPG_2.img	7/28/2020 21:25	Disc Image File	8,192,000 KB
JPG_3.img	7/28/2020 21:34	Disc Image File	8,192,000 KB
JPG_4.img	7/28/2020 21:43	Disc Image File	8,192,000 KB
JPG_5.img	7/28/2020 21:59	Disc Image File	8,192,000 KB
JPG_6.img	7/28/2020 22:15	Disc Image File	8,192,000 KB
JPG_7.img	7/28/2020 22:24	Disc Image File	8,192,000 KB

Figure 10.10   Multiple created 8 GB disk image files which contains fuzzed jpg files.

Please note that this simple example only shows a few commands on how to create a disk image file and fill it with previously generated fuzzed files. With some additional commands, a script can be created that loops through the folders containing the generated fuzzed files in Step 1 and automatically creates additional disk image files of the predefined size when one disk image file has been filled with fuzzed files. An example showing several disk image files, each containing a number of fuzzed jpg files, is presented in Figure 10.10. Please note that this example shows disk image files with a size of 8 GB to emulate USB storage devices of size 8 GB. Suitable sizes for the disk image files can be selected based on what is supported by the SUT.

In Step 3 in Figure 10.4, the prepared disk image files containing the fuzzed files are copied to the *Storage Medium*. This can be achieved in different ways depending on what type of storage medium is used. It should be noted that the disk image files do not need to be stored locally on the Embedded Linux Board, since these Embedded Linux Boards usually have networking capabilities such as Wi-Fi and Ethernet. Therefore, the disk image files may be stored remotely on another system.

It is noteworthy to consider how fuzz testing will be conducted to be able to select the suitable approach for the Storage Medium. Two use cases can be identified:

- The total size of disk image files is limited and therefore the Storage Medium can be attached directly to the Embedded Linux Board.
- The total size of disk image files is large and therefore a fileserver/NAS can be used to share the image files across multiple Embedded Linux Boards and SUTs.

For the first use case, an SD card or an external hard drive can be used as the Storage Medium. In such a case, the Storage Medium can be connected directly to the Fuzz Testing PC by inserting an SD card or connecting the external hard drive over USB, which allows for direct transfer of the disk image files. Alternatively, the Storage Medium can be connected directly to the Embedded Linux Board, e.g. an external hard drive connected over USB or

```
# modprobe g_mass_storage file=$DISKIMAGE
```

Figure 10.11 Command in Linux to emulate a USB storage from a disk image file.

an SD card inserted on the Embedded Linux Board. In such a case, the Embedded Linux Board is connected over Ethernet or Wi-Fi to the Fuzz Testing PC where the disk image files are copied through the Embedded Linux Board and then stored on the Storage Medium.

For the second use case, a fileserver or a NAS could be used as the Storage Medium. In such a case, the disk image files are copied from the Fuzz Testing PC over Ethernet or Wi-Fi to the Storage Medium, which is accessible remotely as a network share.

10.3.3 Phase Two Implementation Example: Automatically Emulate Filesystems

An example implementation of the two steps from Figure 10.5 to automatically emulate filesystems as USB storage is described as follows.

In Step 4 in Figure 10.5, the *Embedded Linux Board* reads a disk image file from the *Storage Medium* and emulates a filesystem containing the fuzzed files. It is important to note that a USB storage emulator is used rather than actual physical USB storage, such as a USB memory, since actual USB storage requires plugging and unplugging it into the SUT. To be able to automate file format fuzzing, this physical activity of plugging and unplugging physical USB storage into the SUT must be avoided and replaced by *virtually* plugging and unplugging emulated USB storage into the SUT. Thus, the Embedded Linux Board is continuously physically connected over USB to the SUT.

One requirement for the Embedded Linux Board is OTG support, which means that the Embedded Linux Board can switch roles from host to device. This feature is required to present the Embedded Linux Board as a USB Mass Storage Device when it is connected to the SUT. Examples of Embedded Linux Boards that support this feature are BeagleBone Black [31] and Raspberry Pi Zero [32].

The Linux operating system supports "USB gadget" kernel modules, which allow emulation of a wide range of USB devices (keyboards, Ethernet adapters, etc.). One of the supported modules is the mass storage class (g_mass_storage, also available through g_multi) which can emulate USB storage. In this setup, BeagleBone Black is used as the Embedded Linux Board and it is running a functional Linux operating system. As such, the following Linux command in Figure 10.11 can be run in a script to emulate a USB storage from a disk image file. The $DISKIMAGE variable would contain the path and filename of the disk image, e.g. /tmp/JPG_0.img.

In this standalone test setup, The BeagleBone Black is connected to the SUT over USB as shown in Figure 10.12. As mentioned above in the beginning of Section 10.3, the SUT is a Raspberry Pi 2 running a specific Kodi distribution acting as an in-vehicle infotainment system. It is connected to a touchscreen that facilitates user input.

In Step 5 in Figure 10.5, after the modprobe command is run on the Embedded Linux Board, the *SUT* recognizes the Embedded Linux Board as a USB storage providing the content of fuzzed files that are stored in the disk image file.

Depending on the SUT, when it detects that a new USB storage has been attached, it may automatically launch the appropriate target application, e.g. a media player which

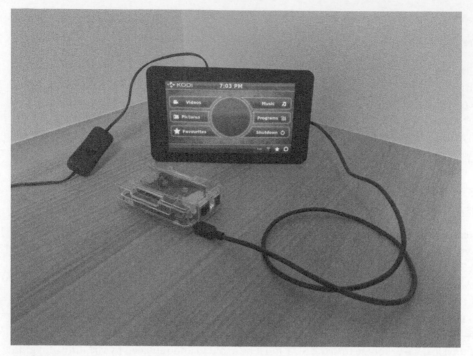

Figure 10.12 BeagleBone Black connected over USB to the SUT following a standalone fuzz testing approach.

loads and starts playing the files detected in the attached storage (i.e. the emulated USB storage). Some SUTs may require user input to launch the target application and load the files in the attached storage. In this case, considerations on how to automate user input are required. Some examples on external instrumentation on automating user input are described in Section 10.3.4.

Moreover, to be able to automate fuzz testing by repeating Steps 4 and 5 in Figure 10.5 by providing the SUT with the next set of fuzzed files in the following disk image file, there is a need to understand when the SUT has processed all the fuzzed files provided in the emulated USB storage.

One approach that can be taken is to monitor read accesses made by the SUT to the emulated USB storage. Typically, the SUT will initially make many read access requests to the emulated USB storage, in order to read the file names, folder structures and corresponding metadata, and present the files or metadata on the display of the SUT in order to play the files. Then as each file is processed, i.e. in the case of media files played by the media player, subsequent read access requests are made to the emulated USB storage to read the relevant media data. When all files have been processed, the number of read requests to the emulated USB storage would typically rapidly decrease or stop.

With this understanding in place, it is possible to use FUSE (filesystem in userspace) [33] which allows running filesystem code in userspace. That is, the disk image file containing

```
# rmmod g_mass_storage
```

Figure 10.13 Command in Linux to remove the emulated a USB storage.

the fuzzed files is mounted as a FUSE filesystem. It is then possible to intercept and monitor the read requests from the kernel module. Please note that the kernel module must be modified to open the filesystem image with the O_DIRECT and O_SYNC flags to ensure that read/write requests from the USB host, i.e. the SUT, are effectively translated to read/write requests to the FUSE filesystem. If these flags are not added, the kernel module would cache the filesystem data and therefore only access the FUSE filesystem once. Subsequent requests from the SUT to access the data would be provided by the cached data rather than accessing the data from the FUSE filesystem. This would prevent being able to properly monitor the read accesses from the SUT to the emulated file system, i.e. to the FUSE filesystem.

By using FUSE on the Embedded Linux Board to emulate USB storage to the SUT, it is then possible to use a script that monitors the read access requests from the SUT to the emulated USB storage. By defining some logic in the script, it is possible to determine when the SUT has finished processing all the fuzzed files in the emulated USB storage, since the script can detect that read access requests have rapidly decreased or stopped for a certain time.

There may be additional approaches to determine that the SUT has finished processing all the fuzzed files by using some external instrumentation on the SUT. There are several approaches for external instrumentation of the SUT to monitor for exceptions described in Section 10.3.5. These approaches may be refined to also monitor the SUT for finishing processing all the fuzzed files included in the emulated USB storage.

Once it has been determined that the SUT has finished processing all the fuzzed files provided in the emulated USB storage, the fuzz testing session continues by repeating Steps 4 and 5 in Figure 10.5. The Embedded Linux Board first needs to remove the existing emulated USB storage before it can load the next disk image file and present it as a new emulated USB storage to the SUT. The command shown in Figure 10.13 can be used on the Embedded Linux Board to remove the emulated USB storage.

After this command is run, the SUT will no longer recognize the USB storage being connected to it. It is possible to create a script on the Embedded Linux Board that would automatically then load the next disk image file containing the next set of fuzzed files using the approach described for Step 4. This script would continue to remove the emulated USB storage when all the fuzzed files contained in that storage have been processed, and then emulate a new USB storage using the next disk image file and continuously repeat Steps 4 and 5 until all the disk image files in the fuzzing session have been processed.

Moreover, besides scripts on the Embedded Linux Board to emulate USB storage to the SUT, the Embedded Linux Board also contains some custom software to allow control of the functionality of the Embedded Linux Board needed to automate fuzz testing. These control scripts provide various features such as:

- Start USB storage emulation (i.e. load a disk file and emulate as USB storage to the SUT).
- Pause/resume fuzzing (i.e. instruct the SUT to stop/start processing the fuzzed files).

- Stop USB storage emulation (i.e. remove the emulated USB storage).
- Log results (i.e. instruct the SUT to provide pass/fail verdict of processing the fuzzed files).

The control scripts used to instruct the SUT may require some additional solutions specific for the SUT. Some examples on how to stop/start processing fuzzed files are given in Section 10.3.4 and some examples on how to determine exceptions and give pass/fail verdicts of processing fuzzed files are given in Section 10.3.5. Additionally, such solutions may be implemented using the Agent Instrumentation Framework presented in Chapter 9.

Depending on the total size of the disk image files there are two different approaches that can be taken for testing the SUT based on two use cases. The two use cases are explained in Section 10.3.2, and can be summarized as follows:

- The total size of disk image files is limited and therefore the storage medium can be attached directly to the Embedded Linux Board.
- The total size of disk image files is large and therefore a fileserver/NAS can be used to share the image files across multiple Embedded Linux Boards and SUTs.

For the first use case, a *standalone* fuzz testing approach can be taken. For the second use case, a *network-based* fuzz testing approach can be taken. The two approaches are described in the following.

An overview of the *standalone* fuzz testing approach is presented in Figure 10.14. In this case the Local Storage Medium, e.g. an SD card or an external USB hard drive is directly connected to the Embedded Linux Board. The Local Storage Medium is large enough to store all the disk images required for the fuzz testing session. The Embedded Linux Board is connected over USB to the SUT.

The Embedded Linux Board also contains the custom software based on scripts required to perform the USB storage emulation and various control functionality for automation. The main advantage with this approach is the simplicity. There is no need for network communication or need to access network storage. The Embedded Linux Board can, in many cases, be powered by the SUT through the USB port, which means that there is no need for an external power supply for the Embedded Linux Board. This approach is suitable for a limited set of fuzz test cases, where there is no need to run tests in parallel and the Embedded Linux Board can be connected to the SUT in an isolated environment where there is no need for network access or external power supplies. It is worth noting that while the main function of the storage medium is to store the disk image files containing the fuzzed

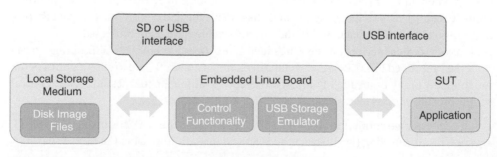

Figure 10.14 Overview of the standalone fuzz testing approach.

files, it is also necessary that the storage medium reserves some storage capacity to store the logs containing results of the fuzz testing. An implementation example of the standalone fuzz testing approach is shown in Figure 10.12. The Embedded Linux Board, in this case BeagleBone Black, is connected over USB to the SUT. The storage medium, which contains the disk image files, is a microSD card plugged into the BeagleBone Black. Please note that since a limited size storage medium containing the disk image files is used in the standalone fuzz testing approach (e.g. a 64 GB microSD card on the BeagleBone Black or a 4 TB external hard drive), technically it would be possible to attach the same size USB storage (i.e. a 64 GB USB memory or a 4 TB external hard drive) directly to the SUT rather than use emulated filesystems since there would be no need to plug/unplug the USB storage. However, such an approach would not allow for automation of fuzz testing. The advantages of this solution is that the Embedded Linux Board contains custom software that, besides emulating USB storage, is able to provide the necessary functionality needed to automate fuzz testing, such as automating user input on the SUT (described in more detail in Section 10.3.4) and monitoring for exceptions on the SUT (described in more detail in Section 10.3.5).

Next, an overview of the *network-based* fuzz testing approach is shown in Figure 10.15. In this setup, the Network Storage Medium, e.g. a fileserver or NAS, is connected to one or multiple Embedded Linux Boards over Ethernet or Wi-Fi. Thus, the disk image files may be accessible on the Embedded Linux Boards over network protocols such as NFS (network file system) or SMB (server message block). The Network Storage Medium is of large enough capacity to be able to store a large volume of the disk images used in the fuzz testing session. The storage medium is typically larger than what is possible for the standalone approach. Moreover, each Embedded Linux Board is connected over USB to an individual SUT.

In this setup, the Embedded Linux Boards also contain the custom software based on scripts required to perform the USB storage emulation and various control functionality for automation. Additionally, the Fuzz Testing PC acts as a control system to be able to control one or multiple Embedded Linux Boards during fuzz testing. The network-based approach is more complex; however, the main advantage is that it is possible to distribute test cases

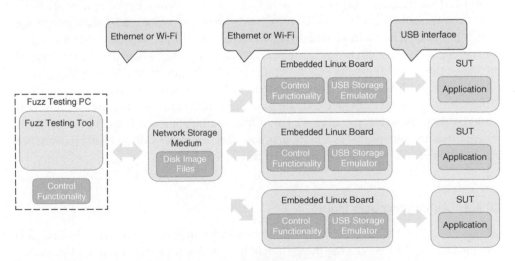

Figure 10.15 Overview of the network-based fuzz testing approach.

over multiple SUTs. Thus, it is possible to significantly reduce the testing time required by running multiple Embedded Linux Boards and SUTs and performing the fuzz testing in parallel.

For example, let's consider a scenario where there are 100 disk image files stored on the storage medium. If two Embedded Linux Boards are used, the Fuzz Testing PC can issue control commands to each of the Embedded Linux Boards and instruct them to use different disk image files. Thus, Embedded Linux Board #1 can use disk image files 000 through 049, and Embedded Linux Board #2 can use disk image files 050 through 099. Each Embedded Linux Board accesses the disk image files remotely over a network protocol or retrieves the corresponding files and stores them locally and emulates a USB storage to respective SUT. Once an SUT is done processing all the contained fuzzed files in one disk image file, the Embedded Linux Boards proceed with the next disk image files. In this case, Embedded Linux Board #1 proceeds with disk image file 001, and Embedded Linux Board #2 continues with disk image 051. Using this approach, the time to perform fuzz testing of the SUT is effectively halved. By adding more Embedded Linux Boards and SUTs it is possible to further reduce the time required for performing fuzz testing. Thus, the network-based approach is extremely useful since it allows one to parallelize the testing and reduce the required test time. Moreover, it is also possible to use the network-based approach when performing fuzz testing of different SUTs, each connected to a separate Embedded Linux Board, where the same fuzzed files, i.e. disk image files, are reused for the different SUTs. This approach saves storage space since all the disk image files can be stored in one central location, i.e. on the Network Storage Medium, and reused for a large number of different SUTs that are tested in parallel. Moreover, the Fuzz Testing Tool can generate additional fuzzed files over time that can be added in new disk image files, which are then stored on the Network Storage Medium. This approach allows fuzz testing to be continuously performed while having the possibility to add new fuzzed files in disk image files that are accessible by all the Embedded Linux Boards.

An example implementation of the network-based fuzz testing approach is shown in Figure 10.16. This setup only shows one Embedded Linux Board, in this case BeagleBone Black, connected over USB to one SUT. The storage medium, which contains the disk image files, is in this case an external hard drive connected over USB to a wireless router which is sharing the storage as a fileserver to the BeagleBone Black. Please note that for faster speed the BeagleBone Black is connected over Ethernet to the wireless router; however, it could be connected over Wi-Fi instead. Please note that the figure is purely for illustrative purposes; if there is only one SUT and one external hard drive, the standalone fuzz testing approach could be used. However, the network-based fuzz testing approach is useful for use cases where there are multiple SUTs and there is a need to use larger storage media that are not accessible over USB, such as remote fileservers or NAS.

10.3.4 Automating User Input

Sections 10.3.2 and 10.3.3 described how file format fuzzing can be automated by first generating fuzzed files and storing them in disk image files, and then using an Embedded Linux Board to emulate a USB storage to present the fuzzed files to the SUT. Depending

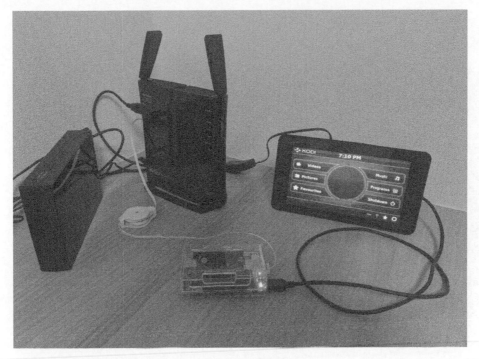

Figure 10.16 BeagleBone Black connected over USB to the SUT following a network-based fuzz testing approach.

on the SUT, the presented fuzzed files in the emulated USB storage may be played automatically when the USB storage is emulated, i.e. when the SUT detects that a "USB storage has been inserted." However, in some cases, the SUT may require manual physical user input to navigate menus, launch the corresponding target application, press a "Play" button, etc. Moreover, if there is an exception indicated visually, e.g. an error screen pops up, there is a need to close the error message screen by clicking an "OK" button or an "X" (Close) button. This type of manual user input is required in order to automate the fuzz testing process to be able to start or proceed with processing the next fuzzed file.

There are multiple approaches that can be taken for automating user input on the SUT. A few different examples are presented in this section.

In a development environment where full access to the internals of the SUT is available, a white-box approach can be taken. For example, the target applications can be instrumented with debug software that allows remote commands to be executed for the target applications to, for example, load, open, or play files. The Agent Instrumentation Framework previously presented in Chapter 9 would be applicable in this situation, where Agents can be used to instruct and control the target applications on the SUT. Moreover, it may be possible to run a VNC (virtual network computing) server on the SUT. The Fuzz Testing PC can then be connected over VNC to the SUT and by using some scripts to transmit keyboard or mouse events would allow automation of the user input on the SUT.

If a white-box approach is not possible, there are other examples that would be useful for gray-box or black-box approaches, as presented below. One of the simplest ways is to enable

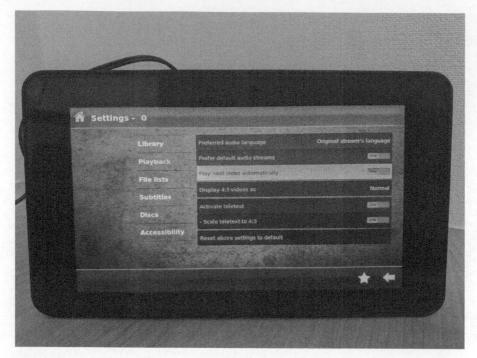

Figure 10.17 Autoplay functionality that can be enabled in the menu settings on the SUT.

Autoplay functionality on the SUT where applicable. Some target systems have an Autoplay functionality that may need to be enabled in the menu settings of the target system. An example of such functionality is shown in Figure 10.17. The Autoplay functionality typically means that the target system will automatically start playing the files available on the emulated USB storage and continue playing through all the available files. It is important to note that different systems may display different behaviors when encountering malformed files, i.e. fuzzed files. Some systems may just skip the malformed file and continue with processing the next file. In such cases, no additional input may be required. Other systems may display an error message and wait for the user input before proceeding. In such cases, there is a need to detect this behavior and automate the input.

Depending on the file format and target application there may be additional ways to control the application. For example, many in-vehicle infotainment systems support Bluetooth AVRCP (audio/video remote control profile), which allows wireless remote control of the media playing on the in-vehicle infotainment system. Thus, the Fuzz Testing PC can be paired over Bluetooth with the SUT and periodically send the "play" command to ensure that the fuzzed audio files are being processed by the target application. Please note that this approach does not work for image file formats since Bluetooth AVRCP does not allow control of applications that are processing images.

For target systems with touch screens it may be possible to provide input using an external component. There is previous work showing how to automate input on a capacitive touch screen using aluminum foil that is taped to the screen and electrically connected to a port on an Arduino board [34].

It is possible to automate touches on the screen by switching the pin state between "grounded" and "floating" (grounded = press, floating = release). Using an Arduino electric switch control it would be possible to, for example, automate playing files or clicking on a button to close an error message window. One challenge is that different touch screens have different behaviors, which means that this approach may need to be adjusted to each type of SUT. For example, on some touch screens, this approach would be successful in triggering the "touch" behavior only but not the "release" behavior, resulting in the touch screen detecting an "infinite or long touch." For situations where this approach works it may be a simple and convenient solution; however, when it does not work, it may require some additional effort to fine-tune the functionality. If the Arduino electric switch control does not work, the Arduino servo-motor control explained next may be more applicable.

As an alternative option, it is possible to automate input on a touch screen using a servo-motor and some aluminum foil. This solution is rather inexpensive and effective. The servo-motor is controlled by an Arduino. Building a capacitive stylus to be used for automated screen input can be a rather difficult task since the stylus may react differently on different screens [35]. Moreover, the capacitive stylus often also relies on the capacitance of the human holding the stylus, thus when connected to a servo-motor it would not work. Instead, a grounded piece of metal, such as a coin or aluminum foil usually works better for most screens. An example setup is explained as follows. The aluminum foil is connected to a servo-motor, which is connected to the Arduino board. The Arduino board can, for example, be controlled by the Fuzz Testing PC which, when necessary, can instruct the Arduino to control the servo-motor to touch the screen with the aluminum foil. This screen touch can in turn control the target application on the SUT, e.g. a screen touch that presses the "Play" button will start playing the next fuzzed file. This solution can help automate user input that may be required during a fuzz testing session. It is an effective solution that has a higher success rate than the Arduino electric switch control and requires less time fine-tuning. Please note that the Arduino servo-motor approach can also be used for automating pressing physical buttons on the SUT if required.

10.3.5 Monitor for Exceptions

To automate file format fuzz testing, Section 10.3.2 describes how to first generate fuzzed files and store them in disk image files, and then Section 10.3.3 explains how to emulate a USB storage with the fuzzed files contained in the disk image files by using an Embedded Linux Board connected over USB to the SUT. Section 10.3.4 then presents how to automate user input on the SUT required to, for example, start fuzz testing by pressing a "Play" button or continue fuzz testing when an exception occurs by closing an error message screen. The last piece of the puzzle to automate file format fuzz testing is performing external instrumentation to monitor and detect exceptions on the SUT caused by processing the fuzzed files, which is discussed in this section.

The main goal is to detect exceptions in the normal behavior of the SUT and its target applications. These exceptions could be caused by bugs and may lead to exploitable vulnerabilities where an attacker could potentially compromise the full system. Examples of exceptions include misbehavior of the target applications and entire system crashes. In general, assuming that access to the internals of the SUT is available following a white-box approach, it is possible to use the Agent Instrumentation Framework presented in Chapter 9 to automate and manage the instrumentation. Generally, there are numerous methods and techniques that can then be used for instrumentation to detect exceptions including:

- Debug access,
- Inspecting processes and log files,
- Simple Network Management Protocol (SNMP) instrumentation.

These methods and techniques are explained as follows. It may be possible to create Agents that use various debug access such as ADB (Android debug bridge) [36] or GDB (GNU Debugger) [37] to perform certain instrumentation of target applications on the SUT. Moreover, it may be possible to use Agents that inspect different processes and log files on the SUT to determine whether a certain application is misbehaving. Additionally, some SUTs may support SNMP instrumentation, which allows a device to collect and store information and make it available over SNMP to a management system.

In contrast, if there is limited access to the internals of the SUT following a black-box or gray-box approach, it may not be possible to use the Agent Instrumentation Framework. Instead, it is necessary to use other methods and techniques to perform external instrumentation to detect exceptions on the SUT, including:

- Absence of response,
- USB storage read accesses,
- Visual inspection.

Probably the most common method for instrumentation is to monitor for an absence of response from the SUT, which can be implemented by simply pinging the SUT and observing whether it is responding to the pings to determine whether the SUT is still alive. Although this approach is simple and may help identify a serious issue that leaves the SUT in a non-responsive state, it may miss more intricate issues on the SUT affecting only the target applications and therefore would not be detectable through pings. Thus, even though this approach is simple it will not be discussed further. Another approach that may be more suitable since the target applications are processing files on the USB storage, is to monitor USB storage read accesses using a FUSE filesystem, as explained in Section 10.3.3 to detect whether read accesses have stopped or are delayed. Finally, it is possible to visually inspect the SUT to detect any abnormal behavior displayed on the screen of the SUT. In order to automate this step, a solution that can detect what is displayed on the screen of the SUT and determine whether an exception has occurred is required.

In order to properly monitor the SUT for exceptions and unexpected behavior, it is necessary to first understand how the SUT and the target applications behave when exceptions occur. For example, many target applications such as media parsers are run as userland processes following the principle of least privilege. If an exception or error occurs in a userland process that causes the target application to crash, the SUT may just restart that process. As a result, there may be some visible effects such as the screen fading through black when restarting the application or a splash screen showing on the screen when the application is launching. In addition, while the application is restarting, the read accesses to the USB storage may also be delayed, which can be detected as explained in Section 10.3.3.

On some SUTs, a target application that crashes may not be restarted but rather the SUT will return to the main menu or the home screen. In this case, there is a noticeable visual change since the target application is no longer displayed on the screen. In addition, the read accesses to the USB storage would typically stop. It is important to note that if only read accesses to the USB storage are monitored, it may not be possible to distinguish the normal case of when the target application has finished processing all fuzzed files and the exception case where the target application crashes and stops processing fuzzed files since, in both cases, read accesses to the USB storage will stop.

In other scenarios, a target application crashing may cause the SUT to reboot the entire system. This is a fairly common approach that works well since in-vehicle infotainment systems are designed to generally boot very quickly to be accessible when a driver starts the car. Although this approach may not be that elegant, however, since there is no need for elaborate error-handling of individual target applications it is the simplest solution for developers of in-vehicle infotainment systems to implement. Once again, there is a noticeable visual change since the entire system is restarting and, additionally, the read accesses to the USB storage will be stopped.

It is worth mentioning that it may be necessary to recognize the correct behavior of the target applications when processing fuzzed files in order to automate fuzz testing. For instance, there may be situations where the target application does not crash but rather correctly displays a warning or error message such as "File cannot be read" or "Invalid file." Typically, the user is prompted to press "OK" or close the message screen before being able to proceed. Similar to above cases, there is a noticeable visual change since a message screen is displayed and additionally the read accesses to the USB storage will typically be at least temporarily stopped. By detecting this correct behavior of the target application processing invalid files and using techniques presented in Section 10.3.4, it is possible to automate the user input to, for example, press the "OK" button to be able to proceed with the target application processing the next fuzzed file. In other cases, the target application may just skip the invalid files when it detects that it cannot be processed and proceed with processing the next fuzzed file. In such cases, there may be no specific need to detect the correct behavior or provide additional input since the processing of fuzzed files is progressing automatically.

Based on above understanding of the SUT exceptions and correct behavior and considering a black-box or gray-box approach, the following methods and techniques for external instrumentation of the SUT are explored further:

- USB storage read accesses.
- Visual inspection.

Regarding *USB storage read accesses*, one can imagine that a read access slower than usual could be caused by a bug, e.g. the target application crashed and restarted which introduces a time delay before the next file is read. However, target applications may behave differently based on the contents of the fuzzed files even if there are no bugs. As mentioned, the correct handling of fuzzed files may also affect the read accesses. For example, a fuzzed file containing multiple anomalies may not pass validation and may be skipped entirely by the target application, which may or may not show an error screen. If there is no error screen, the target application moves on to the next fuzzed file and therefore read access for the next file is immediate. In contrast, a fuzzed file containing a minor anomaly, e.g. a value in the metadata is modified, may still be properly processed by the target application. Therefore, the read access for the next fuzzed file would occur after the current fuzzed file has been fully processed. In both situations the target application exerts the correct behavior, even though the read accesses are different between these two situations, where the fuzzed file is skipped in the first case whereas being processed in the second case.

Moreover, there is a need to consider the fact that many operating systems use file caching to improve performance. This means that a file that is read from the USB storage is temporarily stored in a memory, called file cache. Subsequent read operations of the file on the SUT are performed on the file cache rather than the actual USB storage. Therefore, simply monitoring read accesses to the USB storage may not allow easily detecting exceptions.

Monitoring accesses to the USB storage is definitely a useful approach; however, careful considerations on how to monitor read accesses and how to determine whether exceptions are identified need to be taken. As mentioned, detecting different read access times for the next fuzzed files does not automatically mean that an exception occurred. It could be caused by:

- The fuzzed file being processed by the target application on the SUT, e.g. an audio/video file being played by a media player will be processed for how long the file is, for instance one second, before the next fuzzed file is processed.
- The fuzzed file being skipped by the target application on the SUT, e.g. an audio/video file being skipped and the media player automatically and immediately playing the next available fuzzed file.
- The fuzzed file being cached by the operating system on the SUT, and therefore there are no subsequent read accesses to the USB storage for a certain amount of time.

Therefore, it is important to first understand how the target applications typically access the USB storage and build a profile for the correct behavior. For example, monitoring read accesses when a target application processes several one-second long audio/video files may give an indication on what the maximum delay is between read accesses to the USB storage. Once a profile for the correct behavior has been built, it is possible to perform fuzz testing over USB and compare the monitored behavior to the correct behavior profile to detect exceptions and abnormal behavior.

Monitoring accesses to the emulated USB storage provided by the Embedded Linux Board can be implemented using two different methods. The first method requires modifying the kernel module code (g_mass_storage) on the Embedded Linux Board to be able to probe for read accesses. While this method is more efficient, it requires particular skills to correctly modify the kernel module to provide this additional functionality. The second method is mounting the USB storage in a FUSE filesystem as described in Section 10.3.3. This approach is simpler and allows monitoring USB storage accesses without having to modify and debug the complicated kernel module. Using FUSE also allows more control on disk accesses and can help overcome the challenge with file caching. For instance, it has been shown that it is possible to delay read accesses on purpose to the USB storage to invalidate the cache and therefore force a reread from the USB storage [38].

Regarding *visual inspection*, one can imagine that an exception has occurred if something unexpected is displayed on the screen of the SUT. A simple approach to implement visual inspection is to use a camera and some image processing software. OpenCV (Open computer vision) [39] is library with a set of functions for real-time image recognition. Using the Python programming language and OpenCV it is fairly simple to create a program that can match images to a template image using template matching [40].

Since the SUT is in a static test environment where there is no specific movement or lighting changes, the image recognition algorithm does not need to be very robust and therefore a simple algorithm can be used. There are two use cases to consider:

- Flag an exception when something specific on the screen is detected, e.g. a reboot screen, splash screen, or an error message screen. Where applicable, developers and testers can predefine a number of known "unexpected" behavior screens as template images.
- Flag an exception when something specific on the screen that should always be shown is no longer detected, e.g. a manufacturer logo or a certain text or button in a media player. Where applicable, developers and testers can predefine a set of known "should always be displayed" screens as template images.

For the example SUT used, where Kodi is running on a Raspberry Pi, a template image of the "raspberry" logo was used as an "unexpected" behavior screen. If the image recognition algorithm detects the "raspberry" logo, it would indicate that an exception has occurred, in this case it means that the SUT is rebooting and displaying the "raspberry" logo. This exception detection is illustrated in Figure 10.18.

Finally, as briefly mentioned in Section 10.3.3, it is possible to reuse approaches and methods for detecting exceptions to also detect that all the fuzzed files in the emulated USB storage have been parsed by the target applications. This allows for the Embedded Linux Board to then load the next disk image file and present the new set of fuzzed files

Figure 10.18 Image recognition algorithm detecting the raspberry logo indicating an exception.

to the SUT in the emulated USB storage. Reusing the visual inspection approach, it could be possible to detect that all fuzzed files have been processed by the target application. For instance, if the screen is blank, the screen has returned to displaying the main menu, or the media player has stopped, it can be assumed that all files have been processed. Moreover, by monitoring USB storage read accesses, it may be possible to detect that read accesses have stopped or significantly reduced over a certain period of time, which could signify that all fuzzed files have been processed. It is important to investigate how the SUT ordinarily behaves when it is done processing all the files to create a profile of correct behavior. This profile can then be used to identify whether the target applications on the SUT have finished processing the fuzzed files.

Besides all of these various monitoring techniques to detect that the SUT is done processing all fuzzed files, a simplistic approach is to just rely on a time-based approach. For example, a disk image file could be created to contain a number of fuzzed audio and video files where the total length of all files adds up to a certain amount of time. Once the predetermined time has passed, the fuzz testing session moves on to load the next disk image file and continues testing. This approach is very simple and helps to automate the fuzz testing. For instance, an example disk image file could contain 5760 audio or video files, each of length five seconds, where the total length of the playlist would be eight hours if all files are successfully played. Thus, it can be assumed that after eight hours the target application has processed all files, and the Embedded Linux Board can move on to load the next disk image file, which contains the next set of fuzzed files to be processed for the next eight hours. However, in reality, all files in the disk image file may have been processed much faster because some malformed files have been skipped, or all files may not have been processed because the target application crashes and restarts in between fuzzed files or there may have been timeouts or error screens that delay the processing of the files. Therefore, although this approach is very simplistic, there may be some time wasted where the SUT is standing still since all the fuzzed files have been processed and it is waiting for the predetermined time to run out, or the SUT misses to test certain fuzzed files contained in the disk image because exceptions have occurred on the SUT that delay the processing of the fuzzed files, and there are untested fuzzed files remaining in the disk image when the predetermined time runs out.

Depending on the SUT, a combination solution based on USB storage read accesses, visual inspection and a timer could be used to determine when all fuzzed files have been processed and used to decide when to move on to loading the next disk image file.

10.4 Chapter Summary

This chapter presented a solution for automating file format fuzz testing over USB on automotive systems. First, the challenges with the current approaches, including manual steps to perform fuzz testing such as physically plugging and unplugging USB storage media to the SUT, are discussed. To overcome these challenges, this chapter introduces a system architecture of the solution, including a Fuzz Testing Tool, Storage Medium, Embedded Linux Board with custom software, and the SUT. Moreover, to explain the effectiveness and usefulness of the solution, an example implementation for automating file format fuzz testing over USB on automotive systems is presented. The implementation consists of two phases. The first phase involves preparing the fuzzed files. That is, the Fuzz Testing Tool is used to generate various relevant fuzzed files for the target applications on the SUT, e.g. audio and video files. These fuzzed files are then stored in disk image files on the Storage Medium. The second phase involves automatically emulating filesystems. In this phase, the Embedded Linux Board has access to the Storage Medium and is continuously physically connected over a USB cable to the SUT. Custom software on the Embedded Linux Board is used to load a disk image file from the Storage Medium and emulate it as a USB storage to the SUT. The SUT recognizes the emulated USB storage and is able to read and process the fuzzed files contained in the disk image file. Once the SUT has processed all the fuzzed files contained in one disk image file, the Embedded Linux Board automatically loads the next disk image file and presents its contents of fuzzed files to the SUT. In this manner, since there is no need to physically unplug and replug USB storage media to the SUT, it is possible to automate file fuzzing over USB on automotive systems. Moreover, approaches for automating physical user input that may be required to start processing files on the SUT or to put the SUT in a testable state are presented. Finally, several suggestions on external instrumentation to monitor and detect exceptions on the SUT are also discussed. Since more automotive systems contain USB interfaces that support numerous file formats, which often require complex file parsers, there is a risk that bugs or vulnerabilities that are triggered may cause the automotive system to crash or behave erratically. Besides common media file formats that are supported by these systems, there are also specific update files that allow changing the functionality of these systems, resulting in the USB interface being an attractive attack vector for attackers. Therefore, it is imperative for automotive organizations to have a process and a technical solution in place that allows for automated fuzz testing and achieving greater coverage to help create more secure systems.

References

1 Automotive Grade Linux (2020). What is automotive grade Linux?. https://www .automotivelinux.org (accessed 30 July 2020).

2 GENIVI (2020). Beyond Linux IVI and into the connected vehicle. https://www.genivi .org (accessed 30 July 2020).

3 Android (2020). What is Android automotive? https://source.android.com/devices/ automotive/start/what_automotive (accessed 30 July 2020).

4 Checkoway, S., McCoy, D., Kantor, B., et al. (2011). Comprehensive experimental analyses of automotive attack surfaces. *USENIX Security*, San Francisco, CA, USA.

5 Synopsys (2017). State of fuzzing 2017.

6 QEMU (2020). QEMU the FAST! processor emulator. https://www.qemu.org (accessed 30 July 2020).

7 KVM (2020). Kernel virtual machine. https://www.linux-kvm.org/page/Main_Page (accessed 30 July 2020).

8 Oka, D. K. (2018). Automating file fuzzing over USB. *CODE BLUE*, Tokyo, Japan.

9 Gay, C. and Oka, D. K. (2019). Fuzzing the filesystem layer of IoT devices over USB. *Symposium on Cryptography and Information Security (SCIS)*, Shiga, Japan.

10 Blanda, A. (2015). Fuzzing Android: a recipe for uncovering vulnerabilities inside system components in Android. *Black Hat Europe*, Amsterdam, Netherlands.

11 NIST (2015). National vulnerability database – CVE-2015-1538. https://nvd.nist.gov/vuln/detail/CVE-2015-1538 (accessed 30 July 2020).

12 NIST (2015). National vulnerability database – CVE-2015-3824. https://nvd.nist.gov/vuln/detail/CVE-2015-3824 (accessed 30 July 2020).

13 NIST (2015). National vulnerability database – CVE-2015-3864. https://nvd.nist.gov/vuln/detail/CVE-2015-3864 (accessed 30 July 2020).

14 NIST (2015). National vulnerability database – CVE-2015-6602. https://nvd.nist.gov/vuln/detail/CVE-2015-6602 (accessed 30 July 2020).

15 Drake, J. (2015). Stagefright: scary code in the heart of Android. *Black Hat USA*, Las Vegas, NV, USA.

16 NIST (2018). National vulnerability database – CVE-2017-2575. https://nvd.nist.gov/vuln/detail/CVE-2017-2575 (accessed 30 July 2020).

17 Check Point (2017). Hacked in translation – from subtitles to complete takeover. https://blog.checkpoint.com/2017/05/23/hacked-in-translation (accessed 30 July 2020).

18 Check Point (2017). Hacked in translation, "Director's Cut", full technical details. https://blog.checkpoint.com/2017/07/08/hacked-translation-directors-cut-full-technical-details (accessed 30 July 2020).

19 NIST (2017). National vulnerability database – CVE-2017-8311. https://nvd.nist.gov/vuln/detail/CVE-2017-8311 (accessed 30 July 2020).

20 NIST (2017). National vulnerability database – CVE-2017-8313. https://nvd.nist.gov/vuln/detail/CVE-2017-8313 (accessed 30 July 2020).

21 Unicorn Research Corporation (2002). JACOsub script file format specification. http://unicorn.us.com/jacosub/jscripts.html (accessed 30 July 2020).

22 Miller, C. and Valasek, C. (2015). Remote exploitation of an unaltered passenger vehicle. *Black Hat USA*, Las Vegas, NV, USA.

23 Mazda AIO Tweaks (2020). https://mazdatweaks.com (accessed 30 July 2020).

24 BeagleBoard (2019). PocketBeagle. https://beagleboard.org/pocket (accessed 30 July 2020).

25 USBNinja professional (2018). https://usbninja.com (accessed 30 July 2020).

26 Raspberry Pi Foundation (2020). Raspberry Pi. https://www.raspberrypi.org (accessed 30 July 2020).

27 Kodi. Open source home theater software. https://kodi.tv (accessed 30 July 2020).

28 Synopsys (2020). Defensics fuzz testing. https://www.synopsys.com/software-integrity/security-testing/fuzz-testing.html (accessed 30 July 2020).

29 ImageMagick (2020). https://imagemagick.org/index.php (accessed 30 July 2020).

30 FFmpeg (2019). https://ffmpeg.org (accessed 30 July 2020).

31 BeagleBoard (2019). BeagleBone Black. https://beagleboard.org/black (accessed 30 July 2020).

32 Raspberry Pi Foundation (2015). Raspberry Pi Zero. https://www.raspberrypi.org/products/raspberry-pi-zero (accessed 30 July 2020).

33 Linux Kernel Organization (2019). FUSE. https://www.kernel.org/doc/html/latest/filesystems/fuse.html (accessed 30 July 2020).

34 theUltimateLabs (2012). Triggering capacitive touch screen with an Arduino. https://www.youtube.com/watch?v=JDgDMBquBw0 (accessed 30 July 2020).

35 Instructables (2017). DIY capacitive stylus. https://www.instructables.com/id/DIY-Capacitive-Stylus (accessed 30 July 2020).

36 Google (2020). Android debug bridge (adb). https://developer.android.com/studio/command-line/adb (accessed 30 July 2020).

37 GDB Developers (2020). GDB: the GNU project debugger. https://www.gnu.org/software/gdb (accessed 30 July 2020).

38 Delugre, G. (2017). The path pivot attack. https://gdelugre.github.io/2017/11/06/samba-path-pivot-attack (accessed 30 July 2020).

39 OpenCV Team (2020). OpenCV (Open computer vision). https://opencv.org (accessed 30 July 2020).

40 OpenCV Team (2019). OpenCV template matching. https://docs.opencv.org/2.4/doc/tutorials/imgproc/histograms/template_matching/template_matching.html (accessed 30 July 2020).

11

Automation and Traceability by Integrating Application Security Testing Tools into ALM Systems

KNOW WHAT YOU ARE DOING FROM BEGINNING TO END

This chapter presents how integrating application security testing tools into application lifecycle management (ALM) systems can assist with automation and traceability to help an organization implement a secure software development process. More specifically, this chapter discusses how automated application security testing tools – such as static code analysis tools, software composition analysis tools, and fuzz testing tools – can be integrated into ALM systems, which allows automating the testing, and tracing specific results from such tools to requirements defined in the automotive software development process.

Generally, a number of different functional and non-functional requirements are used during the typical automotive software development process. However, lately, the automotive industry is incorporating more requirements regarding cybersecurity in the requirements for software development. These requirements include various methods for verification and testing to help identify bugs and vulnerabilities in the code, e.g. static code analysis and fuzz testing. Moreover, there may be detailed requirements on the use of coding guidelines, such as CERT (computer emergency response team) C/C++ [1, 2], MISRA (Motor Industry Software Reliability Association) C/C++ [3, 4], and AUTOSAR (AUTomotive Open System ARchitecture) C++ [5]. Besides managing the typical functional and non-functional requirements, there is a need for automotive organizations to manage the security requirements for the software development process. This sentiment is echoed by the National Institute of Standards and Technology (NIST) who published a cybersecurity white paper called, "Mitigating the Risk of Software Vulnerabilities by Adopting a Secure Software Development Framework (SSDF)" [6], in which they highlight the need to define security requirements for software development. Additionally, Microsoft SDL (security development lifecycle), which was first released in 2008, also highlights security considerations that organizations need to address in the development process, and provides guidance, best practices, tools, and processes to improve security in the software development lifecycle (SDLC) [7]. Thus, it is becoming increasingly important for organizations to establish a secure SDLC, including defining security requirements for the software development process [8].

A common approach for managing various activities in the SDLC is the use of ALM systems. By building on this approach of automotive organizations using ALM systems, this

Building Secure Cars: Assuring the Automotive Software Development Lifecycle, First Edition. Dennis Kengo Oka.
© 2021 John Wiley & Sons Ltd. Published 2021 by John Wiley & Sons Ltd.

chapter presents a solution on how to integrate application security testing tools into such ALM systems. In the ALM system, the specific security requirements and corresponding test cases for software development are first defined. Then, using this information from the ALM system, the relevant application security testing tools based on the requirements are launched to perform testing on the software. The application security testing tools are configured accordingly, based on the requirements specified in the ALM system. After the testing has completed, the results from the application security testing tools are incorporated into the ALM system as results to the respective test cases. The major advantage with this approach is that it is possible for an organization to handle traceability in the ALM system to ensure that a certain security requirement has been fulfilled by tracing the results from the application security testing tools back to the specific requirement. It is also possible for an organization to get an overview of all the security requirements for software development, whether relevant application security testing tools have been used to perform the testing yet, and whether the tests have passed, which in turn means that the requirements have been fulfilled. Moreover, since automated application security testing tools are used, it is possible to automate the entire process and have all the security testing managed by the ALM system, which significantly saves an organization time and effort. Since increasingly more software is developed and used in the automotive industry and there are gradually more requirements for secure software development, it is crucial to use a solution which allows for automation. An example implementation is presented in more detail to highlight the applicability and "to" showcase the advantages of this solution. Since this solution allows for automation and traceability, it is extremely beneficial for automotive organizations who are typically already under high pressure to meet deadlines.

The main points of this chapter are:

- We give an introduction to ALM systems focusing on features and functions relevant to automotive software development.
- We discuss the challenges of tracing results from various cybersecurity testing activities to specific security requirements for software development, and the challenges to automate the test process.
- To overcome these challenges, we present a solution based on integrating application security testing tools into ALM systems to allow for traceability of test results to specific requirements and automating the test process using information from the ALM systems.

More details regarding integrating application security testing tools into ALM tools in the automotive industry can be found in Reference [9].

11.1   Introduction to ALM Systems

ALM systems provide a centralized way to manage and monitor all aspects of software development. For instance, ALM systems can be used to manage the different phases of the SDLC starting from requirements, design, development, testing, release, and finally operations and maintenance, as shown in Figure 11.1. These ALM systems often also offer various integration capabilities with other tools commonly used during the software development

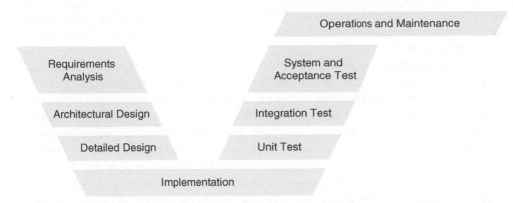

Figure 11.1 Traditional V-model development process used in the automotive industry.

process for the different phases, including requirement management tools, design tools, source code management tools, build automation tools, test management tools, and defect management tools.

There are several benefits for organizations using ALM systems. First, it allows for faster releases since using ALM systems with the right tools allows organizations to better plan their activities and improve the time-to-market for their software applications. The second advantage is that software applications will have higher quality since the ALM systems are used to follow all the necessary activities to make sure quality is not sacrificed. A third benefit is that, by following specific workflows using the ALM systems, it is possible to prove compliance to show that specific requirements have been fulfilled or that certain tests have been executed. Last, the ALM systems provide a centralized, up-to-date view of the software project across the lifecycle, which gives visibility to all involved teams on the progress of the development to better understand, for example, which requirements have been fulfilled, which test cases have not been executed yet, and so on.

In general, ALM systems can support various activities for the different phases below as follows:

- Requirements
- Design
- Development
- Testing
- Release
- Operations and Maintenance

During the *requirements* phase, the requirements for the project are gathered. Besides the functional and non-functional requirements for the software application itself – i.e. product-level requirements, which are mainly the focus of the requirements management – there may be requirements on the software development process, including compliance requirements, i.e. process-level requirements. ALM systems may also be able to import requirements handled in requirements management tools, such as DOORS (Dynamic Object Oriented Requirements System) [10]. Typically, ALM systems allow an organization to get a clear overview of the included requirements to easily do requirements reviews, change management for requirements, and follow approval processes for requirements changes.

During the *design* phase, the application is designed based on the previously defined and gathered requirements. There are various ways to design software applications, including the use of UML (Unified Modeling Language), to create use cases and activity diagrams to describe the general flow and activities of the involved actors. For more specific functions within an application, it is useful to use state machine diagrams and sequence diagrams to describe the different states of a component within a system and the sequence of messages and interactions between actors and objects. Many ALM systems provide functionality to import UML diagrams created in separate design tools such as Enterprise Architect [11].

During the *development* phase, the software for the application is written based on the requirements and design. The development tasks can be planned accordingly to the methodology used for development including Waterfall, V-model, or Agile. For example, for Agile, development tasks based on the requirements and design can be scheduled in two-week sprints, and the ALM system can provide the organization with an overview of development progress, tasks remaining in the sprint, regressions detected after a sprint, etc. Moreover, ALM systems can be integrated with source code management systems such as Git [12] to integrate version control and traceability about code changes.

During the *testing* phase, the software application is tested with a focus on the newly written code that provides the added functionality and where applicable regression testing is also performed. Typically, the application is tested against the requirements to ensure that the functionality has been implemented correctly. ALM systems may be integrated with automation servers such as Jenkins [13], which support automating tasks related to building, testing, delivery, and deployment, to gather information about test results and build information such as source code changes and build times. ALM systems may be also be integrated with various test tools, such as Selenium [14] used for automating testing of web applications or VectorCAST [15] used for automated unit and integration testing of safety-critical embedded systems. Furthermore, defects found during the testing can be handled in defect management tools such as Jira [16]. By integrating defect management tools with ALM systems, it is possible for an organization to get a consistent and up-to-date view of the current issues. It is also possible to maintain traceability and track the progress of bug fixes throughout the lifecycle from defects detected during testing, to bug fixing during software development to including known defects in a release.

During the *release* phase, after the previously mentioned requirements, design, development, and testing phases are successfully completed, the software application is finally released. After the software is released and deployed as a service or product, it will be in operation providing the functionalities based on the requirements from the requirements phase. Depending on the software application, there are different approaches to the release and deployment. Some applications may be released and deployed to run in the cloud that could happen instantly and other types of applications are released and flashed on embedded devices in factories which is typically a more time-consuming process.

During the *operations and maintenance* phases, the software application has already been released and is in operation; however, there may be new requirements to include additional functionality to the software, or new bugs and vulnerabilities have been detected and there is a need to provide an updated version, including bug fixes. Besides managing all the activities during the software development process until release, the ALM systems are also useful for managing updates and maintenance of the software application until its end of life. For the development and release of a new software version, an organization goes through the same phases as mentioned above including requirements, design, development, testing, and release. Depending on the software application, there are situations where it is easy to perform updates during the operations and maintenance phases such as for applications running in the cloud. In contrast, there may be challenges to perform updates of applications on embedded devices, especially if such devices are safety-critical or have limited connectivity. Thus, there is a need for establishing proper processes for performing software updates of such devices during the operations and maintenance phases.

While ALM systems are applicable for software development in various industries, ALM systems are extremely useful in the automotive industry, which is regulated, has strong requirements for compliance and is developing safety-critical systems. To this end, some ALM systems [17] provide templates for workflows that can help automotive organizations achieve regulatory compliance for ISO 26262 [18] and ASPICE (Automotive Software Process Improvement and Capability dEtermination) [19].

While ALM systems are useful for, in particular, requirements management of functional and non-functional requirements for software applications and general testing of the applications, cybersecurity requirements for the software development process and testing using application security testing tools are often not yet managed or integrated with ALM systems. Rather, cybersecurity software development requirements and application security testing are often handled separately, which is a challenge for automotive organizations as described in more detail in the Section 11.2.

11.2 Problem Statement: Tracing Secure Software Development Activities and Results to Requirements and Automating Application Security Testing

With the advancements of standardization activities and regulations for cybersecurity in the automotive industry, such as ISO/SAE 21434 [20] and UNECE (United Nations Economic Commission for Europe) WP.29 Cybersecurity [21], as well as increased public awareness of automotive-related cybersecurity incidents based on security researchers finding and exploiting vulnerabilities on vehicles [22–24] combined with results from an automotive survey called "Securing the Modern Vehicle: A Study of Automotive Industry Cybersecurity Practices" [25] stating that 62% of automotive organizations believe that it is likely or very likely that there is a malicious or proof-of-concept attack against their software or component in the next 12 months, more automotive organizations are increasing the efforts on establishing internal cybersecurity processes and defined activities in their organizations. More details about the automotive survey are presented in Section 1.3. As a result, more automotive organizations are systematically employing the use of application security testing tools in their SDLC.

More specifically, these organizations may establish internal processes and requirements instructing that certain types of application security testing tools should be used or certain test activities should be performed, such as using static code analysis tools (explained in more detail in Section 4.2.1), using software composition analysis tools (explained in more detail in Section 4.2.2), and performing security testing (explained in more detail in Section 4.2.3), including using vulnerability scanning tools, fuzz testing tools, and performing penetration testing. That is, automotive organizations may define specific cybersecurity requirements for the software development process including requirements on testing using certain application security testing tools or performing certain penetration testing activities. To be able to automate these cybersecurity tasks and activities as much as possible, it is required that *automated* application security testing tools are used. Therefore, since the penetration testing activity tries to mimic a real attacker, it is not feasible to automate the penetration testing activity as is; however, there may be some steps in the penetration testing activity that can be automated including the use of certain tools. To consider how to automate penetration testing requires additional understanding of the target systems and the attacker goals and is a topic that warrants a chapter of its own and will therefore not be discussed in further detail. Rather, the focus of this chapter is on the use of automated application security testing tools, i.e. tools that can be configured with appropriate settings based on testing criteria, requirements, and the specifics of the target system, can be run in an automated fashion, and can be run repeatedly over periods of time during the development and testing phases. Examples of such tools include:

- Static code analysis tools
- Software composition analysis tools
- Vulnerability scanning tools
- Fuzz testing tools

As application security testing tools are run more systematically based on requirements as part of the development process it allows for software development teams, QA (quality assurance) teams, and security teams to detect and fix vulnerabilities more efficiently and effectively early in the development process. Since the testing is based on requirements, it is crucial for organizations to be able to trace the corresponding secure software development activities and results from the testing to the specific individual requirements. More specifically, there is a need for organizations to be able to trace the actual results from application security testing tools to verify whether the specific requirements have been fulfilled for the testing related to such tools.

Generally, tracing of activities and results from tools to requirements is a common practice in the automotive industry, known as *requirements traceability*, where there is a bi-directional relationship between a requirement and a test case that can be used to verify that the requirement is fulfilled. The bi-directional relationship allows tracing forward from requirement to test case but also backwards from test case to requirement. In such a manner, an organization can get a complete view from requirements to source code to test cases to test results and, potentially, any identified and remaining issues. The actual test results from the tools executing the test case can be used as evidence to verify that testing has completed and that the requirement has been fulfilled. Requirements traceability is important for several reasons, including *meeting the goals*, *executing the right tests*, and *making informed decisions* [26]. For *meeting the goals*, it is possible to trace requirements through the development lifecycle to ensure that the requirements have passed and therefore the software application fulfills the goals. For instance, requirements traceability can provide proof that compliance requirements have been met for the development of the software application. Requirements traceability also allows an organization to focus on *executing the right tests*. Since test cases are based on requirements, it is possible for an organization to ensure that the correct types of tests are executed to verify the corresponding requirements and improve test coverage. It also helps to verify that there are no missing tests for any specific requirements. Finally, requirements traceability assists an organization to *make informed decisions* during the SDLC, e.g. how to handle change requests on requirements for a software application. As a result, it is possible for an organization to analyze the impact of a certain requirement change to better understand what additional resources, activities planning, and test cases may be required.

Moreover, to be able to handle development methodologies and processes where more software is developed faster and often in shorter cycles, it is not enough to know that a certain application security testing tool has been run once and testing has completed, but it is necessary for an organization to know how often the application security testing tools are running, which versions of the software are being tested, what configurations of the application security testing tools are used, and which results were produced by the application security testing tools for each test run. Therefore, there is a need for automating application security testing as part of the development process where the corresponding application security testing tools are run with the appropriate configurations on the specific target software versions at defined times during the development lifecycle.

However, there are several challenges many organizations are currently facing to properly perform requirements tracing and automating application security testing when trying to establish new internal processes and requirements for secure software development. For example, often multiple different teams – including development teams, QA teams and security teams – are running a set of different application security tools during the SDLC. Some tools are run manually and only occasionally and executed only by certain teams. As a result, often a manual and cumbersome approach to managing traceability across different teams is used where, for example, Excel or Word files are used and shared among teams to trace test results from application security testing tools to security requirements for software development. This manual method is time-consuming, difficult to keep up-to-date and error prone. Please also consider that initially, to create a traceability matrix in, for example, Excel requires several steps [27]. Information about requirements and test cases needs to be manually gathered from requirements documents and test case documents and copied and pasted into the traceability matrix document. Test results from various application security testing tools, used by different teams, based on the test cases need to be manually collected and reflected in the traceability matrix document. Moreover, test cases that successfully passed can be indicated by the color green and test cases that failed indicated by the color red by changing the cell color for the respective rows in the traceability matrix document. This helps with visibility to get a better overview of the current status. Test cases that failed may need to be linked with an issue list in a separate spreadsheet or linked to specific tickets in a bug tracking system such as Jira for the organization to be able to have a clear view of which issues were detected during a specific test run. Finally, once the traceability matrix document has been created which itself is a very time-consuming task, it needs to be continuously updated with new test results from different security application testing tools used by different teams for new versions of the software that are released. Moreover, if requirements change or are added, test cases need to be updated or added, which needs to be reflected in the traceability matrix document. Furthermore, if an issue that has been detected during testing is resolved and subsequently the software is retested and the test passes, the traceability matrix document has to be updated again to reflect this new test result. All of these different activities performed by different teams require the traceability matrix document to be continuously updated, which makes it difficult to keep the information in the document relevant and up-to-date over time. Additionally, since entries to the traceability matrix document – such as requirements, test cases, test results and issues – are entered manually, this approach is error prone and it is extremely likely that human mistakes lead to inaccuracies in the document. If the traceability matrix document contains inconsistencies, an organization would not be able to have an accurate comprehensive view of the ongoing progress, including the number of test cases that have passed, the number of requirements that have been fulfilled, the number of test cases remaining that need to be performed, the number of issues in the software that need to resolved, as well as whether compliance requirements for the software application have been fully fulfilled.

Thus, to sum up, these activities for managing requirements traceability manually are time-consuming, difficult to keep up-to-date, and error prone. In particular, since application security testing tools are run manually or separately in different teams, there are difficulties to keep the information up-to-date by tracing actual results from the application security testing tools to specific requirements over time. Therefore, to overcome these challenges, Section 11.3 presents a solution for integrating application security testing tools with ALM systems to automate the entire process and allow for requirements traceability of security requirements for the software development process.

11.3 Solution: Integrating Application Security Testing Tools with ALM Systems

This section presents a solution for integrating application security testing tools with ALM systems. First, the concept of the solution is described, including an overview of the operation to allow for automation of testing based on the integration of application security testing tools with ALM systems. Next, a prototype of the concept solution is presented showing how an application security testing tool integrated with an ALM system is able to perform automated testing of a target system and provide the corresponding test results to the ALM system. Finally, a discussion on the considerations for an organization to build a solution based on integrating application security testing tools with ALM systems to automate security testing is provided.

As presented in Section 11.1, ALM systems are useful for organizations to manage all stages of the entire SDLC. Especially regarding the software development phase, previous work shows that it is possible to integrate various tool chains into ALM systems [28, 29]; however, the solution presented in this chapter focuses on *secure* software development and on using information available in ALM systems such as security requirements for software development and corresponding test cases to automate application security testing as part of the development process [9, 30]. Thus, the concept and the prototype for the solution presented in this chapter describe an approach for integrating application security testing tools into ALM systems, and highlight the additional benefits of automating the testing of the target software and incorporating the test results back into the ALM systems. There is a need for an organization to be able to trace activities and results throughout the SDLC from requirements to test cases to test results to defect management to remediation to finally source code changes implementing fixes and new functionality. ALM systems can help an organization provide this type of traceability. That is, by using ALM systems to manage the security requirements for software development and corresponding test cases, to control the application security testing tools, and to handle the test results, allows an organization to trace the actual test results from application security testing tools back to the test cases and the corresponding requirements in order to verify that those requirements have been fulfilled.

11.3.1 Concept

The concept for integrating application security testing tools with ALM systems is explained in this section. There are a couple of prerequisites that an organization needs to consider for this concept. The first prerequisite is that the security requirements for software development are fully captured in the ALM system. The second prerequisite is that the corresponding test cases that can be used to verify that those requirements have been fulfilled are also defined in the ALM system. A simple illustration of these prerequisites is shown in Figure 11.2.

There are a number of different security requirements for software development and application security testing tools that can be considered for this concept. A few examples are provided below to give an idea of the type of requirements and corresponding application security testing tools that could be used, especially to automate the testing process:

- Static code analysis
- Software composition analysis
- Vulnerability scanning
- Fuzz testing

In the following, some details for each example, including requirements and corresponding test cases, are given, and finally an overview of the concept is presented.

11.3.1.1 Static Code Analysis – Example

Requirement: There may be a requirement that specifies that the software shall adhere to MISRA coding guidelines or AUTOSAR coding guidelines. The requirement may specify exactly which guidelines the software needs to be compliant with.

Figure 11.2 Overview of prerequisite information available in the ALM system. Source: Reprinted with permission from [9]. © IEEE.

Test case: The test case can be defined as using a static code analysis tool with a configuration to use the specific guidelines indicated by in the requirement. Thus, this test case can be performed by running a static code analysis tool with the corresponding MISRA or AUTOSAR checkers enabled to verify that the software is compliant with the specified guidelines. The test case will fail if any violations to the MISRA or AUTOSAR guidelines are detected.

A deeper discussion on using static code analysis for automotive software with a focus on MISRA and AUTOSAR coding guidelines is presented in Chapter 5.

11.3.1.2 Software Composition Analysis – Example

Requirement: There may be a requirement that states that the included open-source software components shall contain no known critical vulnerabilities at the time the software is delivered.

Test case: The test case can be defined as scanning the software using a software composition analysis tool with a policy configured based on the requirement. The policy in the software composition analysis tool will indicate that the test fails if any known critical vulnerabilities in the open-source software components are detected.

A thorough review on software composition analysis in the automotive industry is given in Chapter 6.

11.3.1.3 Vulnerability Scanning – Example

Requirement: There may be a requirement that specifies that vulnerability scanning shall be performed to verify that there are no critical vulnerabilities for a known service that is remotely accessible on the target system, e.g. an SSH (secure shell) or D-Bus service.

Test case: The test case can be defined as using a vulnerability scanning tool with a configuration based on the known service running on the target system. Using vulnerability and attack pattern databases it is possible to detect whether the running services contain known vulnerabilities or potentially unknown vulnerabilities based on known attack patterns and, if so, the test case fails.

More details on vulnerability scanning with a focus on automotive systems as target systems are provided in Section 7.1.2.

11.3.1.4 Fuzz Testing – Example

Requirement: There may be a requirement that states that fuzz testing shall be performed for a certain protocol, e.g. CAN (controller area network) or IPv4 (Internet Protocol version 4), for a minimum number of fuzz test cases or a minimum duration of time with no failed tests.

Test case: The test case can be defined as using a fuzz testing tool configured according to the requirement. The test case can be performed by running the fuzz testing tool targeting the specific protocol defined in the requirement for the number of fuzz test cases or duration of time indicated by the requirement. The test case will fail if any of the tests executed during the fuzz testing session results in an exception detected on the target system.

A comprehensive explanation of fuzz testing, including technical aspects of a fuzz testing environment, is given in Section 7.3, and specific examples of practical fuzz testing environments are provided in Chapters 8, 9, and 10.

Figure 11.3 Overview of the concept of integrating application security testing tools into ALM systems. Source: Adapted with permission from [9, 30]. © 2019 IEEE. Portions Copyright 2020 Synopsys, Inc. Used with permission. All rights reserved.

11.3.1.5 Concept Overview

This concept is built on the prerequisites that information about the security requirements for software development and the corresponding test cases are available in the ALM system. The concept follows an approach to reuse this information to address the challenges described in Section 11.2, namely that requirements tracing for application security testing is time-consuming, difficult to keep up-to-date, and error prone. Consequently, this concept reduces the effort required, and allows for automation of application security testing, and automation of managing requirements traceability to keep information up-to-date while avoiding manual errors.

To better understand the steps involved in this approach, an overview of the concept is shown in Figure 11.3. In general terms, the idea is to read the relevant information from the ALM system, launch the corresponding application security testing tools with the appropriate configurations, and incorporate the results back into the ALM system. The following describes this approach in more detail. In the first step, information from the ALM system specifically related to the test cases that are defined to verify the security requirements for software development is read out. A few such examples are given in Sections 11.3.1.1–11.3.1.4. In the second step, based on the test cases, it is possible to understand which application security testing tool is required, and what configuration or test plan should be used. Please note that the test cases in the ALM system must be written in such a way that it is clear which application security testing tool and configuration/test plan should be used. For example, for the static code analysis example mentioned above, the test case should indicate which configuration should be used with the static code analysis tool. The configuration should specify exactly which MISRA or AUTOSAR guidelines need to be checked in the target software. Another example is the fuzz testing example above for CAN or IPv4, where the test case should specify the test plan to be used for the fuzz testing tool. The test plan should contain the CAN ID and bitrate for the CAN fuzz testing, and the specific IP address and port number for the SUT (system under test) for the IPv4 fuzz testing. These configurations and test plans should be created in advance for the respective application security testing tools based on the requirements and test cases in the ALM system. In the third step, the application security testing tools are launched with the corresponding predefined configuration or test plan. These tools perform the necessary testing as indicated by the requirements and specified in the test cases. Last, in the fourth step, the results from the application security testing tools are incorporated into the ALM system. The criteria for pass/fail for the test cases in the ALM system are clearly defined, which allows determination of whether a certain result from an application security testing tool results in a pass or a fail for the corresponding test case. Thus, based on the actual results from the application security testing tools, the ALM system updates its test case with a pass or fail indication. By including the ALM system in these steps allows an organization to trace the specific results from an application security testing tool to the corresponding test case and security requirement, therefore achieving *requirements traceability*. While it is possible to perform these steps manually, i.e. executing an application security testing tool with an appropriate configuration or test plan and then manually uploading test results to the ALM system, the focus of this chapter is on automating the approach to reduce the effort required and avoid manual mistakes such as running the tools with the wrong configurations, uploading the wrong results or even forgetting to upload the results.

11.3.2 Example Implementation

This section presents an example implementation of the concept explained in Section 11.3.1 to highlight the practicability and applicability of the concept. This example implementation integrates various tools to perform the four steps in Figure 11.3 and is described as follows. As mentioned, the focus is on automating the entire process of the steps involved in the concept, so one of the goals with the example implementation is to ensure that all the involved tools are running in an automated fashion. A few different examples of application security testing tools are given in Section 11.3.1. For the example implementation which is based on Reference [9, 30], a fuzz testing tool was used; however, it would be possible to use other application security testing tools as well.

The example implementation is based on the following tools and components:

- Defensics
- codeBeamer ALM
- Jenkins
- SUT

11.3.2.1 Defensics

The example implementation uses the fuzz testing tool Defensics [31], which is a black-box generation-based fuzzer that uses an intelligent, targeted approach to negative testing. It supports 250+ test suites, which allows for comprehensive protocol and file format fuzz testing. Moreover, Defensics can be controlled using API (application protocol interface) commands to, for example, load test plans, and start and stop fuzzing, which facilitates automation.

11.3.2.2 codeBeamer ALM

The example implementation uses codeBeamer ALM [32] as the ALM system, which is an integrated platform for application lifecycle management. It allows for traceability since it provides functionality for managing all relevant tasks throughout the lifecycle, starting from requirements management to software development, testing, release, and operations. Moreover, it provides specific capabilities for the automotive industry, including native workflows built into ISO 26262 and ASPICE templates [17].

11.3.2.3 Jenkins

The example implementation uses Jenkins [13] as the automation server, which is a free and open-source automation server. Jenkins can help to automate various tasks included in the software development process related to building, testing, and deploying software. Thus, it is an extremely useful tool to help facilitate continuous integration, continuous testing, and continuous delivery.

11.3.2.4 SUT

The example implementation uses an embedded system with a rich OS as the SUT. More specifically, the SUT is running Automotive Grade Linux (AGL) [33] on a Raspberry Pi 3 [34] Embedded Linux Board. By default, the SUT has a couple of open ports, namely port 22/TCP (Transmission Control Protocol) (SSH service) and port 53/TCP (DNS [domain name system] service). Additionally, the SUT supports wireless communication over Wi-Fi and Bluetooth. Thus, there are multiple suitable protocols and interfaces that could be used for fuzz testing of the SUT.

11.3.2.5 Implementation Overview

The example implementation of integrating application security testing tools with ALM systems is based on the above-mentioned tools and components. These tools and components interact with each other to automate the testing based on the test cases defined in the ALM system and to provide the test results back to the ALM system to achieve traceability. The interaction between the tools and components is depicted in the swimlane diagram shown in Figure 11.4. The swimlane diagram illustrates in more detail the workflow, the activities, and the interactions between Jenkins, codeBeamer ALM, Defensics, and the SUT, and is described as follows.

First, even before the activities in the swimlane diagram start, there are a few prerequisites to ensure that the fuzz testing can proceed. These prerequisites include building and

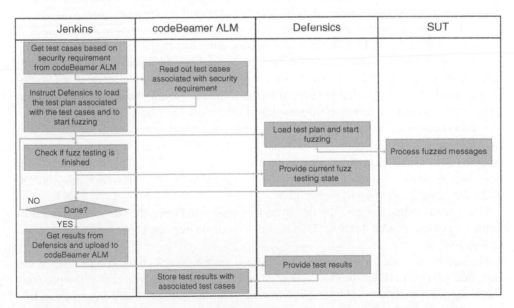

Figure 11.4 Swimlane diagram showing the interactions between the different tools and components. Source: Adapted with permission from [9, 30]. © 2019 IEEE. Portions Copyright 2020 Synopsys, Inc. Used with permission. All rights reserved.

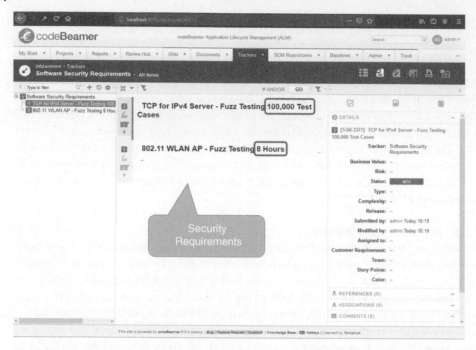

Figure 11.5 Security requirements for software development defined in codeBeamer ALM. Source: [30]. Reproduced with permission from Intland Software GmbH.

flashing the necessary software to the SUT and running some functional tests on the SUT to verify that the service or protocol to be fuzz tested is working correctly from a functional point of view before starting with the fuzz testing. Please note that these prerequisite steps are not shown in Figure 11.4, but they are discussed in more detail in Section 11.3.3.

Once the prerequisites have been fulfilled, the workflow and the activities in the swim-lane diagram in Figure 11.4 can start. Since Jenkins is the automation server that handles all automation and triggering of tasks, it initiates the fuzz testing workflow by executing a script to read out the test case information from codeBeamer ALM, which includes the test case(s) associated with the security requirements for software development. Please note that Jenkins is instrumental in this example workflow since it runs the various scripts that trigger, process, and make decisions for the different tasks. In the example implementation, one security requirement defined in codeBeamer ALM is "TCP for IPv4 Server – 100,000 Fuzz Test Cases" as shown in Figure 11.5.

The corresponding test case defined in codeBeamer ALM to verify whether this require-ment is fulfilled is called "TCP for IPv4 Server – 100,000 Fuzz Test Cases Test" as presented in Figure 11.6.

The success criteria for this test case is defined as "minimum of 100,000 fuzz test cases executed AND zero failed fuzz test cases." Since similar wordings are used in the previous sentence, it is worth highlighting the terminology for the sake of clarity: a *test case* in this example is used to verify a security requirement defined in codeBeamer ALM, whereas a *fuzz test case* in this example is a specific fuzzed message used during the fuzz testing run. During a typical fuzz testing run, depending on the protocol and target system, thousands,

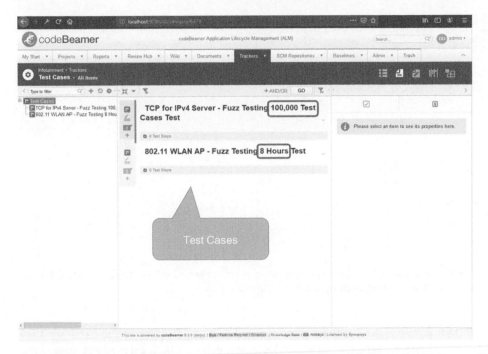

Figure 11.6 Test cases defined in codeBeamer ALM. Source: Intland Software GmbH. Source: [30]. Reproduced with permission from Intland Software GmbH.

or tens of thousands, or hundreds of thousands, or even millions of fuzz test cases can be used. In this particular example, the requirement and test case state that a minimum of 100 000 fuzz test cases shall be sent to and processed by the SUT. After extracting the test case information from codeBeamer ALM, Jenkins launches another script that identifies that the test case information is related to fuzz testing and therefore launches the fuzz testing tool, Defensics. Moreover, the test case information specifically mentions "TCP for IPv4 Server," therefore the script instructs Defensics, using Defensics' API, to load the "TCP for IPv4 Server test plan," which has been prepared in advance since the requirements and test cases are known. This test plan contains the specific IP address and TCP port for the SUT to be used for the fuzz testing run. Furthermore, the script instructs Defensics using API commands to start fuzzing the SUT. The SUT receives and processes the fuzzed TCP messages. Jenkins then runs a script to check if fuzz testing is complete. The script periodically checks the current fuzz testing state of Defensics using API commands to verify how many fuzz test cases have been tested or how long the fuzz testing session has been running. In this example, the requirement and test case in the ALM system specifies 100 000 fuzz test cases. Once Defensics returns a response of the current fuzz testing state indicating that at least 100 000 fuzz test cases have been executed, the script determines that the fuzz testing run is completed. As a result, Jenkins triggers the next script that requests the results from Defensics for the current fuzz testing run. The results are then uploaded to codeBeamer ALM for the associated test case. One example result uploaded to codeBeamer ALM is visualized in Figure 11.7.

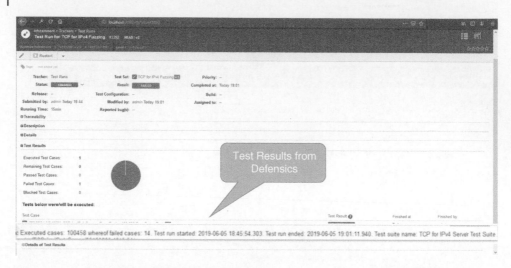

Figure 11.7 Test results from Defensics uploaded as test case results in codeBeamer ALM. Source: [30]. Reproduced with permission from Intland Software GmbH.

As shown in the figure, in this example, 100 458 fuzz test cases of the "TCP for IPv4 Server" test suite were executed, of which Defensics detected 14 failed fuzz test cases of the SUT processing the fuzzed messages. Since the success criteria for this test case is defined as "minimum of 100,000 fuzz test cases executed AND zero failed fuzz test cases," codeBeamer ALM marks the test case as failed since 14 failed fuzz test cases were detected. Moreover, as shown in the figure, additional details from the fuzz testing run, including the time the test was executed, how long the testing took, the name of the test suite used, etc., are also stored in the test case in codeBeamer ALM. This type of information allows for traceability to have a better understanding of when, how, and what was tested. It is possible to include further information such as the specific version of the software being tested to help with traceability.

All of these steps in the process for this example implementation can be automated so that when there is a new software release that is loaded onto an SUT and ready for testing, Jenkins will get the appropriate test case from codeBeamer ALM, launch Defensics with the corresponding test plan and instruct Defensics to start fuzzing the SUT. Once the fuzz testing session has completed, the results from Defensics are automatically uploaded to the test case in codeBeamer ALM, including an indication of whether the test case *Passed* or *Failed*. Thus, in this example implementation, it is possible in codeBeamer ALM to get a complete overview of all the relevant security requirements, the corresponding test cases, and the current status of testing including the related results from Defensics indicating whether the fuzz test cases passed or failed. This allows for requirements management and traceability to verify whether a certain requirement has been fulfilled or not. An example of this overview in codeBeamer ALM is given in Figure 11.8.

This figure shows two requirements, where one requirement is marked as *Failed* since the example test case of "TCP for IPv4 Server – 100,000 Fuzz Test Cases Test" described above resulted in 14 failed fuzz test cases. The other requirement is marked as *Incomplete* since the testing required for this test case has not been performed yet.

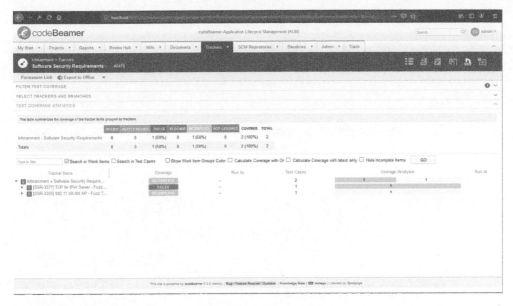

Figure 11.8 Overview of relevant security requirements, test cases and current status in codeBeamer ALM where one test case failed. Source: [30]. Reproduced with permission from Intland Software GmbH.

Once the development teams have fixed the issues that caused the 14 failed fuzz test cases, the updated software is retested. When the fuzz testing run of 100 000 fuzz test cases has successfully completed and the test results from Defensics indicate that no failed fuzz test cases were detected the corresponding test case in codeBeamer ALM is marked as *Passed*. This result is shown in Figure 11.9.

The requirements overview still lists the two requirements; however, now the requirement "TCP for IPv4 Server – 100,000 Fuzz Test Cases" shows that the test case passed and therefore the corresponding requirement has been fulfilled. The other requirement is still marked as *Incomplete* since the corresponding testing has not been performed yet. This overview allows an organization to better understand which requirements have been fulfilled or have not been fulfilled because testing failed or because testing has not been performed yet.

Moreover, for traceability purposes, it is possible in codeBeamer ALM to go into the details for the requirement that has been fulfilled and see the related test case and, additionally, find the necessary information about the test run and the actual test results from the fuzz testing tool. This allows for traceability from requirements to test cases to actual test results from application security testing tools. Furthermore, since these steps can be automated, it reduces the manual effort needed to perform the various tasks, it allows an organization to easily keep information in the ALM system up-to-date, and it avoids the risks for manual mistakes by running the tools with the correct configurations based on the test cases in the ALM system and automatically uploading the relevant test results from the application security testing tools to the ALM system.

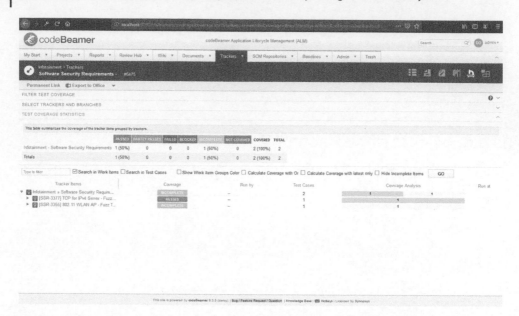

Figure 11.9 Overview of relevant security requirements, test cases and current status in codeBeamer ALM where one test case passed. Source: [30]. Reproduced with permission from Intland Software GmbH.

11.3.3 Considerations

Integration of application security testing tools with ALM systems to automate testing allows automotive organizations to better manage requirements traceability to reduce the time and effort, keeping information regarding requirements, testing, and test results up-to-date, and avoiding potentially costly human mistakes. However, to fully take advantage of such an automated solution requires careful consideration. There are several prerequisites and steps required that an organization need to consider.

It is important for an organization to first define the workflow process and have a clear view of what software targets, requirements, test tools, and equipment are necessary to perform relevant application security testing. It is also useful for an organization to first investigate the manual steps required for the process to integrate appropriate application security testing tools with ALM systems. An organization can then further investigate how the workflow can be automated using various APIs supported by the different application security testing tools to allow integration with ALM systems, especially to help achieve requirements traceability. It may be useful to consider how to gradually integrate application security testing tools with ALM systems to help automate the workflow process, focusing on the tools that provide suitable interfaces and are easy to integrate first.

There are numerous automated application security testing tools that can be used in the automotive SDLC, such as static code analysis tools, software composition analysis tools, vulnerability scanning tools, and fuzz testing tools [35, 36]. Although the example implementation presented in Section 11.3.2 showcases a fuzz testing tool being integrated with an ALM system, it is worth noting that it would be possible to integrate other application security testing tools in a similar fashion. While some application security testing tools and approaches (i.e. static approaches) can be used to scan source code and binaries of the software as is, other application security testing tools and approaches (i.e. dynamic approaches) may require a specific test environment for the target software. Considerations for ALM system integration based on the static and dynamic approaches are provided in more detail as follows.

Some of the application security testing approaches can be performed using only the target software in a static fashion by accessing the source code or the binary, e.g. for static code analysis (cf. Section 11.3.1.1) and software composition analysis (cf. Section 11.3.1.2). By integrating such tools with ALM systems, the examples presented in Sections 11.3.1.1 and 11.3.1.2 can be implemented as follows. For the static code analysis example in Section 11.3.1.1, it is possible to read out the MISRA or AUTOSAR guidelines defined in a test case from the ALM system and then execute a static code analysis tool using a configuration where the corresponding MISRA or AUTOSAR checkers are enabled. Depending on the tool, it may be required to prepare the configuration files in advance based on the information available in the test cases. In this case, it would be possible to create a configuration file with the specific MISRA or AUTOSAR checkers enabled and then launch the static code analysis tool using this configuration file. Once the scan completes, the static code analysis tool uploads the test results to the ALM system. Based on the results, either the test case is passed because no violations to the MISRA or AUTOSAR guidelines were detected, or the test case is failed because the static code analysis tool detected one or more violations to the MISRA or AUTOSAR coding guidelines. Details about which version of the software was scanned, which parts of the software were scanned, which specific guideline violations were detected, which parts of the software contained the identified violations, etc., can be included in the upload to the ALM system as well. This additional information can be used by software developers to better understand what they need to focus on and what issues they need to resolve in order for the test case to pass.

For the software composition analysis example in Section 11.3.1.2, it is possible to read out information from a test case in the ALM system regarding testing for known critical vulnerabilities in open-source software. A software composition analysis tool can be launched with a policy configured based on the information in the test case, e.g. testing that the open-source software should not contain any known critical vulnerabilities. Depending on the tool, the policy configurations may have to be prepared in advance based on the information available in the test cases. For instance, it would be possible to create a policy configuration stating that no known critical vulnerabilities are allowed and then launch the software composition analysis tool with this policy enabled. Once the scan completes, the software composition analysis tool uploads the test results to the ALM system. Based on the test results, the test case is either passed because there were no known critical vulnerabilities detected in the open-source software, or the test case failed because the software composition analysis tool identified one or more critical known vulnerabilities in the scanned open-source software. Details about which version of the software was scanned, which parts of the software were scanned, which specific known critical vulnerabilities were detected, which open-source software components contained the identified critical vulnerabilities, etc., can be included in the upload to the ALM system as well.

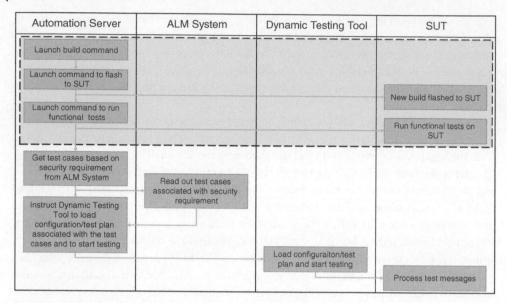

Figure 11.10 Swimlane diagram including prerequisite steps to allow for application security testing in a dynamic environment.

However, some other application security testing approaches are performed in a dynamic fashion and require the target software to be running on the SUT, e.g. for vulnerability scanning and fuzz testing. By integrating such tools with ALM systems, the examples presented in Sections 11.3.1.3 and 11.3.1.4 can be implemented as follows. However, first, before any dynamic testing can be performed, it is important to consider the process for building and flashing the target software to the SUT. Additionally, it is useful to perform functional testing of the target software to ensure that it is properly working before performing the application security testing in the dynamic environment. Therefore, a prerequisite for automation to allow continuous application security testing is that the build, flashing to SUT, and functional testing steps can be automated. Then the appropriate application security testing tools can be executed. The steps necessary for automating the build, flashing to the SUT, and performing functional testing may differ depending on the target software and target system. Details about these steps are not covered in this book, however it is imperative that an organization considers how to perform and automate these steps to allow for continuous application security testing requiring a dynamic test environment. To highlight the necessity of these steps, Figure 11.10 shows the prerequisite steps in gray background added to the top of the swimlane diagram adapted from Figure 11.4.

For the vulnerability scanning example in Section 11.3.1.3, it is possible to read out information from a test case in the ALM system regarding testing for critical vulnerabilities in known services running on the target system. A vulnerability scanning tool can be launched with a configuration based on the information in the test case, e.g. testing that the SSH service on the target system should not contain any critical vulnerabilities. Depending on the tool, it may be required to prepare the configuration files in advance based on the information available in the test cases. In this case, it would be possible to create a configuration file with the target IP address, target ports, scan modes, and vulnerability database to use, and then launch the vulnerability scanning tool with this configuration. Once the scan completes, the vulnerability scanning tool uploads the test results to the ALM system. Based on the results, either the test case is passed because no critical vulnerabilities were detected, or the test case is failed because the vulnerability scanning tool detected one or more critical vulnerabilities. Details about which build of the software was scanned, which ports or services of the target system were scanned, which specific critical vulnerabilities were detected, which services contained the identified critical vulnerabilities, etc., can be included in the upload to the ALM system as well.

The fuzz testing example in Section 11.3.1.4 has been covered already in the example implementation in Section 11.3.2; however, a brief explanation is included below for the sake of completeness. It is possible to read out the information from a test case in the ALM system regarding the interfaces or protocols that should be fuzz tested and then execute a fuzz testing tool using a configuration or test plan for the corresponding interfaces or protocols. Depending on the tool, it may be required to prepare the configuration files or test plans in advance based on the information available in the test cases. For example, it would be possible to create a configuration file or test plan specifying the target address, protocol to be fuzzed, number of fuzz test cases to include, type of anomalies in the fuzzed messages, etc., and then launch the fuzz testing tool with this configuration or test plan. Once the fuzz testing completes, the fuzz testing tool uploads the test results to the ALM system. Based on the results, either the test case is passed because there were no failed fuzz test cases, or the test case is failed because the fuzz testing tool detected one or more failed fuzz test cases. Details about which build of the software was tested, which protocols or interfaces of the target system were fuzz tested, how many fuzz test cases were executed, which fuzz test cases failed etc. can be included in the upload to the ALM system as well.

Moreover, when performing application security testing in a dynamic fashion there may be additional challenges that an organization needs to consider. For instance, there may be timing issues for the test environment that need to be considered when performing vulnerability scanning or fuzz testing over, for example, Wi-Fi and Bluetooth. Moreover, there may be some advanced situations where the SUT requires external input to function properly and additional monitoring capabilities to detect exceptions occurring on the SUT during the dynamic testing. Examples of such approaches and solutions are described in more detail in Chapter 8 (using HIL [hardware-in the-loop] systems), Chapter 9 (using Agent Instrumentation Framework), and Chapter 10 (using an Embedded Linux Board). It would also be possible to integrate these types of advanced test environments with ALM systems to allow for closer control and interaction between the ALM system, application security testing tools, and relevant test environment equipment.

There may also be cases where the SUT stops functioning due to a vulnerability scanning or fuzzed message and requires to be restarted or restored back into a testable state. These situations to handle failed test cases may look different for different SUTs and different security application testing approaches. Furthermore, in some cases, dynamic testing may require manual input to the SUT to control the target application or power cycle the SUT. These topics are not covered in detail in this chapter; however, an organization should consider what steps are necessary to enable application security testing on the SUT and, if possible, how to automate such steps. Some ideas on how to automate user input to the SUT are discussed in Section 10.3.4. It is also worth mentioning that it may be possible to perform some dynamic testing of the SUT in a virtual environment [37]. Similarly, this virtual test environment requires considerations for the SUT on how to enable testable states, how to detect issues, and how to recover from failed test cases. This is an interesting and upcoming topic that requires further research and exploration and will therefore not be discussed in more detail in this book.

Besides integrating application security testing tools with ALM systems, it is useful for an organization to also consider integrating other tools and systems used in the SDLC with ALM systems. For example, bug tracking systems such as Jira could be integrated with ALM systems. In this case, it would be possible to, for example, have a static code analysis tool that automatically creates relevant Jira tickets based on the identified findings from scanning the target source code. These Jira tickets can then be managed from the ALM system to provide an overview of how many Jira tickets are still open, how many have been resolved, etc. Thus, it is possible to achieve traceability from requirements to test cases to actual results from static code analysis tools to the corresponding specific Jira tickets created based on the test results. Moreover, using test coverage functionality in the ALM systems enables an organization to get an overview of which security requirements have been fulfilled based on the actual test results from the application security testing tools, as shown in Figures 11.9 and 11.10. Using this overview, it is then possible to track the progress for fulfilling a certain requirement by observing how many of the Jira tickets have been closed and how many Jira tickets are still open. This information also helps with planning and scheduling as well as requirements traceability. That is, it is easy for an organization to, at some point in the future, trace a requirement that has been fulfilled to the actual test results from an application security testing tool that can be used as the evidence to show that the requirement has been met.

Generally, when integrating application security testing tools with ALM systems and automating security testing, it is imperative to consider the APIs and approaches required to control and communicate between different tools to allow for a straightforward integration. There may be situations where an organization uses legacy systems or tools with limited APIs or there may be complex test environments that require further technical consideration on how to integrate such tools. Moreover, there may be organizational challenges, such as there being different teams and processes responsible for requirements management and testing, and there being different owners for the systems and tools used. Nevertheless, it would be useful for organizations to investigate the possibilities of integrating application security testing tools into ALM systems to help with automation and traceability.

11.4 Chapter Summary

This chapter presented a solution to automation and traceability by integrating application security testing tools into ALM systems. First, the challenges regarding requirements traceability of security requirements for software development and automation of application security testing in the automotive industry are discussed. Mainly, since application security testing tools are typically executed manually or separately in different teams, the related activities required for traceability such as tracing actual test results to requirements are time-consuming, difficult to keep-up-to-date and error prone. To address these challenges, this chapter describes a solution for integrating application security testing tools with ALM systems to automate the necessary steps for application security testing and allow for requirements traceability in the SDLC. ALM systems are typically already used in many organizations to handle various tasks in the SDLC and it would be beneficial for an organization to also integrate application security testing tools into the ALM systems. The solution uses information available in the ALM system, such as security requirements for software development and their corresponding test cases, to launch various application security testing tools with the appropriate configurations or test plans according to the test cases. Once the application security testing tools have completed scanning or testing the target software or system, the actual test results from the application security testing tools are uploaded to the ALM system for the corresponding test cases. Based on the test case criteria, the test results from the application security testing tools are used to determine whether the test case passed or failed. Moreover, if the test case failed, additional details about the findings, violations, or identified vulnerabilities are provided to the ALM system to allow developers to easier understand what the specific issues are and what needs to be resolved in order for the test case to pass. If the test case passed, it is indicated accordingly in the ALM system. As a result, it is possible for an organization to have a complete overview of all the relevant security requirements and see which requirements have been fulfilled based on the passed test cases, and which requirements have not yet been fulfilled due to failed test cases or the fact that they have not been tested yet. Thus, this solution allows for requirements traceability, meaning that it is possible to trace specific requirements to actual test results from application security testing tools that can be used as evidence to show that the requirements have been fulfilled. It is worth noting that while these steps for the test activities can be performed manually, owing to the large volume of software developed and used in the automotive industry coupled with increasingly more requirements for secure software development, it becomes gradually more important for organizations to consider how to automate the steps involved in the process. This chapter also presents an example implementation to showcase the practicability and usefulness of the solution. In this example implementation, an automation server is used to automatically trigger a script that reads out test case information for a specific fuzz testing requirement from an ALM system, identifies the appropriate test plan for that test case, and launches the fuzz testing tool with the corresponding test plan. The fuzz testing tool then automatically performs the testing of the SUT and uploads the test results to the ALM system. Based on the actual test results and the test criteria, it can be determined whether the test case passed or failed, and, consequently, whether the requirement is fulfilled or not. Considering standardization activities and regulations for cybersecurity in the automotive industry such as ISO/SAE 21434 and UNECE WP.29 Cybersecurity, the number of requirements for secure software development will continue to increase. Thus, it will become increasingly important for organizations to be able to manage requirements traceability, i.e. to be able to link security requirements to actual test results that can be used as evidence that the requirements have been fulfilled. Applying an automated approach and building this process into the SDLC using ALM systems allows automotive organizations to more effectively develop and test software and verify that the related security requirements have been fulfilled.

References

1 SEI (2016). CERT C coding standard - rules for developing safe, reliable, and secure systems.

2 SEI (2016). CERT C++ coding standard - rules for developing safe, reliable, and secure systems in C++.

3 MISRA (2013). MISRA C:2012 guidelines for the use of the C language in critical systems.

4 MISRA (2008). MISRA C++:2008 guidelines for the use of the C++ language in critical systems.

5 AUTOSAR (2019). Guidelines for the use of the C++14 language in critical and safety-related systems.

6 NIST (2020). Mitigating the risk of software vulnerabilities by adopting a Secure Software Development Framework (SSDF).

7 Microsoft (2020). Microsoft security development lifecycle (SDL). https://www.microsoft.com/en-us/securityengineering/sdl (accessed 30 July 2020).

8 Synopsys (2020). Secure SDLC 101. https://www.synopsys.com/blogs/software-security/secure-sdlc (accessed 30 July 2020).

9 Oka, D. K., Makila, T., and Kuipers, R. (2019). Integrating application security testing tools into ALM tools in the automotive industry. *IEEE 19th International Conference on Software Quality Reliability and Security Companion (QRS-C)*, Sofia, Bulgaria.

10 IBM (2020). IBM engineering requirements management DOORS family. https://www.ibm.com/products/requirements-management (accessed 30 July 2020).

11 Sparx Systems (2020). Enterprise architect. https://sparxsystems.com (accessed 30 July 2020).

12 Git (2020). Git is a free and open source distributed version control system. https://git-scm.com (accessed 30 July 2020).

13 Jenkins (2020). Jenkins – build great things at any scale. https://www.jenkins.io (accessed 30 July 2020).

14 Selenium Project (2020). Selenium automates browsers. That's it!. https://www.selenium.dev (accessed 30 July 2020).

15 Vector (2020). Automating software testing with VectorCAST. https://www.vector.com/int/en/products/products-a-z/software/vectorcast/ (accessed 30 July 2020).

16 Atlassian (2020). Jira software. https://www.atlassian.com/software/jira (accessed 30 July 2020).

17 Intland Software (2020). Automotive embedded E/E and software development with codeBeamer ALM. https://intland.com/codebeamer/automotive-software-engineering (accessed 30 July 2020).

18 International Organization for Standardization (ISO) (2018). *ISO 26262-1:2018 – road vehicles — functional safety*. Geneva, Switzerland: ISO.

19 VDA QMC Working Group 13/Automotive SIG (2017). Automotive SPICE process reference model/process assessment model version 3.1. VDA QMC.

20 International Organization for Standardization (ISO)/Society of Automotive Engineers (SAE) International (2020). *ISO/SAE DIS 21434 – road vehicles — cybersecurity engineering*. Geneva, Switzerland: ISO and USA: SAE International.

21 UNECE WP.29 (2020). ECE/TRANS/WP.29/2020/79 REVISED: proposal for a new UN regulation on uniform provisions concerning the approval of vehicles with regards to cyber security and cyber security management system.

22 Wired (2015). After jeep hack, Chrysler recalls 1.4M vehicles for bug fix. https://www.wired.com/2015/07/jeep-hack-chrysler-recalls-1-4m-vehicles-bug-fix (accessed 30 July 2020).

23 Tencent Keen Security Lab (2019). Tencent Keen Security Lab: experimental security research of Tesla autopilot. https://keenlab.tencent.com/en/2019/03/29/Tencent-Keen-Security-Lab-Experimental-Security-Research-of-Tesla-Autopilot/ (accessed 30 July 2020).

24 Tencent Keen Security Lab (2020). Tencent Keen Security Lab: experimental security assessment on Lexus cars. https://keenlab.tencent.com/en/2020/03/30/Tencent-Keen-Security-Lab-Experimental-Security-Assessment-on-Lexus-Cars/ (accessed 30 July 2020).

25 Ponemon Institute – SAE International and Synopsys (2019). Securing the modern vehicle: a study of automotive industry cybersecurity practices. Synopsys, Inc. and SAE International.

26 Perforce (2020). A guide to traceability in product development. https://www.perforce.com/resources/alm/requirements-traceability-matrix (accessed 30 July 2020).

27 Perforce (2018). How to create a requirements traceability matrix. https://www.perforce.com/blog/alm/how-create-traceability-matrix (accessed 30 July 2020).

28 Imran, S., Buchheit, M., Hollunder, B., and Schreier, U. (2015). Tool chains in Agile ALM environments: a short introduction. *On the Move to Meaningful Internet Systems (OTM)*, Rhodes, Greece.

29 Markov, G. and Druzhinina, O. (2011). Towards an industrial ALM (Application Lifecycle) tool integration. Masters thesis. Blekinge Institute of Technology.

30 Oka, D. K., Makila, T., and Kuipers, R. (2019). Integrating application security testing tools into ALM tools in the automotive Industry. *A3S'19: IEEE International Workshop on Automobile Software Security and Safety*, Sofia, Bulgaria.

31 Synopsys (2020). Defensics fuzz testing. https://www.synopsys.com/software-integrity/security-testing/fuzz-testing.html (accessed 30 July 2020).

32 Intland Software (2020). codeBeamer ALM is an integrated application lifecycle management platform. https://intland.com/codebeamer/application-lifecycle-management (accessed 30 July 2020).

33 Automotive Grade Linux (2020). What is automotive grade linux?. https://www.automotivelinux.org (accessed 30 July 2020).

34 Raspberry Pi Foundation (2020). Raspberry Pi. https://www.raspberrypi.org (accessed 30 July 2020).

35 Oka, D. K. (2018). Security in the automotive software development lifecycle. *Symposium on Cryptography and Information Security (SCIS)*, Niigata, Japan.

36 Bayer, S., Enderle, T., Oka, D. K., and Wolf, M. (2015). Security crash test — practical security evaluations of automotive onboard IT components. *Automotive — Safety & Security 2015*, Stuttgart, Germany.

37 Oka, D.K. (2020). Fuzz testing virtual ECUs as part of the continuous security testing process. *SAE International Journal of Transportation Cybersecurity and Privacy* 2 (2): 159–168. https://doi.org/10.4271/11-02-02-0014.

12

Continuous Cybersecurity Monitoring, Vulnerability Management, Incident Response, and Secure OTA Updates

BE PREPARED AND ALWAYS IMPROVE

This chapter discusses the importance of protecting vehicles after production, covering the topics of continuous cybersecurity monitoring, vulnerability management, incident response, and secure over-the-air (OTA) updates. While the previous chapters focused on improving security, mainly during the development and testing phases up until release, this chapter focuses on security aspects *after* release and the related processes and activities during the operations and maintenance phases. Considering the fact that vehicles have lifespans of 10–15 years, it is necessary for automotive organizations to conduct continuous cybersecurity activities such as threat and vulnerability monitoring. To this end, it is important to have an approach for how to monitor for new vulnerabilities and be able to track which vehicles or automotive systems are vulnerable.

As the focus on cybersecurity in the automotive software development lifecycle increases, there will definitely be more secure and safe cars on the roads in the future. However, with new vehicles containing large volumes of software, even with the right security tools, processes and training, it is not possible to guarantee that there will not exist any vulnerabilities in the software of a vehicle when it is released, or to ensure that no new vulnerabilities will be detected over the course of the lifetime of the vehicle after production. As explained in Chapter 2, automotive organizations can and should apply various cybersecurity measures and activities during the development process, including cybersecurity requirements review (cf. Section 2.3.1), security design review (cf. Section 2.3.2), threat analysis and risk assessment (cf. Section 2.3.3), source code review (cf. Section 2.3.4), static code analysis (cf. Section 2.3.5), software composition analysis (cf. Section 2.3.6), security functional testing (cf. Section 2.3.7), vulnerability scanning (cf. Section 2.3.8), fuzz testing (cf. Section 2.3.9), and penetration testing (cf. Section 2.3.10) to improve security and identify and reduce the number of vulnerabilities in automotive systems during the development and testing phases. Moreover, besides the cybersecurity activities during the development and testing phases, it is equally important that automotive organizations consider cybersecurity activities after release to be able to identify and fix vulnerabilities on vehicles after production. Activities include incident response and updates (cf. Section 2.3.11) and continuous cybersecurity activities (cf. Section 2.3.12). This chapter explores these activities in more detail

Building Secure Cars: Assuring the Automotive Software Development Lifecycle, First Edition. Dennis Kengo Oka.
© 2021 John Wiley & Sons Ltd. Published 2021 by John Wiley & Sons Ltd.

to explain how automotive organizations can secure vehicles after production. During the operations and maintenance phases, it is extremely important for automotive organizations to employ cybersecurity monitoring as part of the continuous cybersecurity activities. This allows them to identify new vulnerabilities in automotive systems during the lifetime of the vehicle. When new vulnerabilities are detected, it is imperative that automotive organizations have vulnerability management and incident response processes in place to handle said vulnerabilities. Moreover, in order to address critical vulnerabilities in a timely manner, the organization must have an established secure OTA update process, which allows updating the vulnerable automotive systems in the field. This update process should also ensure that no new known vulnerabilities are introduced with the new updates.

This chapter discusses the current challenges and presents solutions to help secure vehicles after production. Specifically, this chapter presents a solution concept that receives alerts on newly found vulnerabilities, maps those newly identified vulnerabilities to existing vehicles and automotive systems that are already deployed in the field, and finally allows secure OTA updates to be performed to patch those vulnerable systems.

The main points of this chapter are:

- We explain the need for cybersecurity monitoring and secure OTA updates based on the current state of the automotive industry and automotive software development.
- We discuss common challenges for automotive organizations in terms of software inventory, monitoring vulnerabilities, and vulnerable vehicles.
- We present an overall solution for securing vehicles after production consisting of release management, monitoring and tracking, and secure OTA updates.

More details regarding securing vehicles after production, vulnerability management, and secure OTA updates can be found in References [1, 2].

12.1 Need for Cybersecurity Monitoring and Secure OTA Updates

As automotive systems contain larger and more complex software, the risk for bugs and vulnerabilities in the software code is increasing. In addition, more systems are no longer developed by a single organization but are often complex systems containing software from numerous different organizations and parties.

There are a number of challenges in the automotive industry especially regarding software development. Results from an automotive survey, called "Securing the Modern Vehicle: A Study of Automotive Industry Cybersecurity Practices", presented in more detail in Section 1.3, helps to understand the automotive industry's cybersecurity posture and its capability to address software security risks inherent in connected, software-enabled vehicles [3]. The survey was commissioned by Synopsys and SAE International and conducted by the Ponemon Institute. In total, 593 professionals in the automotive industry from various regions, who were responsible for contributing to or assessing the security of automotive components, provided input to the survey. One interesting result is that 62% of those surveyed responded that a malicious or proof-of-concept attack against automotive software, technology and components developed by their own organizations is likely or very likely in the next 12 months. This means that there is a strong concern about the security risks and potential attacks on automotive systems expressed by the people responsible for the security of such systems. Another interesting result from the study is that 69% of the respondents say that they do not feel empowered to raise concerns about the security in their organizations. This means that even though the security experts at these organizations may know about potential security risks and be concerned about attacks, they are not empowered to address the concerns and improve security. One reason for this may be that 30% of the surveyed organizations do not have an established product cybersecurity program or team. Moreover, only 10% of the respondents say that they have a centralized product cybersecurity program or team in their organization that guides and supports multiple product development teams. Exploring further to understand why there is a lack of established cybersecurity programs or teams in automotive organizations, the survey presents results indicating that most organizations do not have the appropriate level of resources for cybersecurity to address the cybersecurity threats in the automotive space. Namely, more than 50% of the respondents say they do not have enough resources, both in terms of budget and human resources for cybersecurity activities. In addition, even if the organizations have cybersecurity teams, 62% of the respondents state that they do not have the necessary cybersecurity skills. Moreover, these organizations, which typically employ thousands or tens of thousands of workers, on average only have nine full-time equivalent in their product cybersecurity management programs. The survey also highlights that security vulnerabilities are being assessed far too late in the product development and release processes. Only 47% of the organizations assess vulnerabilities in the early stages of requirements and design phases, or the development and testing phases. Preferably, this number should be much higher where all organizations are performing proper cybersecurity activities in the early phases of the development and testing. As an established best practice, it is recommended that a risk-based, process-driven approach to cybersecurity throughout the entire product development lifecycle is taken. As with any software, there is a risk of vulnerabilities being introduced in automotive systems during development, and of being missed during testing, leading to vulnerable software in vehicles when they are released. According to the survey, the primary factor that leads to vulnerabilities in automotive software and components is owing to the high pressure to meet product deadlines. This may indicate that certain cybersecurity activities are reduced in scope, are not conducted properly, or may even be skipped entirely. Furthermore, the top three factors besides the pressure to meet deadlines are related to *coding*, *testing* and *open-source software*. Regarding *coding*, there are challenges involving lack of understanding or training on secure coding practice, and accidental coding errors. In terms of *testing*, there is a general lack of quality assurance and testing procedures. For *open-source software*, the main factor is using insecure or outdated open-source software components. Moreover, the survey highlights the technologies that pose the greatest cybersecurity risks, where the top three areas include RF (radio frequency) technologies (e.g. Wi-Fi and Bluetooth), telematics, and autonomous vehicles.

Moreover, since these complex systems that make up new vehicles contain software from multiple parties, supply chain management is becoming an increasingly important topic. The survey emphasizes that 73% of the respondents are very concerned about the cybersecurity posture of automotive software and technologies provided by third parties. Given the large volume of software coming from several different parties, this high number is quite alarming. Moreover, 56% of the organizations surveyed do not provide any specific cybersecurity requirements to their suppliers. Even for the organizations that provide cybersecurity requirements to a supplier, 40% of the organizations do not have any formal processes for verifying whether the requirements are fulfilled. Therefore, there is a need to have a proper supply chain management in place, including creating SBOMs (software bill-of-materials) to know what software is provided by suppliers.

This understanding of the current state of security in the automotive industry – with limited cybersecurity resources, skills, and, additionally, the challenges regarding coding, testing and open-source software, combined with the fast pace of developing new, complex software for autonomous vehicles and wireless communication solutions – leads to significant risks that new vehicles will contain vulnerabilities during development and testing as well as that new vulnerabilities will be detected during the lifetime of the vehicle. There are numerous cybersecurity activities that organizations can employ to reduce the number of vulnerabilities during development and testing, such as performing source code reviews, static code analysis, software composition analysis, vulnerability scanning, fuzz testing, and penetration testing.

However, to be able to address critical cybersecurity vulnerabilities detected during the lifetime of vehicles there is a need for continuous cybersecurity monitoring and capabilities to perform updates in a timely manner, often implemented through secure OTA update functionality. Such update processes already exist in many other industries and there are working solutions for target devices such as mobile phones and PCs. However, the automotive industry is not on the same level yet. The survey mentions that 61% of the organizations do not have a software update delivery model that allows for addressing critical security vulnerabilities in a timely manner. Only 37% of the respondents say that their organization currently provides OTA update functionality but more than 50% of the respondents have plans to provide OTA update features in the next five years.

Regarding cybersecurity monitoring, there are requirements in ISO/SAE DIS 21434 [4] and UNECE WP.29 [5] specifying the need for organizations to have capabilities to perform monitoring for new threats and vulnerabilities. Moreover, ISO/SAE DIS 21434 and UNECE WP.29 Software Updates [6] also provide requirements on software updates specifying the need for organizations to have capabilities to perform software updates on vehicles.

Moreover, besides the organizational-level topics highlighted by ISO/SAE DIS 21434 and UNECE WP.29, on a technical level the AUTOSAR (AUTomotive Open System ARchitecture) platform provides standardized approaches for OTA updates of ECU (electronic control unit) software [7, 8]. These approaches allow automotive organizations to follow a standardized process for performing updates for AUTOSAR-enabled ECUs, including considerations for security such as encryption of data in transit and in flash memory, and reliability such as avoiding degradation of ECU functionality and allowing rollback of software if anomalies occur.

To summarize, even though there are effective cybersecurity activities that can be taken during the development and testing phases, it is necessary for automotive organizations to consider solutions applicable for vehicles after production, such as cybersecurity monitoring and secure OTA updates to be able to detect and fix issues in a timely manner. Besides the inherent cybersecurity risks with more complex automotive software as presented in this section, there are also requirements in standards and regulations that define the need for cybersecurity monitoring and updates.

12.2 Problem Statement: Software Inventory, Monitoring Vulnerabilities, and Vulnerable Vehicles

Based on the need for cybersecurity monitoring and secure OTA updates presented in the previous section, this section describes in more detail the current challenges for automotive organizations to fulfill those needs.

There are main three challenges identified:

- Keeping an up-to-date software inventory,
- Continuous cybersecurity monitoring,
- Performing updates in a timely manner.

The first challenge is regarding *keeping an up-to-date software inventory*. Owing to the complex supply chain and large volumes of software in vehicles, there are challenges for automotive organizations to monitor and keep track of which software and which versions of such software exist on which vehicles. As part of inventory management, automotive companies have traditionally often been using PLM (product lifecycle management) systems to manage the hardware BOM (bill of materials) of their vehicles and automotive systems. Thus, from a hardware perspective, there is often a clear view and understanding of the vehicle with its ECUs and hardware components, down to details on microcontrollers and electrical components.

However, from a software perspective, there are challenges for the automotive industry to perform the same level of inventory management. Software in automotive systems is complex and comes from various sources, such as own-developed software, third-party developed software, commercial software, and open-source software. Software also comes in various configurations and versions and, in contrast to hardware, is easily updatable, and therefore a certain software configuration is more likely to change over time and more frequently than a certain hardware configuration. Hence, while the usage of hardware BOMs is common for vehicles, there are many cases where the usage of SBOMs is not prevalent yet. Moreover, software updates may be performed by automotive workshops when bringing in a vehicle, some software may be updatable over the air, and some software may be updatable by the user through a USB interface in the vehicle. Thus, there may be cases where the vehicle manufacturer is not aware of successful updates of the software to the vehicle, so even if there is an initial SBOM created for a specific vehicle it may quickly be outdated. Therefore, there are situations where it is unclear for an automotive manufacturer which software, and specifically which versions of the software, are running on which vehicles.

The second challenge is regarding *continuous cybersecurity monitoring*. The automotive industry has traditionally not had defined processes for cybersecurity monitoring to actively monitor for threats, vulnerabilities, and attacks on their vehicles. As Section 12.1 mentions, there are requirements specified for cybersecurity monitoring in ISO/SAE DIS 21434 and UNECE WP.29 Cybersecurity [9] and since these documents are still in draft versions at the time of writing, many automotive organizations have not been able to establish the proper capabilities to perform monitoring for new threats and vulnerabilities yet. While cybersecurity monitoring is commonplace in other industries such as IT and enterprise, mainly because systems in such industries have been exposed to cybersecurity threats and attacks for decades due to easily accessible online servers and systems, cybersecurity monitoring practices for automotive systems are still in their infancy. Since vehicles traditionally have not been targeted in cybersecurity attacks owing to limited attack vectors, there has not been much need for continuous cybersecurity monitoring activities; however, with the increase in connectivity capabilities and advanced software in vehicles, it is likely that more vehicles will be targeted and thus will be requiring automotive organizations to establish cybersecurity monitoring processes. One example showing the need for monitoring of new vulnerabilities is described in Section 6.2. In this example, an automotive-related software package that was released in October 2017 includes a fairly recent version of the open-source component curl, released only eight months earlier in February 2017 (curl version 7.53.1). However, in March 2018, within just five months after the software package was released, three critical vulnerabilities in curl had been discovered (CVE [Common Vulnerabilities and Exposures]-2017-8816, CVE-2017-8817, CVE-2018-1000120). If a proper continuous cybersecurity monitoring process is not in place, an automotive organization would not be aware of any critical vulnerabilities that may be discovered shortly after software is released.

The third challenge is the lack of capabilities for *performing updates on vehicles in a timely manner*, leading to potentially vulnerable vehicles in the field being exposed for longer periods of time. As briefly mentioned, software updates on vehicles are often performed by automotive workshops when bringing in a vehicle, some software is updatable over the air, and some software is updatable by the user through a USB interface in the vehicle. When a critical security issue is detected and an automotive organization has to act swiftly to reduce the risk of cybersecurity attacks, there may be limited approaches to patch the vulnerabilities on the affected vehicles. As mentioned before, the results from the automotive survey [3] show that 61% of the organizations do not have a software update delivery model that allows for addressing critical security vulnerabilities in a timely manner. Moreover, only 37% of the organizations have OTA update capabilities. Thus, if critical security issues are identified, in many cases users may still have to bring their vehicles in to a workshop to be updated, or users have to download an update from the manufacturer website and install the update through the USB interface themselves.

12.3   Solution: Release Management, Monitoring and Tracking, and Secure OTA Updates

This section presents a solution concept based on a three-step process to address the individual challenges described in Section 12.2. The three steps are:

- Release management,
- Monitoring and tracking,
- Secure OTA updates.

Release management focuses on having a clear view of what software and which versions are being released and to which vehicles and systems the software are released. *Monitoring and tracking* focuses on an organization providing the necessary capabilities to be able to properly monitor for new threats and vulnerabilities and to be able to track specific vulnerabilities to vulnerable vehicles, and more specifically identify vulnerable systems and software versions. Last, *secure OTA updates* focuses on an organization having capabilities in place to be able to remotely and securely perform updates of vulnerable systems and software in its vehicle fleet.

Each step of the process is described in more detail in the following sections.

12.3.1 Release Management

The automotive industry traditionally uses PLM systems to integrate and manage data related to design, manufacturing, and maintenance of automotive systems [10, 11]. The PLM systems also allow management of sophisticated BOMs, where there may exist different variants and configurations that need to be handled. Older methods of managing BOMs, such as using Excel files, have limited capabilities compared with the advanced functionality provided by PLM systems. These systems are often used to manage hardware BOMs, to know exactly what hardware components are included, where the part was manufactured, how many parts were manufactured, etc., so that if a safety or quality issue owing to a faulty hardware component occurs, the auto manufacturer would be able to track the hardware-related issue to know exactly how many vehicles and which vehicles are affected that may need to be recalled [12]. One example is a defective airbag that has led to a recall of more than 41 million vehicles [13]. These airbags were mostly installed in cars from model year 2002 through 2015, and included in vehicles made by 19 different auto manufacturers [14]. Without managing BOMs it would have been impossible to know which vehicles have the faulty airbags installed.

With the increase of software in vehicles, besides managing hardware BOMs, it is becoming equally important to manage software BOMs. That is, it is required to know exactly what software components are included, where the software components are supplied from, and which systems are using which versions of the software, etc., so that if a safety, quality, or security issue is detected, the auto manufacturer would be able to track the software-related issue to know exactly which and how many vehicles are affected and may need to be updated or recalled. Thus, a combined application lifecycle management (ALM)/PLM solution is needed to manage software throughout the entire product lifecycle [15, 16]. One example of a software-based issue is a vulnerability in a head unit that led to a recall of 1.4 million vehicles [17]. The head unit was installed in a number of different vehicle models, ranging from model years 2013–2015 [18]. This example highlights the importance for automotive organizations to be able to track which vehicles and automotive systems contain a certain vulnerable piece of software to know how many vehicles are affected.

Automotive systems contain several layers of software, including low-level drivers, operating systems, libraries, communication stacks, and application layer software that may be developed and supplied by a number of different parties in the supply chain. For automotive organizations to be able to properly create and manage SBOMs it is required that the automotive industry applies *software transparency* in the entire supply chain.

To this end, to support software transparency in the supply chain, there are numerous ongoing activities. For example, NTIA (National Telecommunications and Information Administration) is working on several documents to help provide a common understanding for software in the supply chain [19]. These documents cover topics such as how to identify and name components, how to share SBOMs, and how to automate the creation and usage of SBOMs, based on various tooling and different SBOM formats. For instance,

SBOMs can be generated automatically using software composition analysis tools. More details about software composition analysis is presented in Chapter 6. Regarding sharing and using SBOMs, an example is where the SBOM is provided together with the software delivery to a receiving party who can verify the SBOM to get an understanding of the contents of the software delivery including individual software components and versions.

Besides security, safety, and quality issues in software, if open-source software components are used, there are license compliance issues that need to be considered. To this end, the OpenChain WG (working group) has developed a new standard that was published in December 2020 called ISO/IEC 5230 to help organizations in the supply chain to provide software transparency between the providing party and the receiving party [20]. Specifically to target automotive topics, the OpenChain Automotive WG was established in July 2019 [21].

Although these activities are not finalized yet, they can help automotive organizations define processes for creating and keeping software inventory of their vehicles and automotive systems. Furthermore, since software can be updated and changed over time, it is important to consider processes to ensure that the software inventory is kept up-to-date. With the complex software used in automotive systems and increased usage of open-source software, it becomes increasingly important to have a clear and up-to-date software inventory of what software is included in vehicles and automotive systems.

Focusing on open-source software, it is recommended that the following steps for release management are taken. These steps are described in more detail in Section 6.3.

- Fully inventory open-source software: Generate SBOMs for software packages.
- Use appropriate software composition analysis approaches: binary scanning (when only binaries are available) or source code scanning (when source code is available to achieve more comprehensive results) to identify included open-source components.
- Map identified open-source components to known security vulnerabilities: Use information of known vulnerabilities (CVEs) from vulnerability databases such as NIST (National Institute of Standards and Technology) NVD (National Vulnerability Database).
- Identify license, quality, and security risks: consider legal risks if not complying with open-source licenses, consider quality and security risks if using poorly maintained open-source software components.

A simplified solution for the release process for the purposes of managing SBOMs is illustrated in Figure 12.1. The different boxes in the figure represent different stages and activities in the release process. During *Software Development*, various software is developed and integrated and, where applicable, will run through a software composition analysis tool based on source code scanning during the *Software Composition Analysis* activity. The developed software is then stored in a *Software Repository*. There may be cases where other software such as third party applications or libraries supplied in the form of binaries are stored in the Software Repository and, where applicable, will run through a software composition analysis tool based on binary scanning during the Software Composition Analysis activity. The scanned results from the software composition analysis tool are used to generate SBOMs that are then stored in the *ALM/PLM System*. Next, the software from the Software Repository is used for *End-of-Line Flashing* in the factories during vehicle production to flash the specific software to the automotive systems in the vehicles. At this stage,

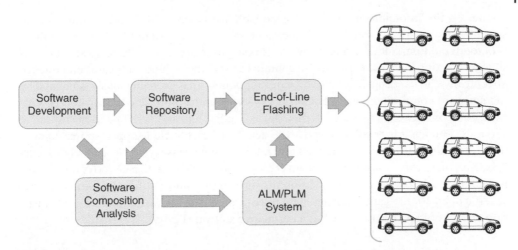

Figure 12.1 Overview of release process including software composition analysis to generate SBOMs. Source: Adapted from [2]. Portions Copyright 2019 Synopsys, Inc. Used with permission. All rights reserved.

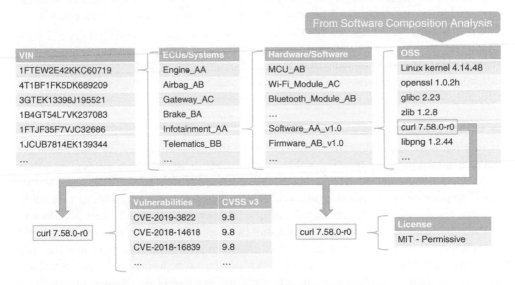

Figure 12.2 Storing relevant information including SBOMs, and vulnerability and license information in the ALM/PLM System. Source: Adapted from [2]. Portions Copyright 2019 Synopsys, Inc. Used with permission. All rights reserved.

relevant information about which software is flashed to which vehicles and automotive systems is stored in the ALM/PLM System.

An example of how relevant information can be integrated in the ALM/PLM System is depicted in Figure 12.2. Starting from the top-left in the figure, the ALM/PLM System contains a list of all vehicles based on their VIN (vehicle identification number). Focusing on one specific vehicle, it is possible to obtain a list of all the included ECUs and systems, such as engine ECU, brake ECU, in-vehicle infotainment system and telematics unit. Exploring further on the infotainment system, it is possible to acquire a list of the included corresponding hardware and software modules such as MCU (microcontroller), Wi-Fi module, Bluetooth module, software, and firmware. Investigating deeper into the software, it is possible to examine the SBOM. The SBOM contains a list of the included software components. Specifically, the list of open-source software components has been previously generated by the software composition analysis tool. It shows a number of different open-source software components, such as Linux kernel, openssl, glibc, zlib and curl, and their respective versions. Finally, it is possible to verify the details for each included open-source component, including the associated known vulnerabilities and license types. Specifically, for curl 7.58.0-r0, there exist a number of known critical vulnerabilities with a CVSS (common vulnerability scoring system) rating close to the maximum value of 10, and additionally this specific open-source software component is associated with the MIT (Massachusetts Institute of Technology) license, which is a permissive software license.

12.3.2 Monitoring and Tracking

After following a release management process where automotive organizations have a full view of software installed on different vehicles and systems, the next step involves the capabilities to continuously monitor for new threats and vulnerabilities and to be able to track the new vulnerabilities to specific vehicles, systems, and software versions. Please note that the continuous cybersecurity monitoring activity also covers vulnerability management and incident response, thus the automotive organization must have the capabilities to manage and respond to detected vulnerabilities and attacks based on the criticality and relevance.

12.3.2.1 Solutions in Other Industries

In other industries, such as IT and enterprise, there are already several solutions for enabling monitoring and tracking of threats and vulnerabilities through the deployment of a SOC (security operations center). A SOC is a centralized function within an organization that is responsible for monitoring, analyzing and responding to security threats, vulnerabilities and incidents. The SOC requires security staff to handle operations, defined processes on the activities that should be performed, and the deployment of technical solutions to aid in their work. For instance, a SOC for an IT organization is continuously monitoring and analyzing activities on, for example, networks, servers, websites, applications, databases, and other systems that house valuable information. If the monitoring triggers any alerts on suspicious behavior, the SOC can analyze the alerts and, based on the priority, decide to perform various actions to respond to the suspicious activity. This may include shutting down systems, isolating targeted systems from the network, or terminating harmful processes.

It is also common practice for many organizations in other industries such as IT and enterprise to have a PSIRT (product security incident response team), which is a centralized function that manages the reporting and handling of vulnerabilities related to the organizations' products. Vulnerability information may be received from various sources such as customers using the products, independent security researchers, and industry groups. The PSIRT then analyzes and prioritizes the vulnerability reports. Next, the PSIRT assesses the product impact of those vulnerabilities and investigates mitigation approaches. The PSIRT also coordinates the resources needed to perform the fixes and finally provides the updated software versions and notifies customers.

Some organizations use bug bounty programs to work with third-party security researchers and the security community to receive vulnerability information. In this manner, security researchers can test certain parts of an organization's infrastructure or products and report any identified vulnerabilities to the associated organization through the bug bounty program. In return, the security researchers may receive monetary rewards in the terms of hundreds of dollars for high severity vulnerabilities, up to thousands of dollars for critical vulnerabilities [22]. While bug bounty programs are becoming more popular, they are not new – one of the oldest bug bounty programs is for the open-source web browser Firefox, which started in 2004 [23]. For some industries, there are also coordinated efforts by industry groups to help manage vulnerability information. For example, for the finance industry, FS-ISAC (Financial Services Information Sharing and Analysis Center) is an industry consortium that provides financial institutions with threat and vulnerability information [24].

12.3.2.2 Solutions in the Automotive Industry

The automotive industry is moving in this direction with the need to establish similar solutions for monitoring and tracking threats and vulnerabilities that have been deployed in other industries for several years already. As briefly introduced in Section 2.3.12, the ISO/SAE DIS 21434 standard describes requirements for automotive organizations to conduct continuous cybersecurity activities, including threat and vulnerability monitoring. To this end, there are various ongoing activities at automotive organizations such as establishing an automotive SOC or a vehicle SOC. The automotive SOC provides similar functions as SOCs for other industries in that it is responsible for monitoring, analyzing and responding to security threats, vulnerabilities and incidents. The main difference is that the target systems being monitored are not the organizations' own systems and networks but rather the fleet of vehicles produced by the automotive organization. The goal is to protect the connected vehicles from cybersecurity threats and attacks.

12.3.2.3 Example Automotive SOC Overview

An example automotive SOC is depicted in Figure 12.3 to highlight the different activities and communications required in an organization. Please note that the names and responsibilities of the involved teams may differ in different organizations.

First, information about threats and vulnerabilities need to be collected from various sources as illustrated in the top-left corner of Figure 12.3. Examples of sources include but are not limited to:

- Auto-ISAC (Automotive Information Sharing and Analysis Center)
- Bug bounty programs
- From the field
- Software composition analysis tools

Auto-ISAC is an industry-driven community that was established in 2015 and includes members from light- and heavy-duty vehicle OEMs (original equipment manufacturers), suppliers and the commercial vehicle sector, e.g. fleets and carriers [25]. The format is

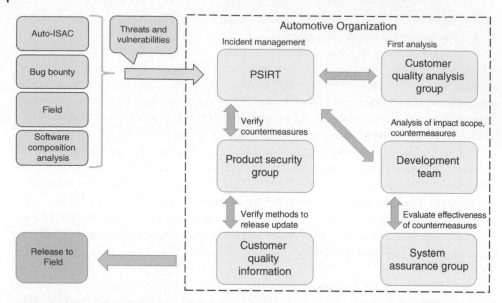

Figure 12.3 Overview of an example automotive SOC showing the different activities and interactions. Source: Adapted from [2]. Portions Copyright 2019 Synopsys, Inc. Used with permission. All rights reserved.

similar to the previously mentioned FS-ISAC, where the goal is to share information about threats and vulnerabilities to improve overall vehicle cybersecurity. Auto-ISAC also provides best practices for vehicle cybersecurity covering organizational and technical topics such as incident response, risk assessment and management, and threat detection, monitoring and analysis.

Regarding *bug bounty programs*, as mentioned previously, such programs have been used in the IT and enterprise industries for several years; however, the concept is fairly new to the automotive industry. Early adopters include Tesla, which started its bug bounty program [26] in 2014, GM (General Motors) [27] and FCA (Fiat Chrysler Automobiles) [28] which started theirs in 2016, and Toyota [29] in 2018. While the focus is mainly on automotive organizations' websites and mobile apps, it is becoming more common to include vehicles as targets for bug bounties.

Receiving threat and vulnerability information *from the field* includes receiving information from vehicles themselves. The information can be based on exceptions detected by in-vehicle sensors or in-vehicle security solutions, which then provide the exception data and alerts through a telematics unit to an automotive SOC. An example is an automotive intrusion detection system (IDS) which is deployed in the vehicle to detect suspicious behavior and events occurring on the in-vehicle network and ECUs, and reports to the organization's automotive SOC. There are also ongoing discussions on standardization of automotive IDS functionality in AUTOSAR, including the specification for IDS sensors and IDS manager [30].

Using *software composition analysis tools* during the release process, as explained in Section 12.3.1, allows automotive organizations to create SBOMs to know which open-source software components are included in which automotive systems, e.g. in an in-vehicle infotainment system or a telematics unit. The software composition analysis tool can then provide information in the form of alerts to the automotive SOC about newly detected vulnerabilities associated with the open-source software components contained in the SBOMs.

12.3.2.4 Example Automotive SOC Workflow

In Figure 12.3, the threat and vulnerability information from these various sources is provided to or collected by the automotive organization, processed internally and, if required, a fix to counter a specific threat or vulnerability is finally released to the affected vehicles. The following steps may differ depending on the internal organizational structure, involved teams and responsibilities, and processes and workflows, but a general approach is as follows. The threat and vulnerability information is collected by the *PSIRT* which is responsible for incident management. A first analysis is performed by the *Customer quality analysis group* to determine priority and relevance to the organization's vehicles and systems. If it is determined to provide a fix in order to counter a certain threat or vulnerability, the *Development team* analyzes the impact of the specific issue and considers appropriate countermeasures. Next, the *System assurance group* evaluates the effectiveness of the countermeasures, including identifying risks for the introduction of new vulnerabilities and any potential negative impacts on other parts of the system due to the countermeasures. If agreed, the Development team proceeds with implementing the countermeasures, after which the *Product security group* verifies that the countermeasures have properly addressed the issue. Then, the *Customer quality information group* investigates approaches and timing for providing the updated software with the implemented countermeasures to the affected vehicles and systems. This includes informing affected customers and releasing information regarding the issue to the public. As part of the final step, the fixed software is released to the field to be applied on the affected vehicles and systems. An example of how this final step can be realized using capabilities for secure OTA updates is described in Section 12.3.3.

12.3.2.5 Newly Detected Vulnerabilities in Open-Source Software – Example

Let us review an example in more detail of when an organization receives an alert about newly detected vulnerabilities in open-source software components from a software composition analysis tool. Based on the information about the open-source software vulnerability there is a need to evaluate the risk and understand how many systems or vehicles are affected. Building on the release management approach from Section 12.3.1, it is possible for an organization to use the information in the ALM/PLM System to perform such an analysis. An example of how an organization can evaluate the risk for newly detected vulnerabilities in open-source software components is depicted in Figure 12.4.

Imagine that an organization during the release management process, while generating SBOMs, identifies that the open-source software library curl version 7.58.0-r0 is included in multiple software packages. These software packages are released and used in various systems on a number of different vehicles. Sometime in the future, security researchers detect a new critical vulnerability in this version of curl. The relevant vulnerability information is reported and registered to, for example, NIST NVD, and a CVE ID is assigned (e.g. CVE-2023-XXXX). As shown in Figure 12.4, the software composition analysis tool provides an alert to the automotive organization, informing that there is a new vulnerability detected in curl version 7.58.0-r0 called CVE-2023-XXXX with a severity rating of 10 on the CVSS v3 scale, which means that this is a critical vulnerability. As mentioned previously,

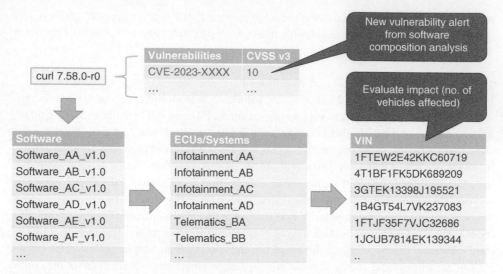

Figure 12.4 Evaluating the risk for newly detected vulnerabilities in open-source software components using the ALM/PLM System. Source: Adapted from [2]. Portions Copyright 2019 Synopsys, Inc. Used with permission. All rights reserved.

the organization has to perform some analysis on the exploitability and the impact scope on how the systems containing this vulnerable version of curl can be negatively affected by an attacker successfully exploiting this vulnerability. Moreover, it is imperative to understand how many systems are affected by this vulnerability, i.e. how many vehicles and systems use software that include this particular version of curl. As illustrated in the figure, using information from the ALM/PLM System, an organization can first obtain a list of all software versions that contain this curl version, 7.58.0-r0. Next, the organization can identify all ECUs and systems that currently have the affected software versions installed. Third, the organization can then map those specific ECUs and systems to individual vehicles that have those automotive systems. This information allows the organization to get an understanding of how many systems and vehicles are affected by this specific vulnerability. Based on this understanding, the organization can decide on an appropriate priority to handle this vulnerability and, if required, provide a fix. For example, an organization may approach the same vulnerability differently based on whether 10 million vehicles are affected vs. 100 vehicles. Thus, using information gathered during the release management process to assist with monitoring and tracking provides added benefits to the organization to know which vehicles and systems are affected and to help with prioritization. If the organization decides to provide updated software, which addresses the vulnerability, and if due to its criticality the update has to be delivered in a timely manner, the organization requires a secure OTA update capability described in the next section.

12.3.3 Secure OTA Updates

Based on following the release management process described in Section 12.3.1 and tracking vulnerabilities to specific software and vehicles explained in Section 12.3.2, the next step in this solution is to perform secure OTA updates on the vulnerable vehicles. While the topic

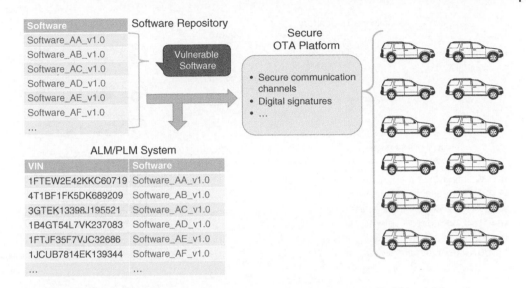

Figure 12.5 Vulnerable software packages in Software Repository mapped to vehicles containing the vulnerable software in the ALM/PLM System. Source: Adapted from [2]. Portions Copyright 2019 Synopsys, Inc. Used with permission. All rights reserved.

of secure OTA updates has been discussed for more than 10 years [31, 32] this section is not restricted to a certain technical solution for OTA updates. Instead, this section focuses on a general approach for performing secure OTA updates of automotive systems and receiving receipts that the respective systems have indeed been updated.

12.3.3.1 Identify Vulnerable Vehicles Targeted for OTA Updates
First, as shown in Figure 12.5, the various vulnerable software packages of version 1.0 in the Software Repository are mapped using the ALM/PLM System to the corresponding vehicles, identified by their VIN, containing the vulnerable software. Based on the information in the ALM/PLM System it is thus possible to know which vehicles and systems contain vulnerable software and need to be updated.

Next, the vulnerabilities in the software are fixed and the new versions of the software packages, version 1.1, are stored in the Software Repository, as shown in Figure 12.6. Through the release management process, a software composition analysis tool is used to scan the updated software versions to verify that no other known vulnerabilities are included before the software packages are released to the vulnerable vehicles.

12.3.3.2 Perform Secure OTA Updates
Using a Secure OTA Platform, the updated software versions are provided to the affected vehicles and the vulnerable target systems are updated. The Secure OTA Platform, described in more detail in Section 12.3.3.4, is based on best practices for performing updates and establishing secure communication channels. In this case, a secure communication channel can be established based on the TLS (transport layer security) protocol, and digital signatures can be used to verify the integrity and authenticity of the software updates packages on the vehicle. Next, after a vehicle has performed a successful update of the target

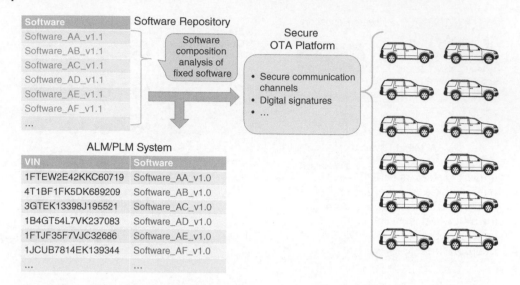

Figure 12.6 Fixed updated software packages scanned using software composition analysis tool and stored in Software Repository. Source: Adapted from [2]. Portions Copyright 2019 Synopsys, Inc. Used with permission. All rights reserved.

system with the updated software version, a receipt is provided from the vehicle through the Secure OTA Platform to the ALM/PLM System. The receipt is used to indicate that the particular vehicle now contains an updated software version on the target system, which is reflected by an updated entry in the ALM/PLM System, shown as software version 1.1 in Figure 12.7. This entry also contains the SBOM for the new software version, including the results from the software composition analysis scan. Using this approach of managing software updates in the ALM/PLM System, it is possible to verify which vehicles have been successfully updated and, more importantly, also to know which vehicles have not been updated yet and therefore still contain vulnerable software. It is also possible to have an up-to-date view of which vehicles and which automotive systems contain what software packages and versions and, further, which software components are included in those software packages, e.g. open-source software components and their respective versions.

12.3.3.3 Target Systems for OTA Updates

The Secure OTA Platform contains capabilities for secure OTA updates, which allows an organization to securely provide software updates to vehicles in a timely manner. While there are still ongoing discussions on which systems should be the target for OTA updates, the automotive industry is general moving in the direction of performing OTA updates.

There are typically two types of embedded systems in a vehicle:

- In-vehicle ECUs
- High-performance IT-based systems

The *in-vehicle ECUs* typically run on small microcontrollers with limited memory sizes and processing power. They often focus on a specific set of functionality, for example, some ECUs are responsible for real-time critical functions such as braking and steering.

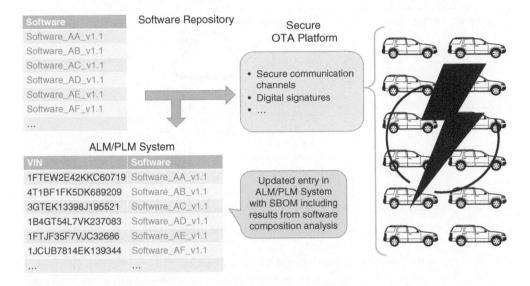

Figure 12.7 Vulnerable vehicles updated over the Secure OTA Platform with fixed software versions which are then reflected in the ALM/PLM System. Source: Adapted from [2]. Portions Copyright 2019 Synopsys, Inc. Used with permission. All rights reserved.

These ECUs communicate over in-vehicle network channels and therefore do not have direct external communication capabilities with an OTA backend. On the other hand, the *high-performance IT-based systems* often run on more powerful microprocessors with larger memory sizes and more processing power. They are typically used for in-vehicle infotainment systems and telematics units and are not responsible for real-time critical functions. These systems can generally communicate with the in-vehicle networks and also possess external communication interfaces such as Wi-Fi, Bluetooth, and cellular communication. The common approach for OTA updates is for the vehicle to establish a communication channel directly over cellular communication with an OTA backend; however, there are also approaches where Wi-Fi or Bluetooth could be used, e.g. by connecting the vehicle through the users' mobile phone or home Wi-Fi network to allow OTA updates.

The update process for these two different embedded systems have different requirements and may be implemented differently. Solutions for the high-performance IT-based systems can utilize best practices for secure OTA updates from other industries such as for mobile phones and PCs, and therefore will not be discussed in further detail in this chapter.

12.3.3.4 Overview of Secure OTA Update Process for ECUs

Performing updates of in-vehicle ECUs requires a specific process, considering the limitations of ECUs in terms of connectivity and memory [33, 34]. A simplified example of a secure OTA update process for ECUs is illustrated in Figure 12.8.

The software update packages are provided by, for example, an *ECU Supplier* or an *OEM* to the *Secure OTA Platform*. In the Secure OTA Platform, the software packages are protected using digital signatures for integrity and authenticity, and encryption for confidentiality. A *Telematics Unit* on the vehicle communicates with the Secure OTA Platform to download relevant software packages for the specific vehicle. The communication between the Telematics Unit and the Secure OTA Platform is secured using the TLS protocol. The

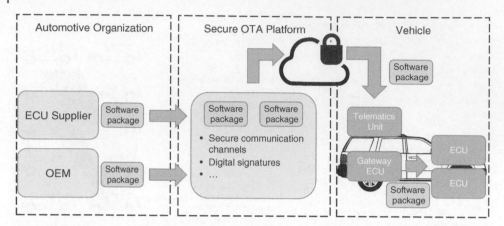

Figure 12.8 Overview of a secure OTA update process for in-vehicle ECUs.

downloaded software packages are stored on the *Gateway ECU* in the vehicle, which contains, for example, an external flash memory that is large enough to be able to store the downloaded software packages and backup copies of previous versions of the software in case a rollback is required. The Gateway ECU is typically a more powerful ECU, which also contains an HSM (hardware security module). Automotive HSMs are described in more detail in Chapter 3. The HSM in the Gateway ECU then verifies the digital signature of the downloaded software and decrypts the contents. The cryptographic algorithms, keys, and operations used for these tasks are securely handled by and stored in the HSM. To perform an update of one of the *ECUs* in the in-vehicle network, the Gateway ECU then initiates authentication with the target ECU by activating the UDS (Unified Diagnostic Services) Security Access service [35]. The HSM also keeps the cryptographic material needed to unlock the target ECUs in a secure storage. After successful authentication, the software update is flashed to the target ECU. Before the new content is executed on the target ECU, a software component, e.g. the bootloader, validates the signature of the flashed software. If the signature verification passes, the bootloader executes the new software and thus an updated version of the software is running on the target ECU. Although it is not shown in Figure 12.8, after a successful flashing of an updated software to an ECU, a receipt is provided to the Secure OTA Platform indicating that the target ECU now contains an updated software version as described above.

In case there is an unrecoverable error occurring during the flashing of the new software, which could lead to the target ECU becoming non-functional, the Gateway ECU can perform a rollback by flashing the previous version of the software back to the target ECU. This software may still be vulnerable but at least it allows the ECU to be in a functional state to try performing the update again or to ask the driver to bring the vehicle to a workshop to have the update performed by a mechanic.

12.3.3.5 Standardization and Frameworks for OTA Updates

There are also standardization activities for OTA updates. For example, AUTOSAR has published documents with requirements and specifications for OTA updates. These documents provide requirements and descriptions of a detailed technical solution for OTA updates for

AUTOSAR Classic Platform, including requirements for memory capabilities, rollback, and diagnostics services [7, 36]. Moreover, there are requirements and specifications for updating and changing software on the AUTOSAR Adaptive Platform, including considerations for safety and security [8].

Besides ensuring a secure OTA update process where the focus is on prevention and detection of attacks, it is also important to consider *mitigation* to make a compromise less impactful. The Uptane framework focuses on mitigation approaches for OTA updates. Uptane has been in development since 2015 and is a new standard for securing OTA software update systems [37]. The Uptane framework is based on TUF (The Update Framework), which is used in the industry by numerous organizations including IBM, Microsoft Azure, VMware, and Red Hat [38]. TUF assumes that servers will be compromised and/or that keys will be stolen or used by attackers. Therefore, TUF tries to minimize the impact of every compromise. For OTA updates for vehicles, Uptane is based on the key idea to use two repositories: image repository with the image files and metadata used for updates, and director repository with the install directions for the image files. The image repository uses offline keys to sign the metadata about all available updates for all ECUs on all vehicles. Thus, the image repository data are compromise-resilient because attackers cannot tamper with the signed contents without being detected. The director repository uses online keys to sign the metadata about which updates should be installed on which ECUs on a specific vehicle. A vehicle would verify that the install directions from the director repository match the updates from the image repository to ensure that the vehicle is allowed to install the updates. By using both repositories it allows for compromise-resilience and on-demand customization for vehicles. Thus, even if one repository or cryptographic key is compromised and an attacker maliciously modifies the contents, the vehicle can verify that the modified contents do no match the second repository and therefore the risk for comprise is reduced [38, 39].

12.4 Chapter Summary

This chapter highlighted the importance of continuous cybersecurity monitoring, vulnerability management, incident response, and secure OTA updates to protect vehicles after production. With increasing sizes of software and connectivity capabilities in vehicles combined with the fact that vehicles have long lifespans of 10–15 years, there is a risk that there are new software vulnerabilities detected after a vehicle has been released that can be exploited by attackers. Therefore, there is a need for automotive organizations to perform continuous cybersecurity monitoring for new threats and vulnerabilities, manage and handle identified vulnerabilities based on criticality and relevance, and – in order to address critical vulnerabilities in vehicles in a timely manner – be able to perform secure OTA updates. However, with more complex software and many involved parties in the supply chain, including the use of open-source software, it is a challenge to keep an up-to-date software inventory. In addition, although there are requirements specified for cybersecurity monitoring in ISO/SAE DIS 21434 and UNECE WP.29 Cybersecurity, since these are draft documents many automotive organizations have not been able to establish the proper cybersecurity monitoring capabilities yet. Moreover, as shown in a recent automotive survey, 61% of the surveyed organizations do not have a software update delivery model that allows for addressing critical security vulnerabilities in a timely manner. To address these challenges, a solution based on three steps, release management, monitoring and tracking, and secure OTA updates, is presented. Release management allows an organization to have a clear and up-to-date view of its software inventory. This includes creating SBOMs during the release process to know which software components and versions are included in a software package. For open-source software, a software composition analysis tool can be used to generate SBOMs which contains information about the included open-source software components and their respective versions, and any associated known vulnerabilities and licenses. These SBOMs can then be stored in an ALM/PLM System during the release process to know which vehicles and which systems contain which software packages and versions. The monitoring and tracking step then provides organizations with capabilities to be able to properly monitor for new cybersecurity threats and vulnerabilities and be able to track specific vulnerabilities to certain software and vehicles. One of the sources for vulnerability input is the software composition analysis tool used during the release management process. If a new vulnerability is detected in the future, in one of the previously scanned open-source components, an alert from the software composition analysis tool is provided to the automotive organization. The organization can then track which software contains the vulnerable open-source component, and further identify which systems and vehicles use the vulnerable software through the ALM/PLM System. The final step allows an organization to perform secure OTA updates of the affected vehicles and systems containing the vulnerable software. Once a fixed updated software version addressing the vulnerability is released, the updated software is provided through a Secure OTA Platform to the affected vehicles. The Secure OTA Platform uses best practices for secure communication, and encryption and digital signatures to protect the confidentiality, integrity, and authenticity of the software update packages. When a vulnerable vehicle has performed the software update, the ALM/PLM System is updated to reflect the new software version, including its SBOM, associated with the target vehicle and system.

References

1 Oka, D. K. (2019). How to secure vehicles after production: vulnerability management and secure over-the-air (OTA) Updates. *IEEE International Workshop on Automobile Software Security and Safety (A3S)*, Sofia, Bulgaria.

2 Oka, D. K. (2019). Securing vehicles after production: vulnerability management & secure over-the-air (OTA) updates. (Webinar).

3 Ponemon Institute - SAE International and Synopsys (2019). Securing the modern vehicle: a study of automotive industry cybersecurity practices. Synopsys, Inc. and SAE International.

4 International Organization for Standardization (ISO)/Society of Automotive Engineers (SAE) International (2020). *ISO/SAE DIS 21434 – road vehicles — cybersecurity engineering*. Geneva, Switzerland/USA: ISO/SAE International.

5 UNECE (2020). UN Regulations on Cybersecurity and Software Updates to pave the way for mass roll out of connected vehicles. https://unece.org/press/un-regulations-cybersecurity-and-software-updates-pave-way-mass-roll-out-connected-vehicles (accessed 30 July 2020).

6 UNECE WP.29 (2020). ECE/TRANS/WP.29/2020/80: Proposal for a new UN Regulation on uniform provisions concerning the approval of vehicles with regards to software update and software updates management system. United Nations Economic Commission for Europe.

7 AUTOSAR (2019). Explanation of firmware over-the-air.

8 AUTOSAR (2019). Specification of update and configuration management.

9 UNECE WP.29 (2020). ECE/TRANS/WP.29/2020/79 REVISED: Proposal for a new UN Regulation on uniform provisions concerning the approval of vehicles with regards to cyber security and cyber security management system.

10 Urban-Galindo, J.-J. and Ripailles, S. (2019). PLM at GROUPE PSA. *Product Lifecycle Management (Volume 4): The Case Studies*, Springer.

11 Firstpost (2010). Chrysler group extends partnership with siemens PLM. https://www.firstpost.com/business/biztech/chrysler-group-extends-partnership-with-siemens-plm-1878831.html (accessed 30 July 2020).

12 Autodesk (2017). Bill of materials management – why the bill of materials is critical for automotive suppliers. https://www.autodeskfusionlifecycle.com/en/resource-center/why-the-bill-of-materials-is-critical-for-automotive-suppliers (accessed 30 July 2020).

13 NHTSA (2020). State of Takata air bag recalls | third report. https://www.nhtsa.gov/takata-recall-spotlight/takata-monitor-third-report (accessed 30 July 2020).

14 Consumer Reports (2020). Takata airbag recall: everything you need to know. https://www.consumerreports.org/car-recalls-defects/takata-airbag-recall-everything-you-need-to-know (accessed 30 July 2020).

15 Barkai, J. (2016). PLM redefined: PLM-ALM integration. http://joebarkai.com/plm-redefined-plm-alm-integration (accessed 30 July 2020).

16 Bosch (2020). ALM PLM alignment all-inclusive platform for embedded hardware and software systems. https://www.bosch-india-software.com/en/products-and-services/business-solutions/enterprise-packaged-solutions/alm/alm-plm-alignment/ (accessed 30 July 2020).

17 Wired (2015). After jeep hack chrysler recalls 1.4M vehicles for bug fix. https://www.wired.com/2015/07/jeep-hack-chrysler-recalls-1-4m-vehicles-bug-fix (accessed 30 July 2020).

18 FCA (2015). Statement: software update. https://media.fcanorthamerica.com/newsrelease.do%3bjsessionid=0B80156E6900AC7963DF86F540855E2C?&id=16849&mid= (accessed 30 July 2020).

19 NTIA (2020). NTIA software component transparency. https://www.ntia.doc.gov/SoftwareTransparency (accessed 30 July 2020).

20 International Organization for Standardization (ISO)/International Electrotechnical Commission (IEC) (2020). *ISO/IEC 5230:2020 – information technology — OpenChain specification*. Geneva, Switzerland: ISO.

21 OpenChain (2019). OpenChain automotive work group – a global solution for a global market. https://www.openchainproject.org/news/2019/07/15/openchain-automotive-work-group-a-global-solution-for-a-global-market (accessed 30 July 2020).

22 HackerOne (2020). The most trusted hacker-powered security platform. https://www.hackerone.com (accessed 30 July 2020).

23 Mozilla (2020). Firefox's Bug Bounty in 2019 and into the future. https://blog.mozilla.org/security/2020/04/23/bug-bounty-2019-and-future (accessed 30 July 2020).

24 FS-ISAC (2020). Safeguarding the Global Financial System by Reducing Cyber Risk - FS-ISAC helps protect the financial sector and the billions of people who rely on it. https://www.fsisac.com (accessed 30 July 2020).

25 Auto-ISAC (2020). Automotive information sharing and analysis center. https://www.automotiveisac.com (accessed 30 July 2020).

26 bugcrowd (2020). Tesla. https://bugcrowd.com/tesla (accessed 30 July 2020).

27 HackerOne (2020). General motors - vulnerability disclosure program. https://hackerone.com/gm (accessed 30 July 2020).

28 bugcrowd (2020). Fiat chrysler automobiles. https://bugcrowd.com/fca (accessed 30 July 2020).

29 HackerOne (2020). Toyota - vulnerability disclosure program. https://hackerone.com/toyota (accessed 30 July 2020).

30 Metzker, E. and Weber, M. (2019). What's behind automotive intrusion detection? Ideas concepts and a software architecture proposal. Presentation at *Vector Technology Days*.

31 Nilsson, D. K. and Larson, U. E. (2008). Secure firmware updates over the air in intelligent vehicles. *IEEE International Conference on Communications Workshops*, Beijing, China.

32 Nilsson, D. K., Larson, U. E., and Jonsson, E. (2008). Creating a secure infrastructure for wireless diagnostics and software updates in vehicles. *International Conference on Computer Safety, Reliability, and Security (SAFECOMP)*, Newcastle upon Tyne, UK.

33 Mckenna, D. (2016). Making full vehicle OTA updates reality. NXP white paper.

34 Oka, D. K. (2015). OTA and remote diagnostics for updating in-vehicle software. https://monoist.atmarkit.co.jp/mn/articles/1511/13/news017.html (accessed 30 July 2020).

35 International Organization for Standardization (ISO) (2013). *ISO 14229-1:2013 – road vehicles — unified diagnostic services (UDS)*. Geneva, Switzerland: ISO.

36 AUTOSAR (2019). Requirements on firmware over-the-air.

37 Uptane (2019). *IEEE-ISTO 6100.1.0.0 uptane standard for design and implementation*. https://uptane.github.io/papers/ieee-isto-6100.1.0.0.uptane-standard.html (accessed 30 July 2020).

38 Cappos, J. (2019). Uptane - securing over-the-air updates against nation state actors. *Automotive Linux Summit*, Tokyo, Japan.

39 Littke, T. (2019). Uptane – open standard to secure automotive OTA updates. *ELIV (Electronics In Vehicles) Congress*, Bonn, Germany.

13

Summary and Next Steps

EXPLORE NEW PATHS TO FIND YOUR DESTINATION

This book presents a number of topics related to building secure cars, focusing especially on helping automotive organizations with assuring the software development lifecycle. Initially, the book gives an overview of the current state of cybersecurity in the automotive industry (Chapter 1). The book then introduces the reader to a number of relevant cybersecurity activities during the development lifecycle of automotive systems mapped to the V-model development process (Chapter 2). Before doing a deep-dive on the software development related cybersecurity activities, the book provides some background on automotive hardware security modules (HSMs) that serve as the root of trust for other solutions built on top of automotive systems (Chapter 3). Next, various security solutions for the automotive software development lifecycle are discussed with a focus on the need for automated solutions to reduce effort and improve efficiency (Chapter 4). These include solutions for the product development phases, such as static code analysis, software composition analysis, and security testing, and solutions for the operations and maintenance phases, such as cybersecurity monitoring, vulnerability management, incident response, and OTA (over-the-air) updates. The following chapters then provide additional details for these solutions that automotive organizations can apply. First, solutions for automotive organizations to use static code analysis with a focus on MISRA (Motor Industry Software Reliability Association) and AUTOSAR (AUTomotive Open System ARchitecture) coding guidelines that overcome common challenges are presented (Chapter 5). Next, solutions, including process steps and technical considerations, for open-source software management and handling of known vulnerabilities in automotive systems are discussed (Chapter 6). The book then provides the reader with an overview of automotive security testing approaches including security functional testing, vulnerability scanning, fuzz testing, and penetration testing (Chapter 7). This book further focuses on fuzz testing since it is an efficient and powerful approach to finding unknown vulnerabilities. First, solutions on automating fuzz testing of in-vehicle systems by integrating with automotive test tools are presented (Chapter 8). Further, solutions on improving fuzz testing coverage by using Agent instrumentation are explained (Chapter 9). Lastly, solutions for automating file fuzzing over USB for automotive systems are discussed (Chapter 10). While the book so far has presented how automotive organizations can use these automated solutions based on application security testing

Building Secure Cars: Assuring the Automotive Software Development Lifecycle, First Edition. Dennis Kengo Oka.
© 2021 John Wiley & Sons Ltd. Published 2021 by John Wiley & Sons Ltd.

tools – including static code analysis tools, software composition analysis tools, and fuzz testing tools – in the software development lifecycle, the book further describes how automotive organizations can achieve automation and traceability by integrating these tools into ALM (application lifecycle management) systems (Chapter 11). Although the focus of the book is on automated solutions that can be applied in the development and testing phases, the book also gives some insight into solutions for the operations and maintenance phases, including cybersecurity monitoring, vulnerability management, incident response, and OTA updates (Chapter 12).

While there are many other cybersecurity-related activities that automotive organizations need to consider and apply, this book focuses on solutions for the software development lifecycle and, further narrowing down, on solutions based on automated tools. It is important that organizations also consider approaches and processes for performing manual activities such as threat analysis and risk assessments and penetration testing. While there are some automated tools that can help with these activities, it is worth noting that these activities often require personnel with relevant cybersecurity skills and experience. Considering the challenges automotive organizations are facing, presented in Chapter 1, including limited cybersecurity resources and personnel with limited cybersecurity skills, it is useful and beneficial for organizations to first consider effective approaches to deploy automated solutions to improve software security and reduce the risk of vulnerabilities in automotive systems.

The automotive industry is going through a paradigm shift. While there are cybersecurity standards, regulations, and best practices providing automotive organizations with valuable information on establishing security practices, these documents are not fully prescriptive. This means that these documents do not provide the level of detail required for an organization to know exactly what to do to on a process and technical level to perform all the activities described in the standards, regulations, and best practices. Instead, automotive organizations have to create their own internal process requirements with more specific details on what type of cybersecurity activities should be performed and defined steps on how they should be conducted. Furthermore, organizations need to deploy appropriate technical solutions to help fulfill those internal process requirements. Moreover, as presented in Chapter 1, the top three main factors that lead to vulnerabilities in automotive systems, besides the pressure to meet deadlines, are related to *coding*, *testing*, and *open-source software*. This book presents numerous technical solutions that address these three main factors and provides several useful implementation examples on how to deploy suitable technical solutions to fulfill the internal process requirements.

Besides assuring the software development lifecycle, as part of the next steps it is equally important for automotive organizations to consider security controls and security solutions to be applied on automotive systems to secure the vehicles. Discussing the different types of such solutions would require several chapters or even warrant a separate book. However, just to give a brief overview of the type of security controls and solutions that automotive organizations should consider, the following examples are given.

A common theme in the automotive industry is to consider a multilayered approach to security solutions for vehicles, often consisting of four layers. The first layer is the outermost layer and includes remote communication interfaces on the vehicle. Typical examples include cellular, V2X (vehicle-to-X), Wi-Fi, and Bluetooth. For this layer, a firewall on the external interfaces can be applied to protect access to the in-vehicle network, and various cybersecurity solutions based on cryptography to achieve confidentiality, integrity, and authentication, can be used, including secure communication protocols. The second layer covers the E/E (electrical/electronic) architecture of the vehicle. This layer includes secure design of the in-vehicle network by segmenting and isolating various domains and ECUs (electronic control units), and applying security solutions such as automotive firewalls and automotive intrusion detection systems. The third layer is securing the in-vehicle network communication. Common solutions are based on secure communication protocols including applying techniques to ensure that messages between ECUs are secured. Finally, the fourth layer focuses on securing the ECU itself. Applicable solutions include the usage of automotive HSMs to establish a root of trust in the ECU, on which other security solutions can build upon.

It is also worth noting that besides securing the vehicles themselves, automotive organizations also need to consider appropriate security solutions for the development and production environments, factories, workshops, and backend servers. Thus, security solutions need to be applied to the entire eco-system of the vehicles.

As a final note, to create all of these security solutions to help build secure vehicles, *software* is required. To this end, to assure that the security solutions and all other relevant software in the vehicle eco-system are "secure," it is imperative that automotive organizations follow best practices for secure software development, establish the necessary organizational and technical processes to enable secure software development, and deploy automated application security testing tools in their workflows.

Index

Printed and bound by CPI Group (UK) Ltd, Croydon, CR0 4YY